A Good of Legs

Walking the World

Christopher Portway

RAMBLERS' ASSOCIATION SERVICES LTD 1999

A Good Pair of Legs — Walking the World
by Christopher Portway   1999

Ramblers' Association Services Limited
Box 43 Welwyn Garden City, Herts AL8 6PQ

ISBN 1 901184 27 7

Cover photos by Bill Birkett

All other photos by Christopher Portway unless stated

Cover design by Sue Lishman, Graphique, London

Printed by Thanet Press, Margate

CHRISTOPHER PORTWAY was born in rural Essex in 1923. He was educated at Gosfield, Abbotsholm and Felsted schools.

In 1942, he joined the Essex Regiment. He was later transferred to the Dorset Regiment, with which he fought in the north-west Europe campaign of World War Two. Captured in Normandy, he later escaped from prison camps in Poland, Czechoslovakia and Germany. He ended the War with the American Third Army.

He first met his Czech wife Anna when her family offered him shelter while he was an escaped prisoner-of-war. After 1945, he made repeated attempts to reach Anna in Czechoslovakia, which by then was virtually sealed off behind the Iron Curtain. In one attempt, he cut his way through electrified fences and negotiated a minefield – only to be caught and sentenced to jail for 104 years! But, following an international incident, he was released after four months. Eventually, Anna was permitted to join him in Britain. The couple have a son and daughter and now live in Brighton.

A member of the British Guild of Travel Writers, Christopher Portway is also a Fellow of the Royal Geographical Society. He has been a recipient of a Winston Churchill Award for biography and travel. He is a frequent contributor to various magazines, newspapers and other publications. He writes about a wide range of travel topics, from holiday travel tours to adventurous expeditions.

Christopher Portway's previous non-fiction books are: *Journey to Dana* (Kimber), *The Pregnant Unicorn* (Dalton), *Corner Seat* (Hale), *Double Circuit* (Hale), *Journey along the Andes* (Oxford Illustrated Press/Impact Books), *The Great Railway Adventure* (Oxford Illustrated Press/Coronet Books), *The Great Travelling Adventure* (Oxford Illustrated Press), *Czechmate* (Murray), *Indian Odyssey* (Impact Books), *A Kenyan Adventure* (Impact Books), and *Pedal for your Life* (Lutterworth Press).

His published works of fiction are: *All Exits Barred* (Hale), *Lost Vengeance* (Hale), *The Tirana Assignment* (Hale) and (as John October) *The Anarchy Pedlars* (Hale).

Publisher's foreword

Ramblers Holidays helps people to travel to destinations around the globe, and to enjoy some of the greatest adventures of their lives. Most of our holidays involve exploration on foot – from gentle strolling to tough trekking.

So, when I read a manuscript of this book by Christopher Portway, I was naturally fascinated by his amazing walking exploits, in locations around the world.

But I realised too that the stories which he has to tell will also fascinate our clients – and probably thousands of other people for whom travel adventures on foot are a primary source of enjoyment and fulfilment.

Thus, when Christopher invited Ramblers Holidays to publish his book, we were pleased to say yes. The content and style of his writing fully reveal his uniquely colourful and courageous personality. On his walks, Christopher has experienced not only satisfaction and conquest, but also hardship and suffering. Yet he always emerges triumphant and eager for his next adventure.

We did ask Christopher to undertake a few of our holidays and to add a chapter about his experiences on them. This he agreed to do, and thus he set forth on a whirlwind tour of tours – from the Lake District to South Africa – in the spring and summer of 1999.

I am sure you will enjoy reading this book. It will surely give you a taste for travel.

Perhaps you will take the book with you on a Ramblers Holiday, to read in the airport lounge while waiting to board your plane – as I did. But be careful. If you are engrossed in Christopher's adventures while he follows the Incas in the Andes, or dodges lions in the African bush, you are in grave danger of missing your flight call!

Stuart Alderman, Chief Executive, Ramblers Holidays*
September 1999

*Ramblers Holidays is the main trading subsidiary of Ramblers' Association Services Limited. More information about Ramblers Holidays is given on page 351.

Ramblers Holidays gives generous financial support to the work in Britain of the Ramblers' Association, which helps to protect the countryside and public access to it. The RA helped with the production of this book. More information about the Ramblers' Association is also given on page 349.

Foreword
by Susan, Queen of the Albanians

Our first meeting with Christopher Portway took place after reading his superb book *Double Circuit*, a section of which is to be found in his subsequent *The Great Railway Adventure*. The author had been to the then fanatically communist and restricted Albania and when he visited South Africa in 1985 we invited him to spend an afternoon with us at our Randberg home. This resulted in his spending the night and a deep continuous friendship ensued.

Christopher's great love is railway travel but one wonders why when some of his resulting tribulations are revealed. As an escaped prisoner of war during World War Two he managed to catch a moving goods train only to find himself travelling deeper into enemy territory, and, even in our own country, Albania, on a rail trip between Tirana and Durres concealed from authority amongst young soldiers who kept him liberally supplied with doses of Raki, he was arrested by the feared Sigurimi secret police.

Now Christopher has produced *A Good Pair of Legs* which tells of similar adventures and experiences while on foot, walking being his other favourite method of motivation.

I, for one, am not surprised that most of his travels are unaccompanied – to read his books is to discover why few if anyone wishes to accompany him! Riding a bicycle in Albania and running over an unfortunate citizen when Tirana could probably raise only twenty bikes in its entirety is but one tiny incident that amused us. And he must be the only man to be arrested breaking into a communist country when everybody else was trying to break out! His adventures have also included spending time in various jails in Eastern Europe, dodging grizzlies in northern Canada and buffalo in Kenya and running into terrorist groups in Peru.

To be in Christopher's company might be fascinating but one certainly does not have to follow him on his travels since his stories are detailed, expressive and enthralling enough to keep a reader safely at home.

Christopher, we – (King) Leka and I – wish you success and survival and fully recommend to everyone the books on your eventful journeys around the world; this one being a hundred per cent typical.

Susan, Queen of the Albanians,
The Royal Court of Albania, Bryanston, South Africa.

Acknowledgements

I extend my sincere appreciation to a multitude of individuals companies and other organisations for the support, advice and help which they gave prior to and during the walking projects which are narrated in this book. There are too many for individual mention but some are referred to in the list of useful contacts which is given in the appendix starting on page 341.

However, I thank in particular Oxford Illustrated Press (Haynes Publishing) for allowing me to adapt extracts from two of my earlier books, as well as Impact Books and Country Life magazine.

Finally, a big thank you to a host of people I came across during my walks who offered spontaneous hospitality to a passing stranger.

Christopher Portway

Contents

		Page
About the author		3
Publisher's Foreword		4
Foreword by Susan, Queen of the Albanians		5
Acknowledgements		6
Location Map		9
Author's Introduction		10
1	Great Britain: Where the Roman Legions Marched	15
2	France: A Writer's Way	28
3	Germany:	
	(1) South: A King's Walk	37
	(2) East: Bigfoot in the Rennsteig	44
4	Greece: Perambulations in the Pindus	49
5	Walks in the Cold:	
	(1) Iceland: Fire in the Snow	57
	(2) Spitsbergen: Archipelago on the Rim of the World	65
6	Clandestine Walking in Central Europe: Smoke Channel	71
7	Road walking in Central Europe: from the Baltic to the Danube	83
8	Trail Walking in the USA: the Trail by Cold Turkey Creek	108
9	Canada: The Ghost Highway	120

10	Indian Sub-continent:	
	(1) India: A Gentle Trek in the Himalayan Foothills	140
	(2) Nepal: Trade Route through the Himalayas	150
11	Kenya: Sundry Exertions in the African Bush	156
12	Peru: Highway of the Inca – a Short Walk in the Andes	179
13	Ecuador: How not to Climb a Mountain	213
14	Walking with Ramblers Holidays:	
	Introduction and note on holiday walking grades	222
	(1) Italy: Eastern Sicily	224
	(2) Spain: Andalucia	231
	(3) Morocco: the Atlas Mountains	242
	(4) Italy: Tuscany	256
	(5) USA: New England	267
	(6) Greece: Samos	281
	(7) UK: Hassness, the Lake District	290
	(8) Austria: The Upper Inn Valley	301
	(9) South Africa: the Drakensberg Mountains	310
	(10) Armenia	328
15	Epilogue	339
Appendix: Bibliography and list of addresses		341
THE RAMBLERS' ASSOCIATION		349
RAMBLERS HOLIDAYS		351

Map showing Christopher's travels

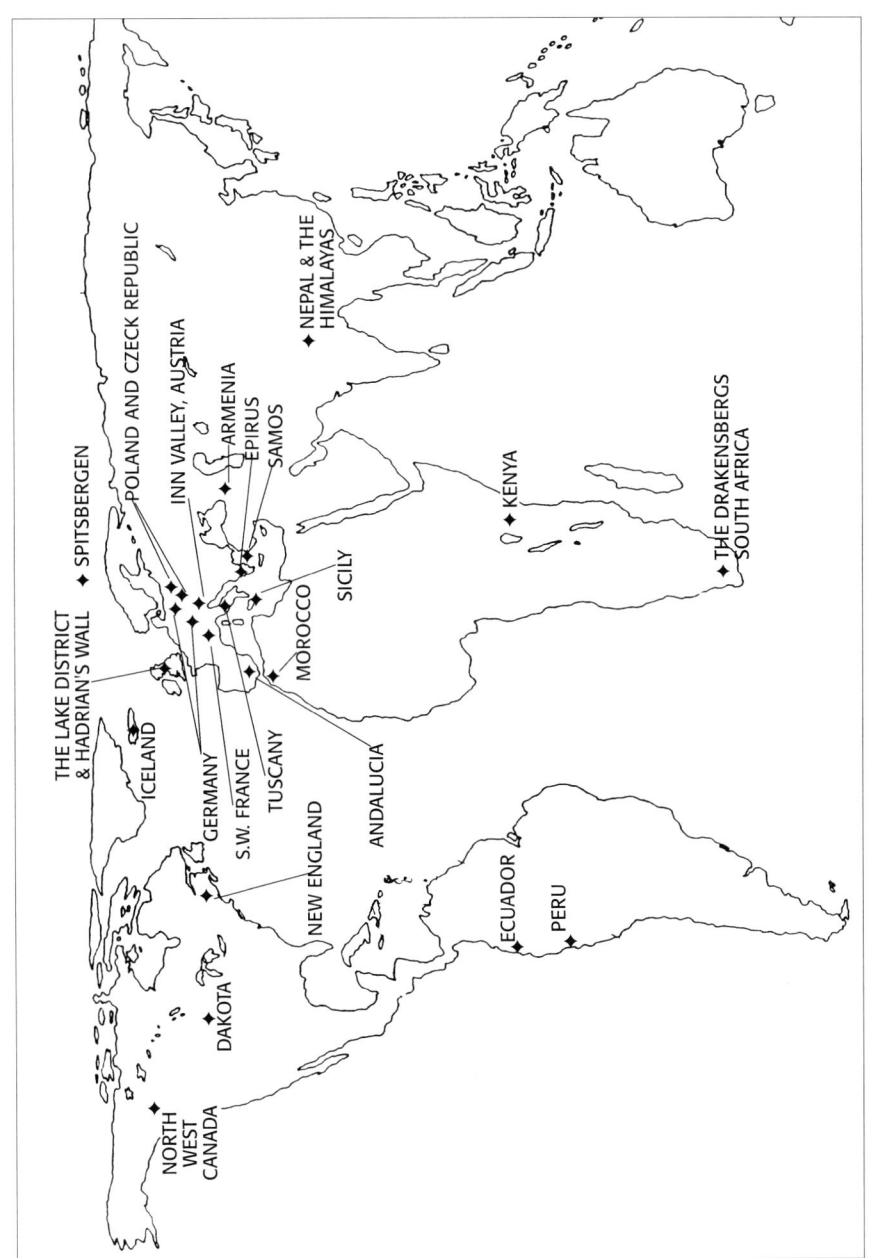

Author's Introduction

Walking, I have heard said, is good for the soul. It is a pace and a movement suited to the human frame and temperament, giving one opportunity to think; to ponder upon a mad world while, at the same time, offering a physical exercise many of us crave but neglect. Its benefits – better than aspirin – encourage the deepest and healthiest of sleep.

Another aspect of putting one foot before the other is the financial one of saving money. Walking is an inexpensive method of moving around and, in our teeming cities, frequently the fastest. It can also be a prelude to and reason for adventure, the calibre or lethality of which can usually be decided, or at least controlled, by the walker. There is no need to follow the crazed footsteps of Sebastian Snow or even the dogged ones of John Hillaby but there is a sense of achievement that riding a mechanical vehicle will never offer when setting out from A to B.

I myself am by no means a serious walker of the sort that enlists in clubs. Neither am I a fanatical collector of the paraphernalia of backpacking. But I do prefer to progress on my two feet with an object in view. Although I have long been partial to walking it is only during the past two dozen years that I have managed to weave this pursuit into the tapestry of my travels wherein I walk for no other reason than walking's sake. And it is surprising how large a proportion of this earth is attainable to those prepared to utilise their legs.

When I came to write this book I pondered long and seriously upon the desirability of a walking book pure and simple or one covering progress maintained by supplementary legs – such as those belonging to the horse, camel, mule, and elephant, plus, perhaps, the bicycle on which one's own legs are used in an unnatural fashion. I finally came down on the side of simple walking; using the legs bequeathed us by the Almighty in the manner he presumably intended since the scope of my foot travels cover, if not a multitude of haunts for the walker, a wide enough one to awake the interest of readers who may wish to follow my example and some, maybe, my footsteps.

I would never attempt to set myself up as a walking, hiking, trekking – call it what you will – adviser. I learnt from my mistakes the hard way and paid for them accordingly. However, there are many walker/writers – some of close acquaintance – who have produced a most excellent and comprehensive range of works covering the 'how to do it and survive' field of wilderness-walking and back-packing and I won't pretend that I haven't picked up a tip or two from this rich source. But my reader may not be aware that he or she is learning the art of negotiating the countryside except, hopefully, through the more interesting and entertaining of my mistakes and near-disasters. Nor is my narrative any kind of guidebook to the footpaths and historic routes of parts of the world my two feet have taken me. But it may arouse reflection in an enquiring mind or allay – or otherwise – the fears and doubts of would-be trekkers. Some of the routes I have walked have been simple footpaths used by weekend hikers like the South Downs Way in Sussex; others were tougher propositions such as northern Canada's dying Canol Road and the equally remote Andean royal Inca road in Peru. East Africa was the venue of a Kenyan jungle walk marked by no visible route as was Iceland and the the Karakorams of Pakistan, while the likes of those of the Himalayas of Nepal and India are arteries that can be followed by anyone with some knowledge of the terrain and a good map – plus the ability to read both properly. The walks narrated in this book are of very different grades, type and environment, and I have intentionally selected those with the greatest variation. The ten recounted in chapter 14 are organised by the touring company Ramblers Holidays who also organise tours to the countries covered by many of the other chapters. Their details are given on page 349.

It was the army in World War Two that taught me to march and I suppose my interest in long-distance walking blossomed from this barren soil of inspiration. Those 40-mile route marches, each of us encumbered with battle equipment, have not been entirely erased from my memory but at least the training came in handy a year or two later when, as a prisoner of war in company with untold millions of other unfortunates, I was pushed onto the refugee-choked, aircraft-strafed roads of eastern Europe in a 1945 winter of unparalleled ferocity. The 'Death March' – as it became known – commenced in Poland when the Soviet Army lay poised to enter Warsaw, and ended, months and hundreds of miles later, deep inside Germany as endless columns of human flotsam, evacuated from the east, poured westwards against a canvas of hideous cruelty on a titanic scale.

This brief mention of my military slogging is suffice to show, in contradictory fashion, how my enthusiasm for adventure walking came about. The experience, I suppose, should have cured me once and for all of taking a step further than my own front gate. For many years after the war my enthusiasm indeed lay dormant and it was not until middle age had wiped away the last clinging vestiges of youth that I discovered the joy of legging it about the world.

Since then I have been bombarded by three questions; Why? How? and Where? I have already contributed my own reasoning as to why but I can enlarge upon it by offering the answer I obtained from an American – a breed not known for energetic walking – who goes back-packing nearly every weekend.

His reply was hardly profound and he was unable to pinpoint what he thought he was accomplishing; nor could he explain just what it was that excited him. All he could tell me was that he loved it. He knew he wasn't a masochist and he knew he wasn't trying to shape himself up for any Olympic marathon. He just knew that he adored being out there in the wilderness, even if that wilderness was only 55 minutes from the concrete security of New York City. He enjoyed driving his body uphill and down, feeling his muscles exerting themselves, feeling the 'country' air fill his lungs, feeling the yards and miles trail off behind him, knowing that everything he needed was strapped to his back. He was unsure what he was accomplishing, but he knew he was filled with a sense of self-accomplishment.

I have a near-neighbour who uses the wilderness to help straighten out his city life. To him – and within him – there was a constant appreciation of an urban and rural environment. At the same time there was a constant dislike of both. He used the wild to help him appreciate the convenience and comfort of the city. Then, in turn, he used the city to help him appreciate the escape – the sensual awareness – that the woods offered him. It is, on reflection, the same with me though I like both urban and rural surroundings perhaps for that very reason; each having their place in the business of living.

Both the city life and the wilderness escape can offer a sense of self-accomplishment. Both environments call for our best survival instincts. Being in the woods backpacking brings out this same sense of survival and accomplishment in most people. Being out there on your own is a throwback to pioneer times. The psyche reaches back across the aeons to gather up a full appreciation of 'I did it; I have survived'.

Which brings me to How? Nowadays we have all sorts of modern equipment to help us survive – super lightweight tents and sleeping bags, pre-packaged foods, sophisticated gadgetry – but there remains the challenge of the wild. A wilderness – even the few remaining in our own island – can overwhelm whatever super-duper equipment you may be carrying. So there are still vital basic precautions one should take in the mountains and there is a different set of precautions to be taken in a desert. Weather conditions – one likely to be too cold; the other too hot. Water – in the mountains there'll be too much; in the desert too little. And sometimes the sun can harm you in both environments even though you may be shivering with cold in the former.

Finally, there is the old adage of walking that is more relevant today than it was when it was coined. 'Leave nothing but footprints; take nothing but memories (or pictures)'. Alas, many attainable trails of modern times are marked not only by indicator stones or painted arrows but by the litter of thoughtless ramblers.

And so to the final question, Where? This book provides one answer, chronicling some footways I have taken that lead to this new experience and, ultimately, if you surrender to the lure, to the possibility of high adventure.

Christopher Portway 1999

1

Great Britain
Where the Roman Legions Marched

No country in the world, for its size and population, has such a wealth of public footpaths as Britain. Its magnificent network of arteries over which a walker has legal right to pass is well in excess of a hundred thousand miles with many hundreds more of quiet green lanes along which few vehicles penetrate.

Walking in Britain has a special fascination. Many of its footpaths have been established for centuries; some were even worn by the feet of prehistoric man. The earliest paths were used for transporting goods; in effect they were trade routes linking isolated communities. The Romans built surfaced roads mainly for strategic purposes of which stretches still survive. And drovers' ways along which cattlemen herded their beasts to market, tracks worn by pilgrims, and 'corpse ways' on which the dead were carried from outlying villages to the nearest churchyard, are, in many cases, still footpaths to this day.

In addition to Britain's network of local paths, some two thousand miles of long-distance footpaths following more than a dozen routes through countryside of outstanding beauty await the walker. These are routes designated by the Countryside Commission to provide continuous off-road walking, well away from urban centres. Each offers varied scenery, wildlife and glimpses of the past.

Not quite so thick on the ground as the footpaths, yet some derived from the same source, is the country's web of Roman roads. All over the

Roman Empire their highways were laid as a carefully planned system linking the centres of occupation, both military and civil, to every neighbouring centre, so as to ensure the most rapid communication possible. The roads were thus more nearly analogous to a railway system, and their layout was planned by well-trained engineers in much the same manner, after a skilful survey of the ground problems to determine the choice of the most practical route. It is the universal evidence of just this skill which constantly renders their work worthy of our admiration, for it should be remembered that no maps or compasses were available to them; the land to be traversed was often thickly forested, and the survey must often have been made in territory only recently conquered and liable to be infested with the remnants of a hostile population.

Today, many a modern road follows the general alignment of the original Roman route for no other reason than there is none better.

Britain is richly endowed with Roman roads, many of them bearing names that are far more evocative than the simple numbering of our present-day arteries. Five of them are virtually household names or at least so in the localities they traverse. Universally famous is Watling Street, much of it today forming the route of the A5 between London and Shrewsbury, and, in the other direction, the old A2 to Dover. And who hasn't heard of Foss Way linking Lincoln to the Devon coast by way of the Cotswolds, East Anglia's Peddars Way and the Welsh Sarn Helen are, likewise, meaningful names to those interested in Britain's Roman legacies as is Dere Street running from York into Scotland.

To follow on foot such ancient routes is not, perhaps, the easiest of tasks for, in modern times, they are apt to cross private land or serve as the bedrock of a road used by 20th century traffic. But an element of challenge enters into it which makes for an intriguing journey. An itinerary that includes town and village and countryside laced with known and unknown Roman remains provides varied, even adventurous walking.

The five Roman roads mentioned above themselves offer the maximum variety; some are rural from start to finish, and in places are only a track. Others, though they carry much traffic, retain grassy sections where the modern road goes its own way. To follow the old routes where they deviate from the existing highway is a task made possible by the presence of sections still visible either in the original stone or in the form of *aggers* – 'ghost' markings – faintly identifiable across hills and meadows, and from the information offered by Ordnance Survey maps particularly their 1: 50 000 sheets. And not only do these maps show the track of the original road but also the Roman and non-Roman antiquities along the way. Maybe you – like me – are not one to get excited about a heap of stones purporting to be a Roman villa or bath-house but come upon such a site in a lonely situation and at the end of a trail-blazing slog and, I assure you, you'll be in the right frame of mind to enjoy the discovery.

The most northerly of the major Roman roads of Britain is Dere Street. Conceived in York it runs, far straighter than the modern counterparts, towards Edinburgh. It was the one I chose to follow in the company of my son, Paul. With York as an appropriate starting point, it is close to Micklegate that Dere Street has its beginnings though the old road fails to identify itself until the bridge across the Foss Stream, some three miles out beyond the factories, marshalling yards and housing estates of a later, less elegant age.

Distrustful of English summers which Byron declares come 'somewhere between the end of July and the beginning of August' we had chosen early spring as the season in which England excels, but the morning we set off from the city was damp and dreary. The gloom made the suburbs drearier still but we persevered to gain Green Hammerton, the best bits of which lie off the Street though we were in no mood to dally. At Aldborough Moor we crossed a tributary of the river Ure to lose the route momentarily because we were unable to reconcile a suddenly twisting course for no apparent reason with our preconceived notions of a road-building pattern that permitted few corners. A local butcher complete with traditional boater emerged from his shop to point us the way. He was pleasantly garrulous to the point of explaining that Aldborough was the *auld* or old fort, *Vetus Burgus*, which the Romans called *Isurium*, seat of the governor of *Eboracum*, the town on the river Ure, capital of the Brigantes who had surrendered Caractacus to Rome. But our butcher's knowledge, alas, was unable to supply the reason for the winding road. We continued through the village, noting its well-kept green, preserved stocks and a row of ancient houses, and set course for Boroughbridge.

Those who drive madly along the Great North Road will have heard of Boroughbridge for it is a name that appears on direction indicator boards many miles north and south of the small town. But few are likely to have turned off the multi-lane highway to see it. And this is a pity. Formerly *Ponteburc* or the bridge of the burgh of Aldborough across the river Ure, modern Boroughbridge, though bedevilled by the A1 and its ceaseless thunder of traffic, is an ancient and sleepy place.

To the north of the town the *agger* of Deer Street is traceable intermittently among fields but since trespass results from sticking closely to it we took to the offerings of a bus bound for Catterick. Fanatical though I can sometimes be I was not going to suffer the asphyxiating fumes of the internal combustion engine by walking Britain's only named arterial highway.

But near Leeming we were tempted off the airless vehicle to investigate the village through which Daniel Defoe declares Dere Street to run. 'The Roman way is plain to be seen, and is now called Leeming Lane, from Leeming Chapel, a village through which it goes through'. We could but take his word for it. Again the route makes some uncharacteristic bends probably for the purpose of maintaining a course on higher, firmer ground. Leeming took its name from the old English *leoma*, meaning 'brightness', a reference to the beck on which most of it stands. This piece of intelligence we unearthed from the church, invariably a repository of information on village geography.

Catterick held some surprises. A shower of rain sent us into the local cafe where a woman in a white overall vouchsafed the fact that there were two available hotels in town where we could stay the night. The County was next door so we called there first – to be met by the same woman and her lofty declaration that 'she was full'. It was as if she had not clapped eyes on us before! Opposite was the Angel and we half-expected the good lady to appear here too in response to our summons. Instead a bright young Irishman, one Denis Doran, late of the Stags Head, Dublin, bade us welcome, offering the best room in the house. The building contained an underground passage to the village church as well as a crypt which now keeps the beer cold. Even a ghost was on the inventory. The bar was well patronised by a mix of locals and servicemen and it was a soldier who told us about Catterick Bridge.

Cataractonium, as Catterick was called, is today wedged between a racecourse and two main roads. As it was over two thousand years ago, so it is today, a military camp though there appears to be nothing left of the earlier establishment. But our pre-dinner leg-stretch along a footpath that followed the course of the Street brought us to the river Swale and a charming old bridge. Scrambling down the side of the massive stone supports we came upon the original Roman flagstones that once formed the Dere Street ford. They are in perfect condition and yet few people know they are there. In fact only one of the several residents of Catterick to whom we spoke back in the Angel bar admitted to knowing that Dere Street passed this way; the others had never heard of it. I was grateful to the soldier for his remarkable knowledge.

Next morning we made our way to Scotch Corner, an important junction of trunk roads and a traffic-snarled roundabout and from there onto the peaceful B6275 making a beeline for Bishop Auckland. At this point Dere Street became a country road, straight as the straightest in Britain. But at the river Tees the new bridge has funked the crossing, its builders having chosen a narrower point a hundred or so yards upstream. Not so the old. For Paul and I the walk had turned into a legion's march which took us straight on down a sunken lane to the remains of the Roman bathhouse belonging to the fort that once guarded the bridge. When the river is low groups of piles can be seen in the bed which formed part of the foundations of the Roman structure.

Piercebridge is the entry into Durham and a lovely village into the bargain. Its green was lavishly sprinkled with a heavy crop of daffodils beneath the bare arms of a number of large elms and in the nearby pub we put down a pint of the local brew with the greatest of ease.

The 'pierce' of Piercebridge refers to the *persh* or osiers beside the Tees. And here the river is a serene waterway, its banks clothed in willows and reeds, threading through the southern end of the village. Its beauty belied the fact that we were entering a county more than half of which had been exploited as a coalfield.

For another eight miles the Street held an unerring course until it reached Brusselton, once a village that became a colliery town but has since reverted to a semblance of picturesqueness. There the modern road forsook the Roman, rejoining it as the main street through Bishop Auckland. It was Man who had sullied the fair face of the Wear Valley with his abominations of the 19th century industrial revolution though the scars are healing on a landscape of far-flung horizons.

Beyond Bishop Auckland the Roman road, marked by traces of its *agger*, plunges steeply down to the river Wear in the direction of Binchester, standing perched on a shoulder of high ground.

Playing hide and seek with a phantom of a road we came upon the excavated ruins of *Vinovia*, a Roman hill encampment at Binchester. Student archaeologists invited us inside the confines of their excavations to inspect the carefully-revealed and sifted stones and hypocaust and to discuss the question of whether Dere Street ran through or only close to the site. We came to no conclusions and little trace of the old road could be found of its northwest course out of Binchester. Its promise, however, led us to Willington, another one-time colliery town, where in vain we searched for a vacant bed eventually being forced to continue to neighbouring Crook.

Now well off course we had the greatest difficulty in re-locating Dere Street and its alignment through Ragpath Wood and a hamlet called Quebec. Except for knowing it would surface once more at Lanchester we had no means of recognising the faint traces and water-worn hollows by which an expert might succeed in following it. A signpost indicated Quebec as '1 mile' but it was well to our right and plainly we had muffed the route here. We were not to rejoin it until Wilks Hill on the B6301 upon which we arrived around mid-morning.

For the final two miles into Lanchester we accepted a lift in a tarmac lorry. It was a sticky ride but the driver was a wealth of information. *Longovisium*, he told us, possessed a great aqueduct for watering the fort though most of the masonry had been used to build Lanchester church tower. At the outskirts of the small town we were dropped to make the steep slog up the hill to view what remained of all this Roman construction. Our disappointing reward was the mere sight of a grassy rise which purported to be the foundation of the fort.

Lanchester itself was an improvement on Willington. A shopkeeper confirmed that indeed a series of aqueducts watered the fort but that its stone had gone into the repair of neighbouring houses and the erection of the church tower. Certainly the most substantial edifice in Lanchester is the church and well it should be.

On again through Leadgate, a town that once had the misfortune to gaze upon the giant skeleton of a defunct Consett Steelworks, to Ebchester which became the parting of the ways; the end of the healing scars and the beginning of unblemished beauty.

The Romans built another small fort at Ebchester called *Vindomora*, the materials of which are, of course, incorporated into the nearby Norman church. But there are enough foundations to look upon even if one does have to obtain permission from a local resident to explore them amongst the brussel sprouts of his vegetable garden. The householder was evidently aware of the novelty of having fragments of his country's heritage on his doorstep and, fittingly, he knew something about Dere Street. A Northumberland man, he had married a Durham lass but paid the price by having to move into the neighbouring county. 'Only by a few hundred yards', he declared with a grin, 'Just down the road you cross the river and are in Northumberland'. Of the route of the Street he was less concise. Across the river the course of the road is not at all clear mainly on account of some recent mining, he told us. But at Morrowfield it is reckoned to materialise again to Whittonstall and near there its course is

A view of Hadrian's Wall at Walltown in the Northumblerland National Park
Photo: Countryside Agency

marked by yet another fort. 'Not much left to see', he mused, 'but it shows you're on the right track'.

We descended the hill to the narrow bridge spanning the river Derwent and marched abreast into Northumberland. Once more a river marked a county border and, ahead, stretched a million acres of fresh air and a territory sometimes gentle but more often wild. GM Trevelyan wrote: 'Northumberland throws over us, not a melancholy, but a meditative spell'. We were to see exactly what he meant.

Through Whittonstall we tramped, feeling the exhilaration of the proximity of exciting country. Our road – the modern B6309 – switchbacked in equally anticipatory mood and an iron notice indicated the few stones of a fort in an adjacent field. Had we been driving a car I doubt if we'd have given it more than a glance but being one of the markers along our path the turf-covered stones made eloquent viewing.

At Stockfield, pointed at by signposts that increased the mileage the nearer one got to it, a plate on a bridge read:

'Does the road go uphill all the way?

Yes my Friend.

Will it take the whole long day?

Yes to the very end'.

But the end came all too soon with the busy A695 paralleling the river Tyne. The density of the traffic and a rising blister on my toe provided excuses for a short bus ride; three miles into Corbridge, the famous *Corstopitum*, a Saxon and Roman town of spectacular display.

The ancient town was once the capital of Northumbria. From about AD81, when the Romans first came here and built their onward northern road towards Scotland, it became a strategic crossing-point of the river Tyne and the junction with their lateral east-west road known as the Stanegate. Back in the third century AD, it was evolving into a military centre. King Ethelred I of Northumbria was slain here by a conspiracy of his nobles in 786. In 918 Regnald, a persistent Viking invader, defeated the combined English and Scottish army, and, at various periods thereafter, the town was ransacked by King John, Robert Bruce, David II of Scotland and others. Today history retains a living presence in Corbridge.

A cottage that forms one of its medieval dwellings became our home for the night with Mr and Mrs Hulse scurrying around their warm and cosy domain attending to our comfort. The equally oak-beamed Black Bull Restaurant fed us a meal of a substance calculated to allay a walker's appetite.

A student of Roman archaeology will have a field day at *Corstopitum*, a mile to the west of the town. The site of the one-time Roman town is laid bare for all to see. Built originally as a cavalry post in AD79, enlarged seven years later to accommodate five hundred horsemen and a thousand infantrymen, the fort was abandoned when Hadrian's Wall was erected. Subsequently a new and expanded fort was constructed on the same site and this is what remains today. Covering about twenty-two acres it contains granaries, temples and two military compounds as well as a well-stocked museum.

Dere Street leaves the fort at *Corstopitum* to merge with the present Corbridge-Portgate road, the A68, which was to lead us for many solitary miles towards the lonely Cheviot Hills. And at Portgate we reached Hadrian's Wall.

The story of the wall is part of that of Rome's conquest of Britain, which began in earnest about AD 71. In the year 121 Britain was visited by Hadrian who ordered his Imperial Legate, Aulius Plautius Nepos, to build a wall as a safeguard against the northern Picts who habitually showed their feelings for the conquerors by making incursions southwards.

The original plan was to build a wall as well as a ditch from Newcastle to Carlisle, eighty Roman (about 73 modern) miles long, effectively sealing the Tyne-Solway line. Additional to the main forts there were to be strongpoints every Roman mile and two turrets or signal stations in between. Reduced in some sections, it finally stood twenty feet above the ground overlooking its ditch of twenty seven feet wide and nine feet deep. Into this formidable defence went the troops, one thousand infantrymen or five hundred cavalrymen to each of the seventeen forts and fifty soldiers apiece to the strongholds, and four to each of the turrets.

At Portgate, alas, there is little to be seen of the remains of the wall and nothing of the gate. But northward, as the Romans discovered, the land was to grow wilder with every mile, the climate harsher, the natives fiercer, the comforts fewer.

A tiny village war memorial offered its martial testimonial to a conflict of our own time:

'Ye that live in English pastures green,
Remember us, and think what might have been'.

It's comforting to know we've been conquered only once.

For miles the road, dead straight, pranced over escarpments to reveal more miles of itself arrowing to the horizon. Cars sped by in bursts of enthusiasm as their drivers, freed from the restrictions of urban driving and winding roads, gave in to their speed cravings. Accomplished walker as I thought I was, my son kept forging ahead to be checked repeatedly by a foot-sore father.

Road walking, particularly on a main road, I do not care for but here, to have the proximity of others, was a certain assurance in such a desolate land. At Bewclay the contours steadied themselves, and for several miles the Street steered west-north-west through countryside that grew lonelier still. North of Chollerton it entered a world older than that of the Romans'; the sites and stones of the earliest builders can be seen in North Tynedale. In the midst of these simple mementoes the road veered east, crossed a burn, then turned west again, but Dere Street swept on, marked by a faint *agger* through stone-strewn meadows.

Though tempted off the road by the proximity of Thockrington where members of the Shafto family are buried we remained on course, passing Hallington Reservoir, in a region rich with ancient earthworks and camps. 'Bobby Shafto's gone to sea', I started to sing in time with our footsteps; the old jingle touching a chord in my memory. Near a farm called 'Waterfall' – isolated houses were marked on our maps in lieu of non-existent villages – we heard talk of a Roman milestone erected as a memorial to an English nobleman and determined to find it. The deserted farmstead lay under a spur of high land but though we searched everywhere we found nothing. Only when I sought concealment in a ditch at the bidding of nature did I stumble across it – literally. Indeed I fell over it, an oblong stone slab like a log on the damp earth.

At the site of the small Roman camp at Fourlaws the road, straight until then, takes a noticeable shift to the right as the Roman surveyors corrected their line towards Chesterhope Common and the modern road slavishly follows suit. However, at Fourclaws village the A68 shakes itself free and veers away from the rigid line of Dere Street, the *agger* of which can be seen as more lightly-coloured herbage across the fields.

So clear was its passage that we followed it with no difficulty, passing Chesterhope Common on our right, and so came directly upon the large Roman fort of *Habitancum* overlooking the river Rede. About *Habitancum* Daniel Defoe is supposed to have remarked: 'Here is abundant business for an antiquary; every place shews you ruin'd castles, Roman altars, inscriptions, monuments of battles, of heroes killed and armies routed.'. The fort consists today almost entirely of grassy mounds with some fragments of finely-worked masonry at the north-east corner. As with other forts in the area, *Habitancum* was rebuilt several times after its foundation in the mid-second century AD, when the 'Barbarian Conspiracy' overran all the country north of Hadrian's Wall and there was treachery amongst the Romans themselves, with some of them joining the invaders. Never again did the Romans garrison such outposts as these, and within sixty years their armies had left the country to its fate.

A couple of miles and we ran into yet another fort, this one neither indicated nor recorded. It was no more than a mound or two; a swelling of the earth, but I was pleased with myself for recognising it for what it was.

Kipling, more than Defoe, catches the timbre of Dere Street here in the silent world of Northumberland: 'The hard road goes on and on, and the wind sings in your helmet-plume, past altars to legions and generals forgotten, and broken statues of gods and heroes, and thousands of graves where the mountain foxes and hares peep at you'. Many times the paving stones of the road must have rung to the marching legions. Twenty-five miles a day they could march, armed and armoured. The order of marching seldom varied. First came the cavalry; jingling a lordly way before the infantry; after them, the baggage, the senior officers, the Legion Standard flanked by auxiliaries and more horsemen. The wind sighed, rising and falling with a pitiful sobbing sound as if it mourned the dead of long-forgotten battles that once raged about this haunted landscape. Even the few stunted trees, their branches keeled over by wind, bowed in supplication.

We were glad of the lift into High Rochester. A lone woman in a smart Toyota picked us up of her own accord and we needed no second invitation. Our legs were weary and we were concerned about accommodation for the night. She would have taken us further but at High Rochester is *Bremenium* – 'Place of the Roaring River' – a strategic Roman outpost that clamoured for attention.

Much of the small village, including the porch of the school and that of the church, was made of Roman stone, a fact that boded ill for what remained of the fort of *Bremenium*. At first glance the ruins, ensconced incongruously in a farmyard, looked neglected and insignificant but there is more of interest here than meets the eye.

The site overlooks Sills Burn (whence the name *Bremenium*, from *Brimo* or 'the roaring one'). But the burn flowed less loudly than in AD142 when the Governor of Britain, Lollius Ubicus, lodged at the fort on his way northwards. The heyday of High Rochester was probably in the third century AD when it was garrisoned by a cohort of the Roman army, with cavalry for patrols and its famous spring guns for defence. Two of the stone balls which the weapon used can still be seen at the village schoolhouse. Today it is possible to recognise the west gateway and bits of the surrounding wall muddled with dilapidated cowsheds and farm outhouses.

At Redesdale Camp, just half a mile beyond *Bremenium*, the A68 swings away from Dere Street never to return. The line of the old road is clearly traceable for three miles arrowing towards the rise of the Cheviots, maintaining its arrogant straightness, but for Paul and I a lift to Byrness, some half dozen miles along the modern road, became prudent. We got it from a grocery van to discover that Byrness was no more than a hotel. But a hotel was what we had in mind and, moreover, there was room at the inn – which was as well for it had begun to rain.

The lonely Byrness Hotel proved an oasis of comfort. We were pampered rotten by Peter and Maureen Scott from whom we learnt much about Dere Street's crossing of the Cheviot Hills. By morning the rain had turned to a sullen drizzle with low grey cloud smudging the tops of the Forestry Commission's dark acres of pine enveloping the hotel. We left with ominous warnings in our ears. In such fickle weather the Cheviots can be a dangerous playground in which to stray from the path.

Our initial route was that of the Pennine Way, the long-distance footpath winding up England's spine, and though this led across part of an artillery range – its red danger flags liberally displayed – we could hear no crump of shells. Unexploded missiles there may have been strewn around the ground but, being a Sunday, we took the view that even the army would respect the Sabbath. More to the point the fog would inhibit useful gunnery practice if the Sabbath didn't.

The Pennine Way, let it be said, is the ultimate challenge to a walker in Britain. For much of it the landscape is rugged, majestic and sometimes breathtaking. The route offers some of the roughest walking in the country on a path that drifts across featureless peat moors and windswept peaks often far from habitation. The climax comes with the Cheviots. In good weather an experienced walker will meet no major problem. In adverse conditions, the going can be beyond the endurance of the toughest hiker.

I have to admit to an abysmal ignorance of these facts at the time though we were offered some awareness of them by the kindly Scotts. However, our progress along a fenced track that deteriorated into a sodden path was swift, mainly on account of the cold mist that penetrated to our bones. The path took on a new name – Gamel's Path – and we knew then we were back on Dere Street.

Who this Gamel was nobody seems to know though somewhere along his path is a point where the English and Scottish met to settle disputes; sometimes peaceably, sometimes not. In the swirling mists enveloping the hills and dales it was easy to imagine the Northumbria of bygone days. Then it was a no-man's land, a region of fierce and wild independence whom the Romans, behind their forts and walls, designated as barbarian. This notion of barbarism coupled with a fast realisation of the dangers that its climate could inflict upon us lent wings to our feet.

At Coquet Head, back with the Pennine Way, we stumbled across the first of four camps which the Romans built near Chew Green, a locality of bleak magnificence in sunshine but brooding menace in cloud. Excavation here has unearthed the bones of a Roman soldier who died more likely of the climate than by a Pictish spear. On nearby Brownhart Law, a mound rising from a hollow, we found the remains of the Roman signal station which marks the border with Scotland. We knew both sites to be there, hidden in the damp grey film, but the thrill of discovery as each appeared was not to be denied. We halted briefly, gazed upon their lonely stones, and pushed on, eager for the sight of the habitation of living souls.

We entered the Scottish county of Roxburghshire and from Shibden Hill the Street ran straight for six miles in the form of a sheep track. The contours of the land pushed apart, making for gentler walking and at the river Teviot I knew from the map that the town of Jedburgh lay within striking distance to our left. A certain relief engulfed me for mid-afternoon heralded a dark and early nightfall. A country lane materialised to give us the comforting certainty that it knew where it was going and, ignoring whatever route Dere Street chose to take, we clip-clopped along its metalled surface into Newtown St. Boswells, there to spend the night at the Buccleuch Arms Hotel.

A typical Lowland township is St Boswells of squat, stony dwellings with trim front gardens and moth-balled 'front rooms'. Only the abbey made it special, the warm sandstone ruin, lawn-laced and tree-trellised, sitting comfortably in the centre of town.

The last three miles of Dere Street were vague and muddled. Parts seemed to concur with the A6091 to Melrose so we took the easy way and tramped purposefully along it with the Eildon Hills humped on the skyline. The mist had lifted, leaving its dampness upon the land.

Melrose, not to be outdone, produced another substantial abbey ruin to add dignity to a town that already wore an aura of genteel respectability. We turned away from its bustling centre onto a B-road to reach a suburb called Newstead. Here a fort – *Trimontium* – marks Dere Street's suspected end, raising more green mounds as its epitaph; an inauspicious finale to a hundred and forty miles of Roman road through large tracts of the wildest territory in Britain. Now only ghosts haunt *Trimontium* for few visitors pause in Newstead.

By way of Galashiels and a friendly coach of Scottish Omnibuses we travelled the last miles to Edinburgh, staring fixedly out of steamed-up windows wondering if Dere Street might, secretly, be coming this way too. But there was nothing to show; not even the faint shadows of an old highway. Even the ghosts were dead.

2

France

A Writer's Way

If you have ever tried to follow one of those fine, broken lines marked 'FP' on an Ordnance Survey map, you'll know what I mean. They look so clear as they stretch across Badgers Dell, march through Maplehanger Copse and wind along the Spindlebrook (Spr); in the flesh – or foliage – you're as likely or not to find that the 'footpath' fingerpost merges wonderfully well with the surrounding trees, that Badgers Dell is three foot high in corn, that the last high wind has left Maplehanger Copse like a plate of spaghetti, and that the path and Spindlebrook are so uniformly dry/muddy that you can't tell if you're on one or the other. And then you notice that the broken line has stopped – in the middle of nowhere. Ah well, at least you won't have any trouble finding your way back.

Footpaths in Great Britain are a gratifying source of head-scratching wonder and confused delight. Our long-distance paths have come into being in specific regions of recognised beauty and interest. They are nourished and protected by the Countryside Commission and, more intimately, by local societies through whose territory they pass. We have our Pennine Way, Offa's Dyke and South Downs Way and others, together with a host of indiscriminate short-distance routes; but there is no attempt whatsoever to link these into a national 'grid'.

France, of course, does things differently: her Federation Francaise de la Randonee Pedestre has been in existence since 1947, during which time it has mapped, protected and prolonged the footpaths of France, organising them into a national complex and teaching people to enjoy them. You could spend a year or more and never leave a route that is designated 'GR', numbered like a main road, indicated by a red-and-white fingerpost, and blazed by cheerfully painted daubs on trees and posts. No chance here of explaining away your pioneering urge with an airy 'Sorry, I seem to have lost the path'. French farmers can order you simply to 'Suivez les bloomin great signes rouge-et-blancs!'

Today, the French long-distance footpaths wriggle across more than 15,000 miles of picturesque France and – with the Gallic peasant's disregard for borders – neighbouring countries too. France's situation as part of the European mainland has encouraged her to introduce international paths – itineraires Europeens, marked green with red that run blithely into neighbouring countries.

Then there are the PDs – itineraires pedestres. These are for both the aspiring walker with little time to spare and for those wanting a pleasant afternoon stroll – often circuits, of one to six hours duration.

Wherever you go on a GR, you can be sure that it will lead you into the cream of the countryside. Walking these footpaths offers a chance to see the real rural France. But additional to this official network is a celebrated 'outsider'; a route blazed by a nineteenth century Scottish author. It is called The Robert Louis Stevenson Trail.

It was a well-publicised event in 1978, the centenary of a walk in the Cevennes of central France taken by our own Robert Louis Stevenson that made Britons abruptly aware that France could offer the hiker some first class walking territory together with amenities of a flavour so exclusive to that country.

The author's celebrated walk, chronicled in his diary in 1879 and entitled *Travels with a Donkey in the Cevennes* has been read and loved by generations of readers even though his *Treasure Island* and *The Strange Case of Dr Jeckyll and Mr Hyde* were more famous still. Yet Stevenson's influence on walkers has been far greater than his own brief and limited walking experiences suggests.

This notwithstanding I am indebted to the gentleman for being the unwitting cause of my following in his footsteps – albeit minus donkey – exactly a hundred years later when the now-extinct airline, Dan Air, commissioned me to hike the 132-mile trail with a view to promoting its flights serving Clermont-Ferrand and Montpellier, the closest feeder airports to the extremities of the trail.

For me, as with Stevenson, the walk commenced from the hillside town of Le Monastir-sur-Gazeille in the Haute-Loire and ended at the town of St Jean-du-Gard in the province of Gard. It follows the red and white fingerposts of the Sentiers de Grande Randonnee in some sections but mostly forges its own way marked with a blue and white cross. It is a route that makes for inspiring hiking.

My retracing of the RLS trail was made in the same daily stages as the author's. With four companions I set out from jaunty Monastir, capital of the ancient canton of Velay at the northern end of the stunning but little-known Cevenne Hills. We carried our own rucksacks, not trusting our loads to the likes of Modestine, Stevenson's permanently obstinate donkey of which he writes so eloquently. It was for very different reasons to mine that RLS had taken to the road. Disagreement with his father which, for him, made home unbearable was the initial impetus and the world had become his oyster. Having voyaged the canals of Europe and following the publication of his views on the subject of walking tours he decided to put his suppositions to the test; putting his legs where his pen was so-to-speak. In his essay he defined various types of walker; by what interests them as they walk, the speed at which they walk and the type of terrain they chose. 'Uneven ground is not so agreeable to the body, and it distracts and irritates the mind. Whereas, when once you have fallen into an equable stride, it requires no conscious thought from you to keep it up, and yet it prevents you from thinking earnestly of anything else', he explains.

Following his dalliance with canals he set out, in 1878, to tramp the Cevennes arriving at Monastir for the start of this particular journey. Together with Modestine, described as the size of a large Newfoundland dog and the colour of 'an ideal mouse', Stevenson intended traversing some of the highest and wildest terrain in France, moving across the remote borderlands of four departments – the Haute-Loire, the Lozere, the Ardech and Gard – and over the top of two notable summits, the Gouley and the Pic de Finiels of between four and five thousand feet. This, then, was the route he had set for us. His journey was to last twelve days, a period we intended to repeat. The itinerary, for one who had been obliged to dissect his books as part of an educational curriculum, read like a litany of household names – Le Monastir, Pradelles, Langogne, Notre Dame des Neiges, Montagne du Tarn and St Jean-du-Gard.

Monastir is a warm-stoned township of narrow alleyways and hidden squares barely changed from medieval times. RLS tells us 'As the name betokens, the town is of monastic origin. It stands on the side of a hill above the river Gazeille, about fifteen miles from Le Puy, up a steep road

Walkers on the Robert Louis Stevenson Trail

where the wolves sometimes pursue the diligence in winter' (*diligence* being a French word for stagecoach).

Following an inspection of the RLS exhibition at the minuscule half-timbered town hall we departed, clattering across the cobbles, bound for Goudet, ten kilometres distant.

Below the ruins of the sombre Chateau de Beaufort, the Hotel de Loire had provided very adequate sustenance as well as bed before the spartan offerings of bivouacking. RLS route signs pointed the way over pleasant rolling countryside though, clear of the town, these began to exhibit an aggravating habit of disappearing at junctions just when they were most needed. The locals were untiring in directing us to each subsequent hamlet though their suggested routes varied with personal notions of the shortest. The late September weather was perfect; a clear blue sky, warm sunshine and an occasional cool breeze rising from nowhere to stir the autumn crocuses in the meadows.

At Ussel Stevenson had experienced a minor mishap when his 'saddle and all, the whole hypothec, turned round and grovelled in the dust below the donkey's belly', as he puts it. Smugly I recorded in my own notes that by stoically carrying our 'whole hypothec' on our shoulders we were immune to such tribulations.

Beyond Goudet the going had become harder, a fact reflected in the RLS diary which, likewise, complains about the steepness of the country roads baked in hot golden dust. At Bargette, however, we were in for a surprise when the village mayor, Monsieur Marrion, a keen Stevensonian, expressed his pleasure at the task we had been set, obviously visualising commercial advantages for his flock were hikers to regularly pass through his domain. He then invited us into his cottage living room to ply us with aperitifs. The heavy furniture hindered our movements as, top-heavy with packs, we moved to the armchairs indicated. Our glasses were repeatedly refilled by our host, egged on by his considerable family who insisted we finish off their home-made sponge fingers. All the while Monsieur Marrion discoursed upon Stevenson in manner that had me looking round for him in the room. 'I would dearly love to come with you – even just to the next village', he said, glancing down at the crippled leg that tied him to his immediate surroundings. 'The trail is a living thing to me though the man himself who gave it birth is as dead as my foot'. I felt a stab of sadness for a man who plainly yearned to go on long walks but was prevented from doing so. We departed in a flurry of re-shouldering of rucksacks, handshakes and 'au revoirs' to steer a slightly erratic course towards our next objective.

Bouchet is all of 25 kilometres from Le Monastir but we, like Stevenson, reached it before nightfall, his donkey troubles and our alcoholic interlude notwithstanding. He stayed at the one and only inn; we camped under an outcrop of pines on spongy turf that, for me, induced sleep better than usual on a first night's camping. Village inn bedrooms in the nineteenth century were communal affairs and RLS slept in the same room as a young married couple. For all his Bohemian manners he was a shy man at heart but was sufficiently sophisticated to feel abashed. 'I kept my eyes to myself as much as I could', he writes, 'and I know nothing of the woman except that she had beautiful arms, full white and shapely; whether she slept naked or in her slip, I declare I know not; only her arms were bare'. No such worrying ponderings disturbed my slumbers.

Our combined route now swung almost due south, up over the last high farmlands of the Velay to Pradelles, then down to the small market town of Langogne on the river Allier. Pradelles turned out to be another ancient township which we reached following a stiff climb that had us sweating copiously between ever-increasing halts for blackberry consumption.

Our day ended at tiny Jagonas where we camped on the village green at the insistence of a group of gossiping ladies who plainly had a say in the running of the community. In the morning, milk straight from the cow provided us with the strength to tackle another uphill grind, this one to Langogne. It was a bigger place than we expected and its historic covered market gave fine opportunity to top up our provisions. The old bridge, where Stevenson crossed the river, was no longer in use; it was broken, crumbling and covered with ivy. Like the old broken bridge at Avignon its message was that one could not cross, literally-speaking, into the past as we were trying, perhaps rather half-heartedly, to do.

Beyond Langogne '...the land kept mounting for miles to the horizon', proclaimed our mentor – and didn't we know it. We succeeded in getting lost on several occasions – as Stevenson did – and were forever enquiring the way. There was no need to inflict our excruciating French upon each passer-by. 'Stevenson?', they would ask before we had barely opened our mouths and direct us on our way (though not always the right way). 'You must be English', became a regular comment, an observation that would hardly please a Scot.

Stevenson tells of becoming lost between the crumbling hamlets of Fouzilhic and Fouzilhac though it is hard to understand how since the two are only a few hundred yards apart. The countryside had become wilder with tree-adorned hills rising and falling like a wind-swept sea flecked with yellow crests of gorse. And at little Cheylard-L'Eveque, following a thirst-quenching session in the single bar, we succeeded in doing so yet again, only just attaining our prescribed destination by dusk.

It was Cheylard and Luc that provided the venue and reason for Stevenson's most famous – if uncomplimentary – utterance. 'Why anyone should desire to go to Cheylard or to Luc is more than my much inventory spirit can embrace. For my part, I travel not to go anywhere, but to go; I travel for travel's sake.'. Lonely country it may have been but hardly bad enough to incur such displeasure, especially Luc which greets its visitors with castle ruins, a statue of the Virgin (mentioned by RLS) and commendable views over the valleys.

We were now passing through the region notorious for the legendary 'Beast of Gevaudan', a so-called Napoleon Bonaparte of wolves, that had terrorised it during the mid eighteenth century, an occurrence that fascinated Stevenson. Roving in the remote hills between Langogne and Luc, the animal had attacked small children and lone women returning from market. There were even rumours of vampirism since the bodies of its victims were always drained of blood. Finally the beast was shot dead by a local woodsman in 1767 though the fear of further giant beasts caused farming to be neglected for years before suspicions subsided. 'If all wolves had been as this one', Stevenson remarked, 'they would have changed the history of man'.

Lying in my tent that night the slightest sound that resembled the snapping of a twig had my imagination running riot.

Nine kilometres ahead lay the Trappist monastery of Notre-Dame-de-Neiges – Our Lady of the Snows. And for those who are weary from travelling this path here is the means of a bed and a meal for the asking and a few francs.

The monks, of course, knew about RLS for he had stayed with their predecessors for two nights and had much to say about them in his chronicles. Our three-course meal in their company was plain but enjoyable with wine to go with it. The night in a severe cell apiece, with the only ornament a crucifix, was but a slight improvement on the bivouac and we felt compelled to attend Communion in their impressive chapel at some ungodly hour the next morning. The monastery had its own wine-producing annex, a warehouse of vats, barrels and bottles, run on a seemingly lucrative and hard-headed business basis. Whether any of us slept in the same cell as did Stevenson nobody could say though a fire in 1912 had destroyed some of the buildings.

One of the Grande Randonnee footpaths – the GR72 – took us in hand thereafter to lead us to La Bastide, a neat town possessing a railway station from which a train can be taken to save more than ten miles of road-walking should one be so inclined. But we were purists, more by necessity than personal choice, so walked.

'About Bleymard', writes RLS, 'the white road...traversed a piece of green valley set with spiry poplars and sounding from side to side with the bells of flocks and herds'. Here nothing at all had changed over the years and, I suppose, he, like us, shared the running water of cattle drinking troughs with cows in the fields along the way.

We were now climbing steadily and were well inside the Parc National des Cevennes created in 1970. It was only when we had cleared the tree-line that the true glory of the scenery became apparent. As far as the eye could see the plateau stretched into the far distance, changing hues from green to brown to a grey and purple; a wasteland virtually devoid of any sign of human presence. In fact the only sign of life, as we gazed around us, was a soaring Lammergeier vulture, a dark speck against the blue of the sky.

But it was between Le Bleymard and Florac with the climax at the Col de Finiels that the most majestic heights of the Cevennes are attained. Stevenson puts it thus: 'These are the Cevennes with an emphasis, the Cevennes of the Cevennes that, in clear weather, commands a view over all lower Languedoc to the Mediterranean Sea'.

We spent a night in a thick-walled stone refuge listening to the wind howling in the darkness. To the north the rounded granite bastion of Monte Lozere, the col of which we had earlier traversed, showed stark against the starlit sky, the highest point of the Cevennes which, for more than a quarter of the year, is covered by snow.

Next day we gradually descended to the charming sixteenth century Pont de Montvert, on the southern flank of Monte Lozere, prior to commencing the hike along the Tarn Valley. And with Montvert we found ourselves in the 'Country of the Camisards', the Protestant rebels of the insurrection of 1702, an incident of history that, again, caught the attention of RLS. Overlooking the small town from a ridge it was all too easy to conjure the writer's gaze sweeping the wild horizon above the struggling Camisards; Seguier leaping to his death from the window of a surrounded house, Roland fighting to the end with his back against an olive tree. For it was here in this tranquil township that the Camisards War broke out.

I vaguely recollect hearing about this obscure, forgotten but very nasty insurrection from my schoolboy youth. Pont de Monvert was just one of a score of villages where the Camisards attempted to maintain their Protestant faith in the face of Louis XIV's efforts to reconvert France to Catholicism. A priest, appointed by the king, had set up a torture chamber in the village to 'persuade' his charges to embrace the 'proper' faith but one night, on July 24, 1702, a group of Camisards attacked and hacked the Abbe to death. And it was this event that sparked the two-year civil war that led to the 'Burning of the Cevennes' in which government soldiers slaughtered twelve thousand Camisards and destroyed their villages.

This neighbourhood of the Cevennes still has a haunted, empty feel. Striding down the steep twisting road towards Florac we passed ruins of stocky Cevennes farmhouses built of local granite that could have been the result of the then government's handiwork.

By way of the Gorges du Tarn we came upon Florac and were reminded of another RLS declaration. 'I think if the Garden of Eden be anywhere, it is here in the Valley of the Tarn.' Together with the Pic de Finiels, flanked by the Goulet and Mars peaks of the Lozere, the real climax of the Cevennes is undoubtedly here in this lovely valley. It is visionary highland country; steep woods of scented pine giving way to bare moorland, heath and scree, dropping back down in precipitous alpine meadows or rocky gorges, rushing streams and deep green and gold terraces of chestnut trees. One walks against the sky, with chain after chain of hills rolling away southwards ahead.

Stevenson had found pleasure in Pont de Montvert nestled attractively around its old stone bridge and had nice things to say, too, about Florac. 'As perfect a little town as one could desire to see', he enthuses. For myself I found it nondescript at first glance but coyly it reveals an attractive heart as acquaintanceship increases.

The valley of the Mimente takes over from that of the Tarn to the Col de la Pierre Plantee which leads, in turn, to St Germaine-de-Calberte, 'a great parish nine leagues about...But the place itself, although capital of a canton, is scarce larger than a hamlet', complains RLS. The place must have grown a little since then though not to any great extent. Our route had led us down the long escarpment known as Monte Mars from which the astonishing panorama of hills continued, dominated by the Plan de Fontmort where the Camisards fought their final, bloody and suicidal battle.

Our last night was spent bivouacking uncomfortably on a grassy slope among a profusion of grapes, blackberries and apples. At least fruit with our breakfast was assured. It was close to the old coaching road – today little more than a track – that leads directly to St Jean-du-Gard and journey's end.

A walk that had turned into a march saw us over the Col de St Pierre, overgrown and undersigned, but the scenery remained but a degree less spectacular as we entered upon a new departement, that of Gard. The stone path descending a shallow gorge made joyous striding, much of it by way of natural steps. 'It was a long descent upon St Jean-du-Gard. Fifteen miles and a stiff hill in little beyond six hours', reports Stevenson. We made it in seven and thought we had done pretty well.

St Jean-du-Gard offered the Hotel Moderne of sublime comfort and the most delectable of cuisines. I could but hope that RLS celebrated the end of his journey as we did.

3

Germany (South)
A King's Walk

Bavaria is many things. It is mountains and hills, lakes and rivers, flower-strewn meadows and mushroom-sprouting forests, historic towns, elegant spas and fairytale castles. It is Farina dumplings, white sausages and white beer. And King Ludwig.

Whether Ludwig II was plain mad or merely eccentric will never be known. But however incapable he may have been as a reigning monarch there is no doubt at all about his popularity today as an extinct one. Bavarians speak of him in terms of tolerant endearment and even make picnic pilgrimages to his alleged death-place marked by a simple cross in the water at Schloss Berg on the twenty-kilometre long Starnbergersee. In mysterious circumstances he drowned in the reeds but did he fall or was he pushed? To this day conjecture as to what really happened is very much alive though what is fact is the legacy of magnificent edifices he bequeathed the German nation.

The acclaimed and much-promoted King Ludwig's Way is but another manifestation of his popularity. Whether the king ever walked any of its route that meanders some 120 kilometres – or 75 miles – across impossibly beautiful Bavarian countryside south-west of Munich is incidental. But the fact that three of his most fanciful castle-palaces lie along the Way between Starnberg and another lakeside town, that of Fussen on the Austrian border, is as good excuse as any for a long-distance footpath.

Schloss Berg itself, more manor house than castle, is technically the start point of the Way. We humans, however, unable to pick up the knack of walking on water, usually commence the walk from Starnberg town the other side of the lake – perhaps from the church of St Josef which also claims to be one of Ludwig's expiry points. Should you insist upon being a purist you can, of course, walk round the head of the lake which will add a few more kilometres.

Without doubt one of history's greatest southern German families is the Wittelsbachs who produced every ruler of Bavaria from Otto I in 1180 to Ludwig III in 1912. When Ludwig I died popular Ludwig II was pitched upon the throne in 1864 at the tender age of eighteen. Two years later he was forced to wage war, a war he didn't want and for which his domain was not equipped and subsequently lost. In spite of this indifferent accomplishment and further reduction of Bavarian sovereignty the highly sensitive and misanthropic monarch came to be the most liked and best-known ruler. 'Death claimed thee all too soon' was the tenor of a song by his subjects – although they had been assured that the king, and most of Bavaria with him, would have been plunged into bankruptcy had he not been declared incapacitated.

The three royal residences – Linderhof, Neuschwanstein and Herrenchiemsee – are today among the most frequently visited attractions in the whole of Germany. They are the legacy of an enigmatic, controversial and – for all his aberrations – undoubtedly notable ruler. 'The last true king of his century' is Paul Verlain's poetic tribute. Neuschwanstein Castle – the favourite German travel poster subject – sits astride the Ludwig Trail which, as all walkers of it are emphatically assured, was his happy hiking ground.

My peregrination down the royal way began somewhat inauspiciously at St Josef's Church, then enmeshed in scaffolding. Prior to setting out I took time off to attempt to admire its celebrated Ignaz Guenther altar when the heavens opened. Hastily I took refuge beneath the scaffolding boards since the church doors were firmly 'geschlossen' – even though it was Sunday. When the boards began to leak I resourcefully removed a white plastic sheet from a pile of bricks, draped it over my head and, astride a grave, prepared to ride out the tempest. Round the corner waddled two elderly matrons beneath a single umbrella. Upon perceiving the white phantom rising, as it were, from the dead both stood rooted to the spot, their mouths agape. They were not amused. My painful explanations rendered in atrocious German failed to pacify them and I received a severe ticking off – and confirmation, if needed, that the popular conception of Germans having no sense of humour is sometime justified.

It wasn't actually raining as I made for the Maisinger Schlucht, the first landmark, but low grey cloud promised a day's damp walking. The forested gorge of mature beech trees dripped in spasmodic manner and the boggy ground clung to my boots. Meadows were ablaze with cowbells bigger than I have ever seen, the wild fruits lushier and the mushrooms more voluptuous. Even the mosquitoes and horse-flies were of a breed that well may have inspired the Stuka dive-bomber of World War Two.

The white and yellow stone church of Aschering was closed – the second closed ecclesiastical building I'd come across on the Sabbath – but that of the larger Andech was open for inspection. Founded in the Middle Ages its rich display of Crusader relics from the Holy Land looked out of place in a Bavarian setting. Directly above the township stood the Monastery of Andech sharing its premises with a brewery-cum-beerhouse providing litre mugs of a special dark brew to go with big fatty pig's knuckles being served at communal outdoor tables. On a weekend one has to queue for everything in company with a horde of trippers out on a Sunday jaunt. Only the beer was delivered; the waitresses carrying three heavy jars in each hand, to deposit them with a thud on the shared tables whereupon a contented hum arose from the diners hunched over their equally hefty stick grenades of pork, or haxen as they call it. I joined in the show of contentment, thankful that I was not a vegetarian in Bavaria.

The path swung away from the monastery and, well victualled, I followed as it plunged downward into another well-timbered gorge, this one forming the steep Kiental Valley, a well-patronised spot for Sunday strollers. In turn it led into Herrsching on the eastern shore of the Ammersee, a small town opposite Diessen in which lay my bed for the night. I debated the notion of walking a half circuit of the lake but an excess of traffic persuaded me to take the ferry.

This at least gave me time to investigate the considerable charms of Diessen's Fischer-designed monastery-church of a bulk out of all proportion to the size of the town. Its startlingly decorative stucco of almost Disneyish abandon was to prepare me for what lay ahead in the realm of church decoration in this part of the world.

My night in the Strand Hotel was surprisingly peaceful for a centre-of-town venue and, blessed by a sun doing its utmost to penetrate a morning mist, I made my way out of Diessen on a route muddled by a rash of new houses and a deficiency of footpath signs. At an unsignposted junction I was directed by a mustachioed and cloaked Bavarian figure who could have been Ludwig himself. Thereafter the path became clearly marked by its motif of a blue letter 'K' topped by a crown.

Uphill and a sombre forest pulled me into its gloomy interior and I felt not the slightest compulsion to rest on the numerous seats provided by a generous local authority. It was a place of eerie shrines and minuscule silent chapels where, peeping through the window of one of them, I jumped out of my skin when a dog, sitting beside its contemplative master, sprang towards me barking at my intrusion.

To behold the sunshine again, to smell anew the grass and hear the comforting sounds of the open countryside lifted my spirits and lent wings to my feet. A stag abruptly cut across my path, paused to stare insolently, and bounded off over a meadow of inquisitive cows.

Wessobrun spelt a lunch break outside a pub sporting a maypole, an ornamentation that is *de rigour* in many parts of Bavaria, together with another church visit, though this particular edifice was, again, more monastery than church and famous for being home of the first German script.

On the way out of the village I was joined by an elderly woodcutter who puffed contentedly on his pipe saying nothing. This was not the slightest embarrassing; I enjoyed his temporary companionship without the necessity to make small talk. The footpath then cut across another smaller gorge before climbing steeply to the nearby summit of Hohenpeissenburg, virtually an outpost peak of the Alps foothills, from which there was a panoramic view on the horizon. With a wave my erstwhile companion left me.

Hohenpeissenburg village lay immediately below the hilltop and its Gasthaus Forelle offered my second night's lodging. It was an exceptionally friendly inn that supplied trencherman fare and, since strangers were then a rarity, I was pressed into conversation with the locals who ensured my glass was never empty.

The third day's march provided a highpoint along the Way, for it led not only through beautiful stretches of forests of mature beech and pine – the ancient German forest of legend with dark brown squirrels leaping through the branches – but also by way of the dramatic Ammerschlucht.

The Ammer is a true alpine river, swift and green-tinged as it forces its way through rocks and debris that form the ravine in which it runs. In one captive pool I managed a swift dip in the nude before a party of canoeists spoilt the solitude. The path's negotiation of the latter section of the Ammerschlucht was by way of trestle bridges and walkways, occasionally slippery but a saving grace for those scared of wet feet. At some points the path descended to river-level, then swept up again to emerge from the tree-canopy at the approaches to Rottenbuch village – the name meaning

A sign near Diessen on Ammersee

'clearance in the beeches'. And here is yet another monastery, this of tenth century vintage and once an establishment of the order of the Black Monks of Augustinian Canons. Its church was open but not the two beer houses, a fact which – heathen that I am – seemed to me to be a case of wrong priorities. But the church's breathtaking eighteenth century decor made some compensation.

Onwards again, thirsty but spiritually-uplifted, I followed a ridge giving further impressive views of the Lechtaler and Ammergauer Alps to the south and east and, by way of a meadowside track, to Wildsteig and my pad at the Gasthaus Strauss where an elder of the tiny community invited me to his home for coffee, schnapps and chat.

The climax of the fourth day of walking was undoubtedly the extravagance of Wies Church – the famous Wieskirche designed by the Zimmerman brothers; a startling masterpiece of Baroque. It is reached by way of low meadows and marshland rich in orchids plus the Schwarzenbach forest. The legend of the weeping statue carved by a medieval monk is a common one but in Wies it has a special significance and today their particular statue forms the centrepiece of the church's flamboyant altar. Personally I found the gold and silver ornamentation to be exaggerated to the point of garishness but it draws the crowds. Having dutifully gazed upon its celebrated battalions of golden angels I continued onwards in anticipation of more natural wonders.

And, nearer now, those distant Alpine ranges had formed into peaks of truly magnificent proportions which repeatedly hove into view as the Way crossed open fields and more marshland traversed by plank platforms. I lunched at a village called Prem where the cemetery held a sad abundance of Second World War tombstones inscribed 'Died in Russia'.

I had hoped to raise a bed at Buching but was forced to walk another three kilometres to Bayerniederhofen where the elegant Hotel Berghof made me exceedingly comfortable in a somewhat formal and soulless manner. Missing the warm-hearted gasthaus atmosphere I went out into the flower-bedecked village to find the place *en fete*, celebrating some obscure anniversary that Bavarians are wont to dredge up as an excuse for a party. All too soon I was roped into a drinking session and was nearly locked out of my posh hotel for my pains. From my bedroom window, even by moonlight, I could make out the white blob of the castle of Neuschwanstein against a jet black setting of trees.

The last eighteen kilometres of the Way I found to be something of an anti-climax; the walking easy, some of it on a tarmac cycle path scything across flat meadows sprinkled liberally with buttercups and ticking with electric fences. The sunshine was brilliant; flashing sparks on the tranquil waters of the small Hergratsried Lake. All the time the fairytale turrets of Neuschwanstein drew ever closer rising dramatically from the forest canopy. The track maintained company with the edge of the narrow lake Forggensee for a while and showed promise of drama to come by climbing the Pollat Gorge, a chasm that climbs right up to directly beneath the battlements of the castle.

Alas, to me, Neuschwanstein was a disappointment when finally I attained its entrance. From a distance – or a helicopter – it is an impossibly romantic sight with towers and turrets straining skywards. But on its threshold it became just another imposing building besieged by sightseers. However, this should not detract from the fact that the castle is a tour de force of both architecture and engineering, perilously perched as it is on its high rock pedestal; a mixture of medievalism and sheer fantasy, a folly on a gargantuan scale.

Ludwig himself seemingly had differing ideas of grandeur. His enormous throne room reflects the rabid fantasy of his kingly power at a period when royal influence was fast waning. Yet he was never happier then when devising a hardly grandiose heat-saving central-heating system for his royal kitchen.

A short driveway leads to another of his castles, that of Hohenschwangau built by Ludwig's father, Maximilian, a modest edifice compared to the former pile though impressive enough. The views from its windows are pure glory; a horizonfull of Alpine splendour acting as a backcloth to the magical exterior of Neuschwanstein.

From the base of Neuschwanstein the Way sheers away towards Fussen. I walked on, feeling a little like Ludwig himself, stealing away from his creation that had become a peepshow for the vulgar hordes. The last five kilometres was a simple following of a busy main road; all the imaginative route-forging bludgeoned out of the Way. I had a blister on my right heel and the horse-flies had got to know the blind spot on my neck. In a Fussen bar overlooking the lake, its opposite shore in Austria, my beer was the nectar of the gods.

Thus King Ludwig's Way – not the longest or grandest of European long-distance paths but one of character and interest together with a fleeting glimpse into the personality of an extraordinary monarch.

Germany (East)
Bigfoot on the Rennsteig

With the eastern half of Germany long-denied the western visitor it has been only since 1989 and the collapse of communism in Europe that the provinces of Saxony, Thuringia and others east of the one-time Iron Curtain stretching from Elbe to the Oder have become attainable to all once more. Looking back, it seems intolerable that for so long after the Second World War countless West Germans and the bulk of travellers from non-communist lands should have been denied the pleasure of visiting a part of Germany which has contributed so enormously to Europe's cultural heritage.

There is a long-distance footpath – the Rennsteig – almost universally known to Germans though to few others that runs near and cuts through not only the greatest of these cultural centres – such as Erfurt, Weimar and Eisenach – but also the spectacular history-laden Thuringian forest. It is a footpath that was even partly denied the citizens of East Germany itself – or the German Democratic Republic as it was called – since sections of it wandered briefly across the fanatically-guarded zonal border into West Germany's Bavaria.

The Rennsteig is actually an ancient road running for 168 kilometres – 105 miles – along the crest of this forest and the Schiefergebirge range of hills. The letter 'R', painted on tree trunks, marks the route which stretches eastwards from Horschel on the river Werra to Blankenstein on the river Saale. In winter the walk becomes a long-distance skier's 'highway' and the route includes a number of winter sports centres such as Oberhof and Lauscha.

In past times the Rennsteig served as natural border between the Franks and the Thuringians and old border stones can still be seen along the way. Altogether 1,300 such stones mark the route, all closely associated with German history, as witness the initials they bear of the many principalities and small feudal states through which the path once led. The highest point of the path is the 916-metre crest of the Great Inselberg.

The town closest to the western end of the Rennsteig is Eisenach. Though still in a state of restoration after World War Two bombing and communist neglect when I was last there it is, to me, a town lacking the picturesqueness of both Erfurt and Weimar though not of distinguished cultural citizenry. Here Luther spent his teenage years, here, in 1685,

Walkers and runners enjoy the Rennsteig

Bach was born, and here, in 1842, Richard Wagner gazed upon the fortress that rises above Eisenach and was inspired to write the opera Tannhauser.

And it is the Wartburg – once the castle home of the *landgraves* of Thuringia – that is the town's most notable edifice. From atop its great crag one can look down on a sea of red tile roofs of pretty pastel houses.

One of them is that of the house where the wife of Ambrosius Bach gave birth to her son Johann Sebastian. Nobody is quite sure which one but it is thought to be the mustard-yellow Bachhaus, as it's called today, and certainly there is a Bachian flavour about its interior especially when a Bach quartet strums his airs there. It is the same with the much larger and more splendid troubadour's hall in the Wartburg where I sat enthralled by a Wagnerian concert to which I had been invited prior to setting out on the Rennsteig.

My companions on the walk were five middle-aged members of a Hanover hiking club with little command of English between them which put my exceedingly limited German to the test. We started out in the early morning from the village of Horschel, lying beneath an autobahn viaduct, our main baggage being fortuitously transported ahead of us. I was, at seventy-two, the oldest of the group and almost from the start my age, plus my size eleven and a half boots, earned me mascot status and the nickname of 'Bigfoot'.

From one of the group's more knowledgeable members I gleaned a few further snippets of information about the Rennsteig. I was told that not only was it a border but also a messenger conduit and medieval trade route from Hessen to Bohemia dating from the tenth century. In modern times it forms part of a European Ramblers' Association long-distance route and, in the communist era, an East European walkway typically titled 'International Mountain Walk of Friendship' between Eisenach and Budapest – though, assuredly, a detour had to be made around the portions that crossed into West German territory.

Our first day's walk was of some thirty-five kilometres, its highlight, quite literally, being the Grosser Inselberg atop a considerable hill and reached – alas – by a road which had brought weekend motorists there in droves. The view was sensational, though the summit itself is marred by not only a rash of snack bars and souvenir shops but a tall radio mast. But the way to it, for us, was along the main ridge of the Schiefergebirge, the wooded hills giving fine glimpses on both sides of Thuringian forest landscapes.

That my companions were good walkers was not in doubt from the very start, particularly Rudolf who was always well ahead, forsaking pauses along the way. But their pace worried me not at all; I have long legs and am loathe to idle. The forests through which we passed were rich in mushrooms, blueberries and wild strawberries; the first day's walk blessed by brilliant sunshine tempered by a late September coolness heralding the onset of winter.

The night was spent in the village of Brotterode the further side of and below the Grosser Inselberg, our evening meal taken in a well-patronised gasthaus. Hardly had I taken a couple of mouthfuls when my stomach, for no reason that I could fathom, rebelled with a violent attack of diarrhoea and sickness that gave me a most unpleasant half hour in the gasthaus toilet. With the greatest difficulty I staggered back to my room there to collapse on my bed, weak and ill.

Though I felt a little better next morning the malady was to continue with varying degrees of ferocity throughout most of the six days of walking which detracted considerably from my enjoyment of it as well as, no doubt, making me exasperating company to my fellow walkers as, periodically, I was forced to dash into the undergrowth at nature's call.

The remaining five days walking became a well-planned operation, our baggage invariably appearing intact at each night's destination which were mostly comfortable and hospitable gasthauses. Oberhof was an exception; the town raising a luxury hotel in this considerable winter sports centre of some sophistication quite a few miles from the footpath. Though the thirty two kilometres of that second day was not a great distance my condition plus several kilometres of tarmac road-walking at the end of it made this stretch of the route particularly trying.

Thereafter the days' walking ran as follows:

Oberhof to Neustadt am Rennsteig : 25 kilometres.

Neustadt am Rennsteig to Limbach : 21.5 kilometres.

Limbach to Steinbach am Wald : 30 kilometres.

Steinbach am Wald to Blankenstein : 28 kilometres.

As was to be expected much of the path runs through forests broken by occasional clearings with, here and there, open meadowlands. 'R' signs, indicating the route, were legion so providing no excuse for losing the way though, now and again, comes a lapse which can put a walker off course. And this was particularly prevalent in the few townships through which the Way passes.

Twice it crosses and re-crosses the old zonal border, the wide sweep of a once-mined no-man's-land cutting ruthlessly through the forestland. The concrete track along which the East German border guards once patrolled remains and it will take many years before this livid scar across the whole of Germany is removed by the healing process of nature. To walk across the old border today remains a discomforting experience; one still expects a challenge; even gunshots and the bullet in the back.

Our only overnight sojourn in Bavaria was at Steinbach am Wald, west of the old border and an attractive little town of true Bavarian warmth. At the head of the town stands a marker announcing the fact that one is standing upon the watershed of the rivers Rhine and Elbe.

At a number of bierhauses close to the old borderline at which we halted briefly for refreshment we were to gain an insight into what it had been like to live in close proximity to a killing ground. For those so situated their world virtually came to an abrupt end just up the road.

Near Brennersgrun we came upon the oldest and most famous of the thirteen 'Dreiherrensteine' marker stones where the boundaries of three territories converged. It dates from 1513 though the track itself – appearing in printed form as 'Rynnestieg' on a then bill of sale – goes back to 1330. 'Rynne' is an old form of 'Rain ', meaning 'border' though in this instance it would seem to mean 'Rennen' – to run 'along an ascending path'. Since then royal personages, military commanders, notabilities and the general public have trodden this stony, sometimes springy but generally gentle highway.

As was the case with King Ludwig's Way, the final day of the walk was to become something of an anti-climax as the trees of the Thuringiawald began to thin out at the approaches to pleasant but unremarkable open countryside. And as the trees cleared so we could see our final destination a good ten kilometres ahead; the small town of Blankenstein being hidden but marked by the tall red-and-white chimney stack of the great paper factory complex of Zellstoff und Papierfabrik, one of the largest of its kind in Germany.

For me that last day saw a recovery from my malady and, such was my new-found energy, I found myself close on the heels of the pause-rejecting Rudolf and, with him, entered Blankenstein far ahead of the others – in spite of taking a wrong road giving us a quite unnecessary five-kilometre detour via the giant industrial complex.

The town, on two levels, sits uncomfortably astride the Saale river, here almost a gorge. Our hotel was, fortunately, on the valley floor close to the railway station.

With the improvement in my physical condition came a rallying of a long-dormant appetite built up over five days of an intake of nothing more substantial than soup and mashed potato which was all I had been able to hold down. That final night I gave it full rein and at the conclusion of the meal I became the subject of a toast proposed by not only my companions but the whole rowdy clientele of the gasthaus. It was 'to Bigfoot, the oldest, illest and finest walker of all'. I hardly deserved the last adjective but coming from a bunch of professional German hikers it was a tribute I much appreciated.

4

Greece
Perambulations in the Pindus

This chapter is not about a specific walk or trek, nor a particular walking route, but its purpose is to reveal an expanse of countryside that is ideal for trekking – and climbing too; one where its small communities and their way of life have barely changed over the decades. I last trekked in the Epirus and amongst the rugged Pindus mountain chain in 1982 but, assuredly, conditions today remain the same.

Epirus lies east of Corfu between the Ionian Sea and the high Pindus, the rugged central backbone of mainland Greece. The province is as large as Kent, Surrey and Sussex together and is a land of limestone mountain ranges, rushing rivers, gorges and upland villages, of Greek and Roman antiquities, Byzantine churches, ruined mosques and minarets. Because of its remoteness from the main lines of communications, it has been the home of much that is most traditional in Greek countryside.

Ioannina is the capital and is situated, as all good capitals should be, in the centre of the territory. To reach it by road today from Igoumenitsa or any of the small Epirus ports, or even from Athens, is no great problem for the roads to it are adequate if tortuous.

Following a swirling descent through spectacular folds of the Pindus ranges my bus had emerged high above the great lake of Pambotis, now known as Ioannina after the town standing at its edge. A rocky promontory juts confidently out from the town, its fortifications punctuated by towers and minarets as if to declare its not uninspiring history. For it was from this base that Ali Pasha, who made Ioannina his capital, carved from the Turks a kingdom encompassing much of western Greece, an act of contemptuous rebellion that portended wider defiance in the Greek's own War of Independence.

As a 'heroic rebel', Ali Pasha – 'Lion of Ioannina' – assumes an ambivalent role for his only consistent policy was that of ambition and self-interest, and as frequent as his attacks on the Turkish administration were acts of appalling and vindictive savagery against his own Greek subjects. He was born in 1741, in nearby Albania, and rose to power under Turkish patronage.

Indeed it is the stories of Ali Pasha's cruelties rather than the glory of his successes against the Turks that seem to hang about the surviving vestiges of his capital. Disappointingly, most of the town is modern and undistinguished with no more than a few crumbling mosques to give atmosphere to the place, their minarets providing nesting platforms for storks. However, a more dramatic site survives on the island in the lake, the monastery of Pantaleimon where Ali expired. Standing in the east of the attractive little island village is the Museum of Ali Pasha which eloquently – even to the fateful bullet holes – charts the 'Lion of Ioannina's' life and death.

For me, as for all trekkers, Ioannina makes a good jumping-off point for Pindus hikes and it was initially to the village of Aristi that my footsteps led me. Increasingly, Athenians have summer houses here, elegant villas with stone porticoes and green shutters, but there was none I remember seeing when I was there. 'What do you all do for a living?' I had asked casually of several seemingly aimless villagers. 'Oh, this and that', had been the gist of the replies though both 'this and that' appeared to cover the hardly arduous tasks of sitting and looking – the favourite pastime in Greek mountain communities.

Onto the twin villages of Papingo – Mikra and Mega – standing at the mouth of the Vikos Gorge and in the heart of the Vikos-Aoos National Park, considered the most beautiful in Greece, a conservation area for rare exotic flora – especially lilies – and the wildlife of this exceptionally lovely region on the flanks of the Pindus known as Astraka.

My road then – a new one has since been constructed I believe – twisted and turned up and down the mountain slopes giving astounding views over the wild, wooded, unworkable country to further mountain ranges whose soaring grassy slopes are summer pastures for sheep. These highland districts are washed by autumn rains and winter snows by boisterous rivers and their tributaries. The Aoos and the Voidthomkatis (Ox eye) run swiftly north-westwards through Zagori, as this whole area is called, to unite in the Konitsa plain before hurrying onwards to Albania and so eventually into the Adriatic near Valona. The Tzoumerka massif rises to over 7,600 feet protected to the east and the west by the Archeloos and the Arakhtho rivers respectively. The sources of these sizeable rivers are the heights above the Zygos Pass, although secondary tributaries of the Arakthos rise in Zagori. In summer, after the mountain snows have melted, these rivers are calm and shallow, but are transformed by the late autumn rains into tumultuous torrents which have carved their imperious way through the mountain limestone to form gorges of which the Vikos is the most spectacular.

The Vikos Gorge – often called the Grand Canyon of Greece – is approached by way of a footpath which leads to what must be one of the finest viewpoints in Europe. The gorge is a little more than 1500 metres wide at its rim and 1000 metres deep. Massive horizontal limestone is cut into vertical walls for half this depth; below that, steep slopes in thinner bedded limestone meet in a 'V' at river level. Directly opposite the viewpoint is the similarly-proportioned tributary gorge known as Kasarma, and rising above the plateau is the 2,436 metre-high summit of Astraka. A tremendous sight.

From Papingos it is a three hour hike to the mountain refuge on the Col D'Astraka. The hut, when I used it, was equipped with beds for thirty as well as all cooking utensils and facilities. While there I managed the ascent of Astraka, a feat of hardly momentous proportions.

My notes of the time remind me of a violent thunderstorm that struck while descending the steep wall of the gorge, loosening the rock and sending slithers of limestone down around me. For three hours I plodded through a solid downpour that soaked everything including the contents of my rucksack. Sanctuary was reached back at Papingo where, in a small taverna, I was wrapped in a blanket while my clothes were dried to much hilarity from the clientele who liberally dosed me with throat-burning brandy.

Two nights I spent in that humble but kindly inn, listening to the wind howling across the col but, thereafter, I managed a hike to the silent pools of water known as the Dragon Lakes situated behind the opposite walls of the gorge, a hike made the more treacherous by a muddied and flooded track and a descent via steep and unstable scree to the delightful village of Tsepelovo. Here, one Alexis Gouris, the English-speaking manager of the general store and plainly a man of influence, took me under his all-embracing wing ensuring I lacked nothing when it came to both solid and liquid sustenance.

Tsepelovo was one of a number of villages scattered about these mountains, villages of fine grey stone houses, white-washed cottages and impressive churches. Others were Kovkouli, Skamnelli, Kipos, Monodendri and Flambourari to name but a few. The original forty-six villages of the Zagori in the eighteenth century developed a special relationship with the Turkish authorities; by forming a confederation they were able to retain a measure of autonomy in return for payment of annual tribute. The mountain people of Zagori, unlike the plainsmen of Thessaly, were never subdued by the Turkish armies nor their initiative frustrated.

My subsequent objective was Mount Smolikas, the highest mountain in the Pindus at about 8,600 feet and, reputedly, the second highest in Greece after Olympus. My road ended at Laista, a large scattered village spread out on green Alpine slopes and surrounded by pine forests. From the main square was a magnificent view to the west of the Timfi massif with Mount Gameela (The Camel) at its northern end, rising to 7,500 feet. And in the north was Smolikas. Few of Laista's houses were occupied then but a preponderance of churches indicated a past prosperity which, possibly, has returned to some extent with the increase in the area's mountaineering popularity.

I am no mountaineer myself but my ascent of Astraka had given me a temporary appetite for scaling peaks and Smolikas beckoned seductively. The village of Brousohori put me in the right position for the negotiation of the massif, a track leading disconcertingly downhill for the initial few miles. But it knew what it was doing since the Aoos river had to be crossed and another village – Pades, clinging to the hillside – was the crossing point. Thereafter it was uphill walking with a vengeance.

The stars in a clear sky made my ceiling that night as I bedded down on a flat grassy plateau on the flank of the mountain. I slept well but a bitter cold and dewy morning had me up and stamping my feet before dawn. And as well, perhaps, since the ascent and descent of Smolikas is not only an exhausting slog but one made tricky by an escarpment and cockscombs of jagged rock that have to be surmounted. The view from the summit is glorious and, with a day as fine and sunny as it was, I sat on the snow with my back against the stone summit marker inhaling the all-round panorama.

Down the other side and the uncomfortable descent brought me to Samarina, a summer-only village of ugly tin roofs and a resident popula-

The author at the summit of Smolikas

tion of characters straight out of ancient Greek mythology. At the taverna I tucked into a well-earned dinner, selecting the dishes I fancied from a series of steaming cooking pots on the spacious range of a diminutive kitchen.

I was to learn that Samarina was a Vlach village. The Vlachs are not easily distinguishable from the other Greeks of Epirus, either in looks or build, but are, perhaps, a little more phlegmatic. Many lived a nomadic life but looked upon the town of Metsovo as their capital and seat of their region though those who left for the big cities soon forgot their origins. The territory included the southern end of Albania and, until the Greek-Albanian border was closed, they moved freely between the two countries. (While in Albania under communist rule I met a Vlach who, even then, regularly crossed the fanatically-guarded border by means I was not to learn).

A day of rest and local exploration and I was on my way to conquer a third peak before the summit-attaining mood left me. The route led through pine forests backed by Alpine-type scenery and past a non-operational ski lift but low cloud negated my reward at the near-7,000 foot summit of Vassilitsa. This and a cutting wind had me scurrying to lower altitudes and another tin-roofed village, this one Perivoli. The hotel there belied its exterior, containing ludicrous inadequacies including water, hot or cold.

Escaping from its inanities I spent a rewarding evening sipping ouzo in a taverna watching the Epirus world go by mostly in the guise of the village elders gently promenading in the main square. Attired in black knickerbocker suits and pom-pom-decorated black shoes and carrying long curled crooks as their badge of office they circuited the square, a ponderous progress invariably ending in the taverna to discuss the business of life.

With the exception of the fine St Michael's church the centre of the village was burnt to the ground by the Germans in the Second World War. And it is the village churches in these parts that epitomise the sturdy character of Epirus communities where the blood of Albanian and Slav has mingled with that of the indigenous Greeks. In such communities the Orthodox Church still has a place of primary importance. The church is where heaven and earth meet; the worshipper, surrounded by the saints on the walls, is in the presence of God. Religion here is a serious business.

Most Zagori villages were largely empty; only the old and the very young remained in the care of their grandparents while their parents worked in the cities or abroad. In Perivoli (which means 'Orchard'), for instance, there were about a hundred fine old houses but only some fifty people lived there throughout the year. More return in summer when the population increases considerably. Others, seemingly, intended to return but never do, yet they prefer their property to collapse through decay and neglect than sell it to strangers. Many of these houses, as I could see, were disintegrating; balconies sagged and creepers strangled peeling walls. Those houses which were occupied held an air of faded charm ; the floor and settees were covered with ancient rugs of local design and a lamp usually glowed before a holy icon.

The village square of Perivoli was of similar design to others. A common feature is an enormous plane tree offering shade to the menfolk when they weren't in the taverna. Their women, of course, stayed at home going about their household duties.

A glutton for uphill walking – for the peaks I had so far climbed were hardly of mountaineering proportions, or at least not the routes I used to scale them – I completed my quartet by 'scaling' a modest mountain called Avgo from the barren summit of which I was able to relive most of my walking of the past week or more. The descent was by way of the Aoos river again and the village of Vouvoussa, the most easterly in Zagori and a Vlach centre of some distinction.

The wood-encircled village has had a long history of brigandage and defiance against the Turks and three of the best-known resistance fighters in the eighteenth century came from Vouvoussa – or Baieasa to use its Vlach name. And as recently as the collapse of the Greek armies in 1941 following the German invasion, the allied Italians attempted to establish a pro-fascist Republic of Pindus with its capital here. Few Vlachs took this seriously but memories hereabouts are long and a residue of bitterness against the families of those who allegedly collaborated lingers on.

Although the Pindus Mountains make superb hill-walking country, trekkers continue to be an unusual sight. Few visitors today discover its hanging valleys in the shadow of snow-covered peaks and watered by icy snow-melt to turn them into grassy swards which, in June, are ablaze with drifts of Alpine flowers.

Shepherds in these high valleys still drive flocks of diminutive sheep in a manner little changed since Byron watched similar scenes well over a century earlier. Wrapped and hooded against icy mists in long wool cloaks, gaunt figures drive their flocks with a series of resonant cries. Guttural commands mingle with the sound of goat bells, the barking of dogs and the bleating of sheep as the flocks follow traditional runs across the mountain flanks. But fewer and fewer young men have taken to the hills with their flocks as industry and the oft-false promise of urban

Walking in the Pindus mountains

employment and reward tempt them away. Yet who can blame them for life is hard for the shepherd and the rewards no more certain. Migratory wolves and bears are a constant problem while in a long winter every sheep will eat more than its market value in feed.

All this was recounted to me by the village priest in Vouvoussa as we sat, Zagori-fashion, beneath the village plane tree. He was an intense young – or at least younger than me – man with sad eyes and a passable command of English. His whole family, he told me, had been murdered by the Germans. Though speaking as if he was not, himself, a member he emphasised the degree of stoicism of the menfolk who continued to display the warrior-qualities which were so necessary to protect their homes and families during the long and troubled years of their country's history. Nowadays their more peaceful occupation remains, as it has since time immemorial, as that of shepherds and wood-cutters and tillers of the soil; their relaxation taken outside the village tavernas, talking politics over a glass of retzina or ouzo.

Next day, following a ridge and via a dense forest, I found my way back to Tsepelovo from whence a clapped-out bus carried me erratically to what is popularly described as 'civilisation'.

5

Walks in the Cold
1: Iceland

Though my thin and angular frame is susceptible to intense cold I have found myself, with some reluctance, embarking upon journeys in the more northerly extremities of Europe, those of Iceland, Greenland and Spitsbergen, but Iceland, in particular, an island to which I have been drawn more by the demands of my job than a deep-rooted attraction. Yet there is something about these remote and frigid lands that refuses to be ignored.

Iceland has claimed me on a number of occasions, there to undertake trekking and motor safari driving. This chapter therefore, is an account of a composite journey made on foot which commenced in 1978.

We angled across the swiftly-flowing river, battling against a strong current, stumbling in the glacial water as we attempted to maintain a precarious balance. Packs weighed heavy on our shoulders, threatening to topple each of us from booted feet placed gingerly among a morass of hidden slippery boulders. Before we were halfway across my limbs were half-paralysed with cold as the group, strung out in line, made its slow motion way towards the opposite bank to emerge onto dry land in squelching boots and in the knowledge that, within the hour, another river would have us doing it all again.

The route led across a snowfield, the whiteness sullied by lava dust, and our footfalls changed to a rhythmic crunch. Sodden boots sank into wet snow, gripping them in an icy embrace and my toes curled with the additional cold.

Above, the clouds were breaking up and, to the east, low mountains tumbled towards the coast. All around, fading into the horizon's haze, was a serrated alpine outline of incredible brutality and awesome loneliness.

Our small group was trekking across southern Iceland dominated by the huge plain that sprawls many miles wide to the southern edge of Vatnajokull, the largest ice-cap in Europe, containing the great Oraefajokull Glacier, one of many. And Vatnajokull itself is but one – albeit the largest – of a quartet of such ice-caps; the others to the north and south of us being Hofsjokull, Langjokull and Myrdalsjokull.

In spite of the desolation of its landscape, Iceland has a homogeneity that few other countries possess. Not only does it seem that everyone in the nation knows everyone else but the Icelander's present is clearly connected with a living past. As they speak of their history one has the notion they are personally remembering events that occurred to ancestors many centuries earlier; things that happened then are related with an immediacy as if they were speaking of yesterday.

Even in Reykjavik, the capital and only urban centre of size, this aura of homogeneity is felt by the outsider but in the 'outback' the sense of blending of past and present becomes infinitely stronger. It is not that monuments of history are strewn over the landscape; on the contrary, most of Iceland is as grandly lonesome today as it was when the first Norsemen found it, the only occupants a handful of Irish monks living in frugal tranquillity on the harsh shores. But the look of the country is young and clear and ever-changing, its very loneliness is evocative. It invites things to happen. Uncomplicated as the landscape is by the clutter of modern civilisation it is easy to see the drama of history rolling across it. The things that occurred then could so easily occur now. Didn't the new-found island of Surtsey, in our own life-time, rise from a volcanic holocaust out of the sea in 1963; a reflection of the emergence of Iceland itself from the ocean fifty million years ago.

This was another aspect of the 40,000 square mile island situated in the North Sea roughly equi-distant from Scotland, Greenland and Scandinavia that had drawn me to it so often. There is no other area in Europe superior to Iceland for the diversity of terrain it offers walkers and climbers. The major difference between walking or backpacking here as opposed to the Scottish Highlands, or the Alps, is simply the remoteness of the place. It is possible to be several days away from the nearest farm thus presenting logistical problems. Everything must be carried; one must

Trekking across a river in south Iceland

be self-reliant and competent. This remoteness and its northern situation also allows weather conditions to be much more inhospitable than those of countries further south. It is all too possible for these to swiftly change, with snow and ferocious Atlantic gales rushing in where blue skies and sunshine existed moments before. 'If you don't like the weather', they say in Iceland, 'hang on a minute'. A common adage but more relevant here than elsewhere.

Hence the reason I chose to accompany a walking group on my first incursion. It was led by one, Dick Phillips, who knows his Iceland almost as well as he does his North Pennines home-territory. A somewhat dour northerner but with a wicked sense of humour, I found him the most affable of companions for such a venture.

On that first day's trek we slogged across about twelve miles of windswept desolation, winding up forbidding gullies and traversing lava scree or snow-burdened escarpments leading from one false crest to another. That twelve miles a day is not, perhaps, a phenomenal rate of progress has to be measured against ever-reoccurring river crossings, the see-sawing weather conditions and harsh environment of the Kaldakofsfjoll region over which we were allegedly passing.

It invariably comes as a surprise to me that humans are at their best in such circumstances of discomfort and fatigue. And perhaps particularly so when these conditions are voluntarily imposed. Almost from the start of our journey in Reykjavik the dozen members of the group became closely fused into a closely-knit team as the warm glow of anticipation and achievement suffused minds at the close of a long day. In spite of a variation in ages, sex, interests and character this comradeship grew the deeper with every mile into the sombre loneliness of a countryside that haunts the souls of those who travel it.

Iceland has been termed a land of fire, a land of ice and a land of contrasts. It is certainly all these and a land of misconceptions too. But above all it is a land of challenge. The island received its chilly-sounding name from a Norse Viking in the ninth century who, after wintering there, climbed a mountain and saw one of the fjords in the north-west coast full of pack-ice in what was a universally cold spring.

The misconceptions must have gone a long way towards the creation of the notion that the island, newly discovered on the fringe of the habitable world, was a land of challenge. Eleven hundred years ago this drew men of stature to a coastline belt that, alone, gave a toe-hold for human life. Men with names like Erik the Red and the resourceful Gnupa Baror who, having established a new home in the north, suspected that milder conditions might be found on the opposite shore. Constructing sledges for his livestock, he loaded them with hay and his worldly possessions and drove south through unexplored deserts and mountains, among ice-caps and over five great glacial rivers, to put his theory to the test. So, down through the ages, we come to modern times, to men like Hannas Jonsson whose duties as postman to the Oraefi district involved him, in 1934, in an eight-hour crossing of the Skeidhararjokull ice-sheet, with a volcano erupting under the ice-cap behind him and the glacier moving beneath him, floated by the force of the melt-waters below.

Icelandic landscape has formed the backcloth to the Sagas and is a fitting match to the stories themselves. Beyond Reykjavik lie the farmlands, the rivers, the fjords, the coastal communities, and behind them, always the mountains, ice-caps and deserts, the everlasting wastelands of black sand, snow-bound and deserted throughout the long, long winter, but in summer, warm under the twenty-four hour sun.

Invariably such facts of geography and history remain uppermost in the minds of all who choose to trudge across this inhospitable land; it nags at the brain as one gazes across an infinity. This certainly was the case with me as we topped each crest and rested in a silence that showed that others too were so affected.

Four more rivers required wading – each one presenting itself just at the point when hard walking had begun to dry and warm our feet – before we reached the little grass-turfed youth hostel at Fljotsdalur, primitive but adequate. With no central heating a weak evening sun had to suffice to part-dry wet boots and socks while sleep came but reluctantly under a twenty-four hour daylight sky. Dick held a food cache here so supper was assured.

Fljotsdalur is classed as no more than a simple hostel and, from it, we walked for three days to Laufafell, climbing steadily, the route hurdled with more glacial torrents, lava-fields of hard, jagged frozen rock, and chasms probed by the chilly fingers of glaciers. Our group was a dozen strong; three women and nine men, the average age being nearer the mid-twenties than my own antiquated – even then – fifty-four – though one of my fellow males was pushing forty-five. Fljotsdalur was a multi-star hotel compared to the bed-time pads in which we found ourselves; an assortment of huts of strictly no amenities, one of them an abandoned sheep shelter at Krokur. On the cold hard floor we lay shivering as the cold seeped through sleeping bags and karrimats. Crowded together for warmth and lack of space our night at Krokur was especially wretched but it was part of the Iceland trekking experience which added to the allure of youth hostels when available. My sleeping bag was far from adequate and though I had brought two – one inside the other – their combined grade of warmth was plainly not enough. Outside, our sodden boots drained on a fence and wet socks stiffened into woollen jackboots.

An ascent of the gnarled peak of Einhyrvingur mountain made a surprisingly easy evening climb unthreatened by the perils of approaching darkness, followed, next morning, by a day of climbing a series of never-ending cols, crunching through snow-fields ever-mindful of the towering Mount Hekla which had last erupted in its terrible wrath just eight years earlier (and was to erupt again in 1991).

Hekla at 1491 metres is not a difficult peak to attain. I reached the summit in company with a Norwegian hiker who, for once, was as old as myself and had climbed it twice before. Why he should have bothered was beyond me for the lava belt that surrounds its higher altitude made most uncomfortable climbing, the black volcanic terrain, some of it hidden under a sheen of snow, not yet worn smooth by age and elements. Eight hours, they tell you, is the time needed for the ascent and another eight hours down so a tent is desirable. We managed it all in one longish day, not feeling too happy about camping near a summit so prone to blowing its top. The main fissure is an intimidating sight but cloud, which hides the mountain most of the time, precluded any worthwhile panoramic reward for our efforts.

The accounts of St Brendan's voyages describe a great flaming mountain which existed on an island reputed to be Iceland and the culprit has been pinpointed as Hekla. The first recorded eruption was during the ninth century, the next in 1104 with devastating results for the early settlers who had established their farms and homesteads in the inviting green valley directly beneath it. Since then it has erupted a further 14 times and even as early as the 1500s Hekla had been designated as the entrance to hell, the expletive of the day in Europe being 'Go to Hekla'.

At Laufafell the group was pampered by two days based at the most comfortable of refuge cabins, this one warmed by permanent central heating piped from a nearby hot spring. Brilliant sunshine, however, lured us from the fug and, to the mournful pleas of oyster-catchers and the laughter of arctic skuas, we trudged the startling countryside raising a greater daily mileage than we had forged earlier. Rest days! They always turn out like that.

Atop another but lower peak, that of Mount Haalda, it was possible to see eight ice-caps including the white eminence of Vatnajokull etched upon a stupendous all-round view. Though southern Iceland is predominantly lowland country, flanked by the sea on one side and the mountains and glaciers on the other, the lowland is far from flat. The mountains that form it are mostly of the flat-topped variety, their ridges running for miles, reminiscent, to me, of an American western landscape. Table-shaped hills – or mesas – are steep and provide the perfect topography for spectacular waterfalls, lesser ones of which we had already come across.

Haalda was but a windswept staging post to Landmannalauger. By way of the Puera and Hitmago rivers, with the inevitable wading of them, and the outer edges of the Myrdalsjokull – its glacier fingers creeping down towards us we arrived there and its palatial youth hostel, a well known refuge for trekkers. We were not the only occupants on this occasion, our fellow-guests being a party of Swedish climbers. Few of us could resist the temptation of prolonged immersion in the series of hot water pools of varying temperatures the subsequent rest day – which, for once, we put to just that – and with Sweden renowned as the chief perpetrator of nude-bathing there was little hesitation about lack of attire. Only a hard core of prim Rock of Gibraltar English females steadfastly retained their knickers.

Food and its attainability is vital to an Icelandic trek and our appetites were wolfish. Dick's system of advance food depots and a complicated method of refuelling them worked fairly well though it did not preclude

A refuge cabin at Landmannalauger

the necessity of carrying a certain amount of provisions, particularly those of a perishable nature. Usually we ate well, the cuisine being basically English with Russian jam, Czech sugar and occasional dollops of delicious Icelandic skyr, or curd.

The onward trek from Landmannalauger towards Porsmork refuge has become the premier walk in Iceland though its fame was only local when I followed the route and refuges along the way were scarcer than they are today.

The inevitable rivers, bogs, soft snow and a minor blizzard accompanied us to Jokuldalir and its hut, something then of a come-down in the accommodation stakes. The route took us over the Laugahraun lava flow before ascending the rhyolite peaks and steaming vents of the Brennisteinsalda area and bringing us down to Storihver. The track led by another hot spring but this one was of more sinister aspirations, a round hole in a rockface choking forth a spume of ferocious boiling water.

Space was at a premium at Jajuldalir and we slept, foot to head, in close proximity which, in a then non-heated refuge, at least helped beat the cold. In all directions the landscape was uniformly forbidding; dark tumbled masses, basalt pillars with a gleam of sunshine striking colour from a garish chemistry of the lava-fields. As a backcloth were the mountain ranges, low, misshapen and disconnected, matching the ungainly heaps of snow which lay on them and the lop-sided formations of cloud which hung above them.

Next day gave us a further procession of hot springs and fumaroles leading to the Jokultungur Ridge and then onto the Alftavatn valley giving startling views of Myrdalsjokull and Eyjafjallajokull as well as strange volcanic images to contort the imagination. And more river crossings too with the 1280-metre summit of Huskerdingur which two of us climbed – mainly for the purpose of drying freezing wet feet – while the others rested. The night was spent uncomfortably in an occupied sheep shelter; the sheep below and we taking over the cramped attic with a vicious draught cutting through the gaps in the floorboards.

Our route now lay along the shore of the Alftavatn lake, one that ensured we got our feet wet at frequent intervals. But there was reward for the mind if not the body at the Alftavatn refuge which was but another sheep shelter, this one with a leaky roof. But at the head of the lake was reputedly the largest fissure in the world climaxed gloriously by the double waterfall of Ofaerufoss framed by a natural bridge of rock spanning a cauldron of liquid fury.

The region is a wonderland of birds and flowers. Iceland turns the luke-warm bird-watcher into a fanatic. There is the puffin which dives and comes up with a clutch of fish in its bill, the arctic tern which makes periodic flights of incredible trans-continental distances, the ravens that nest in the river cliffs by the Gudafoss waterfall, and the rarer white-tailed eagle that soars majestically in the sky. And that's only the beginning. Where the snow has receded a profusion of plants, ferns and wild flowers ignore the cold to grow and often blossom at the very edge of a glacier's lip. Blue sesleria, rosa dumalis and green spleenwort are common

Twelve days and nights in the wilderness were enough to give our group an insight into this amazing land of water and fire. Discomfort, fatigue, the purgatory of cold, ever-wet feet and an unrequited hunger had been our constant companions, yet one acclimatises fast as lessons in survival are learnt the hard way. Very early in the trek I noticed members scampering off semi-naked in the wickedest cold to the nearest semi-freezing river flaunting towels like battle-standards or accepting the most primitive of accommodations without a murmur of complaint. Iceland does this to one; it makes a man – or woman – of you as do few other destinations in the world. It is a harsh, rugged countryside which can be daunting but always magnificent. There can be few finer leisure pastimes than a week or two here with a rucksack and the freedom to go where you please without restriction.

2: Spitsbergen
Archipelago on the Rim of the World

Morketiden, the Norwegians call the days of winter blackness – the dark time, when the sun lies far beneath the distant horizon and the islands of Svalbard lie shrouded in frozen gloom. But, as with Iceland and other far northerly territories, the summer months from June to September bring varying degrees of lukewarm 24 hour daylight often bathing the land in brilliant sunshine.

William Barents, the Dutch explorer who put these arctic islands on the map in 1596, had named them Spitsbergen, Land of Pointed Mountains, but the Norwegian name Svalbard, Land with Frozen Shores, fits it better.

Most of the island's 24,000 square miles is covered by glaciers and frozen snow as deep as 300 metres. Stretching to within 650 miles of the North Pole, Svalbard is so far north that the northern lights reach into its southern sky. Reindeer and virtually all species of wildlife are protected now by government edict but there was a time when sealers, whalers and walrus hunters harvested the Arctic waters surrounding Svalbard. Later came scientists interested in Svalbard's fragile environment. Polar explorers used the islands as a startpoint for ever more northerly incursions.

But for decades the archipelago remained unclaimed since it had little to offer the world. However, in 1925 it was allocated to Norway by international treaty with the proviso that other nations were entitled to exploit the island's sparse resources. Only coal-short Norway and the then Soviet Union did so however and, today, Norway and Russia are the sole countries operating mines there. The first mention of the archipelago is in the Icelandic Sagas going back as far as 1196 though it seems to have remained in limbo for a further four centuries until the arrival of William Barents, a fact that adds to the mystique of this remote and lonely land.

The Isfjord runs deep into the centre of the main island, known universally as Spitsbergen. Along its eastern shores are situated the two Russian mining settlements of Barentsburg and Pyramiden. Between them, up an inlet called Adventfjord, sits the principal mining town – operated by Norway – and capital Longyearbyen. It could well be imagined that the place obtained its name from the slow passage of time in this extremity of the globe suffering so many days of total light and total darkness. In fact it derived from John Munro Longyear, an American mine-owner who formed the Arctic Coal Company of Boston and raised the first buildings in 1906. Even today, though considerably enlarged, it continues to resemble a mid-western township of the nineteenth century onto which a small twentieth century airport has been attached. However, the town is more developed than first impressions suggest with central heating piped to virtually every building. The only roads on the archipelago are those serving the town, its airport and immediate region. It comes as a surprise to learn that so remote a community should experience effects from the Second World War but it is a fact that German warships shelled and destroyed much of the town. The scars have healed and much of the surrounding region has been turned into a national park and nature reserve. Reindeer can be seen wandering the broad gully that cuts through the town; a few musk-oxen still survive while, occasionally, a polar bear will stroll along a side street in search of a garbage snack.

It was in August 1991 that I flew into Longyearbyen from Tromso on the Norwegian mainland. You don't have to be a masochist to go trekking on Spitsbergen but it helps. When I announced to no one in particular that I was going to Spitsbergen for a walk I was pronounced barmy. This in itself was interesting to me for it showed that people at least knew where it was.

A visitor can "do" Spitsbergen in two ways; in a strictly utilitarian boat amongst the fjords or, within a group, on his or her own feet in the permafrosted interior. Both offer supreme rewards if you are made of the right stuff. Germans form the main contingent of trekkers but I was relieved to behold that my small group was graced with the presence of two compatriots even if one fell asleep at Tromso Airport and missed the connecting flight to the island – but we can't all be as efficient as the Germans.

I found Longyearbyen airport to be a remarkably elegant establishment and one out of tune with the capital it serves. The desolate urban centre three miles away is haunted by the ghosts of a dying coal industry that could still raise enough life to cover everything in a sheen of coal dust. The double-walled, treble-glazed houses are threaded by a skein of heating pipes and dotted with derelict conveyor pylons. Most of the miners, I was told, were on holiday when I arrived – probably on some warm Mediterranean shore to whence I evinced a momentary urge to join them. But around the township soared the snow-streaked mountains and a promise of the Spitsbergen experience I had come to sample.

Unless you prefer the expensive offerings of one of Longyearbyen's two guesthouses you will be accommodated the first night in a tent pitched close to the airport runway. Additional to the group of tents that comprise "Camp No.1" is a wooden building that forms a dining room/kitchen, hot water ablutions and flushing WCs. Make the most of them for they'll be the last such amenities you'll see if you have arranged for a trek. And unless, too, you are into backpacking in a big way I advise against the long, three-week, trans-Spitsbergen slog humping tents and provisions, mostly peopled by young Germans equipped with a ruthless determination that frightened the life out of me. Our group were a gentler, more mature breed, with no more ambition than to survive on the twelve-day hike through the valleys of central Spitsbergen based on two established tented camps.

We left under sunshine and an icy breeze unbroken by any tree or vegetation; the breeze blew from the glaciers on both sides of the water. The tallest plant to grow here is the dwarf birch, three to five inches high, but underfoot was soft peat-like ground. Diminutive flowers, deep and bright in colour, and patches of scurvy-grass, a plant with white flowers used either fresh, dried or boiled with soup as a protection against arctic diseases, lay on all sides. Only on the low-lying coastal strip does the snow disappear altogether; but even there the earth remains frozen to a depth of a hundred feet. Many of the flowers continue to survive from a time, fifty million years ago, when this was a fertile country and fossils prove that Spitsbergen once had a Continental Riviera climate.

They call the first day's trek to "Camp No.2" a "warm-up" and it certainly is that for one sweats like a pig, having donned every item of clothing on the assumption that (a) you'll be cold – and it is when you're standing about, and (b) to make your rucksack lighter, for, even without tentage and provisions, it's heavy enough. Actually the distance is little more than sixteen miles along the relatively flat Advent Valley though the walking is punctuated by river crossings and muddy morasses ever-reoccurring when you thought the cold wet wading was at an end.

"Camp No.2" is placed upon an ice-plateau, or "pingo", and is no more than a trio of already-erected tents, one of them containing pre-stored food safely packed in bear-proof containers. Though we held emergency rations in our packs, as well as pocketfuls of chocolate and raisins which were deemed adequate for "lunch" plus the odd snack, we had ravenous appetites upon arrival.

The camp overlooked a substantial river which, likewise, had to be negotiated the hard way. For this we were thoughtfully provided with fisherman's waders but the comparatively shallow channel was known only to our German guide and so made something of an alarming undertaking. In line we slowly crossed, the current pulling at our thighs, attempting to follow the exact designated route since one false step into deep water and both current and the weight on our shoulders could prove fatal.

Though the evening meal consisted mainly of powdered soup, instant rice and potato mash it was wolfed down with the greatest satisfaction. Sleep is likely to be spasmodic since the ground is hard, bumpy and, unless you're possessed of an arctic-resistant sleeping bag, cold.

If your favourite breakfast cereal is muesli you'll enjoy all twelve trekking breakfasts. It's not mine but it's that or nothing. You can have it mixed with instant milk, water, tea, coffee, cocoa, hot or cold, and even dry on its own but since that is what your lunch will be – plus the chocolate – I recommend the wet variety. However, believe it or not, such a diet is perfectly adequate under the circumstances in which you'll find yourself.

A day based at the same camp was followed by a ten mile rucksackless walk across the locality to view strange rock formations forged by ice over the aeons. Reindeer are particularly attracted to this area by a comparative abundance of low-growing vegetation comprising a rare arctic birch, arctic willow and a strange Bonsai-like shrub. An animal disturbed by our incursion into the wilderness was thought to be an arctic fox.

The third day's trek was considerably longer, taking us out of the Advent Valley into another that led to the coast of the Isfjord, Spitsbergen's largest fjord. "Camp No.3" was in view down the bottom of the valley long before we got there. We could see it from atop the new valley and it became a mirage that refused to evaporate or draw nearer as we stumbled through drifts of treacherous snow towards it. The site was close to the coast and the view down the valley and out across the Isfjord and a jumble of glaciers the other side was astounding.

Attempting a short cut across what I thought to be firm frozen snow I was abruptly enveloped in a white straightjacket as my feet broke through the surface. Encumbered by my rucksack I found it a devil of a job to extract myself from the icy embrace and earned myself a good soaking before doing so. Thereafter I resolutely steered clear of drifts.

With the new camp closer at last a sizeable hill had to be negotiated before attaining it, which at least warmed up my semi-frozen body. But that accomplished one is on the threshold of a home from home for a whole week.

The small cluster of tents was situated on a stony and lumber-strewn beach. The lumber is by courtesy of Russia, it having been washed ashore from Siberian lumber camps and timber-carrying shipping. It becomes a useful commodity as fuel for any campfires the wind or/and rain permit or, for those so inclined, for constructing tasteful items of furniture. And since a week is a long time in such an environment any gratis additions to general comfort are not to be despised.

Not that a week was too long for me. Unencumbered by heavy baggage we explored the region. And what a region it is. Across the wide fjord lay the enormous panorama of smaller fjords buttressed by the savagery of glaciers and sharp mountain peaks, their ethereal quality reflected in a myriad shades of colour in the clear water, each sudden change of weather pattern offering a new perspective. Close to the camp a muddy torrent burbled by, spanned by a home-made timber bridge that, incongruously, served also as a treble-seated toilet which we christened the Bridge of Thighs. Excellently drained, it was, nevertheless, a mite draughty. Across it to the north, south and west lay idyllic trekking country bordered by high perpendicular cliffs raucous with roosting guillemots and puffins, and a range of assorted mountains inhabited by inquisitive reindeer. Between were green, marshy plateaux sprinkled with clumps of exquisite wild flowers ranging from white dandelions to a tiny blue flower with leaves that taste of oyster. Geologists will revel in the tortured rock formations and the unlikely debris of retreating glaciers. It is a land of sheer – if chilly – magic.

We saw no polar bears on our explorations; mostly they come south from the colder north of the island during the long night of winter. But precautions are taken; "Camp No.3" is encircled by a trip-wire device that can detonate small explosive charges to the discomfort of unwelcome visitors, and all trekking groups carry a rifle.

With time to spare we made ourselves more at home than had been the case earlier even to the extent of making rough bed-frames out of the available lumber; anything to keep the cold ground at bay. I still found the 24-hour daylight a handicap to sleep and a silly couplet by Edward Lear kept running through my head.

"The sun was shining from the sky,
Shining with all its might.
And this was strange because it was the middle of the night".

The three-day homeward slog back to Longyearbyen could have been a repeat of the outward journey but it was enlivened by two events. A detour to the Jansson Valley, more gorge than valley, to see more strange rock designs as well as the only scented flowers on Spitsbergen amongst clumps of white heather and anemones. And the consequences of an abrupt ending to the Svalbard summer which had transformed the normally fairly dry Advent Valley into a skein of fast-flowing streams and rivers of sullen brown waters which made considerably wetter walking and wading than had been the case before.

But we had become, as I found earlier in Iceland, a fitter, more experienced bunch of trekkers so took the worsening conditions in our stride. And a retracing of a route is hardly a waste in a land where colour and circumstances change hourly offering more to see and experience however many times such a route is covered. In exchange for the odd bootful of water, a muddy dive or two face-down in a bog, and an over-endowment of muesli we had sampled the excitement and charisma of traversing territory north of nearly everywhere else on earth.

6

Clandestine Walking in Central Europe
Smoke Channel

Though I never saw it in daylight I have in my mind's eye a small wood a few kilometres from the colliery town of Zabrze in the industrial belt of what is now Polish Silesia. The copse – and it was no more than that – became the first place of refuge following the breakout by Gordon and myself from the well-guarded prison cage that had held us for many months. The year was 1944; I was a 20 year-old soldier of the Dorset Regiment captured by the Germans earlier that year and, together with Gordon Primrose of his namesake Highlanders, we had escaped from the purgatory of slave labour in a German-run coalmine.

I thought long and hard about bringing clandestine walking into the scope of this book since anyone wishing to undertake a walk in similar circumstances would have to await the unlikelihood of a hot war. And even the possibilities once offered by a cold one – at least within Europe – have now come to an end with the collapse of communism. But one of my walking experiences in the former – though indeed I also have memories of similar perambulations in the latter – might, perhaps, present a thought-provoking interlude.

We *Homo sapiens* are a rum lot. We might not realise it but, just below the thin crust of what is looked upon as civilised behaviour, lies a suppressed urge to break the bonds of that behaviour. All too often, as can be seen from our newspapers, men and women surrender to these cravings to become what the world labels criminals and, when caught, are punished accordingly.

But during a hot war these wayward cravings can, to a controlled extent, be legitimately released and, in the eyes of one's own countrymen, the perpetrator is respected the more for it though he, or she, can expect short shrift from the other side – the enemy – if caught.

In the Europe of World War Two there was ample scope for trespass, theft, infliction of injury and even killing while on a clandestine journey in enemy territory. With these reflections in mind allow me to narrate an instance from those momentous times.

Exhausted from our night-time escape through triple barbed wire fences and running blind in the darkness for several kilometres, the wood became our initial shelter in which to gather our wits. Being in German territory its inhabitants would have little truck with the likes of a couple of fugitives from Nazi rule.

For what was left of the night we spent lying, compressed together for warmth, beneath the trees. It began to rain and, subconsciously, I burrowed under Gordon who had insensibly managed to fall asleep. He awoke an hour later to berate me for keeping dry at his expense but more serious matters were to occupy our attention.

We wore the khaki battledress in which we had been taken prisoner but had covered the tell-tale uniform with our less provocative working clothes. Unfortunately both tunic and trousers displayed a big yellow "K" (for *Kriegsgefangener*, or Prisoner of War), ineradicable and conspicuous, even though we wore them inside out to reduce the brilliance of the stencil. Plainly a change of attire was an urgent priority. We carried a small store of the more durable items saved from the few Red Cross parcels that had filtered through to the camp. We hoped to supplement these with anything edible stolen from field or farm. Our planned direction of escape was eastwards to Cracow then north to Warsaw, east of which advanced elements of the Red Army were alleged to be closing in on the Polish capital. To be frank, our Russian allies were not a first choice of liberating agency, but with the British and American lines many hundreds of miles away on the opposite side of Germany, we had little choice. Our prison camp was of comparatively recent origin so could boast of no escape organisation that could provide the likes of us with natty civilian outfits, forged documents, compasses, maps and the complete escaper's box of tricks. Our one small trump card was the unlikelihood of immediate pursuit. Not only had we concealed the breaches in the camp fences but had arranged with our colleagues for delaying tactics at morning roll call.

Dawn showed us a farm in the distance as we emerged from hiding and came the moment we felt obliged to enter upon a life of crime. In this, Gordon set a far less conscious-stricken example than I. The farmhouse of our initial attentions was remote and, while approaching it, we were able to observe the male occupants departing for work in the surrounding fields. A chained dog barked incessantly which suited our purpose admirably since its bark of real alarm would be masked. Ignoring the animal we sauntered into the yard with an air – we hoped – of casual labourers looking for a job. Reaching the door to a cacophony of fury we found it unlocked so pushed inside to stand uncertainly in an untidy kitchen-cum-living room, mercifully devoid of occupants except for a cat that fled. As if he had done it all before Gordon scooped up a jacket and sundry garments that lay across an ancient sewing machine while I contented myself with a loaf of bread from the table. My companion then swooped on a peaked cap from a hook behind the door and I'm sure, if I hadn't stopped him, he'd have nicked the family silver. Clasping our loot we withdrew, the barking resuming its strident tempo.

Sharing the spoils between us and discarding unsuitable items that had come with the bundle we arrayed ourselves in our new attire with, I regret to declare, some levity. Our working clothes were likewise discarded and I ruefully thought of the heavy punishment authority would impose should we be recaptured. Gordon retained the cap – apparel that is almost *de rigeur* in industrial central Europe – insisting that my blonde hair was Germanic enough anyway and gradually we were transformed into something akin to Silesian peasant workers. Fortified by hunks of bread with Red Cross marmalade we issued forth in search of liberation.

Our blind run from the camp had proved to us the folly of moving by night. Hence we put our mythical Plan B into operation, involving making our way using minor roads, tracks and open fields so long as we could maintain the right direction. We held a map of sorts; no more than a sketch provided by a sympathetic miner, indicating a line of towns through or near which we would have to pass en route to Cracow.

Over the flat landscape towns and villages were easy to pick out, their gaunt pithead shafts as distinguishable as church steeples. We felt obliged to enter one such urban centre for the purpose of pinpointing our position and this we proceeded to do but not without a certain trepidation. The township selected was, like others hereabout, of depressing uniformity; rows of workers' houses, a few dingy shops and an apathetic church. Had its name, shown on a yellow sign at the approaches, meant anything to us we could have avoided its shabby streets but it told us nothing so we kept resolutely on, intent upon locating a signpost offering better advice. The exercise was not wasted for, at the main intersection in the centre, a rack of signs made helpful reading, one finger indicating the road towards Chrzanow, on the way to Cracow, and marked on our sketch map. Our bravado proved something else too. Nobody took the slightest notice of us though I was uncomfortably aware of my bare head, resolving to rectify the omission at the earliest opportunity. The chance came sooner than I expected. Passing a crowded beerhouse, a gaggle of German soldiers abruptly ejected in front of us. One of them asked for a light for his cigarette and the irrepressible Gordon unhesitatingly obliged, babbling happily away in Gaelic to which the soldier turned not a hair. With Europe awash with uprooted nationalities any language, except perhaps English, passed muster even if not understood. On the spur of the moment I slipped into the smoke-filled bar, espied an assortment of headgear on a coat rack, helped myself to the shoddiest cap and returned outside well-pleased with my initiative.

Our most serious shortcoming was our complete deficiency of funds. Acquiring money by theft was not going to be as simple as rummaging around people's kitchens for the odd loaf of bread; cash was usually locked away, its acquisition falling into very different realm. And bank robbery had such a pursuit-raising quality about it.

Heartened by our reception – or lack of it – from the local citizenry we bent our footsteps along the road indicated, leaving the depressing streets with undisguised relief. We were uncomfortably aware that we were on the wrong side of a region, centred by the heavily industrialised town of Katowice, consisting of a complex of smaller, ugly mining communities through which we would have to make our way; a well-populated conurbation lacking open countryside.

We left the road as soon as we were clear of houses. It was a well-used artery and, in spite of the lack of interest shown us in town, it only needed a nosy minion of authority to enquire after our non-existent papers and that would spell the end of our wanderings. The alternative of walking parallel to but away from the road resulted in tiring, frustrating progress, detouring around fences, farms and groups of agricultural workers in the fields. In making one such detour Gordon stumbled into some barbed wire and tore his trousers from the thigh to below the knee. Safety pins being beyond our resources we hastily tied together the corners of the tear with string – and added a new pair of trousers to our "shopping list".

On the bank of a stream we bathed our sore feet in cold, rust-coloured water. Long-unaccustomed walking had produced blisters on our heels and worn holes in already well-darned socks but the water treatment cooled the throbbing and raised morale.

While so engaged half a dozen soldiers and girls with bicycles suddenly appeared, laughing and chatting . We had not realised that a sunken lane lay behind the hedgerow beyond the ditch and it was along this they had come. Their appearance was a shock but we stood our ground, continuing our ablutions, our hearts in our mouths. The girls waved jauntily; the soldiers scowled and they all moved on. Quickly we replaced our boots, reprimanding ourselves for carelessness.

"Bicycles!", I exclaimed apropos of nothing. Gordon glanced at me blankly, holding his torn trousers. "Cycling's faster than walking", I went on cryptically and he got the message. Another item was added to the "shopping list".

The road became erratic, running straight for miles and then taking a corkscrew route to serve a village or two. Sometimes we found ourselves on the road itself and fell to the temptation of its firm surface but the sound of approaching vehicles would send us scurrying into the fields again. At the edge of one such field we came upon the hot embers of a fire in which we baked potatoes gathered from a clamp. This was to be the only time we found food and the means of cooking it in the same place.

The autumn dusk arrived all too early and we cast about for shelter for the night. A barn held more attraction than did the depths of a wood; at least the former could raise both a roof and the warmth of hay or straw.

And hey presto, a barn it was; locked and barred but a window at the rear surrendered to our attentions. We crawled inside, located a stack of clover-scented hay and staked our bed-space. Our eyes, adjusting to the darkness, took in the contents of the building: a derelict tractor, several carts, some harness, a pile of bricks and various agricultural implements. Through cracks in the brick and timber walls we studied a neighbouring house noticing the thin plume of smoke issuing from its chimney.

"Hope they choke on their sauerkraut!" was Gordon's bitter comment and I could not but agree with his sentiments. Potatoes, stale bread and marmalade keep body and soul together but make for uninspiring eating.

With nothing to do we bedded down early and slept extremely well in spite of some irritation resulting from the insect life. However, this was a lot less unpleasant than that caused by lice and bed-bugs that were rampant in the camp. We awoke early, partly from hunger but also from the noise of a horse and cart outside the barn. We lay listening uneasily to rough unintelligible voices, ready to burrow deeper for cover at the first signs of the doors being opened, until the unmistakable sound of the cart being driven away released us from tension.

The morning light filtering through the crevices feebly illuminated the barn's interior. We could see two stalls, one once obviously used by a horse, the other as a store containing a pile of roots. Selecting two swedes, yellow and unhealthy-looking, we cut each into portions to make them more appetising but they proved course and fibrous, and raised a thirst we were unable to assuage. Disgusted, we flung the bits away.

Another scrutiny of the house revealed no signs of life except for the wisp of smoke so we prepared ourselves for another excursion into crime. Aware that bold confrontation paid dividends we made straight for the back door, gently pushed it open an inch or two, and listened. All was quiet; not even a dog barked. The muddy yard and a few outhouses gave no indication of being occupied by man or beast so, encouraged, we stole into another kitchen. Straightway Gordon beheld a pair of trousers on the back of a hardback chair; it was almost as if they had been left there just for him. I homed onto a bread-bin containing a loaf and half a cake which I bundled into a sack brought along for the purpose. Gordon was rummaging through a handbag when voices and the sound of footsteps sounded from the other door to send us into inglorious retreat, Gordon replete with trousers and handbag. We sped across the yard keeping to the lee of a wall to avoid detection.

Assured of no pursuit we made a roundabout return to the barn there to retrieve our other few possessions and for Gordon to don his new trousers. They were far too large but by liberal application of string at the waist and the turning up of the legs the garment made for an improvement on its predecessor. There were even a few coins in the pocket. A search of the handbag produced the equivalent of £8 in German Reichmarks and a collection of women's knick-knacks of no use to us. We hid the torn trousers and handbag and, munching cake, left our night's refuge for the last time.

There was not a stir in the crystal stillness as we climbed down a slope, broke through a hedge, and came back to the road to descend with it into a shallow valley. Two men appeared before we could take evasive action so continued walking , mumbling a reply to their greeting. We felt, rather than saw them staring at us as we marched on not daring to turn our heads. The notion came to me that maybe one of them recognised his trousers.

That second day we made better progress in spite of blisters and stiff calf-muscles but our general weakness from months of semi-starvation and neglect was plainly telling. Pauses for rests became increasingly frequent and, as the day wore on, we found ourselves becoming strangely light-headed and reckless. Too tired to care, we walked straight through villages without the slightest demur instead of detouring round them. A series of mounds by the roadside turned out to be further potato clamps so we dug out some large potatoes, putting them in our pockets with the idea of risking a fire that evening. The only unguarded bicycle we saw was propped outside a shop. It may have been purloinable but what use was one between the two of us?

The town of Mystowice we trudged straight through. We felt safer in the larger industrial centres and far more anonymous than was the case in villages where strangers – even legitimate ones – were objects of scrutiny. A town centre signpost indicated Oswiecim as 21 kms; another arm showed Chrzanow as 24 kms, and it was only because we had designated Chrzanow as a landmark – it being astride the road to Cracow – that we chose the more easterly road. At that time we were not to know that the German name for Oswiecim was Auschwitz.

Soldiers and Volksturm (Home Guard) troops were among the dowdy civilians in the streets but none appeared to be on duty. We remained in dread of the sudden materialisation of a patrol or road block where identity papers would be demanded. But our luck held. Silesia, being then part of Germany, authority had no reason to suppose the population to be anything but pro-Nazi. Crossing the border into a not entirely subdued Poland proper could produce mixed blessings; the hand of friendship as well as the arm of repression. A thought tore at me. Would the border be guarded or merely submerged into the great stronghold of Occupied Europe?

A lone barn provided a third night's bed; this one stagnant and far from any human habitation. The straw was musty, smelt of manure, and dry; so dry in fact we utilised some as fuel for a fire, filling the place with smoke. Straw makes a poor heat source so we dined that evening on lukewarm potatoes as hard as unripe apples.

The ensuing days were pain and grief – and in increasing doses. We had no idea where the border lay; if indeed a border existed, but firmly stuck to our course slowly, oh so slowly, reducing those kilometres to Chrzanow. In retrospect it occurs to me how ridiculous it was that we should have taken so long to cover so short a distance. But memory takes little account of physical condition; how this caused bouts of nausea and vomiting whenever we ate something that disagreed with stomachs that had been ill-treated for a year, and the debilitating effects resulting therefrom. We didn't like the look of Jaworzno so tried to go round the sizeable town only to get lost in allotments and hostile suburbs. Twice we were chased out of gardens and on one occasion had to make a real run for it when Gordon, hunger overcoming judgement, lunged at a skinny chicken. Barns continued to provide shelter – the single plus-element of that excruciating walk – and in only one of these barns were we close to being caught. This was when a couple of labourers invaded our privacy to remove a farm implement stored beneath the stack of hay in which we were concealed. Our further efforts to steal were lamentably unrewarding. The shops in towns held so little stock of food there was hardly anything worth stealing and our haul from shop-lifting amounted to no more than a couple of pears and a tin of spam. We did finally catch a chicken, the unfortunate bird's squawkings being drowned by a dog's barking. That evening we lit a fire amongst trees and toasted the limbs, one by one, on the flames but the smoke drew a pair of boys to the fireside. Their curiosity became too belligerent for our peace of mind so we finally had to stamp out the flames and move on, stuffing half-cooked drumsticks into our pockets.

We could see Chrzanow long before we reached it. The industrial urbanisation of the region was lessening; villages and towns becoming fewer and spread further apart. Cracow, we judged, would be at least another forty-five kilometres and Warsaw God-knows how many hundred after that. But we could think of nothing after Cracow. There we would be firmly in Poland, a land where people universally hated Germans. Anything could happen once we were there.

All our minds could concentrate upon was lessening the pain of walking. We evolved great longings for not only a decent meal but a modicum of comfort; a real bed, a hot bath, a warm fireside, the hand of friendship – all so unattainable, a forgotten condition we once took for granted.

It was about this time that the "train plan" was born. We had discussed the idea of passenger train travel during the planning stages of the escape but had discarded it as too risky, particularly as we held no documentation. But we had not delved so deeply into the concept of freight train travel; secreting ourselves in a railway truck where no questions would be asked or papers demanded. This form of transit was fraught with difficulties, complications and dangers too but, out here in the sticks, getting nowhere and weaker by the hour, the prospects appeared less daunting. Stowed away in our bed of hay the sixth night we discussed the matter at length and agreed to have a go.

Chrzanow, we knew, was on a railway line that was part of a network serving Cracow. That we'd have to look for a stretch of track that fitted all the circumstances of the situation should we attempt "jumping" a goods train was obvious. Alternatively, it was worth investigating the possibility of stowing ourselves away on a stationary wagon in Chrzanow freight yard – if there was such a yard.

It was raining steadily when we left the old barn. The last hunk of bread and a draught of rain-water deluging from a broken down-pipe made an apology for breakfast; all we could raise now that our reserves of food had given out. With no beating about the bush we took the road directly into Chrzanow, intent upon locating the railway station and investigating any sidings or freight yards it may possess. Our stomachs rumbled audibly as we tramped the pot-holed tarmac but our spirits had risen with the prospect of imminent action. An avenue of street lamp standards accompanied us into a maze of awakening streets.

Whether Chrzanow was classed as a border town or not we had no means of telling but, nevertheless, kept our eyes peeled for any sign of a checkpoint. Given warning, we could sheer away into a side road or gaze intently into a shop window as they do in detective movies. People, muffled against the cold mist that heralded winter, scuttled along pavements made uneven by subsidence. A policeman directed desultory traffic at an intersection and a horse-drawn wagon of soldiers clattered over ill-laid cobbles. There was no sign of a border post.

We located the station without difficulty. It was a fair-sized one since Chrzanow was a rail junction where four lines met, only one of which linked directly with Cracow. And there was a freight yard beyond but the entrance was manned by militia while a work gang of soldiers was unloading a truck. There could be no snooping about there; that was for sure.

So it would have to be the boarding of a moving train and for this we would first need to follow the correct set of tracks out of town. A bifurcation of the lines must have occurred the west side of the station, we surmised, for, having walked for some kilometres out of town with the double track keeping firmly to a route following the Cracow-bound road, it seemed that we had hit the right line. Disinclined to walk the trackside path itself we remained on the road for a while but kept the railway in view. However, the road had become too much of a main artery for comfort so we left it, transferring our allegiance to the railway.

There now arose a formidable task. What we had to look for was a sheltered spot near the line where we could lie in wait for a train going in the right direction, where the geography of the terrain raised a gradient to slow the train and where there was a curve in the line to foil vigilance from those who could be aboard the train. Freight trains in those days sometimes carried armed guards both at the rear and with the locomotive crew in the front. It was therefore imperative that both sets of guards were ignorant of what we were proposing to do in the middle.

Both road and rail entered a spruce forest as we walked awkwardly alongside the rails. With nobody in sight in either direction we felt bold enough to do this since we were close enough to the trees to effect a disappearing act if necessary. In this manner we made reasonable progress, the only interruption resulting from an on-coming two-coach passenger train which sent us helter-skelter for cover. From the trees we watched it rattle by, noting its speed which was much too high. Continuing, we located a curve in the line and rested there for two hours to await the passage of another train – a second but longer passenger train moving towards Cracow – but, again, it moved at too great a speed for the purpose we had in mind.

Out of one conifer forest and into another; an uncomfortable night in a wet ditch and it wasn't until late the following afternoon that we came upon a set of circumstances that held some hope. Many trains – both passenger and goods – had gone by since we had joined the track but none was for us.

The rain that had fallen in a desultory fashion most of the night ceased at daybreak but the undergrowth was wet and soggy with a steady litany of drips from sodden trees. We were in a clearing; the row of spruce and fir alongside the line had receded to leave the tracks bare of easily attainable cover. The spot was far from perfect but would have to suffice; hunger and exhaustion were making walking difficult again as well as affecting judgement. We waited, crouched in a hollow.

A heavy goods train rumbled into view and we dashed for the trees again, aware that the dusk was not enough to conceal us in the open. An overworked locomotive engulfed in a sweat of steam headed a long line of wagons that rattled and jerked against each other as if the driver was applying his air brakes. We could see the driver and his mate leaning out of the cab and we surmised that some obstruction ahead was causing a speed restriction. The speed of the train was just right but the thing was going the wrong way damn it. I cursed our luck but then it came to me that the obstruction – if there was one – might work for trains coming from the opposite direction; those that had already been slowed but had not yet had time to cram on speed. We watched the brake van disappear into the distance but could discern no occupants.

Night descended rapidly but the darkness was not complete when the sound of a train from the other – and right – direction lured us from cover. A headlamp pushed a yellow antenna ahead of another large locomotive, its stack belching spark-injected brown smoke. We waited a few seconds to allow the engine to pass our prostrate forms, then rose and sprinted for the track, confident that the gathering darkness would be dense enough to hide our running figures. Crouching as close as we dared against the passing wagons, we desperately searched for hand-holes in the steel walls of the great coal trucks that loomed above us. So close now, the rattle of the train had turned to a sullen growl while, close to our running legs, the iron wheels were cruel and menacing.

Let me say here and now that to accompany and attempt to board such a train in circumstances as these, watching for and avoiding signal cables and other lineside impediments, is no easy task. In the movies the hero nips smartly up into a speeding wagon to the accompaniment of appropriately stirring music. But it's not quite like this in real life – and anyway we were deficient of the Berlin Philharmonic Orchestra for our little epic.

Behind me I heard Gordon pounding at my heels, swearing with the exertion. A lever caught my eye and I lunged at it, clutching the cold metal and holding on tight. It dragged me along the ballast and I experienced a terrible fear that my legs might become enmeshed in those grinding wheels. Trying to swing them clear, my other hand fastened upon another protrusion. My feet dropped again, the toes of my boots bumping along the stones but with two hands firmly anchored I was able to draw myself upwards though the effort cost every ounce of the remaining strength I could muster. A red mist curtained my eyes as I fought to raise my body to the flank of the wagon, my right boot searching wildly for a toe-hold above the wheels. And then it was all over as, with a final heave, I reached the couplings between two wagons.

Gordon was already atop the high side of one of them and he now worked his way round to join me. "Thank Christ for that!" was his breathless comment. Mine are unprintable. We let ourselves down into the interior of the empty truck and lay exhausted on the cold, wet coal-begrimed floor surrounded by four cold, damp walls.

We had earned our ride.

In point of fact our "journey to the east" ran into a hiccup very few minutes later when the train drew to a halt, reversed and carried us in the opposite direction for many miles, taking us back into hostile enemy territory. Thereafter the only method left us of finally attaining Cracow was as fare-paying commuters aboard a passenger train and this we accomplished in spite of our deficiency of identity documents. But these occurrences are outside the scope of this book*.

Cracow, alas, was as far east we got. Picked up by the Gestapo we ended up, via their cells in the city and the transit cage of Auschwitz, back at the camp from which we had originally escaped.

* The full story of these and his other wartime and post-war experiences is narrated in the author's book *Pedal for your Life* (Lutterworth Press).

7

Road Walking in Central Europe
From the Baltic to the Danube

A further aspect, I suppose, of a hike or trek is that it provides a means of looking back on one's life. Not that these considerations are confined to walking; horse-riding and cycling can provide similar parenthetic benefits. I can certainly vouch for that of cycling for, though far from being an accomplished or ardent cyclist, I have, over the past dozen years, undertaken a number of long-distance pedalling forays. The longest and most memorable was in eastern Europe across which I cycled two thousand miles, from Estonia's Baltic coast to the Black Sea, a journey subsequently narrated in my book *Pedal for your Life*. This foray was more evocative than others since it was to mark my seventieth year and was one of recollection as I traversed territory possessing, for me, both sombre and joyful episodes of an earlier epoch of my life.

In 1997, to mark my seventy-fifth year, I reverted to walking, choosing to make a journey that covered central Europe from the Baltic to the Danube. Originally I had hoped to continue to the Adriatic but time alone prevented the extension. The startpoint I designated as the Polish Baltic city of Gdansk which, that year, was celebrating its Millennium, and for the destination I chose Vienna, likewise involved with a celebration, this one being the two hundredth anniversary of the birth of the composer, Franz Schubert. I would be accompanied by my son, Paul, and we envisaged a journey time of six to seven weeks on a route that crossed the whole of Poland as well as the Czech Republic's province of Moravia and that of Niederosterreich in Austria. We would be carrying the bare necessities of life on our shoulders and for overnight accommodation we would rely on our lightweight bivouac plus, in Poland, a trio of hotels offered by Orbis, the state's hotel and touring agency, and one other, in Moravia, courtesy of Best Western Hotels. These would be oases of comfort in a desert of rough living.

Gdansk is a city reborn. In company with Warsaw it was almost totally destroyed during the Second World War, a war that actually commenced here at Westerplatte, the entrance to the port, on September 1, 1939. In March 1945 the Soviet Red Army's westward advance against the retreating Germans reached the city and, during the fierce battle that ensued, Gdansk virtually ceased to exist. Its restoration has taken fifty years and still continues.

The social structure of the city has changed dramatically too. During the post-war era the surviving German majority was expelled; a majority stemming from the fact that Gdansk – or Danzig as it was known – had become a Prussian city, the then Polish minority systematically Germanised. However, with the aftermath of the First World War the Treaty of Versailles gave Poland the so-called Polish Corridor, a strip of land providing her with an outlet to the sea. Gdansk itself was declared a Free City and so became virtually autonomous under the protection of the League of Nations.

In spite of the turnover in population, the spirit of independence remained. In 1970 the city staged a massive strike against the repressive communist regime that had ruled since 1947, a strike repeated in 1980 when it paralysed the shipyards and culminated in the rise of Solidarity, its electrician leader eventually becoming president of a new and democratically-elected government.

For long a Hanseatic city, it merges with the Baltic seaside resort of Sopot and, in turn, the ship-building town of Gdynia, the whole known as the Tri-City. I had visited all three components on a number of previous occasions but it was always Gdansk that inspired the greatest admiration, its houses and streets once more a reflection of those of four centuries earlier. Walking round central Gdansk today is akin to reverting to medieval times, the ancient – but reconstructed – edifices matching, if not surpassing, those of Amsterdam or Antwerp.

I was to see little of the city on this latest occasion, our hotel being on the Baltic coast to the east of it. Because the hotels in the centre of town were fully booked Orbis had found us a guesthouse at Sobieszewo which, as well as being on the coast, was also on an arm of the Vistula River estuary spanned by a pontoon bridge over which traffic had to crawl. But what made the choice of accommodation for the eve of our walk so convenient was its situation as a jumping-off point for our southbound route; one precluding the chore of having to negotiate the city's complicated suburbs.

We spent the evening sorting out the contents of our respective rucksacks. This included a small Vango bivouac, a Gore-tex bivi-bag (in lieu of bulkier sleeping bags) and a ludicrously inadequate (by most camper's standards) amount of cooking gear; just enough to heat water for tea, soup powder and tinned foods. Emergency items included a couple of dozen Mars bars. And since we had both spent thirty hours on a Eurolines coach from London and so were deficient of a night's sleep we were in bed by nine.

Paul's linguistic abilities – he has some knowledge of Russian and a smattering of Czech – were to prove an additional and vital accoutrement. Though both Poles and Czechs are reluctant to listen to or speak the language of the country that, for so long, had oppressed them at least they could understand him a little. My only contribution was a smattering of German plus a little French.

We set out next morning in what was to be the first day of a week-long heatwave with temperatures climbing to the high eighties. Our initial landmark was the town of Starograd Gdanski which could be reached, according to our maps, via minor roads and, for the first half of the day there was minimal interference from motor vehicles. The terrain was flat, rural and unremarkable with plenty of woods in evidence which boded well in so far as camping sites were concerned. Near a village some kilometres south of Pruszoz Gdanski we were approached and asked for our autographs by a small boy on a bicycle who then brought along a horde of his playmates making the same request. Still unaccustomed to the load on my shoulders and in need of frequent halts for rest and re-adjustment of rucksack webbing I hardly felt like a celebrity.

Towards the end of that very first day however we were to become aware of two vital factors. The first materialised as we proceeded along a larger road designated as 222, marked as a minor yellow artery from Gdansk city to Starograd Gdansk and beyond. In fact it had become a busy highway since the map had been published. And thereafter it was all too often the same story with minor routes grown into virtual interstate highways made the more dangerous by being narrow and straight. Try as I could I had simply been unable to procure up-to-date large-scale maps of either Poland or the Czech Republic. The second revelation stemmed from the first. This was that our road-walking project was going to be something of a verge-walking one as vehicles from tiny putt-putting Trabants to hefty trailer-hauling juggernauts ignored any hard-shoulder or carriageway border markings and drove straight at us. We walked facing oncoming traffic so that at least we could see what, if any, avoiding action drivers were taking and act accordingly, i.e. hastily transfer ourselves to the verge. And this introduced a third factor into the equation of road-walking that had to be taken into account; the condition of the verges. Some were of short grass and broad enough to use for soft and comfortable walking in place of the hard tarmac, an important consideration when blisters were at their painful peak. Others consisted of long rough grass hiding all manner of hazards; minefields of discarded bottles, tin cans and dips that could all too easily sprain an ankle. Other verges were a mixture of grass and gravel which made the best walking surface particularly after rain when prolonged use of the wet grass soaked one's boots. Heavy rain also caused lake-like puddles to spread across both verge and the flanks of the carriageway, avoidance of which produced its own dangers. Occasionally there were no verges whatsoever while heavy crash-barriers bordering the larger highways forced a walker to use the tarmac irrespective of what avoiding action oncoming vehicles were taking and this made the most unpleasant and dangerous road-walking of all. In general, with my (fortunately) left foot giving the most pain, I walked using a mixture of verge and tarmac; left leg on the softer verge, right leg on the hard tarmac. Paul, following me and adapting his pace to that of his slower father, mostly preferred the tarmac exclusively.

All these factors were to materialise gradually during our first week of the journey – as were our deficiencies of pedestrian aids. Use clean socks every day, we had been advised; thin inner ones and thick outer ones. But our baggage capacity failed to run to such extravagance, our sum total of socks being two pairs of reinforced hiking socks and two lighter pairs. However, we found this to be entirely adequate, at least from the medical point of view, the donning of wet socks when necessary being purely an unpleasant chore. We had also ignored, to our chagrin, a suggested blisters remedy using animal wool – not cotton wool – teased out of the wedge of tendrils and placed between the sock and the offended skin. Plasters we did possess but these are of little help against the soreness of blisters being simply a method of covering the open flesh of a punctured blister. And the confounded things would never stick for long anyway. But blisters and similar discomforts of the soles of the feet pass if one is strong-willed enough to ignore the pain; the skin turns hard and walking becomes easier once more.

Our first day we accomplished twenty-five kilometres under a burning sun, a daily distance we managed to maintain without difficulty until cooler weather allowed us to improve upon it. Our first camp on the edge of a wood was not a success as we fought to raise a bivouac while under attack from a swarm of vicious mosquitoes. We also made the mistake of pitching the tent facing the setting sun so that, upon taking refuge behind the mosquito-netting within the tent, it was like being boiled alive; sweat running off our naked bodies in rivers. Added to this was our close proximity to one another, space being adequate for a single person but a tight squeeze for two.

Breakfast was a hurried affair of a shared tin of herring washed down by a mug of tea made on our primitive cooker fuelled by hexamine tablets. The reason for the hurry was to be on our way before a new wave of mosquitoes found us and the road traffic came to life. Ploughing through dew-soaked undergrowth we returned to the 222 highway.

We reached Starograd Gdanski well before midday and pressed on across countryside ablaze with scarlet poppies, wild lupins and blue cornflowers. The soles of my feet began aching abominably and the load on my shoulders continued to upset my balance so that I was not quite in control of my movements; a state of affairs that would soon be replaced by a similar lack of control when the load had been removed! At first I had made the mistake of fastening the belt of my rucksack too tight in an effort to maintain the load high on my shoulders but I only succeeded in giving myself a stomachache. On the plus side was the fact that our money-belts, reposing sweatily around our waists, acted as convenient padding for the lower frame of the rucksack.

In the town square of Starograd Gdanski we entertained the local populace to a display of attending to our sore feet which at least brought curious onlookers over to chat with us. "Where are you going?", they asked. "Viden, Vienna, Wien", we replied hoping, usually in vain, that at least one of the name variations of the Austrian capital would be understood. But even if this was the case, no-one would believe it so we substituted the south Polish city of Wroclaw, close to our proposed route, as a more believable destination though even this revelation was met with incredulity. The town provided a hot meal so that all that was needed, foodwise, thereafter that day were provisions for a cold evening repast. These we obtained from a village kiosk surrounded by a bevy of villagers unable to believe we were walking even to the next town. "There's a bus every hour", they pointed out helpfully as head-scarved peasant women of far greater brawn than I tested the weight of our rucksacks, grunting painfully as they did so.

Luncheon meat – which Paul scornfully designated as dog-meat – was usually on the menu of our evening fare plus something sweet such as bottled plums or cream biscuits and, occasionally, soup in lieu of tea. Our night in another forest was a repeat of the previous night's mosquito-infested and sauna-like experiences.

The heatwave had become intense. We sweated profusely day and night; there was no let-up except in the early morning when both temperature and traffic density were at their lowest. By midday on the third day we reached the township of Skorcz there to go in search of a bar and source of a meal. We found both in a small *pivnice* (pub) but not in the circumstances envisaged. Thrusting through the male throng at the bar we ordered beer whereupon, learning of our nationality and mode of journeying, we were plied with glass after glass; as soon as one had been downed another waited on the counter. We were even given lunch by the proprietor – a plate of flaki (tripe), a Polish speciality – and all the while were engaged in complicated conversation carried out in at least four languages. "Had I met Queen Elizabeth?" was one question and when it was learnt that indeed I had – albeit briefly – at a Buckingham Palace garden party it served only to trigger further beer supplies. Under a chorus of directions as to how to continue southwards to the subsequent destination, we staggered out of town, found a shady bank against which to lie and slept off our excesses.

The new road, numbered 214, took us into a green and watery land designated on my map as Bory Tucholskie on the extreme northern edge of Wielkopolska, literally Great Poland, and renowned as the cradle of the Polish state. It was here during the second half of the tenth century that the first recorded ruler, Duke Mieszko I, unified the scattered Slav tribes of the region into a single political unit.

From the time we left Gdansk we had been passing through Pomerania paralleling the lower Vistula valley. Polish history was nowhere so complex as here; various areas changed nationality on numerous occasions with, on balance, more time spent outside the national borders than within them. Germany exerted the strongest influence, the territory bearing the imprint of the Prussians, who ruled it from the early eighteenth century through to 1945.

A wide belt of lakeland is shared by the two regions and our road, shimmering in the afternoon heat, led us to one of the lakes, a broad shallow sheet of water framed by dark forests of pine. It was a weekend which meant that we were not the only people immersed in the cool waters or picnicking on the sandy shore. After a swim we joined the picnickers, cooking our tin of flaki, purchased earlier, then pitched our tent hurriedly in the mosquito-infested pine trees.

Highway 214 made a beeline for the town of Warlube but the route led through sheltering forest with further lakes at intervals though not all were approachable, their shores engulfed in reeds. Traffic was agreeably sparse, the occasional truck raising a buffeting slipstream that at least provided a momentary breeze, albeit one laden with diesel fumes. A midday rest was taken beside another lake, a picture-postcard enclave of placid water alive with croaking frogs, where I bathed my aching feet while Paul found the energy to fill a plastic mug with blueberries. Close to the village of Krzwwiny we were able to partake of an afternoon swim; there to be joined by a trio of men in a grocery van who pressed us to share their picnic meal of cold chicken and warm bottled beer. Before leaving, they even donated a sizeable basket of strawberries which, mashed in our mugs with added sugar, made a delectable desert. All it lacked was cream.

We gained Warlube by early evening and raised camp behind some shrubs on the very edge of the town. The open countryside, suddenly devoid of trees, was also devoid of mosquitoes; a blessing that raised a re-assessment of our belief in forest camping sites. But sleep still remained elusive however; on this occasion a thunderstorm providing the distraction.

Packing the wet tent we made towards the city of Grudziadz on a traffic-snarled E75, there being no alternative road and the Vistula river precluding any possible short-cuts. But at least the highway was well provided with roadside refreshment sources even though their offerings were unappetising and expensive. In one such establishment we met Willi, a German Pole, who joined us for a chat; we were to meet him again a few days hence.

To reach Grudziadz meant crossing the kilometre-long box-girder bridge spanning the Vistula which offered the best view of the city including its celebrated granaries built into the hillside above the river. We avoided the centre of this one-time Prussian town which the likes of Willi visited or revisited in increasing numbers, returning to see the homes of their ancestors or even the scenes of their own childhoods.

Hungry and hot, we searched in vain for a restaurant in endless suburbs finally running to earth a *pivnice* that produced a fine goulash and cold draught beer. Our road was now the 514 and, once clear of the industrial suburbs, was a quiet one carrying minimal traffic. In spite of the storm the temperature remained in the eighties, the loads on our backs making heavy going as we climbed the first hill since the start of the walk.

At the top we camped close to but clear of a wood and were rewarded with a mosquito-free site giving a most satisfactory night's sleep.

Our 514 road narrowed perceptibly thereafter, leaping forward in long straight sections and providing few walkable verges. The soles of my feet hurt abominably; the skin had not yet hardened sufficiently and one of my blisters had spread to form a balloon of skin between two toes. A brunch of liver, chips and salad at a wayside restaurant restored morale as did a cold beer close to a slaughterhouse at Stolno from which emitted beer-curdling squeals. At the junction here we found ourselves back on an old adversary, the busy E75.

At least it was a two-lane highway which prevented following traffic from coming too close; Polish drivers had a dangerous habit of overtaking a slower vehicle just as they drew level so almost brushing us as they hurled by; an inadvertent step off the verge or across the white boundary line and one could end up as another road casualty statistic and roadside memorial of which Polish roads are plentifully endowed. The terrain had changed from forest and lake to undulating plain of far horizons; our road discouragingly visible as it arrowed into the distance.

A night in but the far edge of a wood confounded our mosquito theory by not raising a single biting insect in spite of the proximity of static water. The city of Torun was but another day's march and a scheduled forty-eight hour sojourn there had us drooling with anticipation.

Forests bordered the road once more beyond Chelmza. I was within an ace of spraining an ankle in a hidden dip in the verge as we tramped on, counting the kilometres to the city, dreaming of soft beds and hot baths. A BMW saloon drew up from behind us to reveal Willi who insisted we join him for a snack at a sausage and Coca Cola bar set in a forest picnic clearing though we were impatient to reach the city.

We were several days ahead of our loose schedule though I hoped this would not jeopardise our accommodation pre-arranged in Torun. Through a register of names and addresses of potential Polish hosts anxious to meet west Europeans I had contacted one in this city who had replied inviting us to his home. Additionally, Orbis had also booked us a double room in their Kosmos Hotel.

We phoned Bogdan Burdziez and he met us at the tram terminus at the far end of town. A forty year old lecturer at Torun University he lived with his wife, Ole, and two sons, Alex and Jan, in a block of flats, one of serried rows so common in eastern European cities. The whole family spoke English and a more delightful family would be hard to find. That a bath was a priority item they made abundantly clear. A delicious supper followed and the evening was spent emptying a bottle of a Torun brand of vodka.

The following day was a Sunday and our intended " rest day" was given over to exploration of the city, an activity that involved nearly as much walking as had been our daily stint on the road. But Torun has much to show a visitor.

I had briefly been to the city before so knew a little of its history, the pattern of which is similar to that of other towns along the northern Vistula; birth as a Polish settlement, overrunning by Prussians, take-over by the Teutonic Knights, entry to the Hanseatic League, and final return to Polish sovereignty. Its incorporation within the Polish Corridor early this century enraged Hitler though the Second World War which followed inflicted little material damage; a miraculous occurrence for a Polish city at that time.

Torun is the birthplace of Nicolaus Copernicus, and though the astronomer spent only his youth here, the city is proud of the connection, his name being found all over town; his house enthusiastically open as a multi-storey museum. Having been a wealthy Hanseatic centre, rivalling Gdansk, the buildings, of a multitude of styles, retain a degree of aged magnificence.

Our exploration covered everything from the tiny Church of the Holy Cross in the outskirts to the huge austere St Mary's off the Old Town Square. In between came a Leaning Tower, the Monastery Gate and, of course, the Copernicus Museum, not to mention a visit to the University chambers where Bogdan had his office.

A substantial late afternoon lunch followed by a classical concert in the light, airy and deliciously cool St Mary's Church completed the day's "rest" and, though the good family offered us their hospitality for a second night, we felt compelled to transfer our allegiance to the more impersonal offerings of the Hotel Kosmos, located far more suitably for our proposed early departure next day.

We heard the rain in the night and it was falling heavily as we left Torun. In the southern outskirts of the city a dip in the road beneath a railway bridge had filled with water and only high-axle vehicles were getting through the flood. We waded it, our boots hung round our necks, and though unrealised at the time, that flooded road was a portent of what was to come.

From the day we left Torun the weather began to change perceptibly. However the sun re-appeared that afternoon as we thankfully turned off the busy 54 Poznan highway onto a joy of a by-road that might have been laid for us, so little other use seemed to be made of it.

A military tank range and its churned-up grassland together with the rusted remnants of target T34 tanks marred a tranquil countryside of woods and marshes. Storks flew overhead, colourful butterflies fluttered aimlessly, and, in a stream, a trout swam stationary against the current. We felt at peace with the world as we marched, side by side, in the middle of the little road.

A junction ended the idyll but the new road – numbered 266 – was only a degree larger, the traffic still slight. Clouds obscured the sunshine and a breeze confounded any mosquitoes that might have invaded our woodside campsite that night.

Hardly had we entered the township of Radziejow when down came the rain again. We took refuge in the bus station but could find no welcoming bar or restaurant. The wet streets were devoid of life as if the plague had struck the town. It couldn't have been Sunday; surely it was a weekend we were in Torun? Time and days of the week held no meaning for us anymore. The rain lessened as we continued disconsolately twenty-nine kilometres to Sompolno in one afternoon's burst of speed, moist with rain instead of sweat.

A store was open in another part-deserted town so we stocked up with tinned provisions before taking the road to Konin. But hardly had we cleared Sompolno when the heavy rain returned. Ignoring it we trudged through lush woods indented with lakes; sensationally beautiful countryside in sunnier circumstances. Occasional bus shelters gave momentary refuge and so began a kind of musical chairs progress as we attempted to reach a shelter to coincide with the advent of a fresh downpour. But we were caught out by the mightiest downpour of all; by the time we reached a subsequent shelter our clothes and rucksacks were soaked as water fell solidly out of the sky.

That final bus shelter must have been the runt of the litter. On the verge of collapse, one wall partly missing, it made a dismal refuge as we shivered in its one dry corner. Only in a dusk as black as night did we emerge to enter the village of Kramske. The idea of camping in such conditions failed to appeal so we knocked at a vicarage-farmhouse standing beside the church and obtained permission to sleep in its adjoining barn.

Spreading our wet clothing over the shafts of a wagon in the slight hope of them drying we slept well amongst warm, dry hay, and in the morning were invited to breakfast by the robust priest and his jovial sister. He had to leave straightway to conduct mass, the service being relayed to the kitchen as we tucked into thick slices of bread, ham, cheese and jam. Still damp but revived in mind and body we left under an overcast but as yet non-leaking sky.

The industrial city of Konin has little to offer the visitor though its suburbs refused to give us up until we had circumnavigated the sizeable town, finally ending up on the main Poznan highway 25, a horrifying artery for walkers hemmed in by crash barriers and awash with heavy commercial vehicles that swept by buffeting us unmercifully. Somewhere ahead was a slip-road to the Poznan motorway which, we hoped, would act as a conduit for most of the traffic, but it was a long time coming though, when it did, the relief was considerable.

The following day was something of a repeat performance with heavy rain chasing us into bus shelters as we progressed erratically towards Kalisz. We even acquired another barn for the night though, this time, our passports were taken from us as a security measure by the head of a multitudinous family who tempered his suspicions by insisting we join them for supper prior to dossing down in the hay.

Polish hospitality calls for ample food, and woe to the guest who declines. Yet the guest who grabs food without being encouraged disgraces himself. On this occasion there was a mountain of farm produce on the table with different members of the family joining and leaving the meal at intervals so that our own intake could be as modest as was necessary and yet provide no insult. Finally, locked inside the barn, not even the eternal barking of a dog outside could disturb our slumber.

The prospect of a final Orbis-donated hotel in Kalisz had not been lost upon us these last uncomfortable days; the chance to dry things out irresistible. But jet-black clouds, as black and as widespread as I have ever seen in Europe, darkened the horizon indicating a certainty of more rain in the meantime.

And so it came to pass. Leaving Stawiszyn, the first big drops began to fall, soon increasing to a torrent. The verges, containing their usual quota of dead dogs, cats and hedgehogs, became quagmires and bus shelters but temporary havens. Attempting to acquire the loan of another barn for the night we received a firm rebuff from a group of vodka-swigging youths in the farmyard but miraculously the downpour ceased as we searched, desperately, for a camp site, and on the very edge of the urban build-up of Kalisz, found it atop a bank part-concealed from the road by bushes. Miraculously too, it turned out to be one of our best night's camping with a fiery-red sunset offering a spectacular backdrop.

The rain held off both overnight and into the next day as we entered the city and located the Orbis Hotel Prosna, the other end of town. A flurry of hot baths and scrubbing of clothes preceded a brief exploration of what Kalisz is all about. Held to be Poland's oldest city, it was referred to as Calissia by Pliny in the first century and described in the second as a trading settlement on the "amber route" between the Baltic and the Adriatic. Though sacked and burnt periodically the greatest tragedy, often compared to Warsaw's destruction in 1944, came in our own century when, during the First World War, it was razed to the ground by the invading Germans. Kalisz is no architectural gem but we found it to be an exceptionally agreeable city with the Old Town situated pleasingly in the angle between the Prosna and Bernardynka rivers.

Maybe the unaccustomed comfort and the hospitality we experienced there had something to do with our views for not only did the hotel spoil us but the editor of a local newspaper, interviewing us for a report on our journey, took us to his flamboyant home for a magnificent dinner.

Attempting to find our way out of the city towards Grabow, some thirty-three kilometres distant, was a trial. Enquiries only elicited directions to Grabow street since it was presumed that nobody in their right senses would want to walk thirty three kilometres on a hot day. And it was a hot day under a burning sun which at least helped dry the sodden terrain. The road, when finally located, turned out to be a small and little-used one; just the sort of road we had hoped to find throughout most of the journey. It twisted and turned for no apparent reason for there were no hills. Furthermore it passed through a series of picturesque villages that made the going all the more enjoyable. Unfortunately, I had developed a minor dose of the "runs" which entailed frequent and hurried excursions into fields of corn and barley but the malady lasted no more than a morning. It was the one and only time such an occurrence struck which goes to show how fit one is on a diet of rough living, a regular soaking and general undernourishment.

Our night alongside a half-flooded wood was enlivened by a stag which stood beside the tent barking and stamping in a most aggressive manner – though I don't think it was we who had raised its ire. In the morning I discovered a carton of yoghurt had burst over all my hotel-washed clothes while Paul found a mouse exploring the interior of his rucksack.

From Grabow to Ostrzeszow the road expanded, running through countryside that reminded me of Suffolk's Constable Country. A passing car, travelling much too fast, grazed us on a corner and an old man, wobbling uncertainly on a bicycle in the middle of the road, waffled on about a murder that had taken place in the vicinity – though whether this was yesterday or years ago we couldn't make out.

Then, once more our minor road idyll fell apart as a "red" highway – the 43 main artery to Katowice – took us into its maw. Back amongst searing industrial traffic we could but plod determinedly on, our only pleasurable moment being when a smartly dressed lady driver stopped to present us with a bottle of mineral water. We must have looked as thirsty as we felt.

Kepno, with its promise of a second lodging with a Polish family, was our next objective though we were again concerned that our earlier-than-expected arrival might have denied us the pleasure of their company – and a soft bed. An exuberant forest – plainly a well-patronised picnic and blueberry-picking spot at weekends – lay between us and Kepno, and through it, a religious procession was passing, going the same way as us. It was composed of youngsters organised by a couple of priests and marshalled by orange-jacketed police which had a marked effect on the speeding traffic. There was much chanting and the waving aloft of banners bearing ecclesiastical motifs so, squaring our rucksacks and mouthing the only line we knew of "Onward Christian Soldiers", we joined the rear of the procession and thus enjoyed a brief period of traffic protection.

Eight kilometres short of Kepno the trees thinned as the forest drew to an end so we withdrew from the marching legion and set up camp among the blueberries – which ensured a fruit dessert for our supper.

Next morning we entered the small town which allegedly boasts the largest market square of any other town in Poland. It rained again but only spasmodically as we searched for the block of flats housing the Kaluzny family, our enquiries at a *pivnice* all but igniting a civil war as red-faced drinkers argued amongst themselves over its whereabouts.

The flat was in process of redecoration which made it all the more remarkable that our new hosts could be so lavish with their hospitality. Twenty-two year old Jacub Kaluzny spoke good English and, to a lesser extent, so did his younger brother, Jaceb. Their parents, a most engaging couple, made us feel very much at ease the moment of our arrival and attended to our needs, only too aware how filthy and hungry we were. Both sons studied at Wroclaw University, Jacub having a flat in the city and it was through a concern for his belongings there that we first became aware of the extent of the serious flooding in that city. A television set in the living room revealed the full story in non-stop special broadcasts.

Scenes of devastation on both sides of the river Oder and much of Wroclaw under water with thousands made homeless filled the screen.

And not only Wroclaw either. Many bridges to the east of the city had been destroyed or made impassable by the raging waters; the area declared a major disaster zone. For us, this was a serious check to our continued journey since the route crossed the Oder at Brzeg and nobody was able to say whether its bridge was still there. Reports told too of heavy damage further south and in neighbouring Moravia through which we would be passing. However, there was nothing we could do about the situation except to carry on southwards and see what happened. In the meantime we would enjoy the company of the good Kaluzny family and the pleasures they had planned for us.

Following a walk around their town we were taken by car – a novel experience – back along the road we had come to the small lake resort of Antonin for a swim followed by a visit to the Radziwill family hunting palace nearby. Set in an arboretum of rare trees the unique octagonal timber building was once the summer residence of Poland's richest and best-known aristocratic clan, the edifice now transformed into a luxury hotel. One of its more distinguished visitors was Frederic Chopin who gave concerts there.

The trouble with a brief sojourn of normality; consuming good food at a table, being waited upon and lavishly entertained, is that it makes for something of a shock on a return to rough living. Another interview with the local press delayed our departure until early afternoon though the sunshine did its best to make the inevitable return painless. We had planned to camp north of Namyslow but so invigorated were we from the Kaluzny hospitality that we walked on through this handsome walled town completing a good twenty-two kilometres before raising the tent.

Another encounter with a vocal and aggressively-minded stag got me out of my bivi-bag to behold a dawn of surrealistic intensity boding well for another fine day. And the promise held, making a mockery of the alleged flood disaster ahead. Alas, it was real enough. Beyond the village of Rogatice, fifteen kilometres south of Namyslow, a posse of police barred our way forward. Brzeg and its bridge were under water, they told us; we would have to divert sixty kilometres eastwards to Opole; maybe the bridge there was open.

But it wasn't and half the city lay under water. We reached it with the help of another German-Polish driver of a BMW who gave us a lift to Dobrz, and from there on a bus that had to plough through an area resembling an inland sea through which the upper floors and roofs of villages and farmhouses protruded. And all the while the sun blazed from an azure sky.

Opole had become a bright, prosperous-looking city since I had last seen it during the communist era but now police were blocking all roads leading southwards. A lady in the Orbis office recommended we shack up in a hotel until the flood water subsided but the notion raised no appeal. Krapkovice, twenty-five kilometres southeast of Opole held the next possible crossing point, and to thence we proceeded on a further bus. But it was the same story there. A subsequent bridge was situated at Raciborz, on the southern edge of the Silesian industrial region centred by the towns of Gliwice and Katowice, and we were about to continue eastwards when we learnt of an Oder-spanning viaduct carrying the Wroclaw-Cracow motorway. Surely this could not be inundated? We reached it on foot to find the highway a solid mass of near-stationary vehicles being controlled by harassed police; virtually all the traffic in southern Poland having been directed to this one operational crossing point thus creating a mammoth jam. Walking over the structure proved a far speedier method of gaining the opposite bank; the swollen river below flashing fire, seeming to resent its inability to block this single through route across it. Near the village of Rogow, some kilometres ahead, we left the motorway intent upon walking south-westwards back onto our original alignment, thus keeping to our avowed intent to walk the whole distance from Gdansk to Vienna.

Perversely, I felt a slight pang of regret that we had not been forced to divert still further east since, for me, it would have involved re-visiting an area in which I had been as a prisoner-of-war during 1944/45. Unlike our 1993 Baltic to the Black Sea cycling marathon I had not intended this foot journey to be a perambulation down memory lane but Gliwice was close to the site of the coalmine in which I had been forced to work as a slave miner in 1944. And the Oder bridge at Raciborz I had last crossed while under Russian air attack and in company with tens of thousands of refugees, other captives and broken units of the Wehrmacht fleeing westwards from the advancing Red Army in the dreadful winter that followed. At Rybnik, midway between Gliwice and Raciborz, I had witnessed the hideous spectacle of a mass execution by the SS of naked victims of a concentration camp, the memory of which I can never quite erase from my mind. But now we had floods and their consequences to worry about; it was not the time for dwelling upon the past.

The small 409 road which, later, re-numbered itself 414 became our onward course towards the Czech border at Glucholay, back on our original route. Though narrow and normally little-used, much diverted traffic poured along it; frustrated drivers cutting corners and nearly clipping us in the process. The bulk of the inflated traffic left at the junction at Debina and, thereafter, we had the 414 more or less to ourselves. Many villages had been divested of provisions by the hungry hordes and even at the larger township of Biala the only food we could raise was a hamburger. A cheerful group of road workers gave us a bottle of mineral water and occasionally drivers stopped to offer a lift.

With a rise of hills shading the horizon we entered Prudnik where food – hot and cold – was unaccountably plentiful, and our last campsite in Poland was in a somewhat exposed position beside the road yet seemingly concealed enough for an all-night snogging couple in a small car who never noticed our proximity, nor the audibility of their own amorous activities.

We reached Glucholay before mid-morning to notch up a further five kilometres on a straight but bucking road to the Polish-Czech border. Though a little rain had pattered against our tent's fly-sheet overnight the weather remained fine and warm, almost as warm as it had been the first week of walking. As we sweated our way towards the customs barrier I pondered upon our rate of progress so far. We had covered the whole of Poland, from north to south, inside of three weeks without undue haste. All in all not too bad, I felt, for a seventy-three, nearly seventy-four year-old.

Political borders rarely have much effect on geography but one does here between Polish Glucholay and Czech Zlate Hory. The hills we had seen from Prudnik had been Moravian and hardly had we touched Czech soil and the landscape proceeded to heave itself into almost mountainous proportions. In fact these hills are known as the Jesenik Mountains, foothills of the High Jeseniks which join the so-called Eagle Mountains in eastern Bohemia. The summit of the hill closest to Zlate Hory was topped by what appeared to be a deserted abbey while all around us lay thick forests into which footpaths led enticingly.

We spent an hour or two in the little town satisfying voracious appetites with goulash and *knedliky* (dumplings), of which I am inordinately fond, together with good Czech beer, so much nicer than the Polish stuff. Our next urban landmark was the town of Bruntal, forty kilometres away, and the small "yellow" road that led out of Zlate Hory lived up to the expectation of my Czech map – even though again out of date – once clear of the town. A long steep hill – upwards – made exhausting slogging as we sweated buckets struggling to the head of the pass through which the road ran.

Almost immediately the devastation caused by water became apparent. This was not simple flooding but the result of the titanic force of torrents crashing down the hillsides. Tiny streams had become raging cataracts carrying huge amounts of debris that cut great swathes through the trees, sweeping away bridges, roads, railway tracks and anything, nature or man-made, that stood in the path. In Vrbno the damage resembled that of the aftermath of a wartime air raid with collapsed houses, railway lines clawing skywards and streets blocked by walls of mud. Yet the inhabitants of the region appeared to have taken the disaster in their stride; people still expressed interest in our journey while, in Vrbno, a man who had lost his home insisted we join him in a *hostinec* (pub) for a *pivo* (beer). The police, manning a checkpoint, gave us a couple of bottles of mineral water being concerned for our health when they saw us attempting to extract probably contaminated water from a pump. Overhead, rescue helicopters clattered incessantly.

Twenty-two kilometres south of the border we camped on the gritty but comparatively dry ground of a deserted factory to pass a reasonable night in spite of another shower. And by the following mid-morning we were in the textile town of Bruntal, one of numerous mining centres which originally were set up by the Teutonic Knights. An attractive place this, uncommercialised and typically Moravian, where our substantial lunch cost the equivalent of £1.75 ($4) each.

The road to Sternberk was emphatically a "red" one, numbered 45, turning to 46 as it joined the Opava highway thirteen kilometres short of the town. We had managed to reach the village of Lomnice before the real rains hit us again, resulting in our campsite in a pine forest that night being, literally, a washout. A fast-running, gurgling – much more gurgling than usual – stream ran past our site and we viewed it with suspicion in the knowledge of what such streams could turn into but, nevertheless, put it to use by immersing ourselves naked in the cold water.

Wet roads are an added inconvenience to walkers; not only are the verges sodden but uncaring drivers allow their vehicles to douse pedestrians with jets of dirty water from their wheels. And it didn't take us long to come to the conclusion that Czech drivers were equally as bad as their Polish counterparts, the number of near-misses increasing by the hour. The road had become virtually an elongated cemetery, lined with simple crosses and even stone memorials, which indicated a severe lack of driving ability in a country where, for decades, few had owned a car. Adders and slow-worms together with a multitude of field mice were, however, very much alive at the roadside which provided a little light relief as we pressed on in the rain, dodging death.

It was still raining heavily as we zigzagged down a hill into Sternberk, famous for its thirteenth century castle. A hot meal provided excuse for an hour's shelter after which we hogged rich cream cakes in a cafe. But the rain failed to stop so, fearing for our digestive systems, we made towards Olomouc, the wet, mist-shrouded hills gradually flattening out.

The city lay in sight – even through the murk – as we cast about for a farm that could raise a barn in which to spend the night. But our search was in vain. Here we were in cereal-growing country; storage facilities seemingly unnecessary. A village off the main road, the last before the urban spread of Olomouc, drew our footsteps as darkness increased and we had all but resigned ourselves to a night in a bus shelter when we came upon a half-built house that offered better possibilities. We had observed it as we approached the village but men were still working on the roof rafters. However, they had departed when we returned an hour later so, crossing an expanse of liquid mud, we located the driest portion of one of the downstairs (there was no upstairs) room shells, spread some planks across the floor joists (there was no floor) and lay down in our damp bivi-bags.

It was our worst night ever with the rain finding its way through the ceiling planking, sending down rivulets of water to splash disconcertingly into the muddy puddles that surrounded us as well as upon our recumbent bodies. We lay there miserably; not sleeping a wink, and before dawn had packed our wet belongings and padded into Olomouc before most of its citizens had risen from their comfortable dry beds.

We could, however, count ourselves lucky for many an Olomouc citizen likewise had no such luxury, the city having been badly affected by flooding. The muddied streets were lined with ruined furniture while fire-appliances were busy pumping water out of cellars and basements. Through it all the brown Morava river, which had caused this misery, flowed high, brown and sullen beneath the bridges, only just clearing their parapets. No shops were yet open so we made our way to the central square, sat down inside the portals of the City Hall and waited for Olomouc to come to life.

Once the capital of Moravia before Brno shouldered that responsibility in 1641, the city continues to retain something of a provincial imperial capital, reminding me a little of similarly-sized cities in neighbouring Austria. Its proud square and prim old buildings surviving from different periods lay in a heart which today is encompassed by a mishmash of office blocks and industrial suburbs. The City Hall, a flippantly-coloured edifice, displays an astronomical clock only slightly smaller than the famous one in Prague, its hours marked by parading wooden workers instead of saints since its recent restoration took place during the communist regime. Close by is the soaring St Wenceslas Cathedral and the Premysl Palace to add to the square's strikingly majestic air.

One of the first shops to open was a stationery emporium from whence I was able to acquire a more or less up-to-date map of the Kromerizsko district through which our route to Brno would take us. This helped to avoid the Olomouc-Brno motorway, though we still found some difficulty in locating the small 435 road that made its more rural way to the Moravian capital; our enquiries repeatedly leading us back to the motorway. Eventually we located the reticent little road leading off from the main Prerov highway and thankfully followed it.

The rain, which had lessened for a while, resumed hardly had we negotiated a flood that blocked the carriageway, spreading into the surrounding fields. The road was fine; again just the sort we had always looked for; short on traffic with attractive countryside on both sides. Only the rain spoilt things and this increased to a solid downpour with no let-up as we entered the township of Tovacov which boasted a hotel with no beds. However it did produce a hot meal enabling us to carry on walking another twelve kilometres to Kojetin at which we arrived looking – and feeling – like a couple of half-drowned rats. Yes, there was a hotel just across the square, we were informed by a flashily-attired individual outside the local night-club, his directions leading us to a shabby edifice labelled "Grand Hotel" that had been closed for at least thirty years. Our spirits had sunk to a low ebb, so low that we begged at the police-station for the loan of a warm dry cell for the night since, after two sleepless nights, we hardly relished raising the tent on sodden ground and under the continuing deluge. The young police officer was sympathetic and even spoke a few words of English but, alas, comfort was the reserve of criminals only. We were contemplating breaking a shop window when he told us of a hostel a kilometre out of town and our spirits rose again. They rose even higher when we found ourselves in a four-bed dormitory with clean linen and an electric stove upon which to brew tea. The hostel was simple but perfectly adequate with hot showers all for an infinitesimal sum per night and I think we appreciated that overnight lodging more than any other.

It was only drizzling in the morning and the sky cleared as we followed the slightly larger road 47, passing through a series of picturesque Moravian villages, one such being the larger Ivanice where we halted for a beer. A watery sun blessed the town of Viskov where our road crossed the motorway but the only restaurant we could find offering hope of a hot meal was a small "bufet". The proprietor said that they were not cooking that day but he relented under pressure from the other clients who had gathered round to chat with us.

With the improvement in the weather the prospect of a resumption of camping was less dire and four kilometres out of the town we found a dry site atop a roadside bank shielded by a thin belt of foliage. In the darkness of night a glow in the sky pinpointed the city of Brno and the alluring prospect of another hotel sojourn. But ahead lay a day of perpetual rain which commenced the moment we de-camped.

The 47 parallels the motorway from Viskov onwards and it brought us damply to Komorany where we stoked up with liver plus a double helping of dumplings costing, with a beer, the princely sum of 80 pence ($1). The menu quoted something called "bile" and "grot", neither of which found much favour. In a vain hope of the rain lessening we hung around the bus station for an hour or more then gave it up, striding determinedly into the tempest. In spite of the proximity of the motorway, traffic became increasingly unpleasant as vehicles competed with the rain to soak us the more as they sped unconcernedly by. My boots were full of water that had run down my bare legs and by the time we were within a dozen and a half kilometres of Brno we both felt utterly miserable.

I had crossed the battlefield of Austerlitz before but never have I seen these sombre, blood-soaked acres look so uninviting. It was on these rolling hills that Napoleon fought the combined armies of Russia and Austria on December 2, 1805 and won one of his most famous victories. Here and there a crucifix showed against the rain-swept scenery adding to the desolation and reminding one of the thousands who died in that historic conflict. In all directions not one tree or building gave hope of shelter and I have to say that, though our discomfort was infinitely less severe than that of the Austrian, Russian and French soldiers, this was the day when our own spirits sank the lowest.

And then, cresting a rise, we perceived a stable-like building ahead. There, in the middle of nowhere, stood a McDonald's restaurant, fresh and new as if it were a mushroom that had sprouted overnight. Whether or not such an establishment is a suitable one to grace a soldier's graveyard was no concern of ours as we took refuge in its fuggy interior, our wet clothes, boots and rucksacks forming puddles on the floor.

In the late afternoon the downpour lessened once more, allowing us to emerge and continue towards Brno. But the sodden terrain again precluded the possibility of camping so, at the extreme edge of the city, we took up residence beneath one of the concrete supports of a motorway

The author standing by a road sign in Brno, Moravia

bridge where the ground was hard, dry and sheltered. We never raised the tent but simply lay in our bivi-bags at the foot of a graffiti-adorned pillar and passed a very reasonable night in spite of the constant explosion of sound, like that of a Bofors gun firing next to one's ear, as vehicles overhead hit the expansion channel cut in the carriageway.

Leaving with the dawn we found our way through Brno's considerable suburbs, via a skein of strictly non-pedestrian expressways, before most citizens had sat down to breakfast. And, joy, oh joy, Best Western's International Hotel welcomed us not only at so early an hour but with the offer of not one but two nights in their palatial and centrally-situated establishment. We were to make the most of it.

This was my first post-communism visit – and what a transformation I found. From a drab, lifeless city of food-queues and empty shop windows, I discovered a metropolis of chic shops and tempting restaurants teeming with a smartly-attired populace. And though the restoration continues, the historic squares and facades had come to vivid, eye-catching life. Two specific buildings stand out when Brno is viewed from afar. These are the twin-spired Cathedral of St Peter and St Paul and Spilberk Castle high on their respective hillocks, the latter over which our hotel bedroom looked. The castle dates back to 1287 and its name means a great deal to Czechs who recall the grim days when the Austrians used it as a state prison for anyone who showed opposition to the Habsburg monarchy. To be sentenced to Spilberk was virtually to be sentenced to death. The squat structure is not particularly impressive to look at but its reputation gives it a morbid fascination. The cathedral, on the other hand, is of more cheerful and venerable countenance though its Gothic reconstruction was carried out only at the end of the last century.

The site of Brno was occupied by the Slavs in the fifth century. A thousand years ago an imperial castle was founded here and, in 1243, its buildings were numerous enough for it to be proclaimed a town that later was to become the Moravian capital. The city grew rich in the nineteenth century as the industrial heartland of the Austrian empire; its subsequent ordnance factories, in the twentieth, producing, amongst other lethal ironmongery, the World War Two bren light machine gun in conjunction with the British Enfield weapon factory.

With two days of leisure before us we determined to ensure it remained so though allowing for a few excursions within the city to satisfy our curiosity. Thus we mixed forays into the town with multiple hot baths and clothes-washing sessions. And what made things doubly pleasant was the fact of being, at last, out of the depressing flood disaster zone. Our lunches we took at the stand up "bufet" in the railway station where a hot meal and beer cost 80 pence ($1) after which we spoilt ourselves at open-air cafes devouring those rich cream cakes in which the Czech Republic excels.

The sun rejoiced with us on both days and it was still shining as we left the city. Our road was numbered 52 and though a "red" route on our map it had since expanded into the main Brno-Vienna highway of almost motorway proportions. Somewhere amongst the southern suburbs must run the smaller original artery but we never found it until much later.

Actually the main road made easy, if dull, walking. It was dual-carriageway, had a wide, well-marked hard shoulder, and once the suburbs were behind us, was not over-populated by traffic. The prolonged rest had put a spring in our step so that our rate of progress that day was prodigious. In all we covered nearly fifty kilometres though it was probably the cause of a pulled tendon in my left leg which was not to become immediately apparent.

The first township marked on my map subsequent to Brno was that of Pohorelice, shown astride the smaller road. So at a junction indicating it we left the highway and made for the place, having no desire to continue direct to Vienna on so dull a route. Our intention was to cross into Austria at the border village of Hevlin about fifty kilometres distant.

We now found ourselves on a "red" road 54, long and straight through equally unremarkable countryside but, near Jirice, we managed to leave it on a series of smaller arteries signposted to Hevlin, a winding, picturesque route through flower-bedecked villages with names like Litobatvice and Hrusovany, and it was close by one of these, in an orchard, where we pitched the tent for the night. And what a night. The spell of fine weather came to an abrupt end with a violent thunderstorm that circuited the sky repeatedly returning to pour retribution upon us. The thunder crashed with the intensity of an artillery barrage and the lightning was such that it was well nigh possible to read a book by its vivid illumination. Within minutes the tent was overwhelmed by the deluge and we found ourselves lying in pools of water; our recently-washed clothing soaked; our boots again full of water.

There's nothing much more disagreeable in the outdoor living scenario than having to strike camp in the pouring rain. Donning wet clothes within the cramped confines of wet nylon, to emerge under a steady downpour, and then lowering and packing a soaking tent and equipment is not a joyful process. We had left the site breakfastless at dawn but in a village bus shelter lit our stove, brewed milkless and sugarless tea and consumed our unappetising tin of herring. Whilst thus engaged a number of potential early-morning bus passengers gathered at the shelter but took not the slightest notice of these strange antics.

Upon reaching Hevlin, the Czech border village, the sun reasserted itself to warm up a gently steaming ground. We took advantage of it, spreading items of clothing and equipment over seats on the village green before patronising the local *hostinec* intent upon a last Czech beer. Finally, at a more up-market restaurant than those to which we had been accustomed, we partook of our final hot meal on Czech territory. The terrace was full of Austrians taking advantage of prices eighty percent lower than those in Laa, the Austrian border town, a hundred metres up the road.

An abrupt change of urban environment; the sadly down-at-heel streets and houses of Hevlin compared unfavourably with the spick and span orderliness of Laa, and made an immediate impact as we passed onto Austrian territory and into this visually-pleasing town. I felt a tinge of sadness shared with Paul. But for the stifling hand of communism, Moravia and the whole of what used to be Czechoslovakia could have enjoyed the same high standard of living as that of its western neighbours. It is the same with Poland, of course, as it is anywhere along the one-time Iron Curtain frontier where East meets West.

The one up-to-date map we had brought with us had, unfortunately, been lost, which, together with erroneous information imparted by a garage hand, led us along the wrong Vienna-bound road. Regrettably too, this road was not only the larger and busier one but also would have taken us gradually back to the main highway from Brno to the Austrian capital which, in Austria, had been up-graded to a pedestrian-forbidden motorway. We should have taken a lesser artery numbered 6, not only leading us more directly to Vienna via the town of Ernstbrunn but also giving us a less traffic-afflicted road into the bargain.

Some eight kilometres out of Laa, with the sky again spitting rain, we discovered our mistake. Rejecting the notion of a return to the town, we managed to obtain a lift in a passing car to Mistelbach, twenty kilometres on, which gave us a chance of observing the scenic countryside of rolling hills, together with castle-dominated Staatz, en route. And at Mistelbach we were able to rejoin a "yellow" road that would lead us, for eighteen kilometres, back onto the number 6 route we should have taken in the first place. We were now walking westwards across our original line of march but it would compensate for the lift we had obtained and so satisfied our self-imposed ruling of accepting no rides.

A dry and highly satisfactory camp a few kilometres out of Mistelbach preceded an equally enjoyable walk to Ernstbrunn, only slightly marred by Paul being bitten by a diminutive but raucous dog at Ladendorf and my left leg tendon beginning give pain. A cloudy but photogenic sky complimented the comely terrain of distant horizons; terrain that is surely worthwhile for those with time to explore it. And at Ernstbrunn, crossing over the north/south highway 6, we lunched well, if expensively, at the only restaurant open on a Sunday (it was only then that we realised it was a Sunday). Here our half-litre of beer cost us £1.50 ($2) against the good Czech stuff at 20 pence (30 cents). But we found the people of Niederosterreich and, in particular, this lesser-known part of it called Weinviertel noted for its wine-bearing potential, to be exceptionally friendly; drivers waving and hooting greetings from passing cars and asking questions of us wherever we went.

Back on "yellow" 6, the increasing pain in my leg began to slow me down. We made frequent halts for a rest in substantial village bus shelters and it was while relaxing, semi-prostrate, on the seat of one such shelter that we were questioned and asked for our passports by the suspicious crew of a roving police-car. They plainly disbelieved our statement that we had walked from Gdansk; in fact this only served to increase their suspicions. But they could find no reason to detain us.

The road led to Korneuburg, a town on the Danube barely ten kilometres from Vienna, and it was only the proximity of the end of the journey that gave me the strength of purpose to continue walking. Many Austrian roads – even those as minor as this one – bear not only kilometre markers but one for every fifth of a kilometre, and, for me, each marker became one more to push behind me as I struggled on, trying in vain to transfer my weight to my good right leg. A slug-infested camp site beside a disused railway line and too close for comfort to a derelict house occupied by gypsies made for an uneasy night's rest but the weather remained dry. Castles on hilltops and "Sound of Music" villages gave the sunlit uplands a piquancy I was unable to fully appreciate but when Korneuburg appeared in the distance I knew the end of the long hike was in my grasp.

And those last fourteen kilometres, with the town in view, were as long and drawn out as any of the thousand we had covered from the Baltic coast. With me limping into its streets we celebrated our arrival at the river with a leisurely meal at an open-air restaurant close to the railway station, then, in the late afternoon, plodded on towards Vienna along the wide Danube valley lined with the extravagant villas of prosperous out-of-town citizens. Four kilometres on, the city began to close in on us, reducing the chances of a final night's camping in a rural setting. But an "island" of trees, marooned in what surely must have been the last belt of agriculture this side of the capital, provided our ultimate night under the flysheet and the sky. A few drops of rain fell but came to nothing.

It would seem that Austrian slugs have an affinity with campers; for the second consecutive night we were invaded by these slimy creatures which had to be picked off the tent, our boots and even bivi-bags as we rose next morning. The final tin of herring and mug of tasteless tea consumed, and we were on the way into the Austrian capital.

Over to the right the water of the Danube winked at us as the rising sun dappled its surface. We had attained kilometre zero.

8

Trail Walking in the USA
The Trail by Cold Turkey Creek

White-topped wagon trains, herd-riding cowboys, buckskin-clad trappers, grizzled prospectors, dust-raising stage coaches – all are part of the image of the nineteenth century Old West, an image that still stirs the hearts and imaginations of millions of Americans, and not a few Britishers.

The United States is full of their trails and the word there has more literal connotations than it does in Europe. The Santa Fe and the Oregon are historic trails and, subsequently, stage lines that come easily to mind though, alas, these great routes of American history are now buried beneath the tarmac of interstate highways and the concrete of cities.

With the peace that followed the war of 1812, the tide of migration moved the American frontier steadily westward. The pioneers came by foot, on horseback and in wagons. It was land as well as gold that lured most migrants to the great Mississippi and Missouri rivers and beyond. Canals, stage lines and, later, railways sped the pace. Within a generation industrial cities were thriving – Cincinnati, Detroit, Milwaukee, Chicago, Fargo – where not so long before Indians had hunted and fished.

To locate and follow for any distance the arteries along which this tide rolled is a sad, unrewarding task today even though much of the American West is unspoilt countryside. But with two North Dakota colleagues I had not yet met, researching "on location", and I diligently studying the tomes of the Royal Geographical Society in London, we finally came up with one that held promise – the old Medora-Deadwood stage line running some

A Fort Seward wagon train in Jamestown, North Dakota

230 miles across the Badlands, Butte country and the Black Hills of North and South Dakota. Founded by a titled Frenchman, the Marquis de Mores, who settled on the Badlands with twenty servants to staff the mansion he had built in the town of Medora (named after his wife, New York heiress Medora von Hoffman) the line prospered briefly. However, his ambitions far exceeded his ability to manage the many enterprises in which he involved himself and, around 1885, after hardly a year of operation feeding the human migration from the Northern Pacific Railroad to the goldfields in South Dakota, the line died. Today few people know the route of this one-time stage trail the three of us proposed to follow.

The township of Medora is a living museum of two of the most colourful – and unlikely – characters to be found in the raw badlands frontier, young, bespectacled Theodore Roosevelt and the hot-blooded visionary de Mores. Roosevelt came here in 1883 as part-owner of two of the largest ranches in the vicinity. Long before he became first citizen of the United States, he was, as a lesser president, that of the Little Missouri Stockmen's Association.

North Dakota is a land of prairies, rich river valleys, huge ranches and vast stretches of wheat. Its wealth is still in its soil – agriculture, crude oil and lignite. It is a land through which Colonel Custer's men rode with range grass growing up to their stirrups. It is the state in which to trace nineteenth century frontier history, while, at various earlier times, Spain, France and England laid claim to the territory before it became exuberantly American.

My new companions were generous, casual and friendly. Mike Martin was a young buffalo farmer who, with a degree in American history, had undertaken the bulk of the research for the journey we proposed to make attempting to follow the trail. Steve Traynor was a gruff retired railroad worker, hard-drinking and hard-smoking. And our packhorse was a black stallion of indeterminate breed answering to the name of Beauty.

Unlike the marquis's ventures, Medora had declined to die. It stands, defiant, at the gateway to the Theodore Roosevelt National Memorial Park, beneath the hill on which is situated the de Mores' chateau, now a museum. The small town retains its frontier veneer of timber verandas, lone star bars and Wild West facades with many of its citizens sporting exaggerated Stetsons and riding boots.

Our combined researches had unearthed the approximate line of the trail though opinions varied and much would have to depend upon local knowledge. Throughout the route stage stations had been erected approximately every ten to fifteen miles. The line out of Medora led south, then east up Sully Creek, thence south again to Rocky Ridge – the second station. From this point the trail went further southward by Robert's Springs, continuing to Cedar Creek, Cold Turkey Creek and Crooked Creek, close to the North and South Dakota state line, past another station – O'Dell, the only one still surviving – then south again to Bull Creek, Macey's on the Moreau river, Belle Fourche, Spearfish and Deadwood.

A century earlier a coach had left Medora every day of the week, the route being covered in thirty six hours. Our journey was to take us more than a fortnight. Now, as the four of us clattered out of Medora with only the grizzled Steve suitably dressed for the part in his film-set cowboy outfit, we became the unrecognised, unsung guardians of a stage line's centenary.

Hardly had we cleared the town when a minor disaster struck. Taking fright, Beauty proceeded to bolt, shedding her ill-packed load. I was leading her at the time and my desperate hold on her was simply by reason of the fact that the lead rein was wrapped around my ankle. I held on like grim death but could not bring her under control until after a trail of broken eggs, fractured bottles, broken packets of noodles and a sticky flood of syrup littered the grass verge. Mike and I had aired doubts about the wisdom of a packhorse but Steve firmly vetoed any notions of travelling light.

The Badlands are aptly named by the Indians who once roamed this rock-studded territory which can be remorseless and dangerous for the unprepared traveller. The land was formed from volcanic ash and swamp vegetation after which a myriad streams cut through the soft strata to sculpture a lunar-like formation of flat-topped buttes and deep fissures.

A dust road led us to Gully Creek where an oil company track pulled us southwards over untamed craggy outback. An antelope bounded gracefully across our path and, from a safe distance, halted to stare. Minutes later I caught my foot in a root and pitched forward on my face.

A coil of hate that lay hissing and throbbing in the grass gave me my first sight of a rattlesnake outside of a zoo and this one at dangerously close quarters. But it failed to strike and my luck continued to hold when I took the opportunity to incautiously take a close-up photograph of the reptile. Steve told me off with almost as much venom as the snake was capable of wielding and I learnt another lesson of life. The route continued across a series of valleys and gullies laced with rocks and streams that made uncomfortable walking.

Initially we were following another, very much more famous, trail; that of George Custer and his troopers who passed this way in 1876 according to the preserved graffiti of two of their number inscribed upon a large boulder. Clumps of yellow and mauve daisies splashed vivid on the coarse burnt grass that was the home of bull snakes and rattlers. By late afternoon the sun had dipped below the western hills.

With an estimated twelve miles behind us since our midday start we were content to settle down for the night beneath a clump of skeletal dead trees in Davis Creek, a short distance from where we estimated the first stage station to be. For supper we re-heated our beans left over from lunch, which, though uninspiring to the palate, were adequately filling, and it was while I was bringing in Beauty from a patch of grazing that she escaped. I listened to the diminishing drumbeats of hooves in the gathering gloom and fell into the depths of despair. To lose a load, a horse and possibly nearly one's life to a rattler the first day out was shame indeed and Steve's guff comment, "She'll never come back, you know", hardly raised my morale. But she did come back on her own accord and seldom have I felt so relieved. Lesson two – never let go a horse's rein even for a moment, I learnt that day. Lesson three materialised in the night when the top fold of a flysheet I was using as a combined groundsheet and cover blew off to expose my sleeping bag to an extremely dampening pre-dawn dew. Lessons were learnt by others that night too. When placing my bedding I had noted the precarious angle of the nearest dead tree under which we were lying, particularly the beaver-gnawed trunk, but the others hadn't. Thus when the wind rose and the offending limb overhead produced a series of groans and cracks it was Mike and Steve who felt it expedient to move. I already had.

The new day's march led parallel to the stage route and, as the terrain slowly flattened out, we were content to follow the contours of the land heading south. Big jack rabbits leaped up from almost between our feet, momentarily frightening us as well as Beauty. For many miles we walked, Steve's flashy cowboy boots giving him a crop of blisters.

Our second night was equally disastrous. There was no water source whatsoever until it rained and because we had not bothered to raise tents we spent the small hours huddled together clasping wet sleeping bags around us and trying to re-kindle a dead fire. An early morning start was all too welcome but we lost much time wandering aimlessly about attempting a short cut that wasn't. To add to the debacle, Beauty, shying from a jack rabbit, shed her load atop a windswept knoll.

In spite of our incompetence we were managing some twenty miles a day and our third night saw us at the village of Amidon which raised a bar and a barn to provide both inner and outer comfort. The patrons of the former were amazed to learn of our project; some had never heard of the trail that ran passed their homes. Farmers in the outback were more knowledgeable.

By dint of the close questioning of local ranchers we succeeded in maintaining the approximate route of the line and made steady progress again next day after a morning floundering in a marshy expanse close to a river that trapped us in its valley. Once more Beauty shed her load and we got our feet wet retrieving it from sundry puddles and bog. Our main meals of an evening became the climax of the day with Steve an adept cook using provisions surviving from our baggage plus those purchased along the way. Sunsets made stupendous backdrops to the days' end; they were only equalled by sensational dawns, icy in temperature but inspiring in their radiance.

In the township of Bowman the entire press corps turned out to intercept us for our story, a lanky cub reporter who had heard about the pilgrimage on the village grapevine; its reasons jogging local awareness. From Bowman onwards Highway 85 took us by the hand providing foot-aching tarmac though, since it had been laid over the original course of the line there was no alternative but to follow it for several days. Verges had become receptacles for discarded beer cans and bottles while the mileposts taunted us as we struggled on under an increasingly hot sun. We drew some encouragement from passing drivers who stopped to ask questions and donate refreshment; once even a full bottle of rye whisky.

At the North/South Dakota state border we thankfully swung away from Highway 85 into the Flint Hills to locate Crooked Creek, another stage station, but, next day, the confounded highway enslaved us again.

Beauty cut her leg on barbed wire at Crooked Creek and, consequently, went lame. We got her as far as Buffalo, a small town that has the distinction of being the geographical centre of the United States as well as being the halfway mark of our journey. The temperature was rising to the high nineties so we rested here for a day and night, residing in a cattle market warehouse containing tables that we utilised as beds. And from here onwards it was to be a case of shouldering all our goods and chattels ourselves for Beauty was in no fit state to continue; it would have been cruel to force the animal to do so. The curator of the local museum was not only a veritable mine of information on the subject of the trail but offered to take care of Beauty while we were away. All in all, Buffalo did us proud.

Steve was the one most concerned at the turn of events; the necessity of carrying everything on our backs turning us into mere back-packers, a breed he seemingly despised. Thus packhorseless and under a blazing sun we plodded unhappily along the accursed 85. We carried a bare minimum of food; a few tins of beans, some hard wads of pre-cooked buffalo meat, and a supply of tea and sugar, relying for further variation of cuisine on any township shops we might come across. Had we planned to travel light at the start of the journey we might have got ourselves better organised. As it was, with kettles and pans clanging and rattling from our rucksacks we gave an impression of a trio of orchestral Christmas trees.

At Redig – no more than a service station and a post office – we were befriended by the proprietor of the former who bade us join him for a fine supper of fried egg sandwiches, potato hash, coffee, lemonade and cold tea which was a vast improvement on our midday repast of half an apple. We were also given permission to spend the night in a set of sheep pens across the road but our slumbers were rudely terminated by the most frightful storm I have witnessed. It struck around midnight and immediately raised hurricane-force winds which promptly blew away the corrugated iron sheets that formed the roof of our boudoir. No rain fell but the initial formation of tornado "twisters", spiralling downwards in the not-too-far distance had us wakeful and apprehensive for the remainder of the night.

Breakfastless we took to the road once more and two hours later passed Crow Butte, a flat-topped rock rising from a dead-flat plain, a landmark visible for miles and the site of a famous battle between Crow and Sioux Indians. Today it is no more than a source of Indian legends and a breeding ground for rattlesnakes. For us, however, it was where we finally turned off 85 onto a country road that followed the alignment of the stage route. Its dust surface and grassy crown made for more pleasant walking while traffic was virtually non-existent. We sighted coyote, racoon and deer on several occasions and a golden eagle perched unconcernedly on a telegraph pole watching us go by with evident distaste. We crossed numerous riverbeds, the water long evaporated.

In spite of the storm the heat increased with temperatures nudging a hundred degrees and we were visibly wilting. A brief halt to view O'Dell stage station was a pleasure, though not because of the dilapidated structure with no roof that formed the only standing memorial to the marquis's stage line, but simply for the excuse for a lie-down in its shade. At an isolated ranch house we needed no second bidding to accept the offer of freshly-squeezed lemon juice; the family there had heard of our approach on the local radio and so were half-expecting us.

The day we entered Belle Fourche the temperature rose to a sticky hundred and six degrees and a hot wind made it akin to walking in the face of a giant fan heater. Prior to reaching the quite substantial town we had spent half an hour attempting to relax in the shade of the only tree in sight but flies descended upon us in clouds to bite us back to the task. Far horizons shimmered above delicious mirages of placid thirst-quenching lakes and it was in just this environment that the accursed 85 reappeared to goad us into the town. My attire now consisted of no more than a pair of shorts and even Steve had shed items of his cowboy outfit. We limped through the dusty streets raising curious stares and made for the first bar our eyes clapped upon.

Natives call this cowtown "Bell Foosh" and American history records that cowboys and sheepherders once fought a range war here. It is the seat of Butte country and from it is shipped the largest volume of livestock of any town in the Dakotas, Wyoming and Montana, a record of which its citizens are justly proud. This fact was made noisily clear to us as we gulped down our beer.

We had finally and unequivocally seen the end of 85 and the next day's progress was a positive delight. The fresh smell of hill breezes from the

Black Hills and their virgin forests assailed our nostrils and though breakfast had been but a swig of water the new route – a dust track – lent wings to our feet. It took us through gorgeous country that reminded me, in a way, of lowland Switzerland and it surprised me how abrupt the transformation from hot, baked plains had been. By mid-afternoon we were amongst intimate hillocks agreeably swathed in shady ponderosa pines. Behind, the eternity of the prairie faded into oblivion.

South Dakota is a land dominated by the proud, hard-fighting Sioux, who traded furs at forts along the Missouri river. The Indians and trappers who lived in harmony here slowly gave way to the settlers; the Indians were killed off or put into reservations. Many of the settlers came for the free land offered under the Homestead Act of 1862; others came for the gold discovered in 1874. The early years are vividly remembered. Nearly every native has grandparents who recall the sod homes on the prairies or the gold rush camps in the Black Hills. Three groups of migrants – Germans, Czechs and Scandinavians – retain their original traditions, customs and cuisine while several colonies of Mennonites and Hutterites prosper in the south-eastern areas.

With little warning another mirage appeared when we least expected it. This one took the form of a Holiday Inn in the middle of nowhere. It couldn't be, we reasoned, but it was. A real, bricks and mortar hotel on the edge of Spearfish Canyon just two miles out of Spearfish town and though Holiday Inns don't usually send me into raptures this one made an exception. Immersed in the hotel swimming pool we happily soaked away some of our aches and pains though no doubt sorely taxing the filtering plant in the process. A slap-up meal followed and in the comparative cool of late afternoon we wound a way up the mountain valley laced with running streams that we would have given an eye-tooth for to behold earlier.

Our final night's encampment was within a glade of trees adjoining a gentle torrent, the gurgling water a lullaby to our ears. Mosquitoes were a bane but you can't have everything so we buried our heads in our sleeping bags and thought of tomorrow and journey's end.

Somewhere east of Spearfish we had passed by the last of the stage stations but its location had been lost in the mists of time and we were in no mood to go hunting for it.

But who cared? Certainly not the scurrying citizens of Central City, a characterless suburb astride a lethal highway into Deadwood along which we were channelled. And certainly not those of Deadwood itself who, predictably, could raise no interest in trails or our journey as we marched, ever so slightly triumphant, into town. The place is a well-baited tourist trap with Wild Bill Hickuk and Calamity Jane bars at every turn though, at least, the beer was agreeably ice-cold.

The town was born from gold fever and raised through such Wild West characters after which the bars are named. The main street runs through Deadwood Gulch; the rest of it crawls up the steep canyon sides. At the height of the 1876 gold rush, twenty-five thousand people swarmed over the hillsides to dig for gold and, just as suddenly, the town emptied as new strikes were found elsewhere.

We spent the night, not in the best hotel as we had told ourselves we would, but, inexplicably, beneath the grandstand of the town's sport stadium. Don't ask me why; maybe, when it came, the idea of a soft bed and clean sheets frightened us. It rained like destruction throughout the night with water splashing down around us from flooded gutters but, in our dry but far from luxurious refuge, we never heard a thing.

The concept of the covered wagon, its day and age, is the very core of American history. Countless films and books have told the pioneering story; yet the evocative creaking of iron and wooden wheels has still not entirely ceased today.

A number of organisations continue to run wagon treks along sections of the routes of famous as well as lesser-known trails for both commercial reasons and to evoke a sense of a history of which the United States is in comparatively short supply. And none carries this out so vividly as the annual excursion arranged by the farming community of Fort Seward, Jamestown in North Dakota. Unlike some other similar outfits this is non-profit making and non-commercial; relying upon the participation in and contributions by all who possess a sense of history.

With Steve being the so-called honorary trail boss of the Fort Seward Wagon Train it was inevitable that I would be invited to join the current trek out of Jamestown scheduled to roll some eight days hence. The week-long journey, covering well over a hundred miles, had been running annually since the end of the 1960s and though originally planned as a one-off event, its popularity and support had risen to the extent of the trek becoming a yearly exercise.

For me the ride into yesteryear was to be a walk since the alternative of sitting on a hard wooden seat in an unsprung wagon was not one I particularly relished.

Prior to departure from Jamestown each participant was assigned to a wagon, whatever the chosen method of motivation, and so straightway came under the benevolent charge of a "Big Wheel" and a "Teamster", the whole force being commanded by this year's "Trail Boss" – Steve – who was to lead the long, straggling column, on a fine brown and white stallion. Once on the road the reliving of the "old days" is taken seriously with no radios or modern conveniences permitted while participants are encouraged to dress in the garb of the period, a stipulation that produced a multitude of fancy creations.

Out of the expanding suburbs of Jamestown the wagons and their retinue took to the open fields. Every year a different route is planned; the trail meticulously tracked weeks in advance. Permission to negotiate pastures and establish overnight camp sites has to be obtained though landowners are sympathetic; some even participating in the journey themselves. Many a farmer releases valuable snippets of knowledge concerning local history, Indian legends and characters who shaped the mysticism of the prairie land. This year the route had been titled "The Beaver Creek Trail" and it looped south through open grasslands and the wooded valleys of the James River, a region well immersed in native American and pioneer history.

The wagons on this trek were exact copies of those used on the wagon trains crossing the prairies a century earlier; some, in fact, were originals that actually had carried pioneers into North Dakota. Many of those early pioneers used oxen instead of horses or mules to pull their wagons since oxen were able to subsist better on the short and rough grasses of the plains and had no need of grain to supplement their diet as do mules and horses. Furthermore they were cheaper to buy and, later, could be utilised as food. Today only horses and mules are used with arrangements made to supply hay and feed for them at the overnight camps.

As in the old days a great amount of food has to be gathered and prepared for the trek. Wagon train fodder was not as harsh as is often thought and it is certainly not the case today. A chuckwagon carries food and provisions but an expert cook arrives (discreetly by car) in the evenings to preside over the production of the evening meal. The amount and variability of the food is staggering. Prepared for another week of spartan living I found myself eating better than in many a multi-star hotel. One menu included fresh strawberries and ice-cream while the breakfasts were massive three-course affairs.

Most of the time I walked directly behind my allotted wagon, chatting at intervals with its heavily-jolted passengers who, occasionally, joined me on foot when their hind-quarters became too sore and they could take no more sitting. I walked virtually the whole route, only clambering aboard when the convoy crossed a river. Being the only Britisher on the trek I was forgiven for wearing only my twentieth century shorts – except by Steve who periodically passed by importantly on his stallion to ensure all was going well with his charges.

Every evening the wagons were circled together in the form of a corral and individual tents erected. In this respect today's wagon trains remain authentic – even to a few grisly teamsters sleeping in and under their wagons like their fathers and grandfathers before them. A factor of the Fort Seward Wagon Train is togetherness, with everyone helping with building fires, cooking, meal-serving and camp clean-ups. Activities such as nature walks, competitions, amateur entertainment and sing-songs around the camp fire are part of the programme. My fellow wagoners were mostly from the American Mid-West and a more engaging bunch of people would be difficult to assemble. Being the sole Britisher I was well and truly pampered by all of them.

Travelling is a little easier and faster nowadays, though the pace was a little slow for me. The old wagon trains put in an average of ten miles a day depending upon the terrain, weather and amount of Indian interference. Today twelve to twenty miles is the daily norm – or at least it was on my trek. This allows an early arrival at the camp site, a swim in any available lake or river – including a leech-infested James River – and the preparation of an evening's entertainment around the fire provided by each wagon "detachment" in turn.

The train left from the site of the old Fort Seward (which in 1872 took over duties from Fort Ransom located between Jamestown and Fargo). It returned via Jamestown's Frontier Village, a well-endowed reproduction of a nineteenth century community. Between were days of laughter, the forging of new friendships and a host of open-air activities as original as was the whole concept. We had crossed hills and rivers, and breathed the fresh invigorating Dakota air to which I was fast becoming accustomed.

One of our wagoners was a poet, Betty La Fontaine. She sums up better than any words of mine the joy and sense of occasion inspired by the Fort Seward Wagon Train:

"What you have missed!
You there, in your paper world.
Your hot and cold tap running,
Your data-processed paper world,
Your instant reply, ten to four world.

Come along with us,
Ride up the crest of the hill,
Charge out across the prairie,
Take your fill
of the rain and sun and the sky.
Come know the chill
of a dew-soaked meadow at dawn!"
and
"We creaked and rumbled from horizon to horizon,
Reflecting on those who had gone before.
What power drove them to the farthest sky?
Perhaps we envy hopes so high,
And following their path, expect to win
New lands for the soul, to build new homes within!"

9

Canada
The Ghost Highway

It was in spring 1981 that I was invited to northern Canada to take part in a reconnaissance of a route across the Mackenzie Mountains linking the remote oil-bearing township of Norman Wells on the great Mackenzie river to the state of Yukon. Here I was to join up with three others to traverse the lonely, rugged miles of this forgotten artery with the object of ascertaining whether any sections of it were suitable for the running of small group trekking forays on a commercial basis.

The assignment intrigued me. It had the ring of the pioneering about it and my two Dakota hikes had instilled in me a pioneering spirit. Perhaps the way would not be entirely devoid of the tracks of man, however, for once it had been a road, an old (though not quite old enough to qualify as historic) highway driven through the wilderness. But now it was dead or dying and only its decaying bones would offer a banister.

The water was perceptibly rising. A bright-tinted stone clear of the stream an hour ago, was now submerged. The island upon which we were standing was shrinking fast; there was no doubt about it. The previous night we had waded to the elongated neck of land with the water level no higher than our thighs. Today this backwater had become impassable. The main stream made even more of a formidable obstacle and was frightening to behold. The Twitya river is no placid stream at the best of times and now it was swollen and angry from days of rain channelled into it from the mountains.

Though midnight when we had pitched the tents on the sodden islands there had been no darkness. But the June sun was lost behind heavy drapes of surly clouds vomiting cascades of rain. We slept uneasily as each of us pondered our situation. How were we going to negotiate the Twitya together with our heavy rucksacks? Previous rivers along the route had been fordable affairs even though the bitter cold water and strong currents made the task risky and unpleasant. The Twitya, however, was in a different category. To swim it, fighting a vicious current that would all too soon sweep us helpless to the rapids below the site of the old road bridge, was out of the question, and anyway what of our baggage? No, the river would have to be crossed by raft. There were trees on the island; young saplings too fresh for raft-building and others that lay beached and waterlogged among the flotsam all around. Only some of these were suitable but here another problem had arisen. Amongst our combined stores and provisions we could locate only one small axe and a saw blade. The saw frame itself had been lost. Calculations produced the sum of twenty-six trees, topped and tailed, as a minimum requirement for a raft capable of carrying the four of us and our loads. On the credit side we could raise two dozen six-inch nails and plenty of cord while one of our number possessed knowledge of raft construction. The odds against us reaching safety were uncomfortably high but what was the alternative? We had arrived at the point of no return on our journey, our retreat was cut off and our refuge was reducing by the hour.

We lay nursing our thoughts, hearing the rain beating on the canvas; aware that our refuge might be submerged before we could leave it. David, our leader, was the most worried, the yoke of decision-making on his shoulders. An Englishman, residing in the Yukon town of Dawson City, this project had been his idea. A fellow-citizen but of Canadian birth was Byrun, a fractious character but extremely knowledgeable when it came to survival in the outback. The youngest member of the quartet was Reinhard from Germany; grotesquely fit and never displaying the slightest sign of exhaustion following the most gruelling exercise. I was, as usual, the oldest and weakest, a walker but no backpacker and my concern at our predicament must have been equal to David's – though I fear it was mostly concern for my own skin.

Across the Twitya the opposite bank was another world, an unattainable world flaunting our onward path, a broken banister of a ghost road leading yet another hundred miles to salvation.

The Canol Road; a thin red line on the empty map of north-west Canada that winds from Johnson's Crossing, some thirty-five miles north of Yukon's Teslin astride the Alaska Highway, to the Northwest Territories border. A summer-only route, north Canadians know it as a wilderness road running three hundred tortuous miles into the Mackenzie Mountains to Mackenzie Pass, with a lead-zinc mine and an airstrip as its terminus. The road's history is known only by a generation of older Canadians who will remember the circumstances of its construction over fifty years ago when, during World War Two, the United States Army undertook the building of a pipeline from Norman Wells on the broad Mackenzie river to Yukon's capital, Whitehorse. The object was to supply fuel to Alaska and the military traffic en route from the United States at a time when its far northern state and, more particularly, the Aleutian Islands, were under threat from a Japanese enemy. The project was a fiasco from the start and the price tag of $134,000,000 a fruitless waste that was eventually to undermine the credibility of the United States War Department. Additional to the pipeline was its servicing road but, with the subsequent receding of the threat, very little oil was ever to find its way into the storage tanks of Whitehorse. The pipeline and its road were quietly abandoned.

With renewed oil and gas exploration in more recent years being carried out at Norman Wells and the remoter regions of the Northwest Territories, the spectre of a further pipeline following the course of the old had arisen; the fear of energy shortage comparing ominously with the 1942 invasion threat. But though technology had changed, the savage environment of the Mackenzie Mountains remained constant and had to be taken into account. Thus the lessons learnt by American engineers had to be given serious appraisal by the new generation of, this time, Canadian pipeline builders.

All this, of course, was – and maybe still is – for the specialists and those who guide the destinies of the regions in which we live. However, for all Canadians the idea of a possible repeat of history and the recollection of a road to nowhere are surely of more than passing interest particularly to those who live north of the sixtieth parallel. The Canol Road may not have the allure and romance of the other, Northwest Territories-bound, Dempster Highway, but a rekindled thirst for knowledge of the forgotten road may have indeed arisen. Anyone with a sturdy vehicle can drive to Mac Pass (as it is called) to satisfy this curiosity but the Canol Road does not end there. The road continues as the Old Canol Road Hiking Trail through the multiple barrier of the Mackenzie Mountains for another two hundred and forty desolate yet inspiring miles

Crossing a river on the Canol Road

to Norman Wells bearing, along the way, the mouldering relics of an army's passing.

Although some maps cautiously label the route the "Old Canol Road Hiking Trail" let me warn anyone considering following it that this is an understatement supreme. Rivers have washed away the bridges, landslides have obliterated the road, and rain-storms, cold winds and grizzly bears make the going arduous and dangerous. We thought we knew the score and guessed the path would be hard and hazardous, the elements hostile and the terrain relentless, but none of us was prepared for the physical adversities that nature was accumulating along the way.

This then was the path I had set myself to walk carrying sixty pounds of victuals and equipment upon my back, and in the company of three companions I had never met.

Two weeks previously I had driven the Alaska Highway, but the walking challenge arose following accomplishment of the two rebuilt sections of the Canol Road. This is divided into two sections: that from the Alaska Highway to Ross River (139 miles) is referred to as the South Canol Road; the other from Ross River to the Northwest Territories border (160 miles) as the North Canol Road. Thereafter you are on the phantom Hiking Trail.

David's plan was to undertake the walking of it in reverse – starting at Norman Wells and so travelling back to Mackenzie Pass and the Northwest Territories border. To reach our starting point we had first to drive the 451-mile Dempster Highway to remote Inuvik and from there fly to Norman Wells out in the great void of the vast million-and-a-quarter square-mile state. That bridge-less rivers would have to be crossed was a factor we had to take into account but only one, wider, deeper and bigger than the rest, offered the slightest stirrings of concern amongst us as we unpacked our provisions and gear from the vehicle at Inuvik.

Inuvik is the second town of the Northwest Territories by virtue of the fact that, with Yellowknife the capital, it is the only other town in the state. Even so, Inuvik's population today is not much over three thousand souls. The place has to be seen to be believed. It consists of rows of brightly-painted buildings standing on stilts, of a church shaped like a monstrous igloo, and of bloated metal conduits running in and out of houses all over town. Yet Inuvik is one of the most scientifically-planned places in Canada; it is a government-created community designed to overcome the frightful building problems caused by an unstable ground surface and the bitter cold of a long dark winter.

The piles on which the buildings of Inuvik stand ensure stability. They are driven through the muskeg overlay into the gravel stratum twenty feet down and there frozen solidly into the gravel. The buildings sit on the piles several feet above ground level, this to prevent their interior heat from melting the ground surface and turning it into a mucky sludge. And since underground pipes cannot be laid in permafrost, all utilities, including steam heat, running water, and sewage disposal, are carried through these metal tunnels.

I must admit to finding Inuvik a most depressing town. The only way in and out, besides an unreliable air service, is via the daunting miles of the tyre-lacerating, oft-blocked Dempster Highway which was how the four of us reached it. A sensation of being entirely cut off from even the vestiges of civilisation assailed me. Here the phrase "dead end" has literal meaning.

We spent a restless night under canvas in the town's campsite, a notorious meeting place of Inuvik's criminal fraternity, and next day thankfully flew to Norman Wells.

I found Norman Wells to be more a community than a township, by which I mean that everyone who lives in the expanded collection of dwellings was employed, directly or indirectly, by the oil companies who were the only reason for its existence. Though even more remote than Inuvik and not connected by road to anywhere, it seemed a cheerful spot. Again every house was brightly, even garishly, painted as if in defiance of the staggering loneliness of its situation but the populace was an ever-changing one; their main topic of conversation being what they were going to do when they returned home on leave or expiry of their contract. In Inuvik the people lived there; chained to desolation by fate. Those in Norman Wells were paid considerable sums to exist and work in the outback for a limited period, serving out their sentence based in a house that wasn't home.

I had never flown in a seaplane (or floatplane as they call them in North America) but I enjoyed the short flight, hopping across the mighty Mackenzie river, by which Norman Wells stands, to the Canol Lake, hardly more than an overgrown pond, where we put down. The banks were of soft mud which meant a damp and slimy landing as, one by one with our rucksacks and accoutrements, we jumped from the aircraft's float to what we fondly hoped would be terra firma. Up to our knees in clinging black slime we watched the floatplane heave itself into the air and disappear. We were alone – and rarely have I felt so excruciatingly alone.

The old road lay some miles west of the lake and, shouldering our loads, we staggered across the marshy scrub – a combination of tufts of thicket grass and bog – towards it, intent upon raising our first camp astride the artery. Besides our bulging rucksacks, festooned with cooking implements, we carried coils of rope, a .303 rifle, fishing gear, an axe and a radio-transmitter. Straightway the notion arose in me that I had bitten off more than I could chew as my load turned the act of walking into a drunken slouch.

The Trail, when we came to it, was plain to see, a track, not yet overgrown to extinction, etched into the landscape by tree saplings and alder growth seemingly addicted to its stony surface. As if to emphasise its presence the flattened remains of some wooden buildings lay untidily about a stream crossing. Much of the timber was rotten but made convenient fuel for a fire we soon had blazing merrily, and on this we heated up our first day's supper. Above, the faint outlines of the road could be discerned gently spiralling uphill on its way back to its starting point at the Mackenzie river, just outside our range of vision. The stream offered fresh cold and safe drinking water, a forerunner of many such sources that precluded any concern over supply of at least one vital commodity. We slept, that first night, adequately but uneasily, David, Reinhard and I occupying the main tent with Byron, at his own request, in a small bivouac. "I've been known to snore", he told us. It was the understatement of the year.

Next morning, breakfasted on porridge, toast and marmalade with a choice of tea, coffee or cocoa, we set off down the road, a great deal more confident than we had felt the previous day when we had floundered through the bog. We had re-arranged our loads, adjusted rucksacks so they rode higher on our shoulders and better-distributed the loose items amongst us. And "down" did go the road – but not for long. In the first of many "wash-outs" – a morass of rock carried down by a sometimes raging torrent that was now no more than a humble stream – it disappeared though our maps showed it to have once followed this watercourse. Thereafter the route became an uphill one, made hard going and uncertain by the fact of its disappearance. However, the occasional leaning or broken telegraph pole and attendant coils of cable, making grim entanglement traps for unwary animals, pointed out the general direction.

Halfway up the hill we came upon traces of the road again and, at the same time, a cloud of mosquitoes to give us a sample of what these insects had in store for us. Having liberally covered all exposed skin with an evil-smelling but effective repellent, we spent an energetic half-hour with arms flailing like windmills in an effort to ward them off. In spite of the mosquito menace I wore shorts as I do on most treks since where a soaking by river, rain or sweat is to be a recurring theme I find bare legs an advantage. In this instance so did the mosquitoes.

The road re-established, it then proceeded to bifurcate though no such junction showed on the map. We chose, on principle, to follow the lower route and consumed a picnic lunch in another stony river-bed cleaved by a playful brook in which we found ourselves. As we ate, the sun sank behind a mass of grey clouds and it began to rain. If this was meant as a warning, none of us got the message. Rain, if prolonged, has an awkward habit of turning playful brooks into seething torrents as we were to learn.

The rain on this occasion was no more than a shower in company with an icy breeze and this pattern of sunshine and cold showers remained constant for the rest of the day as we toiled through the Little Keele Valley, finally raising camp close to a deep section of the Little Keele river. In an initial and misguided sense of bravado we immersed ourselves extremely briefly in its paralysing waters to be savaged, as we emerged, by mosquitoes of Stuka-like fanaticism and intent. In future, hygiene was to go by the board with only our feet benefiting from immersion – and this on an involuntary basis when forced to wade un-bridged rivers.

With each meal consumed our packs became that much lighter, a condition that tempted us to make serious inroads into our food supplies. But against this had to be borne in mind the fact that we would receive no further rations for a couple of weeks when an aircraft was scheduled to deliver provisions at one of the Godlin Lakes at least a hundred and seventy miles ahead. David's resourceful Swedish wife, back in Dawson City, had packaged individually-prepared meals – main courses and puddings – to last over that period of time and each plastic-wrapped and labelled pack was to be used strictly on the dates indicated. The fact that we carried a gun – vital for protection against unprovoked attack by grizzly bear – and fishing tackle meant that anything we might obtain for the pot could be looked upon as a bonus.

The night's slumber was interrupted when the tent collapsed; the rocky ground having defied all our efforts to insert metal tent pegs which had bent like hairpins. Thus we had to rely upon boulders as anchors for holding up the canvas and these proved unsuitable for the role. It rained in the night too but fortunately the two events did not coincide.

Our continued progress in the morning was governed by the obstacles in the path rather than by the fading course of the road. The highway itself had long been ravaged by a river that was forever intent upon widening its banks and was nowhere to be seen. So we walked along the centre of the wide valley still partly covered by thick platforms of dirty snow, crossing and re-crossing the Little Keele at its shallowest points. Again fallen telegraph poles and, now, lengths of rusting four-inch pipe (incredible as it may seem the Canol oil pipeline was of no more than four inches in diameter) affirmed we were on the correct route.

Already the journey was becoming a simple march during which the highlights of each day were to be meal stops. Regular as clockwork was the solemn proclamation of our good intentions of rising with the dawn and making early starts but, alas, my companions displayed a disturbing inclination to morning lie-ins which boded ill for our schedule. Thus we usually failed to get away until after ten with a hefty chunk of the day already lost. On the other hand we were in a land and a season of eternal daylight so perhaps our laziness was of no consequence. Our meals too were taken at the insistence of stomachs rather than the clock.

Lunch, on the third day, was served amongst the depressing wreckage of a one-time oil-storage depot overlooking a graveyard of dead military vehicles neatly lined up as though for inspection by the keeper of some ethereal garage. Old machinery – oil pumps, generators and the like – stood directly under the skies, their once-enveloping buildings having fallen away to matchwood. Here and there a shed still stood; a Nissan hut complete with springless beds or workshop without a roof. Strangely a water-closet continued to flush but the graffiti on the wall was of a generation past. While sipping our tea bunched around an oily fire an airline crawled across the sky. Its passing not only accentuated the loneliness but, in a limbo where time means nothing, a link with a world out of reach.

The vehicle parade marked the spot where we turned into a side valley towards the Plain of Abraham. A relentless sun in a suddenly azure-blue sky beat down upon us as we slowly zigzagged our way up a minor canyon liberally sprinkled with the debris of landslides and rain-inspired floodwater. Each obstruction had to be negotiated or detoured, a fiendish test of stamina and avoidance of broken ankles; even of legs, for the appalling loads on our backs continued to upset the normal human sense of balance as we skipped from rock to rock. Hardy mountain Dall sheep grazed, uncaring, on the higher ridges and small herds of caribou stared quizzically, even moving towards us to satisfy their curiosity, as, bathed in sweat, we grimly narrowed the distance to the head of the valley.

Sections of pipe with the ubiquitous telegraph poles became our constant companions as did, later, occasional traffic notices and mileposts that had survived the years and the elements. The pipes were invariably occupied by families of ground squirrels who made their homes in them to escape the attentions of bears and other predators. Their squawks had a strange hollow ring as we passed by. Otherwise a great silence pervaded the air; frightening in its intensity.

But there was beauty too. Whenever sections of the road broke to the surface, recovering from obliteration by avalanche and landslide, it became mottled with colour by reason of a display of wild flowers that was spellbinding. Their delicate blossoms and fragrance amongst the grey dust and in defiance of a fruitless soil lightened our hearts a little. Close to the final ridge at the top of the valley the telegraph poles drew themselves erect in military fashion as if to challenge us to a race to the summit, then keeled over as if the effort was just too much.

Ahead, the scenery opened up to reveal the plain stretching away into glorious flatness to offer last-ditch encouragement to totter the last mile of a now clearly-discernible road. Only one of a number of wooden buildings of the camp at milepost eighty was habitable but it was enough. Over to our left a range of distant mountains shimmered in the haze while the crimson blooms in the road winked at us as, wiping the stinging perspiration from our eyes, we made it to the night's refuge, thankful we did not have to find the additional energy to raise the tents.

The night was cold but bright as day. We lit the little cast iron stove and were glad of its warmth though our beds were no more than the hard dirty floor. Ground squirrels and porcupines scratched beneath the rotting

Eastern Sicily – Part of the Alcantara Gorge (above) and a view of Castiglione (below)

Hiking above Castiglione in Eastern Sicily with the Mount Etna massif in the background

Group picnic in cork groves near Grazalema, Andalucia, Spain

Walking in Andalucia, Spain

Looking out over the Marrakech Plain in Morocco

Picnic on a plateau of Dades Gorge in the Atlas Mountains, Morocco

The spectacular pedestrian suspension bridge spanning the Lima valley at Mammiano in Tuscany, Itlay

Trekking in the snow about the Lago Scaffaiolo, the Rifugio della Doganaccia and the Rifugio della Croco Arcana in Tuscany, Italy (above)

Below — Manhattan Island, New York City

Walkers in the Catskill National Park, New England

Central Park in the heart of New York City

Members of a Ramblers Holiday in Samos, Greece, with Samos town in the background

foundations and other noises caught our receptive ears. With the Plain of Abraham we had reached grizzly bear country. A large specimen had, it was alleged, attempted to dislodge this very cabin occupied by a group of surveyors a month or so before, or so the story went and the threat was not lost upon us. Thus we went to bed with the loaded rifle to hand, half-listening for sounds that were more than the scufflings of squirrels and porcupines. "A Night on Bare Mountain" could well have been the theme of this vigil – and on two counts.

The morning remained cold but dry as we moved away along a dirt road tailing away into the distance. It continued to climb, but gently, for three miles offering, at each bend, a false crest to be attained. The final crest rewarded us with a staggering view of another range of snow-dappled mountains though our admiration was tempered by the knowledge that our path led through them. From the viewpoint, however, it was a downhill course with the road cork-screwing into a new valley, this one designated Andy Creek. We short-circuited some of the hairpins and, risking the grizzlies prone to inhabiting such terrain, cut through a belt of spruce pines alive with mosquitoes to reach the river at the bottom.

Progress down inevitably has to be countered by subsequent progress up but the fresh climb offered fine close-up observation of caribou herds with one handsome bull repeatedly returning to investigate us after the main herd had departed. Immensely attractive animals are caribou and how people can bring themselves to shoot them for no reason except "prestige" is beyond me. Still-warm dung and pug-marks indicated that a sizeable grizzly was close and we proceeded with the utmost caution, the rifle loaded and cocked. Handfuls of bear-fur and porcupine quills indicated where the beast had made its last attempt at a meal but nothing appeared. We camped close to milepost ninety-four in the snow-streaked Carcajou valley with a view one could describe as alpine. Our dinner was mysteriously labelled "Beef & Fusilli with tomato paste & parmesan cheese" which was followed by a sweet called "Pear Brown Betty", and it went down a treat.

Footfalls in the night had us nervously peering out of tents in the small hours but the visitor was only a moose. A rain shower had turned to snow on the mountain flanks so displaying a whiter world than the one we had previously looked upon. The morning's march was marred by an erroneous decision to take a short cut across the valley for which we were punished by an excruciating one-and-a-half-mile traverse of lunar-like rock and a wet negotiation of the Carcajou river. The saving was less than a mile of easy road-walking and the crossing of a river by a bridge that still held. From then on short cuts became strictly taboo.

Whilst massaging sore feet and throbbing ankles David saw a large porcupine which we pursued with the aim of having it for supper. Difficult to catch for obvious reasons we attempted to shoot it but, with ammunition in short supply, our marksman, Byron, had to ensure he got it with the fist shot. Unfortunately he failed to do so and the animal got away – to my secret relief though they say porcupine meat is quite tasty.

A while later a brief sighting of a grizzly had us eyeing the scrub that closed in on the road with deep suspicion but the only animals we met that afternoon were a family of wolverines and more waddling porcupines as we toiled along Bolstead Creek with the warm sun fighting a losing battle with a bitter wind. But the grizzly menace remained. The danger with these beasts is not so much in themselves as of us getting between parents and offspring, a situation that arouses the deepest fury in the former. To fell a full-grown grizzly on the attack is no easy matter even with a high-calibre rifle. A .303 bullet will kill a man with no trouble at all but can be deflected by a bear's thick hide and immense frame. There are few spots on the animal where a single shot is likely to bring it down – and you only have time for one shot. The worry too, so far as we were concerned, was that none of us were all that sure where the weak spot was. On the assumption that prevention is better than cure we made as much noise as possible while continuing on our way, the idea being to frighten the danger away.

Our immediate destination was the long-disused military camp at the head of the valley where we hoped there would be at least one cabin suitable for an overnight stay. Long before we reached it we could see the camp buildings rotting on their timber-strewn site like discarded toys and, as we approached, we came to the skeletal remains of some mouldering Chevrolet lorries, one with its Goodrich tyres in near-perfect condition plus Schroder valves that still held the air in them. A dirty and decaying hut makes a poor substitute for a tent but the one we found at least contained some serviceable spring beds though water for the evening meal had to be brought from a considerable distance.

Up and over Bolstead Creek and into Trout Creek to stumble through a series of "washouts" where rivers of boulders had obliterated the road. The weather turned hostile again to unleash repeated hailstorms from a sky that made the day into as near night as I had seen. The quantity of rivers that had to be forded multiplied, the one-time bridges either no more than driftwood on the shingle or entirely vanished.

There is a technique for wading a river. First, the shallowest section within reasonable distance of one's arrival point has to be located. This is usually where the river is widest. The entry and exit point selected, one can either advance with care into the water wearing boots or these can be removed and replaced with plimsolls but attempting the crossing in bare feet is foolhardy since the riverbed will be treacherous and very slippery. On the Canol Road Trail the rivers were running fast and exceedingly cold so that, at the halfway mark, one's legs lost their feeling and ceased to function properly. And with a heavy load – plus boots swinging round the neck – falling is all too easy, particularly as the movement of water adds an optical illusion to increase the likelihood of overbalancing.

As the trek proceeded – and the weather worsened – so the rivers became more and more of an obstacle. At first they were laughable affairs that could be bounded across with the help of a few well-placed stones but, with the Carcajou and other more formidable water-courses, the problems increased. We helped one another as best we could and the three English-speaking members of our group will not forget the agility shown and firm hand offered by the young Reinhard. It is a strange feature of life that, given a little hardship and danger, a man's character is so often enhanced. David, Byron and myself initially found it impossible to see anything likeable in the somewhat arrogant German who made up the quartet. Always he was ahead of the rest of us, marching determinedly across the countryside pausing only to express exasperation at our more leisurely progress. But the frightening negotiations of those rivers and his unstinting aid had us ashamed and humbled. I like to think that, by the time the trek ended, either Reinhard had become a very credible human being, or we had become more tolerant ones.

Byron, on the other hand, showed a fiery temperament that belied my initial judgement of his character. But his occasional unprovoked bursts of fury never did more than temporarily dent a sustained friendship. We all admired his outdoor living capacities and skill, knowing that, in the company of such a man, we had, in the last resort, little to fear when it came to survival. David, for his part, steadfastly remained calm, reassuring, kind and tolerant. When Reinhard forged ahead and had to be rebuked, when Byron blew his top and had to be pacified, or when I funked a nearly-vertical cliff of scree it was David's action that brought encouragement, understanding and peace. He was the perfect leader; leading without being seen to do so.

We could hear the sullen roar of the major obstacle of the route long before we reached the Twitya river. Prior to plunging into a hillside canopy of trees we even glimpsed it from afar and could make out the white flecks of madness upon its surface. Everyone became unnaturally silent as we descended by a bounding agger of a road to its edge. Our future depended on the state of this river; our plans and expectations were now entirely based upon "after we're across the Twitya". All at once it lay before us.

The previous night's camp had been close to the Trout river, a friendly stream but one already swollen by melting snow and rain in the mountains. We had crossed it with no great difficulty on at least three occasions because the road kept being deflected to the opposite side by sheer towers of granite. But the road, where its route lay alongside the river, had, again, been washed away, forcing us to make a nightmare progress along its treacherous course or by clawing a way along the scree-lined buttresses of the granite walls. Rain fell incessantly adding to the misery so that when at last we emerged upon a shelf overlooking the valley of the Twitya we evoked a feeling that the worst was over. Even fresh grizzly dung and pug-marks in the sandy soil failed to subdue our sense of optimism.

Arrival at the northern shore of the Twitya, however, drained our hopes, like water down a plug-hole. There before us lay a wide, raging torrent of uncontrolled fury, the surface a cauldron of threshing waves. The road strode straight up to this horrifying impasse and disappeared. Of the bridge or its remains that once carried the road to the other bank there was no sign. A short way downstream lay the rapids where the great surge of near-freezing water came hard up against a solid wall of rock forcing a change of direction. We gazed, aghast, at what lay before us, lit a small fire and brewed a pot of tea. It was all we could think of to do.

David's information from those who had been this way before included the advice to proceed upstream some two miles and attain an island formed between the mainstream and a backwater. From the island a raft would have a chance of making it to the opposite shore before disaster overtook it in the rapids. This intelligence was, of course, based upon normal river conditions and the availability of plentiful supplies of timber. For better or for worse there seemed no alternative but to make for this alleged island and then assess the situation from there.

Accordingly began a particularly unpleasant side-trek made, in plimsolls, along the river's edge, rock-infested, slippery, wet and under heavy rain. It was long past midnight when, having waded up to our thighs the wide but only gently-moving backwater, we pitched camp on the sodden soil of a fast-disappearing island.

None of us slept a wink that night as we listened to the rain beating down upon the canvas. Our sleeping bags became soaked from the water-logged ground and, for once, we rose early for there was vital work to be done.

Scene from Canol Road

Our council of war had swiftly decided the only action we could take. With our retreat cut off by the swiftly rising waters we could but go forward – and the only method of going forward was by raft.

Under Byron's expert guidance we set to work. Felling with our ludicrously inadequate axe those growing saplings not already deep in water, and sawing, with a saw-blade alone, those not already waterlogged that formed the flotsam on the island, we heaved each trunk with brute force born of desperation to the water's edge. Four layers of logs Byron had calculated as the minimum necessary to carry the four of us and our baggage across the raging Twitya though we would only discover whether, in fact, this was enough when we cast off. And by then it would be too late to do anything about it.

All day we toiled in the torrential downpour meekly administering to Byron's barked instructions, and gradually the craft on which everything depended began to take shape, though our island fastness reduced by the hour. By evening, soaked and shivering with cold, I experienced the initial paroxysms of hypothermia as exhaustion sapped my ability to maintain a blood-circulation by means of log-hauling while my younger companions were not in a much better condition. At one point David seriously contemplated radioing for help though how help could be given in the present circumstances made requesting it of little use.

In all it took fifteen hours to complete the craft with but one brief pause for a hot meal deemed vital if we were to retain our strength. Another hour and the weird vessel, its timbers lashed together with yellow cord, had been loaded and stood ready at the top of its "slipway" of smoothed-down saplings. The last job was to cut ourselves long punting poles for guiding and pushing the raft to a designated landing point downstream on the opposite bank. Then we took a last look-round, sent a private prayer to the Almighty, named the craft "Pearl" after Byron's girlfriend, clambered aboard and cut the retaining rope.

We hit the water with a great splash, sank to our midriffs, then swirled, out of control, in the scurry of water. Desperately we heaved with our clumsy poles against the river bed, attempting to propel ourselves out of the main stream and towards the far bank but the current held us firmly in its grip, whirling us at high speed towards those terrifying rapids.

Our designated landing point swept by and was gone. "Make for that outcrop!", screamed Byron, indicating a small beach that protruded a little way into the water and, again, we threshed and wrestled with the poles but to no avail. The new beaching point whirled past leaving one last hope, a patch of quieter water the far side of the main stream intimating the presence of shallower water where the river made a slight curve. Already we could hear the roar of the rapids beyond which galvanised us into further action though the cold water was fast sapping our reserves of strength. The foaming waves smashing over us, drenching the rucksacks and rocking the raft in angry little motions that threatened to loosen the bindings. Gyrating madly we spun out of the main stream and, inexplicably, ground to a halt on the shallows. Leaping into the water we hastily removed the rucksacks before the tugging current could release the beached craft. Shaking but jubilant we never even saw "Pearl" slide away into oblivion; only triumph and a heartfelt relief registered in minds that were aware we had attained the promised land, that other bank of the Twitya.

But the nightmare had not quite ended. It was long after midnight and we had a considerable distance to go to reach a Canol Road encampment we knew existed which offered the only hope of a dry refuge from the rain and the cold. We were all shivering violently and were in dire need of shelter.

Judging the direction we plunged into the dense undergrowth, making our way through forest and bog with the deluging rain hissing against the foliage. It took our last remaining strength to fight through this morass, relocate the road and track it back to the broken-down cabin – the only one of several still habitable – a mile inshore from where the river bridge had once been.

Shakily we set about fuelling and lighting the rusty oil-drum stove and soon our efforts were rewarded as we became enveloped in a clammy haze of steam rising from our dripping clothes and bedding spread around the dirty little room. Not even sojourns I have experienced in some of the world's finest hotels have given me greater pleasure than did that simple cabin in the wilderness.

We rose late since it was well into morning when we had climbed into steaming damp sleeping bags. The new day was a brilliant one with a sun lighting up the landscape to make the previous day but a bad dream. Snow covered the tops of the surrounding hills turning the countryside into a scene of ethereal beauty and child-like innocence. Following a substantial brunch we laid out our belongings to air and ourselves to bask anew in our deliverance.

But we had lost time and were behind schedule – we had a tryst to keep with an aeroplane at the Godlin Lakes, our subsequent re-provisioning point. In the afternoon, therefore, we reluctantly repacked the rucksacks, girded our loins and set out to put ten miles of distance between the Twitya and ourselves. The road was a gradual incline, the sun was hot, but to be warm was a pleasure. Byron expended another bullet on a spruce grouse, hitting the target this time but half blowing the wretched bird to pieces. We grilled it for supper to supplement the evening's fare and by the time we had squirmed into our bags it was raining again.

It rained all night but politely dried up before we stirred our stumps next morning. A flooded road and flooded terrain made the going tricky, involving jumping from tuft to tuft of thicket grass "islands" marooned in a marshy sea. It was a time-consuming progress too and none of us escaped wet feet. But the reward was a luncheon of ham in sherry sauce and banana cream pudding taken by the side of a delightful stream pushing its way through a new valley. Alas, full enjoyment of the banana pud was curtailed by another downpour which, if nothing else, provided reason for hastening us on our way. With the appearance of the Godlin river, here set in its picturesque Godlin gorge, movement became really tough. The road had long since ceased to exist, having been washed away by malignant flood waters, and in its place was a two-hour stumble high above the river along a near-perpendicular scree-slope of knife-sharp slate where one slip could send one, in a welter of this odious material, straight to the bottom. It would have been difficult enough to move empty-handed but with sixty pounds of dead-weight on tired shoulders it was positively hell.

We were fast approaching the prettiest section of the Canol Road and our camp site that night reflected this change of landscape. Byron missed another spruce grouse but, luckier with his rod, caught a trout to add to our rations which were showing ominous signs of running out. A belligerent porcupine produced some light relief from the sombre task of surveying and attending to blisters, cold sores, dirty bodies and wet socks with which we were all afflicted. Abed but not asleep we became aware of sounds all too reminiscent of stalking grizzlies but nobody felt inclined to investigate.

Any worries David may have harboured concerning food supplies were dispelled next day when, during the lunch-stop, Byron began pulling arctic thar and greyling out of the Godlin river at a ludicrous rate. We could see them in big shoals in the clear water and, getting down on hands and knees, were able to entice individual fish to a finger and, sometimes, flick them to the shore without benefit of line or hook. In a moment we had a twig fire going and were gorging ourselves silly on the most delicious grilled fish I have ever tasted.

Our route was leading us along a tranquil section of the road which ambled with no broken bridges, cave-ins or washouts, along a valley of sheer loveliness. White-capped peaks made the perfect setting for a river-scene spliced with dark green sentinel pines and moss-covered hillocks. It was all too idyllic to last of course and very soon the river intruded rudely to cross our path, forcing another wading operation. This one, however, was aided and abetted by old bridge supports that stuck incongruously out of the water.

Another encampment, this one in better state of repair, became home for our twelfth night out. The reason for the higher standard of accommodation was that its buildings were in support of an air strip. We had arrived at the Godlin Lakes, and with but two hours to spare. But the aircraft was late and it was not until well into the small hours that we heard the unaccustomed sound of an aero engine. We rushed out of the cabin to welcome the little floatplane as it appeared out of the subdued pre-dawn sky, circled the camp and put down with scarcely a splash on the most northerly of the small lakes past which the road had led. To reach it we had to run a mile over marshy ground but the longing to talk to fellow-humans – besides ourselves – was strong. Until it has actually been experienced, the emotion of enforced loneliness; the results of being shut away in a vast desolation of unimagined remoteness, can barely be understood. Nor can such a visitation by strangers from the outer world arouse the new emotion of intense excitement until the first has been experienced. Like children we waved and shouted, pumped the hands of the pilot and his mate, unloaded the boxes from the aircraft's hold and, with a sickening pain, watched the machine take off again and lift into a sky that, in a moment, became no less empty than our hearts and minds drained of further feeling.

But among the packages was a bottle of whisky and two of wine. "Why do we have to add weight to our loads?" we asked ourselves, so drank the lot and felt better. We were even able to sleep through what remained of the night and, in the late morning, we redistributed the stores and, by midday, were once more on the way.

Three miles brought us to the banks of the Ekwi river and the first of a selection of river crossings that had us in and out of fast-flowing icy water for days on end. The valley was steep, the choice of crossing point restricted and hardly had we fought our way across when we had to repeat the performance as the river coiled about our lame highway. Only for the first day's final crossing was luck on our side. Here the bridge was down but not out and by clinging to rusty spars and splintered timbers we managed a dry passage.

The Ekwi remained with us for three days, its tributaries catching us when the main river failed to do so. Once we became so confused we twice waded it when we didn't have to. If nothing else got washed our legs did and the marvel is we did not end up with webbed feet. In this delta-like environment we were back in grizzly country and sightings became quite common. Whenever we espied these great beasts we gave them a wide berth – even if it involved added mileage. Our ammunition stock was down to five rounds and none of us was too sure how many would be required to drop such a hefty animal if the crunch came.

Entry into the Caribou gorge provided dramatic scenery. There was a prickly detour over it and through thorn scrub since the road through the canyon had vanished. To go with it a sun and showers combination of weather turned to constant shower. At mile two-zero-eight we came upon another dump of derelict military vehicles and, with the Intga valley, we were in sight of the Selwyn Mountains standing straight-backed out of an extensive plain. Excitement swelled once more in our breasts as we pitched camp by the rock-encased narrows of the Intga river. Just behind those Selwyns lay the Mackenzie Pass and the end of the trek. While chopping wood in a surge of anticipation I cut my hand with the axe and bled like a pig.

The previous night we had camped at five thousand feet at the head of the Caribou Pass amongst last vestiges of snow and ice. It had rained all night and the long trudge up the muddy, waterlogged valley had almost defeated me. But on this new morning, a morning that afforded sight of the Selwyns, the sun joined us in silent thanksgiving, splashing their jagged summits an impossible hue of pink.

Plains walking had its points. The terrain was flat, the road surface composed of springy turf and the inevitable rivers were little more than trickles that could be jumped across with little inconvenience. But the Canol is an obtuse road and manages to find gradients in the most horizontal of territory, meandering mindlessly in its effort to locate and climb them. Plains, however, soon become monotonous tramping grounds; there are no surprises – cruel or kind – to anticipate over the next crest, or the next, or the next, for the route being walked can be seen going on forever. And this plain – the Barrens – went on forever, its little rises no more than an aggravation. But the grass verges of the road; indeed the whole endless plateau, sparkled with wild flowers though our pace did not allow for dawdling. Had I sat down I would never have got up since there was not a boulder in sight against which I could lever myself into an upright position again.

Suddenly we were in sight of Sam's place. It was like a mirage. Atop a slightly bigger hill, perversely bypassed by the road, appeared a collection of chalets that were very different from the remnants of a military camp. A handsome, even sophisticated, timber residence stood, solid and square, amongst half a dozen smaller chalets glass-fronted and fresh-painted. With one accord we swung off the road and staggered up the steep incline, taking it the short way – straight up – in our eagerness to reach this outpost of civilisation.

We had arrived at Old Squaw Lodge, a naturalist's paradise built by wildlife biologist Sam Miller and his associates, an away-from-it-all guesthouse attainable by specialist-driven, high-clearance, four-wheel drive vehicles from Mac Pass. And with Old Squaw Lodge we had indeed reached the outer fringes of civilisation.

Sam was not at home but two of his colleagues were and they invited us to spend our last night on the Canol Road beneath a solid roof. In the evening Sam arrived in his jeep-like automobile we had watched approaching from the base of a still-distant Selwyn range as radiant in the evening sun as it had been that morning. In new-found company we talked well into the night watching a sunset of an unbelievable majesty.

What a paradise for the nature-seeker is this lodge named after the melodiously talkative oldsquaw duck that breeds on the arctic coast and the barrenlands of the Northwest Territories. Here among a patchwork of silver ponds, alpine meadows and mossy green tussocks is a heaven on earth. Here it would be easy to ignore the outside world – while yet not quite be out of touch with it – and roam for a magic week or two encountering caribou herds, listening to the soft chirp of bank swallows and langspurs, and glimpsing the flash of white from willow ptarmigan. And roaming amongst a foliage of dwarf birches turning an intense orange in the autumn, and of blue carpets of forget-me-nots and cushions of lichen curled like starched lace. Not all is cruel along the ghost road of the Canol.

The last day's march to the Mackenzie Pass was dictated by the rule of the motorcar. Vehicle tracks scarred the muddy surface of the old road and the serrated channels trapped our feet in a vice that held them in their grip the last dozen miles. There were people at the airstrip too but they took not the slightest notice of us. And why should they? For at this point the Canol becomes a highway of today; albeit a modest one. Just back down the road we had waded the sizeable Intga river, a tributary of the larger Keele, and the last obstacle. But that too was behind us and none of us was to look back. It was as if the past had never been.

10

Indian Sub-continent
Part I
A Gentle Trek in the Himalayan Foothills

When I told my wife that we both had been invited to join a trek in the Himalayas she visibly paled. Not because she dislikes walking – far from it; her daily shopping incursions into Brighton centre clock up a mileage of some twenty a week, half of it uphill, while mushrooming and wild flower investigating in European alpine locations have her prancing around the lower slopes like a mountain goat. No, her initial reaction was that of any comfort-loving being when presented with the abrupt prospect of a first visit to India. Marble temples and mud hovels, maharajas and beggars, lepers roaming the streets, and handcarts making dawn rounds gathering up the bodies of those who had died on the pavements in the night. And on top of that, sweating jungles, baking deserts and icy mountains. These were the images that flashed through her mind. But more vital, and additional to the fact that she disliked camping, was the most daunting problem of La Femme everywhere: what was she going to wear?

The list of participants on the walk was not at all revealing. Every name was prefixed by a sober Mr, Mrs or Miss, with one Captain; not an Honourable or a Sir or Lady this or that amongst them. Only Mr Stratte-McClure and Miss Chabot-le-Conte offered a partnership that struck a discordant note. For an expedition into a fastness of the Imperial Raj and from one of its cherished hill stations we appeared to be a modest, down-to-earth little group.

And so it came about that, under the initial jurisdiction of one Richard Waller, botanist and ornithologist extraordinary, Anna, suitably booted and spurred, and I became fused into the party of twelve and, with them, took the toy-like 1903-built Viceroy's Railcar from Kalka to zigzag playfully up into the hills in similar manner as did that worthy himself when escaping from the summer heat of the plains.

With its green meads of asphodel, of hyacinth and celandine, of carmine rhododendron trees surrounded by solemn forests of deodar and spires of pine, Simla still retains the ghost of its past splendours. To me it was a smiling character of a Sussex market town, its church a faithful copy of those of Burgess Hill or Uckfield. Yet when did Burgess Hill sprout a bazaar? – though implanted on Simla was the most genteel bazaar in all India. Inhabiting it, however, were very un-Sussex-like characters; stately Punjabis, dark-faced southern Indians with rapid gestures, hill people with their Mongoloid features, and an occasional Lama, complete with prayer wheel, tinder and flint.

The Mall was the particular favourite of the memsahibs. Although some buildings still strike a nostalgic note, most of the old shop facades bearing English names have disappeared into the mists of time. Yet, even through the years, the British character of the Mall remains alongside an inlay of Indian detail. It remains the main spur of Simla and continues to be the fashionable venue for a stroll; the place where people shop and, at Scandal Point – named, so they say, after a British commander-in-chief's daughter who eloped with a maharaja – people linger for a while to gossip.

Based for a couple of days at the elegant Woodville Guesthouse, a Rajah's former private residence no less, we took stock of both Simla and ourselves. We strolled the Mall, looked over Scandal Point, gawked at Vice Regal Lodge (which had become the Institute of Advanced Studies), learnt that the church was, in fact, a cathedral, and walked, daringly, to Jakko Hill on the outskirts of town. As for ourselves, no interesting eccentricities initially blossomed. The Stratte-Mclure/Chabot-le-Conte partnership turned out to be young Americans, the captain – army, not RN – showed distinct promise of odd behaviour while "Mr" Champion gave out that he was the former governor of the Outer Hebrides. An addition to the group was one, Kranti Singh, who was to lead us on the trek. A tall sophisticated Indian, his attentions were all too soon focused upon the female half of the Chabot-le-Conte partnership. At a round dozen we were all set for a hike labelled "Venturing to Kulu".

It would have been no arduous undertaking to have walked to Dalash in Outer Saraj from whence the trek commenced but with a road that runs through Narkandah it was thought beneficial to drive us to see a view that is reputed to be ultra-spectacular. If so it was diluted by a heat-haze. The drive into Narkandah was suitably hairpin with frequent warning notices to drivers who ignored them. The village itself is a tiny hill-top place with a little wooden Tibetan shrine, a school, post-office and a scattering of primitive shops. The view, if we could have seen it, looks out across the deep Sutlej valley towards the eternal snows of Spiti.

From Narkandah the road continued along the bottom of the Sutlej valley alongside, and occasionally crossing, the river. We were, we were told, on the Hindustan-Tibet highway and, in keeping with its impressive image albeit unkempt condition, had to push our vehicle over portions of it liberally doused with encroaching sand. Maybe the omitted walk to Dalash would have been less energetic.

Dalash village had been accessible by road for not many years so visitors there were still looked upon as a pleasant novelty. At one time a traveller could follow mule tracks south to the old-established mission station at Kotgarh or north over the Jalori Pass where we were headed. The village contains an ancient temple which we dutifully inspected en route, up a steep footpath, to the resthouse in the boisterous company of a regiment of delightful schoolchildren.

The main attraction to many of this particular Himalayan foothills trek arose from the fact that there are resthouses, sited and constructed by the then British-run forest administration, in commanding positions at convenient intervals along the whole route. That of Dalash was a not very good example of them all. Built in what might be described as Victorian railway-station style, with regular blocks of stone and thick mortar layers, each contained two or three sizeable rooms, mostly plainly furnished. At the rear, small storerooms and bathrooms – with or without running water – and at the front, a wooden veranda. At a discreet distance are a kitchen and staff quarters. Most are now deserted, although the provincial government retains a caretaker at each one.

Until the end of the British Raj they were in continuous use, and equipped with all the minor luxuries of a now vanished society. Some of the items of furniture survive; armchairs with extension foot-rests and chaise-longue type sofas upon which the sahibs could recline in varying forms of horizontal pose while sipping their chota-pegs. The resthouse here had none of these refinements but we were to come across and appreciate others of old-fashioned, strangely out-of-place comfort at a later stage in the trek.

As was to be the case here and on all subsequent sojourns there were too many of us for the bulk of resthouses to accommodate in civilised style so the overflow had to make do with a tent. And with these erected in advance by our cheerful team of Indian cooks and porters there was no tedious boy-scout business of raising and striking camp at the end of a day's walking. A team of packhorses carried our heavy baggage so all we had to carry to give an impression of back-packing was a minuscule knapsack containing no more than a waterproof, pullover and picnic lunch.

Puritans may deplore the idleness of such an excursion but then puritans don't have to do as we did. I found the touch of luxury on trek extremely pleasant, making a refreshing change from conditions found on many of my other walking projects, and though I normally abhor the idea of other people having to do my carrying and dirty work, the route was so easy and our porters so obviously content with arrangements that I could raise no guilty conscience.

We had met our staff at Dalash and were introduced to the chief cook as well as a Tibetan-featured individual called Lama who might well have been a wondering holy man when not humouring the likes of us, such was his demureness and appearance. With no electric light, bedtime universally came with the darkness and we drew lots for a room or a tent.

We rose at five, helped by a cup of tea, to a prepared breakfast of cereal and scrambled egg with chapatis and were on our way well before the cool of early morning had dissipated. Although Dalash was high on

Porters undertaking cooking chores on the Kulu trek

the north wall of the Sutlej valley there was nevertheless a steady climb ahead for the first hour or more to gain the contour-hugging forest tracks connecting the ridge-top villages. Thereafter the walking became more or less level at around seven thousand feet and, though only the first day out, the pattern of the trek began to materialise. Right from the start the American couple proceeded to forge ahead at a great rate of knots as if to demonstrate their indifference to, and indeed contempt of, the remainder of the group, all of whom were well into middle age. I have to admit that the pace was too slow for me but, being past middle-aged myself, I felt obliged to grin and bear it, consoled by the fact that Anna thoroughly approved of the relaxed atmosphere. Richard Waller, the trek's botanist, also came into his own gathering about him those interested in flora and fauna, to dawdle and detour into the undergrowth thus delaying progress the more. Not that this mattered one iota since the day's trek was of only five or so hours duration anyway thus putting time on our side.

The forests through which we walked were mostly of large pines, including the vast deodars; but also ilex, chestnuts with flaky barks, and some bamboo. Through them flitted yellow-billed blue magpies with their distinctive long tails, tiny nutcrackers and white-capped redstarts, while overhead , soaring against an eternally blue sky, were griffin vultures, lammergeiers, peregrine falcons and kestrels. The botanists among us released cries of joy – to the dismay of the bird-watchers – as they sighted ground orchids, geranium and primula of seemingly lesser-known species.

Thus we advanced in a spasmodic manner, usually in two sections with the Americans, exhibiting their impatience, waiting at junctions of the path for us to catch up so that they could forge ahead once more with the zeal of two Livingstones discovering a new Africa. Only at lunchtime would we congregate to spread ourselves on a ridge or in a clearing to consume our tinned fish or meat paste chapati sandwiches.

The second resthouse, called Shila, situated among trees, was in permanent semi-darkness but it afforded a fine view across the valley to the snow-peaks of the Spiti and Kinnaur mountain range far beyond. Darkness transformed it into a landscape of grey undulations; a stilled ocean, with the phosphorescent ribbon of the Sutlej river winding, serpent-fashion, at its base. Anna and I picked a tent for the night; not a success so far as my good wife was concerned since the issued sleeping-bag was one of those models closely-related to a straitjacket. But dinner of soup, curry with vegetables and salad in unrestricted quantity made an appropriate end to the day.

A series of villages provided the high spots – literally – of the next day's six-hour perambulation. The houses were of stone with timber bondings and roofs of slate. A lower roof afforded cover for animals and an upper floor provided living quarters for the family – more often than not a multitudinous one. Around the upper floor were primitive wooden balconies, protected from winter rain by the overhanging eaves of the roof. Many houses had fine stone courtyards adjoining, and forty or fifty such dwellings huddled together at different levels formed a picturesque urban complex of which the central feature was a tall tower of stone and beautifully-carved wood used as a central store. Many such villages possessed a local temple reverently apart on its own piece of ground; sometimes rising from a sacred grove.

There was always time for a pause amongst these communities thus providing opportunity to meet the inhabitants and, occasionally, to be invited into a school or home. All were immensely friendly and our appearance among them seemingly produced as much pleasure to them as they gave to us. Children were released from school to greet us while the head man arrived to lead the grand tour of his domain. The local dress sense was of a high order, the older men of the village arrayed in undyed woollen trousers and coats; the women flaunting brightly-coloured cottons, long dresses and shawls; their shoes made of hemp. Generally speaking, life, though extremely simple, was infinitely better than that of the teeming millions down on the plains.

Each village community cultivated a series of tiny, painstakingly-made terraces on a bi-annual crop system; a summer crop of maize harvested in October, and a winter crop of wheat, harvested in April. They also possessed cows, sheep and goats, but no poultry or pigs which are considered unclean. Drying corn cobs, laid out on every available flat roof, made vivid splashes of orange against the predominately brown background.

Margi resthouse lay at 7,500 feet, amongst apple trees and a belt of cosmos daisies. Flowers that would have cost a small fortune if purchased in a British florist sprinkled the ground among rhododendron trees, cardamom and a profuse selection of mushrooms; one gigantic specimen of which Anna and I cooked for supper. Nobody else trusted the thing but Anna knows her mushrooms. Even our Indian cooks were horrified at our intentions to eat a growth they plainly thought would cause instant insanity, even our demise. The trek was taking us into semi-tropical forest, damp and cool under the canopy of foliage but abruptly hot in clearings upon which a warm sun concentrated its power as if in revenge for being denied penetration elsewhere.

A steep climb to the ridge at over 9,000 feet was a feature of the third day but this was accomplished mostly beneath the sunshade of the trees.

Moreover, much of the way was laid out as if by a landscape gardener with roses, clematis, orchids and gentians excited into exuberant growth. The American couple had been brought to heel by an exasperated Kranti forced to make an energetic detour in search of them when they had anticipated – wrongly – the route at a junction of the path. Henceforth they remained with the main party which was a mixed blessing since they then took out their resentment on us. It was about this time too when the captain began to behave in a most strange and alarming manner as if he had taken leave of his senses though not until later was it revealed that he was, in fact, suffering from some serious malfunction.

An abrupt and stony descent led to the Taralla resthouse from whence the tantalising sound of a rushing stream could be heard, though the source was invisible. Mountain torrents had become another feature of the walk over the last couple of days but they had always appeared in the cool of morning when we least desired a dip in their cold clear water. But near Taralla a torrent had finally coincided with an afternoon sun-ravaged patch of path resulting in delicious immersion by everyone.

Our evening meal – grandly entitled "dinner" – usually consisted of lentil curry, known as dahl, which varied in popularity among the group. Anna adored it but the oft-repeated appearance of the dish on the dinner table earned it the epithet of "DDD" or "damned dull dhal", inspired, I think, by Lady Betjeman, a regular guide on this route. But against any accusation of a monotony of fare must be recorded the improvement of living conditions with resthouses increasing in stature at each consecutive overnight halt.

A case in point was that of Karnag where we were to spend two nights, with a rest day between. Here was not only the luxury of running water and bedrooms with en-suite toilets but a superb view from the veranda to go with it. But such luxury has to be earned and the catch was the longest haul of the trip, an unshaded tramp over a 9,500 foot pass and some uncomfortable walking. But, again, there were compensations en route such as a village temple exhibiting erotic door-knockers, a perfectly-situated pool tailor-made for bathing, and the ruins of an old fort, each offering bliss to their relevant devotees.

As readers might have noticed, group walking rest days have a habit of becoming the most energetic days of all as enthusiasm overcomes fatigue. Anna firmly resisted the temptations of the environment so remained behind to wash her hair and clothes while the rest of us climbed to a holy lake high above a forest of brown oak, the cold but not entirely unswimmable water guarded by a miniature temple. The village of Kot was but

Trekking on the Kulu trail

two miles distant too and its *bhandar* (temple) of striking design made a further objective.

The altitude was enough to ensure nights that were decidedly nippy and, so, with plenty of logs to hand, we indulged in the additional comfort of a dining room warmed by a crackling fire around which we sat, sipping coffee or tea, for long after our usual bedtime. I managed a chat with Lama and some of the cooking staff to learn that they enjoyed these repeated excursions into the foothills though they found it hard to understand what a European sees in a countryside that, to them, is of no consequence. "But the pay is good, the food is good, and the work not so hard", was the verdict with Lama adding, as I had already surmised, that conditions on trek were far superior to life in his plains village.

From Karnag the route swung south-west to contour through some of the grandest fir and dedodar forest in the Western Himalayas. Many villages here lay astride the path, their occupants busy with sheep-shearing and tending huge flocks of goats. A number of us made a side-excursion to the extensive ruins of Jalori Fort built about 1840 in the time of Ranjit Singh, the great ruler of the Punjab. Its broken walls stretched dramatically over several hills, the dead carcass of a century gone by made the more eerie by black thunder clouds and lammergeiers spiralling for thermals above the heat-bleached bones.

With Takrasi resthouse – another contributing astounding views plus some surprisingly civilised facilities for so wild and remote a spot – and a further night behind us, the ridge along the Jalori range led, with only one steep climb, to the pass at 10,280 feet. Actually there are two Jalori passes, the old one crossing the mountains about a mile and a half to the east. The new one was forged just before the First World War as a continuation of the road up the Ani valley. A small hamlet now marks the head of the pass and at a rough and ready "char house" we sat down to a glass of thick sweet tea while gazing upon spectacular manifestations of the Western Himalayas; range after range receding into the horizon. And beyond the head of the Kulu Valley, now well in sight, were the snowy peaks of Hanuman Tibba, Shukerbeh and Mukerbeh. Few travellers traverse this pass, even by the road that runs over it, thus a view that would become a commercial proposition in Europe is hardly known to anyone here, even today.

The top of the pass marks the boundary between Outer and Inner Saraj and the three-mile walk down the other side is by a zigzag road pleasantly shaded by silver fir, spruce and, in places, wild cherry. Clumps of iris growing on the bank above and below the road mingled with bracken and tall evil-looking cobra plants. We passed several groups of men felling spruce firs destined for a bumpy journey down mountain cataracts into the Beas river and along it to the Punjab plains. The captain was now weaving about twice as violently as did the road and had to be helped along. The motherly instincts of Miss Chabot-le-Conte abruptly came to the fore at this juncture and, though her manner challenged the rest of us to mind our own business, there was no doubt that the poor man needed aid.

On arrival at the Shoja bungalow, a guesthouse beautifully situated in a grassy glade thick with iris, we found tea ready on the lawn and the *chaukidar* (caretaker) eager to show us our rooms. And no wonder for they were quite the most luxurious while the wicker armchairs and sofas in the drawing room were positively rapturous.

Thereafter the route was nearly all downhill but made doubly sweet by the glades of iris through which the Jalori river tumbled. As we descended into lower climes so the temperature rose accordingly but the deodars continued to provide shade while the brown oaks were replaced by green holly oaks, white oaks and huge walnut trees. Patches of cultivation appeared, many plots containing cannabis which we had seen as hemp being made into rope.

Jibbi resthouse lay at six thousand feet, only two and a half hours downhill walk from Shoja which made the day's hike an easy one. Next morning we turned off the road onto a path that led along the right flank of the Jalori valley, winding through woods and fields to bring us to Chaini. And Chaini is a very odd-looking village indeed.

It contains an assortment of two hundred-foot white stone storage towers – "sky-scraper treasuries" as they are known – one actually a temple. We were permitted to climb the unbanistered stair-ladders to reach their high-above-the-ground entrances, explore their strange dark interiors and, from the viewpoint of the roof, look down upon the colourful but haphazardly-lain tiles of the village housetops, many, again, the repository of drying corncobs. The village reminded me a little of the medieval Italian town of San Gimignano though its towers are far more substantial than these somewhat rickety campanile-like edifices. The temple tower was firmly locked so, our investigations completed, we slowly wound down to five thousand feet to enter the township of Banjar, the principal centre for Inner Saraj. The place was hot and repressive as we toiled through the long main street abruptly aware of snarling traffic and its attendant smells, of people whose interest in strangers never rose above indifference, and whose open-fronted shops and government offices brought us back to a world of commercialism. Outside the urban boundary the air was alive with multi-coloured butterflies – Indian Red Admirals, Painted Ladies and Newabs, many of enormous size – but our eyes were on the resthouse, this one flaunting its superior grade, aglow with electric light, hot water at the command of a tap, and a lounge of deep-seat leather armchairs in which to sink.

At the gates of the Kulu Valley we had reached the end of the trek as such, our further northward travels bringing little further walking. Kulu, it should be explained, is an ancient kingdom giving its name to the valley of the Beas river which rises near the Rohtang Pass. The original name of the valley was Kulanthapitha meaning "The End of the Habitable World" – as anyone who has stood at the top of the Rohtang Pass, bounding Kulu and Lahoul, will understand.

Our Kulu walk does not pretend to be a test of strength and stamina or a lesson in masochism. However, nature and the countryside such as offered by the foothills of the Himalayas need to be appreciated from ground level; not by occasional glimpses through the window of a speeding vehicle. By observing it of an evening favoured by a rising moon and the promise of a myriad stars, pleasantly weary but well-victualled, is as near perfect a condition for so doing as can be devised. And for those who have their sights set upon the mighty giants of the Nepalese Himalayas it makes a useful run-in to a more gruelling type of progress.

Part II
Nepal
Trade Route through the Himalayas

When I made my first Himalayan trek at the end of the 1970s, a circuit of the Annapurna massif, the route along the upper valley of the Kali Gandaki and Ghorapani Pass, as well as that to the Everest Base Camp, were comparative novelties and one met few fellow-trekkers along the way. These days many a trekker cuts his Himalayan teeth, so to speak, on the circuit I made, yet not everybody has the good fortune to look upon and feel underfoot the greatest mountain range on earth.

When I first saw the Himalayas I was in a Russian aeroplane flying from Novosibirsk to Alma Ata in the then Soviet Kazakhstan. The enormous barrier of mountains upon which I gazed was called the Pamirs and the Hindu Kush, part of the great Himalayan chain that stretches across the thick neck of the Indian sub-continent for one thousand, seven hundred miles, from Afghanistan in the west to Assam in the south-east. Roughly a hundred to a hundred and fifty miles wide, it straddles six countries, dividing India from Tibet and consisting of three major ranges; the Himalayas, the Karakorams and the Hindu Kush.

I next gained the satisfaction of looking upon the most famous range – that of the best-known of the three, the Himalayas – early in 1979 when flying from Kathmandu to Delhi and my first sight of the Nepali Himalaya notched a memorable moment in my life. Too sharp to be clouds, the huge peaks floated, ethereal, above the brown haze of the plains. In both directions, the line of great white massifs marched away into the distance, growing smaller and smaller until my straining eyes could no longer discern earth from sky. Their scale, their extent and their seemingly complete dissociation from the real world beneath us, had me bewildered and dissatisfied.

My dissatisfaction stemmed from the fact that I was coming to Nepal for the first time in my life and that, during the course of my stay, I would approach hardly nearer to the mountains than this, for I was on a visit to the lowlands; the towns, rivers and jungle. There and then I promised myself I would return and walk upon those mighty Himalayas.

I came back sooner than I dared hope; the end of October of the same year. On this second flight into Kathmandu I could make out Everest, but my eyes were for other peaks. One of the world's most wonderful prospects is the sight, as the morning mists dissolve, of the glittering ice-hung southern ramparts of the Annapurna Himal, rising above the mirrored lake and lush green fields of Pokhara, Nepal's second town. Annapurna is more than a mountain. It is a complex of mountains, and no fewer than eleven 23,000-foot and more summits plus a score of other great peaks adorn this incredible massif.

I had been given the chance of making the trek to the Everest Base Camp, now almost a shanty town I believe, but my desires were not satisfied with this. Sensational as that trek is, the route, to my mind, was, even then, becoming over-subscribed, while the idea of attaining an altitude which, even at 18,000 feet, is but the bottom of a mountain left me strangely unelated. Thus I chose a trek round Annapurna and through a region that had only recently been open to foreigners.

Trekking in Nepal is possible at any time except during the monsoon, the winter months being probably the best walking season. And it is precisely because of the monsoon that Nepal is, basically, so green and fertile both in its sub-tropical lowlands and the more arid mountain regions up to 12,000 feet. Cultivation extends up to 9,000 feet with rice paddies and terraces of millet, buckwheat, maize and barley thriving in the wildest places. Deep in the hidden valleys are the communities of little people, in a fastness I had thought to be penetrated only by the occasional climbing expedition. Even "behind" Annapurna there are people busy living their simple, precarious lives.

Our trek circuiting the Annapurna massif was by way of the Marsyangdi Valley, Manang, the Thorung La Pass and Muktinath, with the return via Jomosom, the upper valley of the Kali Gandaki and the Ghorapani Pass; some two hundred miles and twenty days of tough walking along ancient footpaths that are vital trade routes and still heavily used. Transport is on men's backs or, in the northern reaches, on yaks.

It was this facet of the route that particularly fascinated me. I found it difficult to comprehend that it could be one of the main trade arteries of Nepal – a narrow footpath broken by boulders with room only for one person to walk comfortably. Nevertheless it carried a weight of traffic, all on foot and heavily laden.

The first few days after leaving Dumre, on the Kathmandu to Pokhara road, we trekked along tropical valley bottoms passing cultivated terraces that looked like the corrugations of a crocodile's back. Villages were numerous in the initial stages, each house arched around the inevitable peepul or banyan tree collared by a stone seat. Dwellings are made of adobe with timber slats, their veranda and floors of hardened mud kept scrupulously clean. Sanitation is non-existent, however, and as a result all villages swarm with flies. This is a primitive land supporting a hard way of life, but a contented one. Only the fit survive, but the villagers have sufficient to eat and a capacity for enjoyment. Disease still takes a deadly toll, and all too many people are marked by smallpox and goitre. Moving up the Marsyangdi, the handsome face of Himalchuli smiled in the sunshine, providing us with our first encounter with a great mountain.

On the fifth day we entered an area entirely different in character. North of the Annapurna Himal, and cradling the headwaters of the Kali Gandaki, is Mustang, a strange area of desert country, a salient of Nepal pushing into the Tibetan plateau. Mustang was closed to foreigners when I was there and maybe still is. Before us was a broad valley, with towering mountains on each side, but in the broad plain ahead was the stunted pine and juniper and the stony type of terrain associated with that mysterious land. Accompanied by the music of running water, though no longer the great crashing crescendos of the cataracts that had been a constant symphony earlier, we pressed on. Here and there these cataracts had been spanned by flimsy rope bridges which swayed alarmingly as we inched across trying not to look down at the foaming, boulder-strewn waters beneath, yet being forced to do so by virtue of the fact that there were terrifying gaps in the footway planking. Villages became few and far between, their appearance like miniature Lhasas; people displayed Mongolian features and wore Tibetan costume. On the patches of stunted grass sheep, goats, small wiry ponies and shaggy fierce-looking yaks grazed with a certain desperation.

The peaks around had grown to awesome proportions. The huge bulk of the Annapurnas dominates the Manang Valley, their gigantic buttresses formidable mountains in themselves. Gangapurna (24,457 ft) and Glacier Dome (23,405 ft) together with Tilicho Peak (23,405 ft) offer astounding views, their snowbound crests rearing skywards from a morass of impregnable rock. The Manang Valley came to an end, the Marsyangdi shrank to a trickle and the Thorung La Pass (17,200 ft) confronted us together with a new range of mighty peaks barring all ways except one.

Its ascent was a long painful slog, the thin air making breathing difficult. We stumbled up, each of us at his own pace, and were rewarded at the summit by bitter cold and stupendous fresh horizons of mountains. We camped at the top and I remember panicking slightly when I found

Muktinath on the Annapurna trek

breathing difficult; my first experience of the initial symptoms of altitude sickness.

Down to Muktinath, a pilgrim centre of shrines and temples strewn about a community of mud dwellings. A rest day here, but, as usual, for the more active of us an optional side trek, this one the ascent of a nearby hill liberally sprinkled with fossil ammonites, there to look upon a panorama that, in all my life, I have seen nothing to equal in splendour.

Shining in the distance was a mountain of crystal – Dhaulagiri – so beautiful as to leave one breathless. Together with its retinue of towering crags the great massif overshadowed the Kali Gandaki Valley, its winding river a fluorescent serpent writhing in the dark bottom. Rising from the other side of the valley were the proud Nilgiris, while bolstering the magnificent scene was the Great Barrier, its flanks falling to the basin of the upper Miristi Khola, and, far above, the soaring might of Annapurna, resplendent, proud, dominating everything as a goddess should. The wind tore through us as we gazed, spellbound, upon the scene.

The Kali Gandaki was our way home. The valley is reputed to be the deepest gorge in the world. It separates two of the world's largest mountain massifs – Dhaulagiri and Annapurna – each of which has a main peak of over 26,000 feet. The distance between them is twenty-two miles and the bed of the river at its central point lies 18,000 feet below.

But the word "gorge" needs some qualification: it suggests a narrow slit cut by a river between near-vertical rock walls. The Kali Gandaki certainly has its dramatic passages, but much of its upper course, carved by glaciers, is a mile wide, and its banks, though often nearly perpendicular, are also quite gently inclined in parts. Along it there is a precipitous path that can be followed from village to village by men and pack-animals. Again, the route has been known for centuries to traders as a breach of the Himalayan chain. The upper end of this colossal corridor is afflicted by violent gales that blow down the high-walled funnel. These rage all the year round, preventing any kind of growth. Columns of dust whirl up into the air, and the stinging wind howls round the gloomy, rocky inferno making it arid, cold and dry.

The Kali Gandaki claims another distinction. The valley becomes a semi-desert only 20 miles beyond a point where its vegetation is riotously tropical. High in the sky, cranes, storks and eagles soared on thermals as we crossed yet another river, a tumbling torrent grey with cold.

In the space of a day's march we descended from the sharp dry sunshine and wind-blown Tibetan flora around the village of Jomosom to the steady humidity and sub-tropical monsoon flora below Ghasa. The abruptness of the change was astonishing.

The people of the mountains and their villages changed too. One such village was Tukche, a maze of alleys, its houses little fortresses against heavy snow. These dwellings were mostly caravanserai where passing travellers can find lodging for the cruel nights. The inhabitants are Buddhists, whose piety can be judged from the walls of prayer wheels fifty feet long.

We ourselves never omitted, when passing, to give a joyful turn to the metallic cylinders upon which sacred texts are engraved – a far more practical idea than the reciting of lengthy prayers. Our turning of the wheels was not entirely for a sense of curiosity and fun. In these rarefied and lofty altitudes, between heaven and earth, there exists an inherent awareness that a traveller needs every bit of help from whatever source.

So gradual was the descent I was scarcely aware of losing height; the walking easy along the flats of the widening valleys or on narrow paths cut from cliff walls. Along the ridges from the south strode the advance guard of an army of conifers as the path began to climb again to the next village flaunting sacred streamers flying from its housetops, their prayer texts agitated by the incessant wind. Each village had its gompa, or temple, and numerous prayer walls around which we learnt to walk on the left so as not to offend local beliefs.

But suddenly we were back in the tropical zone. Thick forests of pine

Crossing a river in the Marsyangdi Valley

clung to the valley slopes and, crossing the Ghorapani Pass (9,300 ft), we trudged for a day through a great forest of rhododendron trees. Subtropical Nepal rose to meet us with the descent from Ghorapani, and the mountains were behind us. We still had stiff gradients to negotiate for we were crossing the grain of the foothills to reach Pokhara, the end of the trek.

Our last sight of a great mountain peak in close proximity was that of Machapuchare, the "Fish Tail" (23,000 ft), with its twin summits, and one of the world's most perfectly proportioned mountains standing, as it does, isolated before the crystal wall.

For us the return to base was tinged with a sense of loss. From south to north and from north to south we had walked clean through the Himalayas, and were now saying farewell to the greatest natural barrier on earth.

11

Kenya
Sundry Exertions in the African Bush

I look upon the three months of the 1976 Tana River Expedition in East Africa, of which I was a member, as one of the highlights of my life. Some twenty-nine strong, the membership mainly comprised young student scientists of the Polytechnic of Central London (now the University of Westminster) under the leadership of one Nigel Winser, who has since risen to eminence as deputy director of the Royal Geographical Society.

The invitation came out of the blue, my role being pronounced chronicler of the expedition, press and public relations officer and general dogsbody. I had absolutely no experience of expeditioning; neither, until then, had I been to East Africa. The object of the enterprise was to undertake a source-to-mouth investigation of human, animal, water, land and other resources with a view to their being utilised to the best advantage by the newly-established Tana River Development Authority and various other Kenyan governmental bodies who were concerned with the introduction of large-scale irrigation schemes along this remote, four hundred and fifty mile-long river. Our means of transportation was to be paddle-powered inflatable dinghies in which we were to convey ourselves between half a dozen encampments that we were to establish at different sites along the river's course and from which the youthful boffins would go about their week-long investigatory tasks. The first such camp was to be set up at Kora Rock, in the middle reaches of the waterway.

Initially our complement was divided into three action teams: the Mountain Team, the White Water Team and – the largest – the Scientific Team, each with their supporting elements. The two smaller teams were stiffened by a brace of serving soldiers and a few members – myself included – were expected to participate in both the ascent of Mount Kenya there to locate the source of the Tana, and, subsequently, to continue down the river accepting the challenge of its adolescent tantrums prior to our unification with the main scientific party at Kora. Thus, right from the start, I was pitched into the adventure element of the expedition.

It was Lake Hohnel, reached following a stiff climb up and over the southern wall of the Teleki Valley on Mount Kenya's flank, we found to be the Tana's birthplace, an oval gem of water from which a single stream emerged. With Hohnel revealing its offspring and the Mountain Team's unremarkable disclosure confirmed, its military elements – budding mountaineers all – were unable to resist the challenge of the trio of peaks that make up the summit of 17,058-foot Mount Kenya. Thus Richard Matthews, the expedition photographer, and I, having accompanied the climbers to the comparatively easy-to-climb Lenana peak of 16,300 feet, were forced to hole up for ten miserable days in ludicrously un-African snow while our military companions did their thing on the more inaccessible peaks. Our home for that period was a draughty, rat-infested cabin known as Two-Tarn Hut at an altitude of 14,730 feet.

Climbing appetites appeased we began an excruciating descent through a morass of bog following the course of the infant Tana to eventually return to the sort of climate and environment that I had always imagined Africa to represent.

Came the white water bit as the river grew in stature and flexed its muscles with the joy of youth. Kicking itself free of mountain restrictions it bounded noisily through lonely bushland – taking us with it. But since my narrative concerns only walking I do not intend to berate my reader with lurid prose describing the hair-raising events of the ensuing week as our two Avon inflatables progressed backwards, sideways and occasionally even forwards through one cauldron of wild water to another. Suffice to say that, with one boat torn to pieces in the watery maelstrom, most of our provisions lost, and my own life close to termination by drowning in a whirlpool, we found ourselves beached and stranded. From this predicament we were saved by a trio of spear-wielding Wakamba tribal hunters who led us to their village, there to provide refuge until our rescue could be affected.

Arrival at Kora and reunion with the main body of the expedition brought the adventure teams to heel and, thereafter, our day-to-day activities were to run on a less erratic course. Here the river had become a docile artery meandering serenely through the forests that looked so innocuous by day but which came to raucous life with darkness.

To me the dawns on the Tana were pure magic; the birth of the very first day; a radiance and a richness streaming over the golden sand and ethereal trees that shimmered like molten wire. Those dawns are surely one of Africa's greatest gifts but, as with Africa in general, things are not always what they seem. For a start the Tana's often tempting waters were disease-ridden and we were advised, where possible, to have no contact with it – particularly its static backwaters.

Paddling downstream from Kora, our respective teams finally drawn together and distributed amongst the remaining inflatables, life took on an unreal quality punctuated by both frequent wonder and, occasionally, fear. Hippos submerging and crocodiles scurrying into the water at our approach were, invariably, cause for apprehension and sometimes consternation but other animals, birds, and the flora of the jungle-enveloped river banks never ceased to provide joy.

All large but shallow rivers possess a deep-flowing channel but these have an infuriating habit of following the outer curve of every bend which precludes the cutting of corners. Frequently too we grounded in the shallows which meant enforced wading, diseased water notwithstanding, and the hauling of the well-laden boats along the croc-infested and uneven-bottomed river. Thus, for us, voyaging the Tana was not simply a case of idly drifting downstream whether it was along the river's smoother reaches or, as on the earlier occasions, the white-water sections where portaging the heavy boats across rock-bulwarked gorges made for the most exhausting and painful walking of all.

Our week-long sojourns in self-made encampments gave us a rest from these exertions and plunged me into a new world of animal, insect, bird, fish and plant investigation there to learn much I had never known before. Our camps bore such names as Mulango, Korokora and Kipendi, each a world of their own.

At Kipendi we were within the territory of the Mangabey and Colobus monkeys and the rare Pels owl. The Mangabey species is found only along the Tana and resembles the more common white-checked variety except for the pointed tuft on the top of its head. It feeds on fruit, nuts, leaves and bark in the trees, or on insects on the ground, and varies its social habits accordingly. One of the scientific tasks was the observation and reporting of their existence.

It was from the Kipendi camp, situated within the Tana River National Reserve, that three of us, Major John Richardson, our doctor, the young Sandy Evans, ornithologist, and myself, departed on a project of our own; a somewhat foolhardy sixty-mile foot safari to the subsequent designated riverside campsite. Originally it was to have been a larger walking party but a prolonged plod, unarmed, through game-infested bush and forest beneath a burning African sun failed to appeal, and volunteers were hard to come by. Our scientific brief and reason for the hike was a multiple one. We would track down and observe the Pels owl and report its location. We would look for a species of butterfly – a gold-banded forester – which changes colour with the environment. And, finally, we would leave messages of the forked-stick variety along the riverbank indicating anything of profound interest which could be investigated by the boat contingent who would be continuing their voyage a couple of days hence.

Since we had to carry our own equipment and provisions our rucksacks contained the very minimum of personal effects; food being the most vital element. Even so, fully loaded, it was as much as I could do to raise mine off the ground. The day prior to departure I had, characteristically, sprained an ankle, while its opposite member, pierced by a thorn, had turned septic. Hence I was hardly in my best walking condition. However, the inflammations and sores well-strapped and smeared with evil-smelling ointments and my pockets filled with pain-killing pills and Paludrine tablets, I deemed myself fit enough to go.

Years later, participating in commercially-orientated big game safaris in both Kenya and Tanzania where tourists are not even permitted to leave their well-protected outback hotel grounds or set foot outside their Land Rover vehicle, I was to realise that our perambulation into the hostile wilderness was a unique experience. Viewing game from a vehicle (or even a boat) one is essentially a passive witness. Travelling on foot through the game's territory one enters their world and on their terms.

We received a rousing send-off from our comrades as we forced a path through an overgrown banana plantation together with knife-edged grass from which zebra ticks had a field-day transferring themselves to our bare legs. We negotiated small groups of *manyattas*, around which families of Pokomo tribespeople sat cooking or relaxing while their excited offspring attached themselves to us, following in our wake. Stepping over pots and pans, walking between thatched "igloo" houses, I felt something of an intruder into private lives, but everyone was exceedingly gracious, polite and helpful; some villagers even offered us mangoes as we tramped by.

Continuing along a track we came upon an elephant graveyard; a sort of Stonehenge of bones in which John, in his medical capacity, was soon in his element sorting out and identifying the bits and pieces of the skeletal jigsaw puzzle.

The moment our juvenile retinue left us I cut a new notch in the yardstick of my African experiences. Here we were, just the three of us, alone, unarmed, uncertain, in the savage African outback. All around us, unseen but undeniably present, were the beasts of the jungle, river and bush. Here was the most abundant and varied life still existing on earth; we were surrounded by the immanence of death: the horns of rhino and buffalo and elephant, the teeth and fangs of crocodile and snake, the claws of the great cats. A jumble of emotions licked the pit of my stomach : excitement, insecurity, alarm and sheer dread.

However, the track that was to lead us to the village of Maroni, an outpost and last habitation, we imagined, before the lush jungle of a newly designated but not yet "tamed" game reserve, showed us no more than baboons, Sykes monkeys, jackals and dik-dik. The jackals we were surprised to see for they are mainly nocturnal animals. On John's recommendation we walked in single file, keeping a sharp eye open for movement and marking the position of climbable trees. Those initial hours every bush held menace; each sigh of the breeze in dead foliage was a lion tensed to spring. Bulbuls flickered in the branches of trees, agitating the leaves to cause me involuntary gasps, and snake tracks in the sandy soil kept my eyes darting everywhere. A bird called a tauraco flew up close to my feet to give me near heart failure, the afternoon sun glinting through its blood-red wings.

Maroni was a near-dead village, a community of deserted mud houses dilapidated or collapsed. Yet a prosperous-looking Christian church topped by a golden cross on its stubby tower made an incongruous impact as well as shade for a goat chewing firewood in the imposing portal. But Maroni was still kicking. As we halted in the square beneath the canopy of a tree we were aware of a family group staring from an aperture in a mud wall, and could feel other inquisitive eyes upon us. Using sticks of dead wood we made a small fire on which to brew a cup of tea to go with our biscuit and squirt of greengage jam. Whilst we were doing so a handsome young African, spear in hand, materialised to give us instructions how to get to Makere Ya Gwano, some four miles on, where the game warden lived. There lay our destination for the first day's walk.

I felt vaguely annoyed. Here we were, getting to grips with Africa, and along comes someone not the least surprised to see you and able to converse amicably in near-Harrovian English. This, plus afternoon tea in the village square. All we needed now was a silver teapot, daintily-cut cucumber sandwiches and a Maroni First Eleven cricket side to wreck everything.

I was in this bolshie mood when we bumped into the elephants. It was quite obvious that none of us had been observing properly, for, abruptly, the great beasts were all around us. Eight of them, with two babies, were over on the left; a couple of tuskers were munching the scrub on the right; only the track ahead and behind was empty. Personally I was all for minding our own business and pretending we hadn't seen them, but John and Sandy, of course, had other ideas. John, aware of his responsibilities as leader of the patrol, only wanted to take photographs, but young Sandy, off the leash from the more staid members of his team, was up to no good. The family group of elephants over to the left offered the greatest photographic attraction, and we zigzagged from bush to bush to get near. John took a few shots, then Sandy performed a kind of jig before the brutes attempting, presumably, to alter their docile expressions for the camera. That they failed to approve much of Sandy's performance was made quite plain, and a charge, feint or in earnest, became all too likely. Then they seemed to have second thoughts, turned tail and disdainfully stalked away. My relief was profound.

The track continued towards a dense patch of jungle that promised all manner of surprises but, to reach it, we had to run the gauntlet of more elephants. They were everywhere. Some were close to the path, half hidden behind clusters of scrub, and we had to veer away to keep our distance from them. As long as elephant can see you everything is plain sailing. They don't like being caught off guard.

A gazelle got up suddenly and sped towards the horizon. Peters', Thomson's or whatever variety it may have been, there is an elegance and dignity in all such gazelles and antelopes and this was no exception. But we were not going his way. Somewhere behind the thick belt of jungle was the abode of the warden and a European or two Nigel Winser had asked us to contact. One of them was Jim Alloway, who was undertaking an elephant survey, and we were eager to tap some of his knowledge. We entered the gloom of enveloping foliage.

At once we were aware of the birds. The trees were alive with their screech, trill and song. Something with iridescent green feathers and a breast that flashed into flame caught my eye but, mostly, it was just noise.

Rounding a substantial thicket of growth that looked like over-indulgent rhododendron we walked into the rump of another elephant.

It never saw us. Or if it did it gave no sign. An enormous beast, its form loomed over us as we crept away. There were others among the thick scrubwood and we had the very devil of a job avoiding them. One did catch sight of us, trumpeted loudly and made towards me, but stopped in its tracks wildly flapping tattered leather ears as if in indecision. A baboon screamed and hyenas wailed like fog-bound ships. All through this tableau of sound, the other elephants noisily ripped off branches and toppled young trees as they devoured the stalks and leaves.

The sun lay low in the sky as we came into a clearing where two bungalows made up the sum total of Makere Ya Gwano. A herd of frightened impala streamed by within a few feet, almost knocking us over in their flight, and we peered uneasily into the dusk, wondering what it was that had frightened them. The bungalows proved to be unoccupied though plainly in use. While we waited to see if anyone would turn up, we ambled down to the river bank to renew our acquaintance with the Tana and found a herd of five hippos, four crocodiles and half a dozen zebra close to the water's edge. In a welter of stamping hooves and farts they took off at our approach.

The first humans to appear were Jim Alloway's two servants and the brother of the game warden. He confirmed that Alloway would, in fact, be returning shortly with a couple of guests from an elephant observation stalk. (We didn't think he would have to go far for this since one specimen was grazing noisily just yards from his front door).

Jim Alloway turned out to be a lean young American when he eventually arrived in an ancient Toyota. He was also not at all pleased to see us. The guests – both Englishmen – showed more amiability, though it was the game warden's brother who offered us the use of a tent situated two hundred yards away and reserved for official game conservation visitors.

We made a fire and cooked ourselves a substantial tinned meal for the dual purpose of assuaging an appetite and lightening our rucksacks. The mosquitoes were equally hungry, whilst, to add to the discomfort, my inflamed ankles throbbed and ached in unison. We must have been in a breeding ground of monster crickets too, for they were everywhere; one even managed to join me in my sleeping bag. And if all this hadn't contributed to keeping me awake, the night noises of the enveloping jungle and river would certainly have done so. Hippos burping, lions sighing, elephants grazing, small mammals squeaking and night birds creating such a racket that they set off most of the day birds as well. It was all something like Disneyland on the fourth of July.

The next day we sallied forth to see Jim Alloway and friends again. He must have slept better than I had, for he was more disposed towards us than he had been earlier. It was arranged that he should drive John back to Kipendi later in the day to report the attractions of the reserve so that a photographic team could stop off as they came by in the boats. Alloway rather reluctantly agreed to this on condition that he and his guests could attend a camp supper. This business concluded, we decided to spend the rest of the day investigating some of the creatures that had contributed to the night's sound effects.

At first we followed the shore of the river, enjoying – in my case at any rate – a certain security in the knowledge that the steep bank could offer some protection in the event of sudden attack by something of the calibre of buffalo or rhino – particularly buffalo, for which, I don't mind admitting, I hold a healthy respect. Experienced hunters will smile at my alarm, but then hunters have guns and know what they are about. Of course, if a land animal failed to get you on the bank then a croc might do something about it under the bank. But things don't happen quite like this, though one's imagination in these circumstances works overtime.

Turning away from the river we entered an eerie world of shadow: tall trees rejecting the strong sunlight. We began noting each trunk in earnest, assessing the branches as a ladder upwards and away from some fanciful pair of viciously wielded horns. But every cluster of undergrowth we passed yielded nothing more deadly than dik-dik, to become just one more empty chamber in a game of zoological Russian roulette. A rustle of leaves would jerk us into fleeing in different directions but it would be only a stirring of monkeys as they leapt from branch to branch, twittering as they did so. Forest guinea fowl, chortling fiendishly as they ran across the path, made us jump. What had frightened them? Baboon, wart hog, elephant, lion, buffalo?, We stood at the base of our chosen tree refuge waiting and listening for something to emerge before sheepishly regrouping.

A putrid smell led us to a dead elephant in a clearing. This one had met his end but a few days earlier; the corpse was revolting in death, blown up with gas, crawling with maggots, a turgid liquid emanating from the bowels. Sickened, we turned away to re-enter the twilight, a patch of jungle dense with grey-green lichen festooning the trees. Again, the strange, mournful call of hyena arose. The call may have been part of its mating ritual or an announcement that it was being stalked by a lion. The king of beasts is thought to loathe the hyena, perhaps because the lion is haunted by the presentiment that, in old age, those same hyena who fear him now will pull him to the ground and tear him to pieces as they sometimes do his cubs. The spotted hyena is, however, not the coward it is reported to be; it hunts in a pack and will drag down a wildebeest. Spotted hyenas have the strongest jaws of all mammals, and their boldness grows with the night: then they will even bite a piece from the limb of a sleeping human.

There came another kerfuffle in the tree tops. A pack of monkeys leapt across a gap between two branches, then another and another. We stared up at them, shading our eyes from the sun that pierced the shield with daggers of light. Without a shadow of doubt these were Colobus, the shyest and most acrobatic of the tree-dwellers, moving with great rapidity and skill. They travel through the forest, venturing out to the furthest extremities of branches and hurling themselves into the air to land with a great curtsying and swishing of boughs twenty or thirty feet away. Black with a white fringe draped low across the back, like an academic hood, tails a long bush of pure white thicker than a fox's brush, and black faces severely framed in white as though they wore the closest fitting of a nun's coif. Yes, these were certainly Colobus, though still not the red ones.

They were gone in an instant, so we sat down on a log to see if more would come along. Idly I watched a butterfly hover on a twig then flutter a few inches off the ground to another perch. A beautiful insect, the wings were.. I looked again with a more analytical eye and, glory be, there before us was the golden-banded forester! The three of us dashed about trying to catch it, and in the process disturbed two more. All that was wanted now was a Mangabey and a Pels owl to parade themselves and we could go home and put our feet up. Then a wart hog dashed by, grunting indignantly, and I was surprised to see John halfway up a tree – more surprised still that I hadn't beaten him to it.

We came out of the gloom into the sunshine again, marvelling how a little brilliance can restore one's equilibrium. It was a clearing of dead trees, stark skeletons of rotting wood that could have offered morbid fancies but for the midday sun. A maniacal snicker did have us imagining shapes again but the elusive hyena was not to be seen. This one may have been the more timorous striped variety, which local people say changes its sex every year. If true (which I doubt) it may or may not have something to snicker about. Sandy climbed a tree – voluntarily – to look for elephant that had advertised their presence by leaving visiting cards of still-steaming droppings (which, incidentally, when dry make good fuel for camp fires) but, again, nothing was in sight.

A tornado of vultures led us to the river and along it to a sandbank alive with maribous, woolly-necked storks, two crocodiles and more vultures. In their midst lay a pathetic grey mound that was another not-long-dead elephant. Squabbling and squawking, the birds were tearing at the main carcass, except for the maribou storks, which cannot tear the meat off but have to wait for the crumbs, and which stood quietly by with beady frustrated eyes. The biggest vultures had taken command and were chasing intruders away, stalking in Prussian-style goose-step fashion towards them, the big capes of their wings spread out menacingly. The air was filled with noise of gluttony. It was horrible, macabre, yet engrossing to watch, and when one thought about it not ferocious at all – simply using as food whatever had died, leaving the earth clean and fresh. All the same, we shooed them away to give them indigestion for their pains: but the moment we walked off they were back, minus the crocodiles who played it more coolly.

To the croon of a distant lion we crossed one of the Tana's tributaries and, at the edge of the river, beheld a mighty crocodile – the daddy of them all – fast asleep beneath an overhang of the bank. John crept forward, intent upon obtaining a photographic close-up. In this he succeeded brilliantly, barely managing to get its full eighteen feet in the view-finder. Unable to resist it, he uttered a low "Boo!" and the croc had the rudest awakening of its life. It lifted into the air all four legs frantically paddling and was gone. A moment later the overhang gave way and, in a shower of sandy turf, John found himself where the reptile had been seconds before.

Returning the way we had come we glimpsed more Colobus. They gave us little chance to identify them but the afternoon sun had shown up the ginger-red crown on their heads before the monkeys had thrown themselves out of sight. Red Colobus. Our day's perambulation had not been in vain.

The game warden had returned during our absence and we were able to call on him at his office. And here, to our chagrin, was another initially hostile character. Suspicion appeared to be at the root of his unfriendliness. He was displeased to learn that we were occupying the visitor's tent, and when John came to the bit about the expedition's desire to film in the reserve he exploded. Expounding regulation after regulation he found every reason to forbid probing cameras onto his patch. What with the unsociability of the few authoritative humans we had so far come across in the reserve, combined with the number of dead elephants, I began to think nasty thoughts. I was later to meet the warden in happier circumstances and find him quite charming. But that was on neutral territory outside the game reserve.

At dusk the warden, Jim Alloway and his two guests, plus John and Sandy crammed in the old Toyota, whirled away towards Kipendi in an angry storm of dust. I had volunteered to stay behind since someone had to. They would be back before nightfall, they said.

Left to my own devices, I built up the fire and prepared to chalk up yet another experience in my life. From three in the jungle, here was I by my own sweet self. And never have I felt so alone in all my days. Lonely no, alone yes. And there is a difference. Loneliness is a gradual melancholic emotion; being alone in such circumstances can build up into something approaching stark terror. Tripping down to the Tana to refill a bucket with water, I found a monster crocodile leering at me together with a quartet of hippos blowing raspberries. And before they disappeared, more reluctantly than usual, I noticed the expression on their faces were different: a sort of there's-only-one-of-you-now-isn't-there look. I retired, chastened, to the tent and attempted to cheer myself up with the prospect of three tinned treacle puddings and a bottle of beer that John and Sandy promised they would bring back with them later.

Throughout the hot day the elephants had been musing and swaying in some cool recess of the forest, but now they began to rouse themselves and drift to their night-time feeding grounds like great grey shadows, their bodies moving through the undergrowth so gently that the only sound was the faintest whisper of leaves rustled by a tiny breeze. Sometimes a herd of elephants will move so silently through the tangled undergrowth that you are only aware of their presence by the one noise over which they have no control – the prolonged, often-sonorous rumbling of their tummies.

A herd of the great beasts began grazing their way in line abreast, moving in the manner of a fleet of battleships, slowly but relentlessly towards me, munching raucously, pulling great chunks out of the vegetation. As the line approached, the nocturnal noises of the jungle abruptly turned to full volume, each howl, squawk and scream a drumbeat of menace. The hairs on my neck rose to attention. From the direction of the Tana my riverine companions got into the act with a chorus of belches and farts that defy description.

The trouble was I couldn't see anything. I am something of a man of action. Let me see the foe and I'll have a go at him. I searched the night shadows till my eyes ached, but nothing moved. The fire shrank to a glow; to replenish it would mean a lone walk towards those evil noises, which was out of the question. Frantically I blew on the dying embers and raised a tiny flame to kindle a spark of courage within my breast. A military maxim arose in my mind offering a clarion call to action: To attack is the best form of defence.

The nearest of the elephants loomed out of the darkness; a shadowy outline as big as a house against the greater darkness. I picked up a faggot that had burst into feeble flame, wielded it about my head, uttered a banshee war cry and hurled myself at the foe. I felt better now. My tormentors were phantoms no longer. I knew where I was going.

The big tusker was too intent upon stuffing his face with trunkfuls of fodder to notice me at first. Then it looked round, perceived a miniature ape-like figure fast approaching emitting strange sounds, opened wide its eyes in disbelief, turned and bolted. A thunder of hooves, a smashing of undergrowth and, what is more, the whole herd was routed. To consolidate my triumph I flung my smouldering faggot at the retreating elephantine rump and had to spend the next half-hour extinguishing the forest fire I'd started.

I would say here and now that my actions are not to be recommended to anyone getting into a similar situation. Remaining quite still would have been a wiser course. But you live and learn in this jungle business.

My foes never moved far away. I heard them resume their interrupted feasting over at the other side of the warden's house. They were still there close on midnight when I heard the Toyota returning and realised that an unsuspecting John and Sandy would walk right into the middle of the herd on their way to the tent. I crept along the path, moving from bush to bush with sounds of munching all around me, to gain Alloway's house. In this way I managed to guide the two back by a circuitous but less risky route.

Again it was elephants that wrecked any hopes of a peaceful night. We listened uneasily to them tiptoeing about right up to the guy-ropes of the tent, and any moment I expected a great foot to descend through he canvas – which goes to show how little I know about elephants. In the morning we discovered that one of them had sucked dry a whole bucket of water positioned by the tent flap in readiness for our morning tea. There had been two bucketfuls there, the other untreated, and as luck would have it, the animal had consumed the treated one, which meant we had to go through the whole purifying performance again. And to make matters worse I drank a whole mugful of the wrong stuff – straight from the disease-ridden Tana – before we had worked out which was which.

We left following a delayed breakfast and a session of first aid in which John had the odious task of extracting about a pint of pus from my poisoned ankle. We moved south via an ox-bow – where the river had changed course – and across the territory of the game reserve with commendable rapidity but still considerable caution. Here and there were tiny communities of Pokomo living in stockaded acres of cultivation and *shambas*. In a sandy hollow we came upon the spore of what Sandy took to be a leopard. These cats are rarely seen, being frequently nocturnal. Their favourite food is baboon and there were plenty of these about, yapping at us at intervals. Another cat we kept our eyes peeled for was the cheetah, for these, though elusive and fast, hunt by day. Nearing the village of Baomo, a confusion of tracks nearly led us astray, but a charming black lady, stoically undertaking a man's job of reroofing a house, directed us with much graceful gesticulation.

Baomo was an interesting little place. No more than a compact group of mud and wattle-daub houses it exuded an atmosphere of a true African tribal village more than most. We were at once the centre of attraction for a host of children, their shy, wide-eyed faces radiant with excitement. To the eldest we gave a "to whom it may concern" letter requesting that it be delivered "in person" to any of our compatriots who might be stopping off in the village. This was more for the boy's benefit than anything else, and it was a joy to see the look of pride suffuse his face with the sudden shouldering of responsibility. Beneath a huge mango tree lay a massive dug-out canoe under construction among a thick carpet of wood chippings: the co-operative effort of the village males.

In spite of steadily eating our way through the tinned rations, our packs remained consistently heavy, our sweaty backs indelibly staining the fabric. On the credit side we were seldom without the reassuring presence of a tribesman, who would appear in the most unlikely of places and always as we were having trouble deciphering our outdated map. From dense jungle to banana plantation, from river bank to bushland we trudged, my ankles standing up well to the heavy punishment. Twice we were provided with an armed escort by fellow-travellers who would insist upon accompanying us carrying a spear at the ready, appalled at our own lack of weaponry. These courteous fellows guided and protected us through many a hostile strip of forest to put us on the right path to a neighbouring village. They asked for nothing in return but were appreciative of the cigarettes and few boiled sweets we were able to offer them.

We would have been more than appreciative ourselves of their protective measures during early afternoon when we made the brief but dramatic acquaintance of a wounded rhino. The meeting occurred in a dense portion of jungle bordering the Tana. The thicker the undergrowth the more care we applied and were dutifully marking our respective climbable trees in the forbidding gloom when it happened. We were walking parallel to the river, some fifty yards from it, when Sandy, in the lead, raised his hand to bring us to a halt and an instant state of readiness. I saw the animal first: simply a large rump behind a palm clump. "I think it's an aardvark, I'm not sure," I whispered in a voice not my own. John and Sandy were better at the animal recognition business. "It's a bloody rhino!" they exclaimed in unison. "Quick. Drop your rucksacks and up your trees. Hurry!." This put the wind up me to such an extent that I was unable to disentangle myself free from my harness, and while struggling to do so failed to make the silent getaway intended. The cymbals of a military band could hardly have made more din as the tin mug and mess-tin strapped to various buckles clashed together and the rhino turned about in some concern. As I finally shook free my harness I glimpsed the beast's head lower for a charge and it came to me, even in that instant, that for the rhino caught between the river and a trio of dithering humans, the humans provided the line of least resistance. I saw the great horn point straight at me, turned and ran.

The smash of trampled undergrowth coupled with a series of low-pitched snorts drove me forward on winged feet. My chosen tree became the single goal at the further end of a vortex of my life, the heavy breathing running with me. I was not alone in my fleeing for, in the next instant, all three of us were struggling up the same tree. In spite of my advanced age I had beaten John to it by a short head, to scramble up the slender boughs neck and neck with the agile young Sandy.

From a safe height we peered down to see the bewildered rhino hurtle by beneath us and discerned a spear wound in its flank. The Black Rhinoceros is a solitary animal and a vegetarian, but will charge and overrun anything – even a train – that its poor eyesight is able to make out.

The danger seemingly passed, we descended shakily from our eyrie and re-shouldered our discarded loads. But hardly had we ventured more than a hundred yards we found ourselves cheek by jowl with the same iron-clad bottom. Recognition was mutual and instantaneous and, once more, we took off, this time in all directions. But climbable trees had abruptly become scarce, and I had to run back to the river bank before I could find one. Behind us the rhino hesitated, unable to fathom what was going on. It remained stationary, ears cocked and grotesque head raised, nostrils dilated as it searched the wind. Uttering a couple of blast-like snorts, looping a stringy tail over its rump, the beast trotted away at a slinging, zigzag pace through the trees, to wheel round and stare once again. Then it gave up and lumbered off.

The path led out of the trees to a patch of bush. In it we brewed a mug of tea, which, with a couple of biscuits liberally spread with marmalade, went some way to restoring our shattered morale. A herd of more than forty oryx and waterbuck occupied our attention in the late afternoon and as the sun ripened and lost its sting we performed a little stalking of our own. Oryx are powerful and fierce. They are beautiful beasts, reddish-brown in colour with black-and-white face markings. Their companions in this instance were waterbuck, which wear friendlier expressions, shaggier coats of brownish-grey and a tail their creator forgot to complete. The herd had smelt our presence but could not see us as we crawled towards them intent on getting as near as possible for a photograph. Only when we could see the whites of their eyes did they catch on. Promptly the herd wheeled and thundered off to less disturbed pastures.

Pressing on, we forged a way through some dingy pine and palm forestry, walking at speed, conscious of the fast approaching night. According to the map Mnazini was a village of a stature that might rise to spare accommodation for the weary traveller. But we were fast losing confidence in the map, though the absence of big stretches of green was no fault of the cartographer. Instead, it was a sign of the times and evidence of the Pokomo's destruction of the forestry. Close to the river again we finally managed to obtain our bearings and strode on with new-found confidence.

Mnazini was, in fact, something of a Wild West village, complete with one main street, a beer house and a couple of shops with colourful facades in compensation for the drabness behind them. Interspersed between the mud huts were an occasional plaster wall and rash of corrugated iron sheets that raised the village from a rural community to an urban one. At the end of the street was the faithful Tana tolerating a fleet of dug-out ferries, open-air laundering facilities and, upon its scarred banks, a sort of village riviera in which everybody sat around in cheerful inactivity. Placed at a strategic position betwixt beer house and river was the public loo which, I was to discover, produced cockroaches of such size as to constipate a European for life.

For our next few days' hiking we would no longer be in an inadequately protected game reserve, though this fact would make little difference to events. In a way it was no more than a case of moving from a frying pan into a fire.

Upon arrival at Mnazini, John, Sandy and I were received by the chief. He was a fat little man with a cheap ball-point sheathed in his curly black

The author makes notes as dawn rises over Mount Kenya

hair. He owned the local stores and was plainly a man of substance judging by the hangers-on engaged upon menial tasks in his backyard. He was also boss of the small bar, but, it being Ramadan and most of his flock being of the Muslim faith, he had allowed his beer stocks to fall to zero, which resulted for us in a diet of Seven-Up. In mysterious dark outhouses and recesses a fever of cooking, baking and washing was going on, which at least provided us with an intermittent source of hot water during our stay. The chief graciously offered a storeroom in which to sleep: a bare concrete chamber adequate for our needs, for which he declined payment.

So for two days we became temporary citizens of Mnazini. The chief's son, an intelligent youngster, was a constant visitor, who arranged for a supply of his friends to sit and chat with us over the evening social hour. From them and others we began to accumulate facts and figures concerning kings, sealing wax and Pels owls, and it was our quest for the Pels that was the reason for our remaining at Mnazini so long. Willing as he is, an African so often exhibits that annoying habit of replying to a question with an answer he thinks the questioner wants to hear, whether it is accurate or not. Many of our informants had a smattering of English, and from them we learnt of an old man who lived in the forest who could lead us to this owl. The difficulty was to get across to them the correct species of owl we wished to observe. The fact that it had no ears hardly made the bird a universally popular subject for study. Yet everyone claimed to know it.

From owls the conversation switched to buffaloes, for in the African world of the bush this was the animal that had the most effect on people's lives. That we had walked from Kipendi unarmed and often unescorted raised many eyebrows in Mnazini since, allegedly, we had passed through very dangerous country thoroughly infested by these vicious brutes. In a manner reminiscent of World War Two bomb stories, the villagers had a nice line in buffalo anecdotes, and we were treated to some pretty grizzly tales of attacks on humans by wily bulls who anticipated every effort to escape them. In the woods supposedly harbouring our precious Pels would be many buffalo we were energetically informed, particularly in the wood named Katherine Homeward (after a lady who had studied Mangabys in the area) and in others across the river. In fact, according to popular opinion, worse terrors lurked on the east bank than on the west.

In spite of mosquito netting, everyone was bitten that first night in the village. John's attackers were a brand of tree lice emanating from a timber store adjacent to his bed space, while Sandy sustained his usual working over by ants, to which he seemed particularly susceptible. Breakfast was porridge, bacon roll and tea cooked on a small fire in the main street. In place of the eight o'clock news we were treated to the views of the local political agitator, a forceful character in smart European dress with a strong line of English patter. His wrath centred upon those who had forcibly evicted innocent families from the new reserve without, according to him, offering any compensation. He waxed bitter on the subject of the primates that lived there for centuries (as if it was all their fault) in harmony with the Pokomo villagers, and could see no reason for the sudden uprooting of the human populations. If there had to be an uprooting, why not the monkeys? To him it was a simple case of *Homo Sapiens* v *Colobus bardius* and the rest. And with the threat of an importation of urban communities to Pokomoland it could be that the Pokomo themselves were becoming the real endangered species. He had a point.

We crossed the Tana by dug-out, I willing myself to remain absolutely still to prevent capsizing the boat, and climbing the opposite bank, we promptly walked into the very man we had set out to find. He was a fifty-year-old African named Komora Bashova of gamekeeper-like appearance, who had once been a companion of Katherine Homeward. He spoke a little English, knew the woods like the back of his hand and, of course, recognised the brand of owl we were searching for. With us too had come a youngster who had designated himself as general dogsbody and hanger-on. The *Msee*, as the older man was respectfully titled, immediately dropped whatever he had been doing to lead us to the elusive bird, which, he vouchsafed, could often be seen atop the highest trees.

The whole morning was spent combing woods and thickets, seeing several red Colobus monkeys and Mangabey but no Pels. At every isolated shamba enquiries were made of its whereabouts, and we were led to places where the bird would surely be – but wasn't. Ever sensitive to the presence of buffalo, my eyes wavered between possible owl perches and climbable trees. I got the shock of my life when, crawling about in a thicket, I looked round to find myself staring between the eyes of a mournful light brown face. Buffalo! The message flashed to my brain, but, prostrate under an entanglement of brambles, the normal reaction got short-circuited and I remained glued to the spot. The same kind of reaction must have afflicted the waterbuck – for that is what the animal was – and five long seconds were to pass before it took to its heels.

With one of my ankles swollen to twice its normal size, I was glad to return to Mnazini shortly after midday, we having arranged with Komora to institute another search at dawn next day. Meanwhile, John and Sandy, full of vigour, took themselves back to Katherine's Wood. When they had gone I attempted an overdue wash in a biscuit tin of water, but a bevy of local lovelies came to watch the performance. "Why not you wash everywhere?" one of them asked, and I had to look hard at her to find out if she was being serious.

I suppose I should have rested my ankle for the remainder of the afternoon, but, being what I am, I found more worthwhile activities to pursue. The construction of a mud villa was in process next door and I was allowed inside to watch the creation of the inner walls. Rough and ready construction it may have been, but, inside, the house was beautifully cool. Once the framework of wood had been erected, interior work consists of little more than throwing fistfuls of mud at it. Someone took me to see the interior of his *manyatta* at the rear of the village and, again, I was able to marvel at the coolness of its dark interior – even though, in this case, the roof was but straw and wattle. Furniture was home-made, right down to an ingenious article I eventually recognised as a washstand of the sort my Victorian grandparents used.

Back in the high street I visited the two shops which were, of course, the meeting places of those in the village with nothing to do, i.e., the men. In one of them I was invited to join a "sit-in", during which community affairs were aired. Probably for my benefit the subject of the game reserve arose and very soon I was made aware of how unpopular the concept was.

But though the accusation hung heavy in the air I could obtain no concrete evidence of families being ejected without compensation.

Our dawn awakening next morning was a belated one, with all three of us oversleeping. Komora had nearly given us up as we met at the ferry landing under a weak sun and, together, proceeded to a wood we had christened "Hell's Pels Park". We observed many owls, including some intriguing breeds of considerable size, but they all sported ears and so were not for us. From wood to wood we went, coming upon monkeys, waterbuck and a leopard which we were fortunate to glimpse if only for an instant. This cat hunts by night, but, otherwise, is more doglike in its habits. It is wary and extremely dangerous when cornered or wounded and, in company with the cheetah, is the fastest animal on earth. As we returned to the river an impala watched us, head raised alertly, a fine tautness in its glossy flanks and slender neck. But of Pels there was no sign.

The inevitable happened as we re-crossed the Tana, this time at a lesser ferry point upstream of Mnazini. Our dug-out was a smaller and narrower craft than before, and in mid-river a ferocious horsefly settled on my naked back. Forced to knock it away, my impulsive movement upset the boat, tipping everyone into the water. An audience of Africans – as well as a ferryman grievously scarred from a hippo attack – thought it all extremely funny, but John and Sandy were not amused.

We partook of a late and very public breakfast, providing an hour's entertainment for a sizeable portion of the community full of unhelpful suggestions about what to do with the baked beans. Then we were off again to the west bank on a last-ditch search. Once more Colobus and Mangabey of all hues exhibited themselves in profusion, but the confounded owl wasn't caring a hoot. It was not until late afternoon that a wildly excited Komora made a dramatic gesture towards the sky as if he were Abraham beholding a miracle. "There, look! On the furthermost bough!" he shouted so loudly that it awoke the thing from its slumbers. But it wasn't a Pels, and we all returned crestfallen to the village aware, as we had half-suspected all along, that we had been led on a wild-goose chase.

Next morning, consigning the wretched bird to its ancestors, we loaded ourselves up and struck southwards, escorted by a platoon of children who slowly dropped away at the "outer suburbs" of Mnazini.

At a hamlet – Bubesa – we rested beneath a mango tree. Finding the way out of a village invariably involved a high percentage of guesswork owing to the multiplicity of tracks running in all directions. However, in

Bubesa we were lucky for a tall Somali was on the verge of leaving for Mwina, about eight miles distant and on our own route. He graciou sly allowed us to accompany him.

He set a gruelling pace taking no account of our heavy loads, but we appreciated the fact that it was vital we reached a habitation before nightfall so we uttered no complaint. The way, too, was composed of long flat stretches of bush and thicket – perfect buffalo territory – and the Somali's spear was not to be spurned; the chap himself looked the type able to use it.

We reached Mwina exhausted but unassailed. While we were resting weary feet on the edge of the village the young chief arrived, greeted us cordially and showed us to his house, which he handed over for the night. We had made no request, asked no favours, but there he was assuming us to be travellers needing a bed. We were deeply touched by this act of spontaneous hospitality. The house was of neat mud and wattle construction, our boudoir containing a number of straw mats which, to a village African, is all the furniture deemed necessary in a bedroom. The one concession to high living was a decoration of painted palm leaves serving as a picture on the brown mud wall.

Though dusk was settling upon the sky, the sun was still warm and my longing for a swim in the forbidden waters of the Tana was not lost on John. He had mentioned earlier that he had seen the locals bathing at the point where the river came nearest the village, and the pleading in my eyes overcame his medical strictures. "It's moving water," he opined and, glancing at the ingrained filth on my body, added "If I save you from bilharzia you'll only catch typhus," which was assent enough for me. I dashed for the river and caught the other bathers completely by surprise. They were the ladies of the village, about two dozen of them and all in the nude. Pandemonium broke out and I was made to turn my back while they emerged with much shrieking. But one lady was too slow so took cover by ducking into the water. And there she remained, too frightened to go deeper because of the crocodiles and too embarrassed to emerge because of me.

John plus any number of helpers had our supper well in hand. All sorts of offerings kept appearing from bananas through plates of cooked peas to chicken pate. These gifts were shyly presented by the women of the village who were extremely curious to discover how and what the white man ate, though I fear they took away with them some pretty poor impressions. Sandy was busy playing with a squad of kids and, judging by the squeals of merriment, making a good job of it.

The men with a smattering of English joined us over tea for a chat and general airing of their linguistic abilities, an area in which, rather naturally, the local schoolmaster shone the more brightly. As I expected, the way we had come was pronounced very dangerous: a sort of "black spot" for buffalo, and one where nobody went at night.

It was my turn for a bad night, though it resulted less from attack by creepy-crawlies than from anticipation thereof. By the light of my torch I found one aircraft-carrier of a bug – all masts and antennae – and a vivid imagination did the rest. John was not going to get it all his own way either: the secret of his medical prowess out, a patient came wandering in during the small hours intent upon being first in the morning surgery queue.

And morning surgery it became with a vengeance. While I made breakfast in the house next door (which was, in fact, the chief's kitchen) John dealt as best he could with the onslaught, Sandy acting as receptionist and nurse. The villagers of Mwina seemed, in general, quite a healthy lot. However, treatment by a *hakimi* – the first, probably, ever to practise in Mwina – was an experience to be enjoyed even by the healthy. Genuine ills, of course, there were too: malaria, venereal disease, liver complaints, open sores, scabies, a host of eye disorders and an assortment of ailments resulting from dietary deficiency.

While John ministered to the sick, I fed him mugs of burnt porridge made in a series of mess tins over a smoky fire. My assistant was the chief's father, a charming, gentle man who controlled the fire, the smoke from which was supposed to exit through the roof. But for virtually the first time on the expedition it rained solidly, and the smoke was reluctant as we were to go anywhere. Outside, everything turned to sticky mud.

Leaving John to repay our debt to society, Sandy and I returned to the forest in company with one of the village hunters in a desperate bid for the Pels. Instead we came across the usual plague of red Mangabeys twittering and flinging themselves about in the trees, and when we were back in the village, a boy brought us one he had caught. The poor thing was tied up like a dog, but, with the cord out of sight, made a fine photograph.

The sky was black and ominous, but the rain had slackened as we evacuated Mwina. The chief accompanied us to the ferry crossing point downstream of my lido of yesterday and his personal ferryman poled us across the browner-than-normal Tana to the east bank. There he proudly showed us his shamba and "workhouse" of palm leaves, from which emerged his mother and two sisters to be solemnly introduced. As a farewell gift he presented us with six eggs for which we could repay him with but a few boiled sweets and a book of matches. The four of them stood watching us go, waving all the time; we hoped that messages addressed to our compatriots would result in a beneficial visit to Mwina by the boat party as it came by. The most pleasant and hospitable people, these villagers possessed yet another virtue: honesty. Earlier John had dropped his compass, though the first he knew of it was when a man came running to return it.

The rain held off just long enough for us to get far out into open countryside, then down it came in cascades. In moments we were soaked through, which in my case meant little since I wore only shorts and a singlet. John and Sandy, however, sported more conventional attire: bush shirts, khaki denim trousers and a sun hat in lieu of a pith helmet. All of us wore safari boots. Ignoring the rain, we pushed on, the river to our right swinging towards and away from us as we cut across its corners. The countryside changed from bushland to open savannah.

Even without an escort to set the pace we walked hard and fast. The plain, dead flat, would have made monotonous though easy walking in dry conditions but the rain had turned the ground into a quagmire, the water and clay-based soil producing a glutinous mixture of mud, known – and dreaded – by the motor-rallying fraternity as "black cotton". And what this substance can do to tyres it can, on a modified scale, do to boots. Within minutes the weight of our footwear had doubled and trebled as the sticky soil adhered to the soles and spread outwards to form snowshoes of packed mud. To attempt to kick the stuff off was tantamount to tearing a leg from its socket; yet to ignore the build-up not only anchored feet to the ground but caused blisters from contortions of the canvas uppers. Thus, to add to the afflictions of my ankles came blisters as big as acorns on toes and heels.

Gradually I fell back, halting every now and again to wrap agonised toes in fresh strips of sticking plaster that refused to stick. Blood stained my filthy socks while boots, once off, exhibited a marked reluctance to go on again. Sandy likewise was showing signs of wear but solved his problems by removing his footwear altogether and walking barefoot. It was a sensible move but my feet were in such a poisonous mess already I felt it would do more harm than good if I followed suit. Only John seemed impervious to the conditions, striding on towards the limitless horizon. Imperceptibly the distance between us lengthened.

With the onset of the savannah we had noticed the spoor of lion, and their presence in the clumps of undergrowth that clung to the plain was periodically confirmed by their coughing grunts, low and muted. That they were close added to my unease, though lions are indolent, lazy creatures, preferring as little exertion as possible in the attainment of their food. Nevertheless, I felt myself to be a sitting duck. A lion will eat anything, no matter how "high" or maggot-infested – which offered me no comfort either! When really hungry, lions become extremely bold and determined, stopping at nothing to bring down a victim. Normally they prey on the larger antelopes and zebra, ostrich and buffalo, and occasionally giraffe, but, when pushed, nothing is too small or insignificant for them to catch and devour, thus man himself may fall a victim under such circumstances. And once a lion has tasted human flesh, and found how easily man can be stalked and killed, it very quickly becomes a confirmed man-eater. Me, I had not the slightest desire to become a source of addiction.

More dead than alive we staggered into a hamlet. The place had about it an air of decrepitude, but a track led out of the cluster of silent mud dwellings scarred by tyre-marks, which offered the notion that we were back on some sort of channel of communication. There were people on the route, too, seemingly intent on getting somewhere: presumably Kulesa, a larger community we could now make out in the far distance. Gritting our teeth, we battled on.

A sizeable school complex characterised the new village, which showed more life about it than the previous one. As we sprawled, licking our wounds, beneath a tree, we were subjected to a barrage of questions concerning our mission and destination. Most of the questions came from local off-duty schoolmasters and we were to learn from them that Weme, the district centre close to our final destination, was "just down the road". We asked the reason for a lack of children in so scholarly a community and were told, with some surprise, that they were working on the shambas. By a combined effort of will we worked out it was a Sunday.

"Just down the road" represented two miles on the map and nearer six on the ground. The savannah had surreptitiously given way to forested country, well cultivated and inhabited. And Weme, when we reached it, showed us a general store, a tractor depot and a missionary church. It was the store that satisfied our immediate cravings in the guise of Fanta orange squash and thick, creamy goat's milk unearthed from a damp cellar.

We debated the option of spending the night in Weme, which to our individualistic minds promised more interest than a barren camp site, but the Church intervened. Its representative was a forceful Irish Methodist priest who insisted upon running us the last couple of miles in the back of his van. And just as well perhaps for, alone, we would never have found the site. The boats had not arrived, so no one witnessed our ignominious entry on wheels.

12

South America — Peru
Highway of the Inca
A Short Walk in the Andes

The revelation that we had bitten off more than we could chew struck me as David and I struggled up our umpteenth boulder-strewn ridge; just another of many behind us and countless more to come. But the highway – here no more than a wide grass thoroughfare bordered by stone drainage culverts – remained a hard taskmaster binding us to its course. In the distance, etched against the blue sky, aloof and mocking, lay the enormous bulk of the Cordillera Huayhuash stretching across the horizon in a glorious panorama of snow peaks. The explorer, Colonel Fawcett, might have been standing by my side for, through dulled senses, I heard his words: "Never had I seen mountains like these, and I was crushed by the grandeur – speechless with the overpowering wonder of it."

I don't quite know when the idea of tracing the royal road of the Incas in the Peruvian and Ecuadorian Andes first took root in my mind but at school the story of the Spanish conquest of the Inca Empire in 1532/33 by a cavalry force just a hundred and seventy-strong never ceased to fascinate me. Of course it was the Spaniard's secret weapon – horses, of which none existed then in South America – that was a major contribution to the collapse and flight of the thousands-strong Inca army which invoked in them supernatural powers. Yet this notwithstanding it was a remarkable achievement since, earlier, the Incas themselves only completed their conquest of the hotchpotch of tribal fiefdoms after centuries of fighting.

The Inca empire, at the zenith of its power, stretched over much of western South America. In order to hold the huge realm together and convert great territories of mountain, desert and jungle into a close-knit entity, communications had to be of the highest order. This was where the system of their renowned roads came in; the hub of the enormous complex being the Inca capital, Cuzco.

The complex was based upon two trunk highways, one following the coast; the other, running parallel to it, along the mountain chain. The coastal road stretched from Tumbes (the frontier town now close to the Ecuadorian border) southward through the coastal desert and the entire length of Peru down into Chile. The Andean royal road ran along the spine of the mountains from Colombia's Ancasmayo river, down through present-day Ecuador, Peru, Bolivia and into Argentina. The total length of the former artery was 2,520 miles while the royal road could boast an astonishing 3,250 miles.

Between these arterial roads ran numerous laterals to connect the two highways. These pushed into the high east-west valleys of the mountain chain while side routes and "slip roads" led to the characteristic gold-bearing regions on the Andean flanks.

The original royal road had been built to connect Cuzco, now in southern Peru, with Quito, then the Inca's northern capital and, today, the capital city of Ecuador. This was the route that David and I planned to follow. David, I should add, was not only far younger than I but something of a student of Andean history.

We actually began the journey further south than Cuzco, tracking the southerly extension of the road from Bolivia northward, using rail and road transport where it followed the route and circuiting the reed-bordered shores of Lake Titicaca. We had spent a hot and humid week in Lima amassing large-scale military maps of our proposed line of march, effecting final research (one source of knowledge being Nick Ashestov, then Lima correspondent of the Daily Telegraph) and sightseeing in the Peruvian capital. The remains of its Spanish founder and Inca conqueror, Francisco Pizarro, still lay in a chapel of the twin-towered cathedral in the Plaza de Armas, for Lima feels itself to be a Spanish city and continues to honour the man who, legend has it, was suckled by a sow.

All who go to Peru find their way eventually to Cuzco. It breathes its Inca history as can nowhere else. Founded by Manco Capac it has become a shrine to the Incas, the place where the visitor can do the

A rural scene on the Royal Road

rounds of its museums and edifices. Almost every central street holds a remnant of Incaic wall that has managed to survive the centuries, the climax being the amazing structures – a third of a mile long – that is the fortress called Sacsahuaman built of monolithic blocks, some weighing up to a hundred tons, yet fitted together perfectly without benefit of the wheel or mortar. Other substantial remains lie in and around Cuzco including Ollantaytambo, Pisac and, of course, Machu Picchu, the famed "Lost City of the Incas", understandably Peru's chief tourist site. For all its Incaic glories Cuzco unaccountably neglects its founder's greatest accomplishment. A dirt track, which we were assured was the royal highway, crept out of the backside of the city wandering lamely towards a great panoply of mountains shining white in a warm sun. We followed it, shouldering our heavy and unwieldy rucksacks containing what we thought was the very minimum of survival gear and emergency fodder.

Two days' march had us at Limatambo. The village lay in the frigid shadow of Mount Satantay which hid the Inca temple and rest station of which little remains. Tahahuasi was once such a *tambo*, par excellence, the equivalent to a three-star motorway hotel, that formed part of a chain of rest stations of varying grades of comfort.

Though progressing at but a walking pace the geographical changes were discernible but we were still unprepared for the intense dryness as we neared the Apurimac river. Its bridge, of course, was that immortalised in Thornton Wilder's novel *The Bridge of San Luis Rey*, originally a hanging structure erected by the Incas from cables of braided straw over which many an Inca army poured as did the Spaniards in the other direction. We crossed on a modern steel structure within sight of the supports of the previous colonial one.

The subsequent landmark was Vilcas-huaman, the so-called "Sanctuary of the Hawk", a celebrated Inca town containing the only one of a thousand and more sun temples to survive almost in its entirety. We had some difficulty in locating it for the royal road in these parts was not an artery of clarity but our efforts were not wasted.

The temple was magnificent. A great truncated pyramid, it rose in tiers to a small terrace reached by a flight of cyclopean steps while the massive stone doorway which faces the plaza stood dignified and lonely. Framed by the foundations of ancient buildings the immense square offered a sombre sight, accentuated by an oppressive silence. Once twenty thousand Indians gave it a spectacle, a colour and a sound that reverberated through the Inca empire.

That the royal road runs through Huancayo is emphasised by its main street, Calle Real, which is actually part of it. The Lord Inca once rode in triumph through the town on a golden litter, preceded by heralds and musicians and attended by Virgins of the Sun who strewed the road with flowers. Today few luminaries visit a town that holds little opulence.

Lake Junin is Peru's second largest lake. Adjoining it an obelisk marked the battlefield where the Peruvians under Bolivar defeated the Spaniards in 1824. The surroundings were bleak but, beyond, was Bonbon, once an Inca command post, and the river that drains Junin led us there across the flat Pampa de Junin, criss-crossed by foot-tracks and laced with ditches half-hidden beneath thick tufts of sharp grass.

Bonbon itself was no more than a scattering of stones but it marked the start of a hundred-mile section of royal road, plainly visible, that accompanied us on a three-day march initially to Yanahuanca. Here we camped on somebody's veranda and restocked with provisions since no further urban centres appeared on our maps for many miles.

The Yanahuanca river bubbled through a ravine along the side of which the road had been cut. The road itself was not only emphatically in evidence but was doing duty as a farm track and confined within recently-constructed walls. At the hamlet of Huarautambo we spent a couple of nights at the simple abode of the Spanish-speaking schoolmaster, Valentine Inge, who took us to see a cave-tomb carpeted by human skulls and bones over which we crunched. The tomb had only recently been discovered and was not of Incaic origin though the nearby *tampu* most definitely was. Our meals with Valentine consisted of potato with a little *charqui* (sun-dried meat) moistened by one of our package soups and during the first we were advised of an expected pack-horse convoy going our way that could be persuaded to carry us and our rucksacks. The weight of our loads was becoming unbearable and, with the imminent approach of very much more difficult terrain, would be beyond our physical capacity.

While in Huarautambo we came into the scheming orbit of one Jose, whose sole interest in life revolved around gold and the acquiring of it. He thought he knew where a cache of the stuff lay buried, the problem being that his superstitious nature forbade him to dig for it. But for gringos – unbelievers – it was different. Jose was as wily as he looked, a mean-faced little man with a shifty manner – but a persuasive one. Thus before dawn next day he had us out of our sleeping bags; the three of us, armed with two long-handled spades, proceeding in darkness to the base of an escarpment and a small marker cairn of stones. We dug for more than an hour but, as expected, found nothing so slunk back from whence we had come having risked the wrath of ignorant villagers whose obsession with gold, hidden by the Incas, led to greed, petty jealousies and, in extreme cases, murder.

The third day the convoy arrived. Our rucksacks were loaded, adding to bulging sacks of potatoes that formed the cargo of a fleet of skinny horses. Only the convoy leader, a cana-swigging, ill-tempered Peruvian called Ron, was permitted to ride, the rest of us lesser mortals, including a woman, walked, David and I deferentially in the rear. One of the men was a dab hand with a whip which he intermittently cracked across the horse's backs with a noise that echoed between the valley walls through which we wound our way.

For mile after mile the royal road never let up. Fording ice-cold rivers, stumbling up Inca-constructed steps where high ridges had to be surmounted, and avoiding loosened flag-stones laid across areas of bog, we followed it. At nightfall we made camp, the stoic bowler-hatted woman making fires out of handfuls of dry grass over which her menfolk's stew was heated in a blackened cooking pot. She never spoke; her wrinkled Indian features never changed their resigned expression as she went about her tasks. None of our companions was exactly brimming over with the joy of life which, perhaps, is understandable in the circumstances in which they probably existed. As we lay in our sleeping bags directly under the stars David and I slept little, envisaging the distinct possibility of being robbed and having our throats cut into the bargain. Just occasionally Ron had shown a spark of bonhomie, insisting we partake of mouthfuls of his fire-water; refusal unleashing spasms of anger and a threatening display of weaponry.

Oro, the word for gold was pointedly aimed at us once more while passing a complex of caverns, their mouths half-buried in the ground. Ron dismounted and announced that oro was to be found here and, of course, David and I had to dig for it while the others looked on. But again in vain and Ron vent his frustration by swigging more cana from a seemingly never-empty flagon. Though it meant a return to shouldering our rucksacks we were not sorry to pay off our fractious companions and continue on our own along a still clearly-defined highway that kept changing its surface consistency to suit the terrain.

I suppose we must have covered some thirty miles from Huarautambo with our convoy though it was not so much the distance or the irregularity of the route that affected us as the fact of not being able to undertake it at our own pace. And in the rarefied atmosphere of an altitude that hovered around eleven thousand feet this was a major consideration.

And it was all too likely to be a continuous disadvantage of travelling in the company of the locals since Andean Peruvians have greater lung-power than low-altitude Britons. The best solution lay in the possibility offered by the acquisition of a pack animal – either on purchase or loan – though, with the potato-gathering season in full swing, the likelihood of purchase appeared slight, particularly for the sort of money we could raise. Simple hire, therefore, offered the only alternative though this would entail the services of an accompanying horseman over whom we would, at least, have some control.

A heavy frost sheathed our bivouac in clusters of diamonds that flashed and twinkled in the early morning sun. In spite of the intense cold the tremendous sight of the Cordillera Huayhuash range lured us out of bed to watch a procession of clouds like flocks of sheep climb up the ravines between the peaks behind which streaks of sapphire were appearing. We performed the very minimum of ablutions from a water hole that also served as a source of drinking water. Breakfast was baked potatoes we had managed to procure from one of Ron's bulging sacks.

Our campsite for the night had been close to a village that our map indicated to be Gashapampa, a motley collection of mud and wattle hovels. The immediate goal was the Inca ruin of Tunsacancha approximately eight miles ahead. Here David wanted to investigate the remains of another *tampu* and former Inca habitation.

Passing through the village our progress was watched by two youths who plainly beheld a source of income out of our stumbling gait for they pursued us and offered to carry our loads to the next habitation. A deal was struck and our cargo distributed to four backs instead of two.

These bearers too hardly inspired our trust. They were equally shifty-eyed and carried sheath-knives which they toyed with lovingly as they walked. One of them, in a combination of Quechuan and Spanish, asked if we carried pistols and I was about to shake my head when David, faster on the uptake, nodded and patted a bulging pocket in which reposed a battered copy of the South American Handbook.

We had been warned in Cuzco of the dangers of terrorist gangs – the embryo Sendero Luminoso, or Shining Path guerrilla movement – that were alleged to have bases in the remote villages through which our route was likely to pass, but we had not taken this too seriously.

A line of quinel trees, rare at this altitude, gave us the first glimpse of vegetation since we had started to climb in earnest a week earlier. The trees were windswept and spindly but any tree in a desolation of grassland and rock made a comforting sight. The royal road, broad and clear, offered easier walking though, again, the necessity of keeping up with our porters exhausted us and by the time we reached the single farmhouse that seemed to constitute a hamlet which might have been Gasacucho our legs felt like rubber.

The *tampo* of Tunsacancha is not of great drama to the layman of the likes of myself but its ruins wore a jaunty air and were set where two valleys met. David roamed the old stones for hours necessitating an early pitching of the tent well before dusk since it was hardly worth going further that day, a set of circumstances that paid a handsome dividend. The householder of the farm, learning of our proximity, invited us to purchase some fresh meat from a recently-killed sheep. This, it was arranged, would be cooked for us that evening.

Presenting ourselves at the house at the appointed hour we were shown into a communal room that served as kitchen, bedroom and slaughterhouse occupied by a woman, eight men and a bevy of nose-running children. In their boisterous company we experienced a veritable banquet, the memory of which we would carry for weeks to come.

The meal commenced with sweet manzanilla "tea" and a round of potatoes roasted in their jackets. The notion arose that this was to take the edge off our appetites so that we would not eat our full entitlement of meat and, indeed, this was probably the case. By the time the "meat course" came it was too dark to perceive from which section of the sheep's anatomy it originated but hunger precludes fastidiousness. We ate with our fingers, the fat dripping from our jowls, the darkness hiding the blemishes of dirt and unhygienic handling. Around our legs guinea-pigs lunged for the odd dropped fragment.

Before returning to the tent we negotiated the hire of a packhorse and minder for our onward day's journey and retired to bed in a contented mood hardly reduced by the patter of rain on the fly sheet. Alas, the dry hacking cough I had developed some days earlier was to have me in paroxysms of choking which became most wearing for the both of us. This had followed a spell when I had gone down with altitude sickness, an affliction that can only be alleviated by a solid forty eight hours of complete rest. David was to be struck down similarly in the days to come but, in the meantime, his cross to bear was a painful rash on the back of his hands followed by a bout of fever he diagnosed as hepatitis.

Dawn was a depressing one with low clouds spitting rain and hiding the brows of the low hills. Our spirits, so high the previous evening, sank into our damp boots as we plodded dismally behind the horse which looked equally miserable as, indeed,. did its accompanying youth. Our morning wash had been taken in a near-freezing stream and was more promise than lick.

The royal road wandered along through broad sweeping valleys of grass and swamp. The stream we followed widened and had to be crossed at intervals while the swamp forced us into detours that, for a while, lost us the route of the road. Large ugly birds soared overhead. They were not condors and were probably buzzards but, to me in my depression, they were vultures.

By midday the sun had poked bright fingers through the stained cotton wool of the clouds to cheer us up as we approached the Banos valley together with plots of cultivated land and crops. We halted to watch a team of peasants hand-ploughing a meadow, working in unison to turn the soil in swift, methodical movements before our presence distracted them.

It was at a point several miles beyond Banos that the royal road finally dropped into another valley, doing so by way of a series of finely-cut stairways, wide and regal. The road remains a thoroughfare to this day, marching across the countryside in arrogant fashion, the only substantial man-made object around. At the bottom of the valley the river Nupe, fast-flowing and deep, barred the way, with no sign of an Inca or any other bridge. Eventually we tracked down a modern timber construction a couple of miles upstream, directly beneath the hillside village of Pilcocancha and made our way towards it, dismissing and paying off our two- and four-legged companions. Barely had we gained the centre when the heavens opened to send us hastening for shelter in the local bakery.

The prospect of another wet night prompted us to accept the invitation to spend it in what the baker termed a "spare room". This turned out to be a bare store with a filthy floor that contained a counter and a shelf of empty lemonade bottles. Ensconced with our baggage in this dreary lodging we were pointedly locked in following a frugal supper of stale rolls and a tin of herrings. Our host turned out to be yet another unsavoury character who reeked of rum and he not only charged us for the room and his stale rolls but also for our own herrings of which he showed himself to be particularly partial.

The night was a dismal one; the windowless chamber stank of urine including our own, the only receptacle for which were the empty bottles on the shelf. Between us we filled more than half a dozen during a night spent trying not to roll off the counter-top onto the filthy floor.

Being windowless the room remained in darkness at daybreak and so we were still abed when the door was unlocked to admit not only the baker but a group of customers. Swept off our counter in the rush we attempted to dress as best we could and collect our scattered belongings amongst a score of customers-turned-gringo-watchers. We left hurriedly, suddenly aware that the bottles we had been using as urinals were being distributed for less utilitarian purposes.

Buying eggs from an emporium in a side street we boiled them on our Primus stove, a magical piece of equipment that, of course, drew hordes of new onlookers, many of whom appeared to be high on rum even at so early an hour. So that's what the bottles were for! But with the stuff cheap by any standards I could appreciate that living out a life in such poverty, in damp houses and on a diet of potato and stale bread would be dismal enough to turn the staunchest teetotaller to the bottle.

Our negotiations for onward baggage-carrying facilities came to nought so we retraced our steps to Banos. "Banos" means "Bath" and the prospect of immersion in hot water took on a distinctly ethereal hue. And since Banos consisted of no more than a series of natural warm springs emptying into Inca-sculptured stone baths locating them was not difficult. Our multi-hour soak in ever-flowing, constantly warm water made an idyllic interlude.

Thereafter, for us, water became less of an attraction as incessant rain became a nightly event and, more often than not, a daily one too. As we neared the township of La Union we gained another horse and minder to help with our loads. Initially they were a grumpy pair, but the latter, on longer acquaintance, turned out to be a pleasant old man, his weather-beaten face alive with character. When it wasn't raining the lowering clouds accentuated the threat but the storm that finally hit us as we descended an escarpment came without warning. A junction had deflected us from the royal road which swung away from La Union to cross the Pampa Huanuco to the Vizcarra valley ten kilometres west of the town. At the onset of the first drops of rain we should undoubtedly have taken the old man's advice and sheltered under the eaves of a shepherd's hut. But La Union was, we wrongly estimated, only nine kilometres ahead and its imagined bright lights and culinary expertise beckoned.

What fell out of the sky as we hurried on was more, much more, than a mere downpour. It was a prolonged cascade, virtually a solid sheet of water that soaked us within seconds. The temperature plummeted to zero and the track became inches deep in liquid mud.

The way wound down into a culvert and night merged with the angry black storm clouds. The river, when we came to it, was hidden in darkness. From a hundred yards on the old man shouted something, mounted his horse, and disappeared, and when next we perceived him he was on the opposite bank. To reach it he must have waded the river at some point and for a moment we imagined he was abandoning us.

The river was the Guytuc, normally no more than a substantial brook when not a dried-up water course. Now, swollen by heavy rain, it had become a raging torrent. Apprehensively we removed our boots, tied the laces together and hung them round our necks, then entered the ice-cold stream. In an instant the water level reached our thighs pulling at our taut legs and threatening to topple us into the sullen depths. I took a cautious step, lost my balance and floundered into deep water. Out of my depth, I threshed wildly and was dragged forward by a vicious current, my boots swinging against my face. I heard David shout but ignored it. The dark outline of the opposite bank showed close so I lunged for it, grabbed some foliage, lost my hold, tried again, and scrambled on all fours up a slippery shore. Light-headed with relief I turned to help David but he too was safely across the maelstrom.

Our shouts brought back the old man, now leading his horse. He waited, mumbling to himself, as we struggled back into our wet boots. "Keep moving! keep moving!" I kept repeating, for the numbing inertia of exposure was paralysing my limbs. Plainly neither of us was in a fit state to reach La Union that night but we had no alternative but to stagger on to keep hypothermia at bay.

Then, miraculously, the dark outline of a farmhouse showed before us, our arrival drawing people from the shadows. Upon learning of our plight the good household swiftly went to work in the rudimentary kitchen to produce a hot meal while an elderly man helped us spread dry hay on the ground beneath a lean-to roof that partly covered a small courtyard. We peeled off our soaking clothes replacing them with items that were merely wet. The stew of potato, vegetable and macaroni with manzanilla tea was disposed of in record time to the accomplishment of our heartfelt expressions of appreciation. Optimistically we hung out our wet garments before settling down in none-too-dry sleeping bags liberally encased in stale hay. A litter of pigs, some hens and a dog found their way onto our beds at different times during the night but their warm-blooded presence was welcome and sleep came easily.

A brilliant sun opened our eyes and within the hour we were progressing across a broad open plain, the Pampa Huanuco, stretching in all directions with but a blur of hills on the horizon. Another hour brought us to the edge of a sharp descent leading into the Vizcarra valley; here more a gorge than a valley. An excruciating path of jagged stones brought us into La Union where our ravenous appetites led us to the nearest restaurant. It was an unsavoury place and the choice of food limited, but six fried eggs each made a satisfactory start to breakfast after which we paid off our companion before returning for more. The old man had enjoyed his breakfast as much as we had and our parting was warm. We had ignored his advice and paid the price but he bore no grudge.

Leaving the restaurant we went in search of a hotel intent upon a taste of the soft life.

La Union, let it be said, is no metropolis. The little town, divided by the river Vizcarra, was drab, lifeless and smelt of boiled cabbage. We spent three days there, however, after which we ran out of restaurants and the rats had become too intimate for comfort in the hovel of a hotel. On the second day we retraced our steps, making an excursion to the Inca ruins of Huanuco Viejo which we had by-passed on our way to the town.

And what the Inca had constructed in the middle of the open grassland is truly magnificent. A huge fort-like edifice or *isnu* stood intact, its massive walls – like those of Sacsahuaman – a marvel of construction. From the parapet the whole complex was spread out before us, each building in a very fair state of preservation since, without interference from subsequent house-, dam- or bridge-builders purloining its stones, the finely-assembled walls had only the elements to withstand. We wandered for hours among the substantial remains of old temples, storehouses, barracks and dwelling houses marvelling at the grandeur of the stone arches and staircases. With us were the ghosts of Incaic soldiers, priests and the multitude of citizens who once inhabited this lonely, spectacular place.

Horseless, we left La Union intent upon picking up the means of onward baggage-carrying at the point in the valley where the royal road crossed it some ten kilometres north. Our next objective was the township of Huari which we calculated as about a hundred and forty kilometres distant or five, maybe six, days of walking.

And Lady Luck was with us for she produced Manuel. He displayed the flattened features and coloured face of the Red Indian though his slanting eyes gave him an eastern appearance. He had turned up out of the blue together with a horse and expressed his willingness to accompany us as he intended covering part of our route anyway.

With him we were on the road by midday. The climb out of the valley was steep, but the new horse was the healthiest specimen that we had seen to date; so much so that Manuel was forced to rein it back when we showed signs of lagging. By evening we had reached some scattered adobe dwellings that rejoiced in the name of Chogolagran. It stood at the head of yet another valley, this one that of the river Taparaco, a tributary of the Vizcarra.

It became apparent that Manuel was a regular commuter of this route and, accordingly, had contacts at various points along it. Those in Chogolagran were a farmer family who offered us their roof but, with five children as well as their livestock under it, we felt that we would be straining their resources by accepting. The tent, accordingly, again became our shelter for the night but our supper of sardines and bread was supplemented by soup and potatoes which Manuel and the family pressed upon us. The family were born of a younger generation than Manuel; there was nothing eastern about the young father replete in jeans, black shirt and black trilby while his wife looked older but probably wasn't. Their children sat in a row watching our strange cooking operations, their heads cocked on one side like mystified puppies.

We left early and were on the hoof hardly had dawn tinged the sky. The royal road closed in towards the narrow river leading us easily along the western flank of the valley. The hamlets of Estanque and San Lorenzo de Isco produced their quota of inquisitive citizens plus a garish cemetery, oddly out of place in so poverty-stricken surroundings. At San Lorenzo a friend of Manuel appeared with what I thought was a welcome mug of water but which turned out to be some home-brewed fire-water to provide an eye-watering aperitif for a frugal lunch.

The road, well-defined and engineered, took full advantage of the contours of the land and seldom was it forced to deviate from the level it first selected when entering the valley. Here the great road of conquest had no need to be guessed at. We were walking over low hills, treeless and bare, the wind blowing in unobstructed from the Amazon jungles to set the *ichu* grass in motion. As we marched we spoke of the epic of this rural highway's construction for only by staggering human effort and endurance could it have been built.

By late afternoon, weary but jubilant, we reached a scattering of hutments called by a name – Taparaco, after the river – where a relic of some earlier civilisation was alleged to stand. If so we never found it. But ahead lay the *tampu* of Torococha, some twenty kilometres distant, this one a relic of Inca durability.

Close, but not too close, to the wretched houses we bedded down, tentless, in a mound of last year's hay, strong-smelling, slightly putrid and very prickly. Even here we were invited to share in the evening meal composed almost entirely of the ubiquitous potato provided by a childless couple to whom Manuel seemed to be related. The woman wore plaited hair which she modelled into a castle-like structure upon her head; not at all the usual Indian hair-style of single or twin pigtails swinging free. The man constantly chewed coca that produced a most colourful spit.

Two days of fine weather gave way, on the third, to ominous clouds but no rain fell. We were on the right bank of the river and, by midday, came to a marshy patch of land that had us dodging about between rocks and dry tufts of *ichu* attempting to keep our feet out of water. We had swung away from the river but the swamp caught us in its slimy maw whatever direction we took. Manuel told us that we were between two lakes atop of each wall of the valley and that the swamp was a result of their overflow. We found a decrepit building but its stones were certainly not Incaic, even to my inexperienced eyes. Any further investigation was discouraged by the depressing swamp and I wondered why anyone should choose to build anything at so moist and inhospitable a spot.

I did not have to wonder for long. Further up the valley were definite signs of road drainage stone formations of obvious Inca origin. No doubt, at some earlier stage, the whole area had been devoid of this morass of liquid mud. The ruin that could only have been that of a *tampu* stood, away from the village, dauntingly exposed to the cyclonic winds. It was a square block of a building of substantial stone and without windows. Even David could find no reason for dallying there for more than ten minutes.

The end of the swamp brought a steady climb out of the valley and, somewhere, we left behind our river which must have risen at the behest of the twin lakes. Came the parting of the ways around mid-afternoon, with Manuel bound for a hamlet called Manca Peque a mile off to the right on a slope overlooking more marshy ground. He suggested we accompany him there to spend the night while, additionally, he would use his good offices to arrange for a replacement horse. This seemed a sensible course of action so we assented.

A lonelier habitation I have yet to see with everlasting hills bucking away in every direction and not even the drama of a true mountain to quicken the pulse. The night meant a return to the tent and, of course, a diet of potatoes this time moistened with our own uninspiring packet soup. All too plainly, the sad remote people of Manca Peque existed at near-starvation level, their pinched faces and suspicious eyes devoid of humour and the milk of human kindness. Manuel himself was obviously unhappy at our reception and I wondered what reasons brought him here but didn't like to ask. A clutch of ragged children, to whom we offered some picture postcards brought along for the purpose, had to be urged to accept them; not the vestige of a smile flitted across their solemn features as they gravely made off with their prize.

Manuel was as good as his word and procured both a horse and a youth to accompany us. The boy, unused to the sly bargaining of his more money-conscious brethren, was content to let Manuel fix the price while Manuel himself charged us only a one-way fee.

Once more we left bright and early. Socially the lad was not a patch on Manuel though he was willing enough. Communication was difficult as he spoke only Quechuan while Manuel had possessed a few words of Spanish. The horse was part-mule and the pace was steady as we walked in near-silence at an altitude of about thirteen thousand feet, the route firmly sticking to the 4,200 and 4,000 metre contours.

It became noticeable that, as we progressed northward, village dwellings increasingly exhibited more substantial construction that incorporated worked stone taken from ancient ruins and, possibly, the royal road. Most were roofed with grass thatch but the living conditions in these hovels were still surely worse than those of the time of the Inca since, in many cases, entire households slept in one room and generally in one bed made of untanned cattle hides.

A larger village below some great bastions of rock became the end of the marked "Camino Incaico", the route of the royal road, as shown on the map. From henceforth onwards our eyes and gleaned local knowledge alone would have to show the way. The name of the large village was, as we expected, Huancayoc, but it was good to see the fact confirmed. Where the old road terminated and the modern track commenced we never learnt for the transfer was a gradual process and we had to accept that they were one and the same. Huancayoc was, by past standards, a centre of some prosperity for it possessed a couple of shops and our potato lunch was supported by biscuits that might well have been a leftover from a Spanish soldier's haversack to judge from their antiquity.

If the bigger village indicated a return to civilisation the environment showed otherwise. It fast became more difficult and devious while rock outcrops, steep and black, pushed us from one minuscule hamlet to another. People and houses appeared with increasing frequency, it is true, and David was forever enquiring in his demanding, no-nonsense voice for the whereabouts of the Inca road. The replies we got from the locals were baffling. Invariably we were given an affirmative; that we were on the right road, corroborated with much head-nodding but we were well aware this might mean nothing. Gradually, however, we evolved a system by which we could gauge the sincerity of an answer or just the simple desire to please us.

A leaden sky and an icy wind kept us walking hard for warmth. That night we camped on a patch of ground out of range of any village. A swiftly-moving stream offered a water supply and another contribution unleashed itself from above. The thunderstorm that struck during the night hit us soon after we had heated our ubiquitous soup.

We persuaded the lad to join us in the tent rather than rely on the doubtful waterproof qualities of his woollen poncho. This made a tight squeeze but ensured we remained warm and reasonably dry while the thunder rolled among the hills and lightning licked the wet rocks with throngs of fire. Rain hissed down, forcing its way through the nylon of the tent, to finally cease with uncanny abruptness. We lay uneasily listening to the drips.

A morning's walk brought us down from the hills past immense boulders hoary with spongy moss and sections of eroded rock fallen from sheer sections of cliff as if sliced by a giant cheesecutter. The descent led to the village of Pomachaca at the bottom of a three-way ravine where two angry rivers met head on to continue their flow as one. David was delighted when his feverish enquiries elicited the fact that, certainly the royal road honoured Pomachaca with its presence, and a villager pointed out the escarpment down which we had come adding that there was now a real road to Huari. He was referring, of course, to the dusty street that bore the corrugated imprints of tyre tracks.

A patchwork of cultivation mottled the fertile green valley of the Huari river we now followed and the open landscape beyond made a cheerful consort after the recent geographical hostility. To the east the gigantic mountain complex of the Cordillera Blanca occasionally offered a tantalising glimpse of its highest peaks, evocative with snow and altitude.

Huari is half the size of La Union but its position overlooking the Alpine-like valley was a joy. Impatient to continue on the move and delighted by the improvement in our fortunes and progress we had no thoughts of a prolonged stay. Ahead lay another hurdle in the obstacle course of the Andes and, though we had a broken banister of the royal road, it was all too likely that, added to the exertions of walking it, would be the exasperations of trying to find it.

Like the routine of living the pattern of our journey emerged and became itself a routine. Stumbling endlessly along rough tracks behind a plodding horse led by a succession of characters from the tediously cheerful to the depressingly morose our spirits rose and fell accordingly. Rain squalls drenched us, wind scoured our faces, sun drew sweat from our bodies and the bitter mountain cold lay in wait at every nightfall. Our days were not measured in hours but by occurrences that became low spots or high spots in the tedium of fatigue and, occasionally, despair.

A high spot usually evolved from an evening descent from a mountain track for a night amongst the tiniest kraal of houses, the simplest community. This was not so much in abeyance to a craving for the amenities of urban living as to a longing for the company of fellow humans. Though neither of would admit it, we desperately needed this antidote to a loneliness which, in the remoteness of the northern Peruvian Andes, has one by the throat.

But we had not completely ignored the warning of a danger that lurked among such isolated communities. "Steer clear of bands of armed horsemen", we had been advised. "They are not to be trusted and if they think you might report their presence they wouldn't hesitate to dispose of you." That a guerrilla organisation lurked in these spectacular and intensely beautiful surroundings seemed unreal.

Huari was a high spot for it offered a solid "biftec" for our bellies and an earthen roof over our heads. Our "bedroom" was no more than the dirty floor of a three-table restaurant but, while there, we became temporary members of the large, cheerful family who, unstintingly, shared with us the treasure of their companionship.

Prolonged stays in such centres were resisted, for, as La Union had shown, their attractions quickly pall. It was from Huari, however, that we made an excursion; a detour on wheels, to Chavin de Huantar off the royal road but a centre made historic by an earlier culture.

We got there aboard a grossly-overloaded lorry, squatting in the buck clutching our belongings so that they would take up less space amongst the assortment of other passengers and cargo. The road was excruciating, an engineer's nightmare of wrongly-cambered bends and a neglected surface though the scenery was awe-inspiring. We corkscrewed up one side of a pass and, near the top, found a mountain barring the way through which a quite respectable concrete tunnel had been expensively bored. Its dripping darkness might have been an omen for the storm that struck as we emerged the other side but, if so, we were slow on the uptake. Huddled, compacted together under a few square metres of torn canvas, we were thankful for the soft, yielding paper sacks beneath us until swiftly-multiplying rents in them revealed their contents to be lard. As we wound slowly into the Mosna valley, semi-drenched by rivulets of water through the leaking canvas and greasy from fatty lard oozing from the damaged sacks, I was reminded that walking had its compensations. And it was not as if the ride was free. In the mountain districts of Peru any vehicle serves as a public transport conveyance with fares to match the calibre of comfort. Gringos are, of course, fair game for cash-conscious drivers and tariffs rise with the fairness of one's skin.

There are many pre-Inca cultures; it is recorded that for two thousand years prior to the Inca there was in Peru a long steady cultural growth but few facts have emerged from the chronicles of time. There are no dated coins such as the Romans conveniently left to posterity; even the Incas had no money, but there is evidence that man was involved with weaving and agriculture as early as 1000 BC. But the first culture of prominence to have been unearthed – literally – is that of Chavin, its leitmotif a ferocious-looking cat god found on pottery and stonework. Here at Chavin de Huantar was the heart of this civilisation and, today, the dusty remains of impressive buildings characterised by well-laid stone walls decorated with stone-carved human and animal (mostly cat) heads have been exposed for all to see.

David was taken ill with stomach cramp during our morning's investigations of the dark tunnels and silent chambers still but partly excavated so, repeatedly, had to return to the comforting sunlight for air. With both our torches lost we had to rely on a limited supply of matches for our advances along the dismal labyrinths and catacombs beneath the site and at each bend the tiny flickering flame revealed a leering cat's head with an abruptness that had us suffering near heart-failure.

As expected the shabby township of Chavin held a minimum of attractions. All afternoon we waited in vain for conveyance back to Huari so were forced to spend a night on the floor of the police station that appeared to double as the local doss-house. Finally, crammed in the back of a Datsun van with two substantial ladies sitting on our feet, we made it.

The fertile valley that accompanied us out of Huari was well-populated with both people and horses. The royal road ran along the right flank of it but at Yanapubouio we were channelled onto the present-day artery where it crossed from one valley to the next. Our subsequent horse and its minder hailed from a Huari farm and the young man considered the three-day trek to San Luis to be not beyond his capabilities. The night's camp was by the lake of Huachococha, beneath the mountain peak of the same name, a most inspirational setting in complete contrast to the odorous cell of the previous evening though we were thankful for even that.

The sheer ruggedness of the terrain further emphasised the extent of the Incas' achievements for it seemed incredible that any communication system with the means available to them could ever have been established with sufficient efficiency to control and administer so huge an empire. But the system of roads was not just for the purpose of the passage of armies or, indeed, that of the Lord Inca, his retinue, officials and traders. With their establishment lay the means of effective communication so vital to a regime that lived by war and conquest. Since the swift transmission of messages was of paramount importance and the distances over which they had to be passed so enormous, a courier method called *chasqui* was developed. It was not new; the Romans relied on relays of horse-riders, but the *chasquis* could run in relays to better effect than their mounted Roman counterparts.

Impossible though it may appear, records show that the *chasquis* could cover the 1,250 miles between Cuzco and Quito at altitudes ranging from 6,000 to 17,000 feet in five days! This meant that runners had to run an average of some 250 miles a day which was very considerably faster than the Roman couriers on their metalled roads.

For us the end of a day of severe plodding brought its rewards with the knowledge that for a few blessed hours one's feet could remain motionless. Plainly I was not *chasqui* material even had I the lungs to defeat the demands of altitude. The wear and tear of the passing weeks might have been having its physical effects but, at the same time, it was honing David and I into a team; oft working with irritation, but working. We now knew the ropes and undertook our small tasks and chores in support of our daily existence and survival amongst one of the most terrifying domains in the world. And here, near Huachococha, came the close of yet another day exhaustingly filled. We were asleep before a single star pierced the heavens.

Aldo – as we came to call our latest companion – had not been reluctant to invite himself into the tight confines of the tent or to share our frugal fare. He was the most talkative of henchmen and would blather on in an unmelodious mixture of Quechuan and Spanish. He was, however, full of rural wit and confidence, a humorous figure in his baggy trousers, short white Cordova jacket and black poncho together with a battered straw sombrero. In the morning it was he who had us out of our sleeping bags at an ungodly hour with much chivvying and demonstrations of impatience to be off. There was a long day ahead, he would warn, and most of it uphill. They all were and it always was.

The present valley we were following widened into a featureless plateau and the carcasses of sheep and goats littered the grass in unexplained profusion. Most had been reduced to skeletons by the attentions of condors so that only the weathered hooves remained to indicate their origins. We climbed steadily, traversing the broad side of a convex slope, with the horizon in front of us ever receding as if intentionally denying us access to the skyline.

Quite suddenly we gained the top. We stood on the very crest of the pass with the whole cordillera becoming the landscape towards which the still higher passes lay in wait. The air was remarkable for its clarity and the magnificence of the view tempted us to pause awhile until the cold drove us on.

It was hard to fathom the path ahead. At our feet was a precipice below which, a seemingly infinite distance away, we could see the foam-flecked course of a sizeable river of melted snow. Unquestionably we followed Aldo, leading his horse, along the ridge towards a point where the precipice gave way to a forty-five degree slope.

While he halted to adjust the animal's load, David and I set off on our own, anxious to escape the cold of the wind-swept ridge and because the path manifested itself on a downward gradient. The descent was painful. Though we traversed the incline in the professional manner we found ourselves skidding and slipping alarmingly, starting minor avalanches of stones that rattled down the slope.

We were almost at the bottom, breathless and aching, our boots full of pebbles, our eyes full of dust, when we looked back. There behind us, but away over to our right, Aldo and horse were comfortably negotiating the hump of a spur which provided a natural and well-graduated line of descent to the river. With the realisation of how disagreeable and unnecessary our descent had been came a reflection upon the folly of hiring guides and then not letting them guide us. Eventually we were reunited on the river bank which we followed for a few miles until it sheered away towards a point of the compass not on our set alignment.

Next day, firmly behind Aldo, we made better progress along a line of switchback hills and a route that our man plainly knew well though, for most of it, there was no sign of a path. But we had chosen the shortest distance between Huari and San Luis, of that there was little doubt, so we could but presume that the royal road too had made the same choice of course. By early evening the habitations of San Luis showed up in the lengthening shadows of the surrounding heights and a small road materialised from nowhere to lead us by well-cultivated smallholdings into the little town.

Almost at once we were taken in hand by a stalwart of the local constabulary. It was as if Aldo had been in league with the law but, on reflection, I think not. More likely it was our appearance that activated the fresh-faced patrolman of the Guarda Civil. The entry into town of two extremely dirty foreign devils offered the moral obligation of apprehension. Watched by a gaping crowd of citizens we were marched to police headquarters, our escort dramatically fondling his Smith & Weston .38 in its holster. Once inside the door, however, the show of authority was replaced by extreme overtures of friendship and the plain longing for a chat. The unfortunate youngster, it transpired, had only recently been moved from Lima for a two-year stint in the sticks of San Luis without his wife and so was, unashamedly, homesick.

Thus, once more, our "hotel" for the night turned out to be the local nick though, on this occasion, the reasoning was pure compassion – for our host as much as us. For what remained of the day, our baggage safely stowed in an empty cell, we became the constable's guests and were pressed to endless glasses of beer and a meal at the local pub. No more than a large village, San Luis lay in the shadow of the great snow peak of 19,000 foot Nydo Huandoy, a sobering sight with the sunset ablaze behind it.

Before we turned in – on the floor of course, but a clean one of the guardroom – we made the acquaintance of our host's superior, the chief of police of San Luis. It was in fact that worthy's home-made cream cheese – a local speciality – we had been fast consuming to help down a night-cap of a fiery liquid that followed the beer. Not the least put out the officer invited us to have breakfast at his home next morning.

Speaking for myself, the night was not as restful as it could have been for not only did David and the policeman snore at varying pitches but a prisoner in the cell below was given to hawking to an extent I never thought possible in a human. But the breakfast, consisting of a whole bull's heart with tomatoes and chips, in the company of the inspector and his buxom wife made amends.

In such circumstances as these the acquisition of horsepower was no problem. The meal consumed, appreciation shown and farewells effected we departed from San Luis with some reluctance but with a game little Patagonian mare and a would-be cowboy in tow. If both had been pressed into service on the express orders of the Peruvian Police Force no resentment showed.

Our researches had indicated that the royal road passed close to the town of Piscobamba, our next landmark, some two days hence. The track grew smaller and rougher and though Ricardo, our new colleague, insisted it was the old Inca route, we were far from convinced. At Yanama township, to which the track led, we met an American agricultural technician and a group of Peruvians unloading furniture from a lorry. We offered a hand thus earning ourselves a beer, or to be more accurate, a whole succession of beers in one of those midget shops that sold everything from transistor radios to hairpins. By dusk everyone was too far gone to know how to start the lorry let alone drive it, so we all slept in the buck amongst bags of cement which I don't recommend as a mattress or pillow. The lorry was destined for Piscobamba where the American had his quarters and we were sorely tempted to accept his offer of a lift. Firm in our rejection we said that we would see him there a day later.

In the event it was another two for, in meandering about attempting to locate definite signs of Inca origins we wasted precious time and increased the mileage among a confusion of low hills and rivers. We camped the second night in a gorge-like cleft through which the Piscobamba river ran and by the third were within sight of the township. At the first house our quadruped and its owner left us, the latter clearly bemused by our indecisive wanderings

Piscobamba's construction would hardly win a prize in a town-planning competition. Built in the standard Andean urban mould of a row of buildings grouped round a central plaza, the square in this case was an affair of ugly concrete, cracked and flaking.

In the patio of someone's house we cooked our midday meal by invitation thus having to share it with its multiple occupants. Released from these activities we went in search of our American friend, running him to earth in his office-flat, the cold bare place of a bachelor's pad. With his help, we raised our porterage to Pomabamba, the neighbouring town on our itinerary. The royal road, we were assured, was on the east side of the valley astride the ridge of the first escarpment parallel to which we had been walking the last couple of days.

Another night in the now empty lorry and we gleefully escaped from Piscobamba, ascending a hill out of town to find a track that was muddier and rougher than the "main road" to Pomabamba. Our horseman pronounced us crazy from the very start and made it abundantly clear that he did not suffer fools gladly. He was an older man, reserved and spiky, who finally accepted what we were trying to do. So sparse were any Inca-like relics or indications of their highway that he had us doubting our own sanity at times though beyond the valley of the river Vitcabamoa, which forced the modern road into a long detour, we came upon the confirmation we were looking for. Not only did the track take on the authoritative aura possessed of any Inca artery but, here and there, showed the familiar bordering stone and, at one spot, the remains of a drainage system. A line of ruined forts excited our curiosity but these were plainly pre-Inca.

Close to one collapsed and over-grown ruin we set up camp; it was not to be one of our more successful sojourns. A downpour of rain extinguished the stove, our candle burnt a hole in the tent, "Old Grumpy", squeezing in with us, insisted on sleeping with his dirty feet in our faces and, finally, we lost the horse necessitating a morning spent searching the hillsides.

Replete with truant steed we came down from the wilds about midday drawn by the magnet that was Pomabamba but holding little hope of it being Valhalla. Nearing the town, I tripped over a stone, sprawled headlong, cut my leg and knocked myself out. The incident shook me up more than I realised and, with blood seeping into my boot, the lure of a night in Utopia had me in its grip once more.

Our subsequent rest and recuperation extended to three days such was the calibre of the good people and environment of Pomabamba. Yet again it was the police who provided us with accommodation; not a cell or guardroom this time but a guestroom equipped with two beds. Hardly Savoy standards perhaps but beds! We had almost forgotten such items existed. The little room adjoined the police station, the staff of which not only allowed us to use their ablutionary facilities but even provided an old woman to make our beds. But, again, it was the chief of police who became the real friend.

El Jefe introduced himself to us as we revelled in our new-found luxury. A middle-aged man with a neat moustache and greying hair he showed a keen interest in our journeyings. He spoke Spanish and invited us to dinner at his home on the outskirts of town. His wife could speak English, he told us with unrepressed pride, and would be happy to have the opportunity of airing a language she seldom found opportunity to use. In the meantime would we care for a hot bath and, if so, he would take us there now. We could hardly believe our ears.

Our last immersion in hot water had been weeks before in Banos and, providentially, Pomabamba was blessed with hot thermal springs likewise which ensured that every house in the town could raise piping hot water – even if it was the very devil to get hold of cold. Initially we thought the bath would be in the family home but were taken to the public baths in a depression just behind the town. The huge stone chambers were pre-sixteenth century though it would seem likely the Incas made use of them too, as do the present-day populace of Pomobamba. Wallowing happily like hippos at play in the big vats the grime of weeks peeled off our pink boiled bodies.

In the evening we accompanied El Jefe to his home encircled by massed ranks of fruit trees edged by an honour-guard of funeral lilies. Here we were introduced to a smiling lady, small, intelligent and vital, who straightaway launched into a monologue of English small-talk for all the world as if she was having the vicar to afternoon tea.

Dinner was a banquet by any standards. The main dish consisted of as many roasted guinea pigs as we could put down and, rich and indigestible as the meat is, we did ourselves proud. To drink was a hot concoction that had a cherry brandy base and for the dessert, great hunks of honeycomb fresh from the beehives we had seen at the bottom of the garden. Oranges and tangerines quenched a thirst generated by the cherry brandy and the honey.

We experienced some difficulty in finding our way back to our bedchamber, a state of affairs possibly not entirely due to the darkness. The beds were hard but not uncomfortable and we slept the sleep of the just – and the well-fed, ignoring the scurry of tiny feet beneath us.

Pomabamba town we discovered next morning to be of considerable charm, particularly so when measured against other townships we had encountered. And it was its attraction – human and architecturally-inspired – that held us there for so long. Its scanty shops offered a source of provision replenishment, the few restaurants were a cut above the average, while the little church provided a haven for an interlude of spiritual contemplation. Our last evening we were again invited to dinner by El Jefe, a repast rudely interrupted when he was called away to investigate a murder.

The incident again brought home to us the realisation of the dangers from fellow-humans. In this instance it was so-called "cattle rustlers" who had murdered an innocent bystander – possibly because they had thought the victim had witnessed their nefarious deeds. And the fact that the victim was a relative of our kind hosts made an even greater impact. Upon the police inspector's return the good man added his warnings to those we had already received. "Be careful when you are up there," he told us, jerking his head towards the darkness. I thought long and hard about the killers in the hills that night.

Our intentions were to leave the following morning and resume our escarpment route. The map showed Sihuas to be the subsequent township north of Pomabamba though, in spite of her considerable knowledge of Inca history, our hostess had been unable to pinpoint the actual course of the royal road sweeping by above her town. "It's up there somewhere – as you've discovered," was her only comment.

Her husband had obligingly arranged for horse transportation as far as Sihuas and, in the morning, introduced us to the new horseman prior to seeing us off from the plaza. Leaving Pomabamba was an undoubted wrench. For the first time on the journey I felt really sad to leave a town that had little enough to offer a traveller other than its kindness. With a strong horse and a burly farmer's lad in tow we returned to the silence of the mountains, climbing each false crest until we had attained the summit of the final ridge and were back onto what we took to be the route of the royal road. It welcomed us with a display of Incaic-shaped kerbstones edging the wide grass artery, a ghost expressway not evident as such unless you are specifically looking for it.

Fearful of losing it, David continued to ply questions concerning the route of all who passed by. Few even knew of the road, fewer still showed any interest – even if they understood what David was asking which they probably didn't. Children, away from the urban influences, replied not a word to our questions and, sometimes, women on their own shook their heads as if not wanting to understand and hurried away. A tiny village school produced a pock-marked schoolmistress of sterner stuff, however, who knew all about it and was as voluble with her information as her students were mute in their wide-eyed dumbness.

Between every contact we stumbled on. And here on the flanks of this beautiful valley, the clear air revealing the massive peaks beyond, all life was present. Wild flowers tangled in a riot of colour; peasants on the plots of cultivation below looked like toys as they tilled the soil behind toy buffaloes and, far away, carried by a soft breeze, came the shrilling of children's voices released from the paralysis of fright. Visions of a Swiss mountain path I had once walked kept superimposing itself on the verdant heights as the old road, fading and then faintly reappearing, strode on.

On the occasions it faded from view there were horse tracks to follow and, since no other way northward was conceivable for either road or path, we had no hesitation about using them. Each was hemmed in by valleys which gradually narrowed and became shallower, driving us ever upwards back into violent convulsions of rocky desolation.

We camped where a valley petered out into a horizon full of the magnificence of the Cordillera Blanca. Our replenished stocks of food, including an abundance of oranges and honey, increased the calibre of ensuing camp meals for a while, their very consumption giving added comfort since it was lightening the load. A jar of honey we retained as an emergency item.

Our companion saw fit to leave us next day in sight of a hamlet in which his cousin was reputed to live. He had not been a bad lad but his estimate of what we understood as "just a few more hours to Sihuas" was something of an understatement. Perhaps he meant days – and in the event it took two. Attempting to obtain a replacement lost us a lot of time and by the time we were successful we had lost the royal route. Fortunately, the new man knew the whereabouts of the dust road that led north though it was late afternoon before we were firmly on the march again. The replacement was another morose individual; his mule was better company.

There is nothing at all Incaic about the road that runs from near Chullin to Sihuas. Its tortuous course was as nightmarish as its construction and surface. Potholes and bogs lay in wait for the unwary traveller, while every small village across valley, gorge or ravine, though just a mile or so away, is reached only after a crazed display of spirals and detours around the smallest obstacle. On foot it was often advantageous to take short cuts but, for all its gyrations, the road knew a thing or two and a reduction of mileage had to be paid for in sweat, blood and tears.

It took the full two days to reach Sihuas and for much of the second one we had the township in sight but, maddeningly, out of grasp. A number of unfordable rivers too confounded our efforts and, twice, the road was not where it was expected to be which meant an exasperating doubling back to go in search of the thing.   The final miles we accomplished after darkness with the sparse lights of Sihuas laughing at us at the end of the corkscrew road.

The township was assuredly no Pomabamba; a village of few amenities though we saw little enough of it in the dark. In the one and only snack bar a lorry driver offered us his vehicle in which to spend the night, following up the invitation with another to join him on his proposed drive to Chimbote, a sizeable town on the coast.

We had no hesitation in accepting the first. The second we debated for only a moment.

The offer was unturndownable. We had both evolved another yearning for the balmy warmth of the seaside and here was a further side excursion to it being presented to us.

The night in the lorry ought to have told us what we were in for. Its buck was half full of crates of Coca-Cola bottles and what space remained had to be shared with a woman eternally breast-feeding a baby (which at least kept it quiet) and a man afflicted with a weak bladder. Sleep, in these circumstances, plus the bitter cold, was elusive.

The twenty-four hours drive was the most terrifying I have experienced. Andean B-roads are little more than pot-holed tracks at the best of times and the ones we took were buttressed on one side by granite cliffs and by sheer drops on the other. Our vehicle, moving much too fast, relied entirely upon the decibels of its horn and the supposition that no oncoming vehicle would be approaching at every bend of the spiralling, zigzag route. And when something did the squeal of brakes heralded a series of reversing operations on the narrow road that often had the rear end of the lorry overhanging space. Landslides had eaten away sections of road surface too while ominous cracks in it further added to the nightmare. The wreckage of vehicles that had failed this motorised assault course littered the ground hundreds of feet below; but travelling in the back of the lorry at least offered a chance to jump for one's life if ours was to follow suit.

Chimbote, when finally reached, was a dead loss. Industrialised, squalid and smelling of fish-meal it offered no comfort except for warmth.

A truck travelling north on the thankfully-flat Pan-American Highway took us the ninety miles to Trujillo, third city of Peru, which was infinitely more pleasant. What's more it held the crumbling ruins of Chan-Chan, imperial city of the Chimu dynasty. Basing ourselves at the "Lima Hotel", an establishment of basic amenities, we set out to explore it.

The pre-Inca ruins consist of nine great compounds built by the Chimu kings whose kingdom stretched a thousand kilometres along the coast from near present-day Guayaquil to Paramonga. The city was almost certainly taken over by the Incas in about AD 1450 but not looted; the Spaniards it was, however, who despoiled its burial mounds of all the gold and silver statuettes and ornaments buried with the Chimu nobles.

What David and I found was a vast mud city – the largest adobe city on earth – fallen into decay, the outer walls nevertheless towering so thick and solid that, after the better part of a millennium, they were still standing eight or nine metres high; only the ramparts showing the erosion of time. The old city stood in virtually desert terrain; no tree or fragment of greenery to be seen anywhere. Inside the adobe walls was a chocolate-coloured world with fifteen kilometres of streets bordered by crumbling houses, public buildings, cemeteries, storehouses and pyramids. From the apex of one such pyramid was an astounding view of sea, old and new city, and a desert backed by peaked and desiccated mountains.

A second night in the hotel and we began the gradual return to the mountains, an operation that took all of three days and involved the services of a local bus, a Toyota pickup, a Volvo truck, a private car and a massive lorry with sides so high that it became a feat of mountaineering just to get ourselves and our packs in and out of it. All this finally brought us to a point near Corongo, parallel to Sihuas. In Trujillo, amidst much heart-searching, we had taken the decision to jettison a good fifty percent of our loads. This hurt David more than I since he had carried around with him a number of text books on the Inca civilisation which, though desirable, were not vital to the execution of our project. Thus, henceforth, we could look forward to progressing entirely under our own steam, a method of progression I had always envisaged in the first place.

As was to be expected, the locals of Corongo displayed genuine ignorance of the presence of any Inca relics – roads included – which was, perhaps, not surprising since their township does not lie on the royal artery. However, the track north provided easy walking, rising slowly but offering no great feats of physical endurance. Traversing the broad side of a convex slope, the horizon in front receded while a cool breeze indicated a return to rarer altitudes. Our aim was a gradual return to the line of the Royal Highway.

A cleft in the perpendicular wall of crags and we stood upon the crest of a pass with a whole cordillera rolled out like a rucked carpet to the north. A number of guanacos – the most timid but also fiercest of Andean animals – looked up from their grazing and froze as if hypnotised by the sight of us.

Our lighter loads made all the difference to progress; our liberation from the dead-weight on our shoulders initially had us spontaneously rejoicing though all too soon the accustomed exhaustion and shortage of breath set in to blunt the elation. And now, all around was inspiring viewing to switch our minds from one emotion to another.

The colours of the landscape were everywhere different; slopes of slag-heap grey flanked by others of coral-red rock; peaks of black and blue granite above emerald-green foundations. Only at eventide did the land merge into a single hue when the last rays of the evening sun transformed the cordillera into a rose-red corrugation that would have earned an artist the accolade of surrealist.

We had eaten little all day; no more than a bar of chocolate, a packet of dry biscuits and some over-ripe cheese washed down by cold clear water from shimmering pools among the rocks. Setting up camp close to but below a ridge we made ourselves a substantial supper of macaroni and, because it was a heavy item to carry, a tin of some unidentifiable meat. A kind of blancmange followed but, by a mis-reading of the instructions, it became a beverage. We had chosen an attractive site though it offered no presentiment of the turbulent night ahead.

It started with a row; one of those bitter dissensions that break out between humans for no real rhyme or reason. I can't even remember how the fuse was lit – and it matters less. We shouted at one another, blew our tops, then smiled sheepishly. But it triggered the weather to bigger things. The darkness of the night was the more intense by virtue of storm clouds blown in our direction by a wind that, minutes before, was no more than a breeze. We fussed around the tent placing small boulders over pegs and tightening guy ropes, then crawled into our bags to ride out nature's tantrums, still aware of our own. About midnight we found ourselves struggling in the folds of nylon but, in both gale and darkness, could do little about re-erecting the tent. We settled down again with the material draped around us and prepared for sleep. But not for long.

"All we want now is for it to rain," I grumbled, and the heavens promptly obliged with a stinging torrent. We lay miserably listening to the hailstones striking the rocks, feeling the cold wetness seeping through the nylon and wondering how long the storm would last. I attempted putting on more clothes but was unable to locate them as rivulets of water leaked their way through those I wore.

Duplicating the form of our own dispute, the rain squall ceased as abruptly as it had started allowing us to re-erect the tent, don more clothes and crawl back into damp sleeping bags. But sleep had fled.

Morning was a relief and we celebrated its dawning with a breakfast of egg powder and beans; its warmth better value than the taste. Glad to be away after a prolonged study of compass and map, we strode off at high speed intent on re-galvanising stiff, damp limbs.

Rain clouds still dominated the sky, scudding and changing shape as they headed the way we had come. No more rain fell but what did descend around our ears was a gale-force wind that swept up the valley to engulf us in a cloud of powdered grit. I struggled to don my balaclava, soggy from the night's damping, and promptly lost it to the violent gusts.

We pressed on, collars up and heads down into the gale. Patches of hard, off-white snow lay strewn along the sheltered spots of the mountainside above us, not unlike the clusters of whitened bones of sheep we had passed earlier. The new valley into which we descended widened, the walls became less steep and the rounded peaks soared above our heads. As we neared the bottom, the wind dropped to a whisper and rents in the clouds showed a petticoat of blue sky.

The pattern of the subsequent days changed little. Our switchback progress made clear we were moving against the "grain" of the mountains; crossing valleys and not following them. The path had petered out the second day and what we were following became no more than a succession of ridge saddles, each selected by the demand of the compass. The weather, for us, remained dry, more by good luck for we frequently observed rain falling elsewhere; heavy squalls deluging the peaks within grey mantles of waterlogged cotton wool. Not another living soul or animal did we come across; it was as if we were alone and fortuitously alive in a dead world. Only the great condors, gliding effortlessly overhead, assured us that life breathed in the universe.

It was while we were atop one of the interminable crests that we caught sight of fellow beings. There were five of them; five men riding horses or mules, leading pack animals. They were a good mile away, had not seen us, but were coming our way. There was something about them that prompted caution; a suspicion that these fellow-humans might not be so glad to see us as we had, initially, been to see them. A grassy dip offered cover so we crouched down in it and watched the band as they moved nearer. Two of them carried what looked like rifles slung over their shoulder and, from the direction they were riding, we judged they would pass no nearer than five hundred yards. We remained silent, thoughtful and concealed.

As soon as men and beasts were out of sight we moved on again feeling a little foolish. Maybe they were perfectly innocent riders on legitimate business between villages with whom we could have conversed advantageously. Alternately, we may have avoided having our throats cut.

A while later we came upon isolated sheep; a sure sign of an approach to human habitation. And not a false sign either since a ragged, poverty-stricken little community hove into view with the onset of evening. We camped out of sight of the place, our suspicions unabated.

We entered the village warily next morning but the suspicions now belonged to the villagers. The first of them we saw took hasty refuge in their houses and even the children – usually more inquisitive than timid – took to their heels. It was impossible to get near enough to any of them to attempt a conversation and, again, it was up to a schoolmaster to come to the rescue.

At least we think he was a schoolmaster though we saw no school. Anyway, the man spoke a little Spanish and, after words of greeting, David probed his knowledge of Incaic matters. The man pointed to the east, to a low range of hills, grass-covered; almost homely and putting me in mind of my own Sussex Downs. Their crest, he indicated, marked the royal road's alignment. The revelation came as a huge relief and showed that we had not gone too far to the east as David feared. We thanked the gaunt figure profusely, pumping his hand with exaggerated fervour.

Two hours later we stood on the new crest, our eyes searching the rolling land. And sure enough, a grass track of familiar straightness softened by a few nature-formed indentations materialised. Our doubts not fully abated we followed it for many miles until the clarity weakened and the route veered to the west. Still unconvinced of its origins we sheered away where a junction offered a more northerly alignment.

We were reminded again how distances in these parts can be deceptive. Sihuas to Huamachuco may have been a hundred miles as the crow flies but as two hikers slogged it – weaving about looking for landmarks and avoiding the more impossible walls of granite – it must have been in the region of two. At times we could see the great Cordillera Blanca with its twenty-two peaks of more than 19,500 feet, one of them – Huascaran – at 22,205 feet, Peru's highest. Even at our average altitude of around twelve or thirteen thousand we were buffeted and half frozen by a succession of high winds, bitter cold nights and stinging downpours during the days that followed. Only in the late morning was the sun warm; the ground in the shadows remaining firmly frozen. The thin, stony soil gave a minimum of sustenance to defiant clumps of coarse yellowing grasses and alpine plants – often bearing minute, delicate blooms – hugging the ground. There were no trees; only tall ferns of the slow-growing, cactus-like puyas.

In such an environment animals are rare though there are rodents, lizards and tiny birds finding cover in the low vegetation, among rocks or in burrows. We never saw a puma but they exist here as do the guanaco and the fast-running vicuna. These we had seen, as we had Andean condors, the largest bird of prey in the world. The bird's great wingspan, which has been known to reach ten feet, enables it to glide effortlessly to eighteen thousand feet on up-currents of air, covering large distances with little exertion.

How we envied them the freedom of the sky. Our way ahead stretched eternally into infinity, a horrific, yet stirring panorama of mountain ranges and escarpments that, we were all too aware, would give us no respite even by the time we had conquered those we could make out in the far distance. But there was beauty too; beauty on a gigantic scale coupled to the compelling drama of isolation. Together they offered a combination that, on occasions, reduced us to a condition of suppressed terror and near-panic; a kind of agoraphobia.

Food, or the lack of it, was an ever-present concern. Our luxury items, purchased at Trujillo, ran out inside of a week as did our basic provisions. Whenever we came across the smallest hamlet we would top up with potatoes, the staple diet of the Andean peasant as it became our own. Our emergency foods – oatmeal cake and tins of sardines – were exhausted by the time the environs of Huamachuco began dotting the hillsides with villages and the chequerboard of cultivation.

Before Huamachuco, however, we were deflected off our route by the proximity and promise of a smaller but attractive-sounding town, Santiago de Chuco. Our map indicated but a short detour and we located the place with no great difficulty. But it soon became apparent that the charm of the township was vested solely in its surroundings. For us it became the location of a disturbing incident.

Walking along a street, intent upon re-provisioning our food stocks, we were accosted by a mean-faced individual who flashed a laminated card in our faces. "Special Criminal Police," he hissed in Spanish to reinforce his status. "You will come with me," Not even a "please" accompanied the order.

Thus our introduction to the dreaded P.I.P. of which we had heard; the Peruvian equivalent of the one-time K.G.B. With ill-grace we followed the stranger to a building off the main street, speaking not a word.

The interrogation was little different to others I had experienced in similar circumstances in other parts of the world. But it was shorter this time though equally threatening, and after two hours we were released with obvious reluctance. What the man suspected remained a mystery; maybe he thought we had links with the Sendero Luminoso guerrillas that were becoming increasingly active.

The township was to show a kinder face in the guise of one Alberto, an agricultural executive with his own office, the floor of which he put at our disposal for the night. From Alberto we learnt of a farmer who was making a foot journey cross-country to Huamachuco the following morning and he promised to make arrangements for us to join him. He would be glad of our company, we were assured, in view of the rising guerrilla threat and the distance which was all of a hundred kilometres.

The night on the office floor made a pleasant change to the recent heavy dose of camping and it was the farmer himself, together with four horses, who appeared at the door next morning. Though we no longer were relying on horse transportation, here it was being handed to us on a plate. Moreover, we were even expected to ride the horses.

"Call me Pedro," had been the stocky, Indian-featured farmer's greeting in English; his entire vocabulary, so Pedro he became. The horses were sturdy, bad-tempered brutes, not the least affected by our friendly overtures or clumsy riding techniques. With our rucksacks piled awkwardly upon the back of the fourth animal we clip-clopped out of Chuco, feeling like cowboy extras in an amateur production of "High Noon".

The journey to Huamachuco was a two-day hack taken at no great pace, the intervening night spent in the cowshed of a friend of Pedro high in the hills. Both he and the host made every effort to give us their beds in the two-room shack that seemed to be the latter's home but we would have none of it though happy to share their modest supper.

The second day we followed the bank of the Yomobamba river which could well have been the original route of the royal road though, of this, Pedro could raise no supporting opinion.

One of those impossible sunsets illuminated our entry into Huamachuco but darkness was complete by the time we reached the plaza lit by a necklace of electric bulbs. We bid farewell to Pedro, giving him a great bear hug; straightway feeling lonely and naked without his company and horses.

There was no doubt now about being back on the royal road. The town is mentioned frequently in the chronicles of the Incaic conquest while Pizarro's Spanish army is known to have rested here for four days after leaving Cajamarca for its southbound march of conquest in August 1553.

As yet untiring of urban living, we repaired to the best restaurant in town, a sizeable Colonial building of large rooms and wooden balconies inward-looking round an internal patio. Most of the rooms were locked and deserted but seemed to form part of some sort of hostel, albeit a superior one of ornate doors and gilded mirrors. The meal was a friendly affair with the few diners and staff joining us at a big table, and everyone helping themselves from an enormous tureen of stew. Invited to lay out our sleeping bags on the restaurant floor we were to pass a further night without the necessity of having to raise the tent.

Before taking to the floorboards, however, we took ourselves for an evening stroll in the small town and had entered a store with the object of acquiring a toilet roll when P.I.P. struck again. The representative of the breed on this occasion was a viciously drunk moron who demanded our credentials and openly accused us of being vagabonds. He produced no warrant card or proof of his calling so, initially, we ignored him though some sixth sense told me he was a "politico". The chap followed us around, weaving a slightly erratic course, then disappeared to return later with a saner colleague as we were enjoying a hot rum punch at a well-patronised bar. The atmosphere in the establishment, all chat and gaiety one moment, abruptly froze into silent hostility the next as the two men scrutinised our passports and went through the contents of our pockets. All the while a barrage of questions directed at David had to be coped with as best he could. Then, once again, we were unaccountably dismissed. But Huamachuco had suddenly gone sour, so, downing our rums, we returned, subdued, to the restaurant and bed.

Forty kilometres away lay Cajamarca where Pizarro's men had rested for two days on their southbound march. The road, fairly straight, ran through groves of eucalyptus, their silvery trunks silent sentinels lining our progress in the opposite direction to that taken by Pizarro's small army. We pressed on, with frequent halts in a series of townships astride the road to Cajamarca. At Cajabamba we spent a night in a stable which offered yet another change of venue though an attack by a dog, saliva dripping from its fangs, had first to be beaten off with a stick and a handful of stones.

The road thereafter took the only practical route by following a wide and ill-defined valley. Imparted morsels of intelligence wrung out of local people showed an encouraging awareness of their Inca heritage, the more so the nearer we approached Cajamarca. At Ichocan we camped in the plaza close to an assured water supply of an erratic fountain that donated a soaking every time we attempted to fill a kettle. No P.I.P squads here; instead the police were most obliging even to the extent of helping in the erection of the tent on an empty flowerbed. Had we arrived a little earlier I have no doubt they would have offered us the best cell at the local nick.

From Ichocan onwards the landscape deteriorated into one of dry and barren semi-desert made the more disagreeable after days of lush, often cultivated vegetation. At San Marco a kindly lady pressed a cold guinea-pig steak apiece upon us and the townships of Matara, Namora and Llacanora became the final urban stages to Cajamarca, the road unfolding into a ribbon of Incaic ruler straightness. We camped the final night beside it amongst brown hills above the town.

That treachery can become a legend is nowhere shown so eloquently as at Cajamarca; the 16th of November, 1532, is a date made infamous in the chronology of Inca annals; not only is it that of the biggest double-cross in history but also the point in time when Spanish exploration turned to Spanish conquest. For it was here that Francisco Pizarro ambushed and captured Atahualpa, the Inca emperor, promising to release him for a ransom of a storeroom of gold. The emperor's order to scour his realm to amass the ransom was obeyed whereupon Pizarro had him murdered prior to his army commencing the march of conquest southwards.

For David and I, entering the suburbs of Cajamarca at first light, the town notched the halfway point of our journey, and our elation could only have been matched by that of Pizarro arriving, in the opposite direction, in Cuzco.

The author's trek continued into Ecuador and Quito, its capital – and once the northern capital of the Inca realm. Finally, he continued by public transport to Colombia and its capital, Bogota.

13

South America — Ecuador
How not to Climb a Mountain

If I have to be labelled anything I am a walker, a trekker, a cautious scrambler perhaps, but decidedly not a climber. My feet are for the more or less horizontal terrain of this earth; not the vertical. I don't particularly mind how high my feet might take me but when a sheer or near sheer wall of granite blocks my path I go round it, the challenge notwithstanding. Not for me the paranoia – or the paraphernalia – of the mountaineer. However, mountain climbing does involve putting one foot in front of the other which, after all, is walking. So perhaps my reluctant ascent of Mount Chimborazo in Ecuador at an age when the Sussex Downs would have been a more suitable mountaineering prospect is worthy of a page or two in such a book as this.

Mount Chimborazo, every miserable 21,000 feet of it, is actually a volcano. In the Indian language the name means "Mountain of Snow" which is no overstatement. A massif of overwhelming scale, Alexander Humboldt only nearly succeeded in scaling it in 1802 while Joseph Dieudonne Boussingault, in 1831, likewise failed; halted at 19,290 feet by "an impossible ravine".

At that time Chimborazo was believed to be the highest mountain in the world before Everest claimed the distinction. Eventually Chimborazo was conquered by Edward Whymper in 1880 and today it is climbed fairly frequently – but not, I declare, by elderly men in glorified gym shoes.

My acquaintance with the mountain came about towards the end of my four months of tracing and following on foot the royal road of the Incas between Cuzco and Quito (part of which is described in the previous chapter), my colleague, David, and I having arrived at the town of Riobamba, at the head of the majestic Valley of the Volcanoes from which rise at least ten sensational volcanic peaks.

Our subsequent preoccupation with volcanoes began with an ill-fated attempt to reach the base of Mount Sangay, a 17,500-foot monster that, unlike Chimborazo, was treacherously active to the extent of it having killed two British climbers earlier that very year. One of the injured survivors of the party was Richard Snailham, explorer, author and instructor at the Royal Military Academy, Sandhurst, whom David and I knew quite well. When told that the route of our journey would pass close to Sangay he had suggested that we might care to try and reach it with a view to giving a proper burial to the dead climbers if the lava flow had not done so already.

The actual ascent of Sangay peak is not difficult; the challenge lies in reaching the base of the mountain through an almost impenetrable belt of forest bush. This challenge seemed to be more in my line of possible accomplishment and for days we hacked and tore at the thick undergrowth with machetes, our semi-naked bodies drenched in both sweat and non-stop tropical rain until utter exhaustion forced our abandonment of the attempt.

Physically and mentally drained we returned to Riobamba, and it was here we met Willi, an experienced twenty-nine year old Bavarian climber, whose single-minded aspiration was the conquest of the highest peak in the Peruvian and Ecuadorian Andes – Chimborazo. To attempt the climb alone, he explained, would be foolhardy since, with but a then single refuge cabin at the halfway mark and no mountain rescue facilities whatsoever, even a minor mishap could be fatal. So would we accompany him? The young impetuous David agreed at once; the novelty of a snow and ice climb attractive after months of rock and rain plus a defeat inflicted by Sangay. "No way!" said I, my protestations loud and clear. But when Willi, looking pityingly at me, remarked "You're too old anyway" my blood was up. I bridled and swallowed my protest. Wild horses, I declared to myself, couldn't prevent me from scaling the confounded mountain, even though a thousand miles of walking and weeks of semi-starvation had me far from the peak of fitness. It's always the same. Germans have this disconcerting effect on me.

Our initial move was to make contact with the Andean Mountaineering Club of Chimborazo which had its office in Riobamba and this led to an amiable meeting with its president, Enrique Valez, who was all too forthcoming with the loan of equipment vital for making the ascent. But either Ecuadorian feet are characteristically small or my feet are unusually large for they defeated every proffered climbing boot in his store. A pair of crampons were dubiously offered, however, in the pious hope that I could find a method of fastening them to the canvas-topped jungle boots I had been using for rough country walking. Signor Valez was also lavish with advice and proceeded to frighten the life out of me by explaining that, because of the equatorial bulge, the summit of Chimborazo was the point on the earth's surface that is furthest from the centre and that only experienced mountaineers should attempt the ascent. "We were all experienced climbers of course?" he asked and my attempted denial was painfully kicked into silence. The good man then stressed the vital necessity of attaining the single refuge cabin at 16,000 feet before nightfall prior to a pre-dawn assault on the summit. "Miss the refuge and you will almost certainly succumb to exposure. It's cold up there." he had added, though tempering this, for me, heart-stopping declaration with the comforting fact that the path to the refuge – and there was only one – was easy to follow and should have us at the cabin within three hours. He didn't actually say "You can't miss it" but this one rosy feature of the whole dismal catalogue of revelations was all I had to cheer me up.

Loaded down with crampons, ice-axes, coils of rope, snow-goggles and gauntlets, we caught a bus that passed through the village of Pogyo from whence the path was alleged to start but nobody had mentioned that the place consisted of no more than five stucco dwellings and that it was sometimes known as Poggios. Needless to say we missed it and were finally dropped at a village some distance beyond. The error was to prove our first disaster although, alighting from the vehicle, Chimborazo, hiding its head in thick grey cloud, looked deceptively close.

Our fellow bus travellers had added to my growing unease by loudly expressing the view that we were attempting the climb entirely at the wrong time of year, that we'd assuredly lose ourselves in the virtually perpetual fog and that our carcasses would lie on the hillside for months before being found. However, at the point where we had left these prophets of doom a trail did indeed lead up the side of an escarpment in the right direction and we followed it in the knowledge that there were more than six hours of daylight left us to locate the correct route and reach the cabin. "There's no problem," announced the alpine-experienced Willi, "Keep going and we'll hit the right path."

Arms of lava soil, softened by gaunt springy thickets, pushed down to meet us before the false track petered out into a morass of volcanic rocks and scree made the more treacherous by isolated patches of snow. It was cold and the cold increased as we progressed upwards.

For a while the way ahead, steadily rising, showed clear but, around mid-afternoon, the grey cloud descended to obliterate everything in an icy embrace, moving steadily across the face of the mountain blown by a rising wind. The realisation struck even Willi that we were lost so we fanned out as best we could, like beaters at a grouse shoot, attempting to locate a non-existent track or, better still, an elusive cabin.

Hours later Willi's altitude-meter, together with the emergence of the snow-line, confirmed the fact that we had exceeded 16,000 feet; too high above the level of the refuge, and so switched to a downhill search. My breath was already turning to agonising pants and my movements limited to bursts of a dozen footsteps between pauses. David too was surprisingly distressed having not yet found his second wind, but Willi, born and bred in the Bavarian Alps, was hopping about like a mountain goat.

Above us a local peak abruptly emerged from the mist and, perhaps because it was the only visible ground in the clear light of a dying day, we made for it as one, climbing and scrambling with a certain desperation. My feet were already cold; my socks saturated. Underfoot the ground was solid snow and ice hiding sharp lava rock. One moment all was grey nothing; the next the cloud had parted to reveal a glimpse of a wondrous panorama.

Far below, the Valley of the Volcanoes was hidden by the grey blanket. Protruding from it were the peaks of other volcanoes and mountains. Directly to the southeast was 16,000-foot Altar and, behind, less distinct but recognisable, was a cone that could only have been Sangay. Their snow-capped glory was tinted an amazing blood-red which turned deeper with every second as the sunset matured and faded. The sight was dumb-founding and eclipsed for a moment the dread welling up within me. At least I could be thankful to my Maker for showing me a manifestation almost worth dying for.

With the setting sun came a terrible cold and hastily we scrabbled to a lip of level ground. Here we held council, consumed some food and squirmed, fully-dressed, into our sleeping bags to prepare, it has to be said, for the "Great Beyond". " It's imperative you reach the hut," I heard again Enrique's warning. Childhood recollections of Captain Oates going out into the blizzard of the South Pole to die assailed me and, as if we had all been struck by the same notion, there began a surreptitious scribbling of last wills and testaments on scraps of toilet paper for the benefit of our next-of-kin and those who would eventually find our frozen bodies. "Get in close. Hug one another like bears," commanded Willi, " We must generate all the warmth we can. It's our only hope." The German was firmly in control and I, for one, had no objection. I snuggled close to my companions and thought about death. Above, the myriad stars made a heavenly ceiling and I no longer felt the cold. All in all it seemed not a bad way to go.

I came to with a bursting bladder and what appeared to be a fever. So it's to Hell I've been despatched; I know I ought to have gone to church more often. I started to wriggle free from the cocoon of bodies and straightway felt the biting wind. But what startled me most was that not only was I still on earth but sweating like a pig. My movement had awakened the others and gradually David and Willi sleepily inched away from one another content to finish the night in less fetid conditions.

Daylight, clear of cloud, showed us the refuge cabin, a wooden octagonal structure painted a brilliant orange, directly beneath and barely a hundred yards distant. It seemed to be laughing at us as we rose sheepishly, screwing up and discarding our paper wills as we did so.

Thereafter everything went more or less according to plan. We spent the new day alternating between cooking and eating in the filthy little cabin which we cleaned as best we could. All around were discarded tin cans and food wrappers; some almost vintage Edward Whymper. The name of the refuge was "Fabian Zurita" and he's welcome to it. I'm told a second refuge cabin has since been constructed but doubtless it's equally filthy.

To attain the summit and return to the refuge before nightfall it was necessary to set out by three o'clock in the morning. At dusk we therefore climbed back into our sleeping bags intent upon getting in as much sleep as possible before the pre-dawn start. In the event we spent a sleepless night warding off the overtures of friendly mountain rats that emerged from the floorboards to investigate our cooking appliances and nibble our hair and ears. Willi, in true Teutonic fashion, murdered a couple with his ice-axe and it was he who chivvied us out of bed at one o'clock to laboriously melt snow to make tea before setting off at three. Outside was pitch darkness but the wind had died and the cold not so painful. Our early breakfast of stale rat-nibbled rolls and packet soup had not been appetising but Willi, exerting his mountaineering authority once more, forced us to swallow it. "Food is warmth. It'll keep you alive," he pronounced, sounding like a survival manual.

Though dawn was nowhere to be seen a feeble moon illuminated the snow to dilute the darkness. We made slow progress up steep escarpments of more lava rock and across sharp black scree frozen solid in a cement of ice. Ten paces. Stop. Ten paces. Stop. It was the best I could do. At intervals I retched, my head between my knees, as altitude sickness struck. We rested ever more frequently in spite of the gathering cold that crept insidiously through our layers of clothing. Willi and David remained ahead of me so that their halts commenced before I could reach them, a state of affairs which coaxed me into new paroxysms of effort to catch up and so obtain at least some of my entitlement of rest. Two steps up. One slip back. Stop. Ten paces. Stop.

We reached the glacier at 18,000 feet and clumsily affixed our crampons. I had never worn crampons before and they, in their turn, had never had to be affixed to jungle boots. Hardly had we moved off again, when they parted company to slide impishly down the sloping glacier floor with me limping and cursing in hot pursuit. The corrugated ice surface cracked and groaned ominously, putting me into a sweat of terror. Willi tried to be reassuring. "I think it's safe," he observed, "Bending ice is usually safe ice", a rejoinder that might have been more appropriate for an afternoon's skating on the village pond.

I never thought we would ever get off that glacier. Even Willi showed signs of exhaustion as we finally stepped onto soft snow into which, of course, my boots sank to dislodge anew my crampons. Dawn had broken though we had hardly noticed it. The wind rose again to cut through our long-johns, double socks and gauntlets while, through our snow-goggles, we perceived a grey world instead of a black one. My hair and beard turned me into a caricature of Jack Frost.

Beneath the overhang of a cliff known as "Red Wall" we paused to eat some biscuits and chocolate. The cold was so intense it had even me raring to move. We circled the base of the great bulwark hung with long icicle daggers pointing down on our heads and swung again upwards. The soft snow turned to hard snow once more, hiding deep gashes of ice. Willi unslung his nylon rope and attached it to the three of us. This is where I really make a fool of myself and let the side down I thought but, heavy slog though it was, I had at last found my own second wind and so made reasonable progress behind David, stepping into his footprints as he did in Willi's. In front the German was moving forward with great care, testing each footfall with a view to avoiding the many awesome crevasses, some virtually invisible.

The breach in the wall was easier to find than expected. I was not to know that Edward Whymper had written into his report the warning: "Thus far and no farther a man may go who is not a mountaineer." Thus I was about to trespass into a realm of the chosen few as we started up the steep slope of frozen snow punctuated by outcrops of slippery, ice-coated rock. We moved at a snail's pace partly on account of the necessity for extreme caution on the climb out of the "Red Wall" but mostly because of the laggard at the end of the rope who could move no faster had all the hounds of hell been snapping at his heels.

The nausea that had slowed my footsteps on the glacier returned with a vengeance. This time it was more than exhaustion. I had been sick earlier but now my condition worsened and I vomited uncontrollably at ever-increasing intervals. The symptoms of the malady were not those described by Sebastian Snow who gained Chimborazo's summit in recent years. He called it *soroche*; it had him shivering from head to foot to very nearly defeat him. With me, as long as I could rest at frequent intervals, I was able to continue. But as with all climbers of this mountain, we were working against the clock and, should darkness fall before return to the refuge, our chances of surviving a second night on a bare mountain above 20,000 feet would be virtually nil.

It was this fact and the fear of risking the lives of my companions that pushed me to the limits of endurance. At times I was even able to keep pace with momentary bursts of super-human energy.

The gradient steepened as we shuffled towards its crest, our heels and toe-caps kicking for holds. All feeling had left my hands and feet, and movement became no more than a mechanical reaction to my will. I had long since discarded my crampons which I had slung around my neck.

Willi's altimeter recorded a height of 19,650 feet when we came to the largest crevasse, possibly the one that defeated another French climber, Gault. My eyes saw it but my brain refused to function so that the revelation of the consequences of its existence failed to register. We approached with extreme caution and, keeping away from the treacherous edge, Willi tried to gauge its depth. The width was certainly in excess of fifty feet though the depth of this snow and ice ravine was anybody's guess. Working our way along the fissure we discovered, to our relief, that it narrowed dramatically to an ominous crack no more than a few feet wide.

Willi selected a spot that he considered a reasonable crossing point and, thrusting his ice-axe into the snow, inched forward on the anchored rope to as close to the rim as he dared. Satisfied that the gap was leapable, even if he had to trust to providence that the landing point would hold, he turned to David and me. "If the lip gives way and I go down, brake my fall and haul me up," he charged. "Come on, let's go." Retrieving his ice-axe he watched while David and I played out a few more yards of rope.

Gingerly Willi stole to the very edge of the crevasse in the knowledge that, in all probability, it was an overhang that could crumble at any moment. He bunched himself, and leapt.

He landed safely with a foot to spare, sprawling forward as he did so. The rope tautened, pulling him back towards the opposite lip and feverishly we played out more to allow him to scramble away. He turned to give a "thumbs up" signal, intimating that it was our turn to negotiate the obstacle.

David, utilising Willi's footprints, repeated the German's movements and, without a second's hesitation, jumped to land easily on the other side. He scrambled to Will's side.

I too forced myself to undertake a carbon copy of my colleagues' actions, inwardly blessing the good Lord for having favoured me with a commendable schooldays long-jumping record. Then I too hurled myself towards the opposite lip, landed clumsily and started to fall back but was restrained painfully by the rope which bit into my flesh. We were across the chasm and all still in one piece.

The snow grew softer and deeper. Chimborazo's southern summit – the Whymper Summit as it is sometimes called – was but a slog of a few hundred yards distant. The three of us forged on, each footfall a struggle to remove a leg from the clinging snow.

Reaching the head of the ridge a wind of intense ferocity rose to sear the exposed portions of our faces. Frozen flecks of ice stung my ears and the bitter cold numbed anew my inadequately-covered limbs. The snow grew deeper still; the struggle to free our legs more frantic. Maybe the effort of combating the trapping of our feet served to prevent the cold from overwhelming us; I don't know. All that my crippled mind would register was the necessity to conquer the accursed mountain now that I had got this far. Nothing else – nothing at all – mattered. Life itself had become subservient to the single aim of putting myself on the summit. Never before had I experienced such strength of purpose for so unimportant a reason and I hope I shall never again, for it is a kind of madness; a spasm of insanity that turns the famed champions of geography into an elite of men and women.

But the spasm goaded me to the southern summit. Less than fifty yards separated us from the western peak, the true summit of Chimborazo. Time was inexorably ticking away but all rational thought had been cast aside.

We made for the final ridge in line abreast, still roped together but no longer working as a team. The snow rose to our thighs so that, at times, we were crawling; lying flat on the surface; attempting to avoid having to make a downward thrust on a leg that would only be trapped in a freezing cast. The wind increased to a shrieking crescendo; a sound akin to maniacal laughter at our feeble threshings.

I have never used an ice-axe before or since but the one I wielded clumsily that day on Chimborazo – reaching out to sink the blade into virgin snow ahead of me and hauling myself bodily towards it – taught me a new method of motivation. Gradually, painfully, it narrowed the gap until all three of us attained the crest. Our combined crazed laughter – a song of triumph – was instantly carried away by the wind. Unable to stand on the peak I could only sit on it.

The way down to the base of the "Red Wall" made for something of an anti-climax; to me the happiest event of the climb. Willi brought his disciplinary measures to bear and bade us exercise the greatest care on the descent which involved less effort but was the more dangerous. Still roped, we returned across the great crevasse and beyond, David and I again slavishly utilising Willi's prints to avoid other pitfalls that lay in wait, hidden by the snow.

Cloud obscured the view below, as it had from the summit, and I did not like the look of the wisps of mist building up and rising from the base of the mountain. I was eager to return to less spectacular altitudes, preferably around sea-level. The moment of triumph had receded and though, years later, I was told by an eminent climber that, for my age and lack of proper climbing gear, I had broken some sort of Chimborazo record, I retain the firm conviction that mountaineering is not for me under any circumstances whatsoever.

14

Walking with Ramblers Holidays
Introduction

When Ramblers Holidays, the touring partner of the well-known Ramblers' Association, invited me to participate in a series of their group walks about the world I jumped at the chance. Here was yet another aspect of how one's legs can provide both accomplishment and pleasure; in this instance perhaps more pleasure than accomplishment. The venue for Ramblers walks are usually the hill districts of a variety of countries in Europe and beyond; only a few of the walks are of great physical endurance, most being, in the main, hikes pure and simple, each graded according to the hours of walking per day and type of terrain to be traversed. Based at unpretentious hostelries, participating walkers are not obliged to cover vast distances or undertake the total length of specific routes as has been the case of my journeys described in earlier chapters of this book. Instead, with a knowledgeable leader at the helm, they can undertake relatively gentle perambulations through the most picturesque and interesting portions of the countryside.

For me it would be a pleasurable change.

Publisher's note

AT RAMBLERS HOLIDAYS we grade our holidays according to the nature of the holiday and according to how strenuous the walks are.

Sightseeing holidays (Ss) mostly involve sightseeing outings to monuments, historic cities, etc. But they often also include some easy walking.

Walking holidays range from those graded as E (terrain easy; walking for an average of three hours a day and for no more than five hours a day), to those (graded as A and B) which involve tough, full-day walks over hard, usually mountainous terrain.

Grade D holidays are on moderate terrain with each day's walk being for five hours or less. D+ holidays involve more energetic walking, with outings of up to six hours per day. In C grade holidays, the terrain is moderate to hard and each day's walk lasts for about six hours. Grade C+ holidays are slightly more challenging, with walks of about seven hours a day. C+ walks may occasionally include some scrambling.

Some holidays combine walking and sightseeing. They are graded, for example, as D+/Ss or Ss/D. (If the Ss comes first, it means that there is more sightseeing than walking).

For more information about Ramblers Holidays, please see page 349.

1. Eastern Sicily (one week, Grade D+)

My first assignment was to participate in a series of walks designated in the Ramblers Holidays brochure as, simply, "Walking in Sicily". My guidebook somewhat gushingly promotes this southern extremity of Italy as "sun-warmed, it is the largest island in the Mediterranean, a haunting land of evocative, varied beauty – and dramatic extremes; a country of forbiddingly harsh mountains and beguilingly soft beaches, of isolated hilltop villages and colourful teeming cities... of a people warm and gregarious", all of which is true and I couldn't put it more enthusiastically myself.

The base was the Hotel d'Orange d'Alcantara in the township of Francavilla; our group, 16-strong including my wife, Anna, and myself, a mix of men and women, about equally divided, in the higher age bracket. Though one could hardly describe them as professionals, many belonged to hiking clubs, taking their favoured mode of locomotion with a certain serious intent.

The hotel was just the sort of establishment one would expect of a small, off-the-tourist beat, Sicilian town. Evening meals were four-course affairs frequently including delicious pasta dishes of which second helpings were liberally and gladly donated. The bedroom suites with balconies were on the small side but perfectly adequate, and for the whole week we had the hotel entirely to ourselves so that when an Italian couple booked in for a night they were looked upon almost as interlopers. Breakfasts were nothing if not original; personally I'm not keen on chocolate cereal and omelette but the fresh rolls and orange juice made amends. A family-run establishment, the manager, who was often to act as driver of one of the hotel's pair of minibuses, was a cheery fellow full of bonhomie and wild gesticulations while his staff were the friendliest imaginable.

Francavilla itself is well off the tourist circuit. Typically Sicilian, its menfolk spent the days smoking and gossiping inside or outside the numerous bars, and when outside contractors came to repaint the road-markings (which no true Sicilian would take any notice of anyway) the whole police force turned out to control the traffic watched by much of the local population in carnival mood.

Besides new road-markings the town possessed a convent (which can be visited only for the purpose of attending a service) and, atop a hill, the dilapidated ruins of a Norman castle. Some very ancient latin inscriptions on the old stonework of a bridge might be of considerable archaeological

The party picnics at Castiglione

importance but, if so, the elders of Francavilla are too busy doing nothing to promote it.

Our leader was a delightful and knowledgeable one-time schoolmistress named Julia who was to handle us with the greatest tact and consideration. As on all Ramblers walking holidays a participant can do as much or as little walking as he or she cares to undertake; if one prefers to hire a car, as two of our couples did, and do one's own thing there's absolutely no problem and, in our case, Julia leaned over backwards to help with arrangements. In short Julia was angelic.

The first day's walk could be described as a run-in. Our initial objective was the castle, a stiff climb from the edge of town. The ruins looked even more dilapidated than they did from below; the remaining arches heavily cracked and on the verge of collapse. A finger of masonry that was once a tower stood out from the rest of the ruin offering a remarkable likeness to our own Corfe Castle in Dorset. By way of the sundry backsides of seemingly extinct factories and an assuredly extinct railway line we made for the hilltop township of Castiglione that had drawn our eyes as we roamed the castle ruins. With Mount Etna in view behind it Castiglione made a handsome spectacle and a promise of rewarding exploration. And in spite of considerable exertion demanded by a steep uphill track that had once been a pilgrim's road we were not to be disappointed.

The little town still preserves the charm of the medieval urban setting. This extended around the castle, likewise Norman, its fortifications daringly wedged in among the crevices of the granite ridge at the top end of town so that it's difficult to gauge which is living rock or man-installed stone. The view over the surrounding countryside, including Mount Etna, is superb whilst, towards the main town one can only but admire the incredible assortment of shapes and colours of the numerous bell towers of the churches.

The elderly and decaying buildings themselves would, without doubt, have been expensively restored were Castiglione situated in prosperous northern Italy. But here in rural Sicily there is no money to spare for such adornment. One of the churches – St Antonio I think – contains a season-indicating sun-dial inscribed upon the floor in such a position that a ray of sunlight penetrating a hole high up in the wall alights upon the correct day of the month, a piece of date-keeping that must have taken a lot of mathematical calculation to design. Embellishing the narrow lanes are balconies and portals made of volcanic stone that wind and cold have seriously eroded.

The town was once a stronghold of Roger of Lauria, ruler of Sicily during much of the 9th century. He, more than anyone, was instrumental in building the many beautiful palaces and churches on the island and the southern mainland.

The second day's walk took us into more rural climes. It started on a ridge above Castiglione to which we were driven by one of our slightly lame minibuses. The rough path followed the ridge-top of a range of high hills giving fine views of Etna against a blue sky on a sunny cloudless day. The clarity of the air made every detail sharp and distinct.

Ramblers Holidays have a policy of requesting a volunteer from every group to act as rear marker or, in RAF parlance, tail-end Charlie, to ensure that the faster, more energetic walkers don't leave the slower ones behind. Fortunately, I was the volunteer this day so could keep an eye on Anna who later was to suffer seriously bruised toes, particularly on the stony downhill sections of the route. Carpets of wild flowers – Osteospermum, anemone, orchid and white iris – drew excited exclamations and brief pauses from the botanists among us – which included Anna only too happy for the excuse to pause for a few blissful moments.

We remained on the ridge for the full day's walk, the path rising and falling with each peak and trough. Here and there were rough stony patches particularly on the final descent to the road and the most welcome cafe designated as the pick-up point for return to the hotel.

Taormina, the nearest town of note to Francavilla, cries out to be seen. The cry was answered but we were to earn the visit there by walking most of the distance. We started from a point on a small road that leads to a saddle directly beneath 2,600-foot Mount Veneretta that overlooks the town and for the first hour it was plain road hiking. But at the saddle we took to the rough upward path to Veneretta's summit. The weather was cloudy and distinctly cool; the higher we rose the cooler it became while at the top a near-gale was blowing, strong enough to buffet us unmercifully. And the wind was icy. However, the view of Taormina together with the whole shoreline of the Bay of Naxos was wondrous. The descent to the town was initially hard with no visible path and sharp jagged rock underfoot while the icy wind howled and gusted, knocking us off-balance. Only when we reached Castelmola, an upper Taormina suburb, did the going become easier and the terrain conducive enough to allow us a picnic stop sheltered from the wind.

The Cadogan Island Guidebook to Sicily quotes Taormina as " one of the most perfect places for a honeymoon or a seduction". Whatever your reasons for going there just to observe its fine medieval buildings, bougainvillaea-filled squares, bustling cafes and shady groves of oranges and lemons is reason enough. And all this is enhanced by the intense luminosity reflected in the sea and echoed by Mount Etna which, as always, looms in the distance.

The Greek theatre is the centrepiece, though actually what exists is more Roman than Greek since it was rebuilt by the former a century after its original 3rd century BC construction. The town is built on several levels extending over the terrace of a crag jutting into the sea.

It was here in this "authentic pearl of Sicily" that we spent the rest of the day walking through the network of lanes and stairways that frequently expand into small squares bordered by ancient houses and *palazzetti*, imbibing the enchanting atmosphere of this quite small town.

On most Ramblers walking holidays there is an optional excursion to a well-known city and for this one most of the party went to Syracuse. Having been there on earlier occasions I chose not to join them; instead, with half a dozen others plus Julia – even though it was her "day off" – we undertook a walk that commenced from the village of Roccella Valdenoe – which translates as "Rock Valley of the Demon".

A vague path led us up onto the snow-line atop a range of hills on one side of the village peaked by the Pointe di Casteluzio of over 3,000 feet. A further series of ridges more than actual paths conducted us down an excruciating escarpment well-endowed with pitfalls to Malvagna, known for its convent. The day was warm and sunny and noting that we were unsure of our bearings in the village the good citizens, ever helpful, repeatedly attempted to direct us to their showpiece though all we were looking for was the pub.

Well-watered, we left Malvagna along a paved highway of almost motorway proportions fringed with expensive crash barriers and ornate lamp standards that zigzagged down the hill to the small river straight into a giant cliff. A highway to nowhere. From there, following a riverside picnic, we trudged across undulating country for many miles back to Francavilla.

Those of the party who visited Syracuse found a city sometimes described as the New York of the ancient Greek world, the thriving metropolis of Magna Graccia, and one of the most important centres of the western hemisphere for over a thousand years. Here is the city, founded in 734 BC, that thrashed Athens in the Peloponnesian War to put an end to her imperial ambitions. The city also defeated the Carthaginians which further increased its prestige.

Close to Francavilla – just three kilometres away – lies the dramatic Alcantara Gorge, an unexpected deep cleft of basalt prisms carved by its namesake river and fashioned by one of Etna's ancient eruptions. Sixty feet deep and a mere nine wide in some places, its walls resemble a multi-layered cake that, in the sunshine, reveal a variety of colours when sliced. An hour spent gawking at this geographical phenomenon and we were off again next day on a walk taking in the nearby hill range.

Following its ridgetop we worked our way along it, admiring the fine views over Francavilla and beyond to the intrusive Etna. The volcano, with its smouldering summit, simply refuses to be ignored. It frowns; sometimes sneers. No wonder the mountain is, by some, thought to be the most disturbing sight nature can offer on this planet. It draws the eye like a magnet.

Ridge-walking is usually fairly easy-going with no more than undulations to traverse and so it was as far as the village of Mota Camastra just below it, the houses packed together on a ledge overlooking the Alcantara valley. In place of a picnic we partook of a hot lunch here in a restaurant clinging to the ledge by its teeth. This put us in good stead to tackle the rocky defile that formed the descent to the river which, in turn, produced another climb the other side to attain our base at Francavilla. A reasonably easy day I suppose you'd call it.

It is possible to cock a snoop at Etna by going for its jugular and that's exactly what we did for our final day's hike. On the mountain's eastern flank the terminus of the winding road leading to it is the ski-centre of Provenzano to which we travelled by minibus. From there we walked up through snow, lava dust and coke grains, passed a number of subsidiary and long-extinct craters, to within sulphur-smelling distance of the fiery head. Walking in soft snow is a fatiguing business; snow and sand have similar walk-resistant properties, but clear of the tree-line the snow, inexplicably, lessened while the coke and lava dust proved easy to negotiate.

Strangely enough Etna's summit had been virtually clear of cloud for the whole week, a rare occurrence in my experience since, on the multiple times I've visited Sicily, seldom was it visible. In this instance it was the rest of the island that was blotted out by cloud below us though the sun above shone brightly.

We made a circuit of the two snow-filled subsidiary craters, named Margherita and Umberto I believe, the stiff climb to them – one step forward, two slides back sort of progress – defeating one or two members of the group who sensibly retired to more comfortable altitudes. An icy wind cut through our clothing so that we were all none too unwilling to follow suit. To attain the live main crater on foot in winter is an entirely different ball-game; virtually it is a mountaineering project and, without permission, is probably forbidden. In the summer months a four-wheel drive vehicle with a knowledgeable driver carries visitors there.

Climbing Mount Etna in the snow

And no doubt Etna, which the locals call "She Devil", takes a perverted joy in reminding us puny humans how small and insignificant we are. This great smouldering boil that pushed itself 9,000 feet up from the sea covers a larger area than metropolitan London. As unpredictable as any live volcano, it has the power to bring death and destruction to tens of thousands in their villages and towns below whenever it has a mind to do so.

The way down led through patches of rarer blue-tinged so-called peacock lava the more colourful bits some of us collected before returning through the snow-bearing pine woods to our vehicle and homeward through the low-level but lifting mist. If Etna was sneering at least we couldn't see it.

Anna never came on any further walks following the second day's punishment to her toes. Instead she happily spent the time exploring Francavilla and, since she speaks some Italian, conversing with the locals who are always delighted when a foreigner speaks to them in their own tongue. Thus it can again be noted that a participant in a Ramblers Holiday is not duty-bound to join the group walks; there is much to do and see in the locality of the hotel.

And in a region such as eastern Sicily there is assuredly plenty both to do and see. The hill villages are untouched by tourism; their alleyways, tiny piazzas and the houses with their individual balconies have barely changed for decades. Turn a corner and there stands a crumbling but beautiful medieval church. Step into an old-fashioned bar and order a cappuccino with a slice of almond cake and the clients will want to know your life story. It has to be said, however, that using one's legs is the best way to appreciate a landscape like that of Sicily in which there is nothing particularly grand or exotic but which is full of detail – orange groves laden with fruit, satiny black cattle grazing in the mountain flanks, wild narcissi, walls made from volcanic rock, the stumps of Norman castles, the occasional abandoned Baroque church, and the morning mist lifting from the hills. This is the real Sicily where, on a more prosaic note, prices are a third of those in the north of the Italian mainland.

And if you're worried about the Mafia forget it. You may observe the occasional lounging Godfather figure sporting a homburg hat and dark glasses but the odds are he'll not be carrying a violin case.

2. Andalucia, Southern Spain
(one or two weeks, grade D+)

There is what might be described as a possible hidden bonus in undertaking a one- or two-week walking holiday with Ramblers in southern Andalucia. This lies in the fact that the closest airport to the initial destination is Gibraltar whence a minibus coveys you across the Spanish border to the first week's walking base. It is a good idea, if you can spare the extra day, to spend 24 hours prior to the start of the tour on and about this famous rock bequeathed to Britain through our expansionist history. Sometimes there is also an opportunity to do this on the last day of the holiday.

Gibraltar, in spite of the restrictive confines of its territory, is full of interest, much of it vested within the great rock itself honeycombed with tunnels, gun emplacements and a gigantic cavern where concerts are held against a background of enormous stalactites and stalagmites; a venue that can never be surpassed by the most decorative of concert or opera houses. But, more to the point, an ascent of the rock itself by way of the multiple-hundred so-called Mediterranean Steps not only offers astounding views over the town, harbour, Algeciras across the bay and the Andalucian coast but provides a warm-up for the walks ahead. And if you make the climb on a warm sunny day in March as I did it'll have you sweating like a pig.

But I digress. The road journey to the Ramblers initial base of Zahara de los Atunes takes about one and a half hours and enables one to attain the Hotel Gran Sol in time for a late supper – and in Spain all meals are late. I liked the Gran Sol. It is homely, compact, wears a slightly Moorish air and is family-run. And the family Quirola were invariably amongst the guests, helping the bar staff or chatting with their Spanish-speaking clientele while the good-looking daughter, Ines, who spoke English, acted efficiently as receptionist. The only disappointing factor, for me, was a typically Spanish breakfast that never varied though the four-course dinner compensated.

The town of Zahara de los Atunes (something of a mouthful but there are a number of Zaharas hereabouts – this one translating as "Town of the Tuna" since this fish was, and maybe still is, processed here) is exceedingly friendly and equipped with a supermarket and basic shops. And though this southern Atlantic coast is beginning to suffer some development Zahara seemingly has been overlooked, at least for the moment.

Little old ladies in black still walk the streets and one wizened old man (though probably no older than I) in a flat cap took my arm and guided me with old-fashioned courtesy to the post office when I made efforts to enquire of its whereabouts. Everyone has a "holas" greeting for you.

Andalucia, let it be said, is an intriguing mix of history and geography that has left its mark on both the countryside and its people. In addition to world-famous cities of the likes of Seville, Cadiz, Malaga and Cordoba there are innumerable smaller towns and villages virtually untouched by tourism; small rural communities where the way of life has barely changed over the centuries and which are seldom visited by outsiders. And all this in a province with a Mediterranean coast awash with package tourism.

Long before the Romans defeated the Carthaginians in the 3rd century BC there had been invasions and occupations of Andalucia by, among others, Iberians, Celts and Phoenicians. In their turn the Romans lost out gradually but remorselessly to various incoming European tribes and finally the Visigoths became the new masters. But their reign was soon usurped by the Moors from Africa and, for the subsequent three centuries, the area flourished culturally and economically, eventually breaking up into small kingdoms which, one by one, were conquered by the Christians to terminate nearly 800 years of Moorish rule in Spain. And it is the Moorish influence that, today, shows the strongest in Andalucian architecture.

So much for the potted history lesson. Back to Zahara de los Atunes and the less significant activities of our group of ramblers. The leader was one David, highly efficient and knowledgeable, whom two of the group had met before on previous rambling holidays. And it is worth mentioning here that many clients participate in the company's walking holidays year after year to become old hands. Just for a moment I felt like the new boy at school. Our group was 21-strong and comprised those participants who had chosen to undertake the two-week, two-centre stint. A smaller group of 15 one-weekers under Gordon, their leader, we saw only at mealtimes. The wide sandy miles-long beach and an Atlantic Ocean of white-capped rollers adjoined the hotel. I was the only one of both groups to test the water by process of immersion and wish I hadn't. It was freezing.

A small fleet of smart taxis was to be our mode of transportation to and from the subsequent week's hikes; our first dropping-off point being the interesting and ancient hilltop "white town" of Vejer de la Frontera. A word of explanation concerning these Pueblos Blancos, so prevalent in southern Andalucia. The name derives from the dazzling whitewashed walls that are common to all such villages where every household is expected to maintain the whiteness of its dwelling so that, over the years, house walls are so thick with whitewash their corners have become rounded.

A walking tour of the town allowed us to observe its fortress-like church, a stone castle with its thick walls melting into the surrounding white balconied houses, a handsome civic hall lording over a tree-shaded square, and some good views over the countryside.

The day's itinerary led along an easy path to the edge of a regional park of umbrella pines where we stopped for a picnic lunch at a tiny community of houses barely numerous enough for it to be classed as a hamlet but which, happily, did boast a pub. Actually it was closed but hurriedly opened with the prospect of 16 thirsty customers. Wild flowers were in abundance though not of the distinction of those my wife and I had enjoyed in Sicily. The beer and sandwiches consumed, walking conditions deteriorated as soft footstep-retarding sand gave notice that we were approaching the coast. And this was a foretaste of more sand-walking to come while we were based by the seaside.

At the cliff edge marking the coast were startling views over the Bay of Barbate in one direction and that of Trafalgar in the other with sheer heart-stopping drops at our feet. The walk continued along the coast with the park to our left and more sand underfoot to make progress heavy-going until arrival at the sizeable town of Barbate together with its very active tuna-fishing port. Our taxis awaited us at the far end of town.

For once I was not the oldest participant of the group; the male member of one couple being in his 80s. The day had been warm and sunny but, being March, there was a cool nip in the air especially noticeable when the sun hid behind a cloud.

The second day's walk was a little more ambitious. It commenced from an old lookout tower converted into an automated lighthouse north of Zahara. The objective was the remnants of the Roman town of Baelo Claudia at Boloma reached after more sand-slogging including the descent of a huge dune which, of course, filled our boots with sand. By the 1st century BC Baelo Claudia was at the height of its prosperity, a prosperity probably attained through the industrialisation of its fishing trade in which salted fish was the chief product. The foundations of its brining factory are to be seen amongst more substantial ruins of the basilica and theatre. Our normally somewhat frugal picnic lunch materialised into a more substantial one at the nearby simple restaurant, my intake being a tasty tripe and bean stew, after which we tramped back to the lighthouse along a blessed sand-free lane, through sandy scrubland and along another little-used road. Gluttons for punishment half a dozen of us chose to walk the best part of six miles along the beach back to the hotel, a slog that really tested our stamina. The softies were picked up by taxi.

As if to reward us for our show of bravado the third day's perambulation was just that; a mere stroll. A living town, that of Tarifa, was the target, one distinguished by the fact that it is the southernmost tip of Europe. To get there involved little more than flat track-walking through cork groves and across open countryside liberally sprinkled with wind-powered generators rising from the tops of the hills. These machines (one can hardly bestow upon them the romantic-sounding nomenclature of windmill) stem from the fact that the Tarifa hinterland is allegedly the windiest and draughtiest corner of Spain and though some may deplore the disfigurement of the hills they make a unique spectacle.

A "cattle cemetery", a patch of open ground displaying an assortment of bones picked clean by vultures as well as evil-smelling carcasses halted us awhile as our photographers attempted to obtain close-up shots of these great birds partaking of their free meal. But they saw us coming, took to the air and circled patiently in the sky above awaiting our departure. We picnicked within the grounds of the whitewashed Sanctuary of Nuestra Senora de la Luz Patrione de Tarifa; another wordy mouthful, this one designating a religious establishment used mostly on local festival occasions.

Tarifa town I found to be rather dull. From atop its ramparts we looked across the seven miles of strait to North Africa winking at us in the clear air. The town centre is graced with a statue of Sancho the Brave of Navarre but the castle of Guzman el Bueno, commander-in-chief of the Spanish Armada, was unattainable since it lay within a military compound. The port from which passengers and cars can be ferried to Tangier was not yet open for business.

Rest days with Ramblers Holidays can be anything but restful, as I had discovered in Sicily. However, on this one most of the party partook of an excursion to Cadiz city, some 50 miles distant. Though years had gone by since I had visited this home-port of many a famous Spanish explorer I remained "at home", pottering about in Zahara and relaxing as best as I am able – which is not saying much.

The itinerary next day took us, via the straggling village of El Soto, its simple peasant dwellings contrasting oddly with the sophistication of the Hickstead-like horse dressage arena in its midst, through a countryside that was plainly a favoured roosting area for storks whose nests littered every treetop, back to Vejer de la Frontera. Here we imagined the walk

Viewing the remains of the Roman town of Baelo Claudia at Boloma

was to end following a sweaty climb up the 600-foot hill on a stone donkey path. Instead, on we were to go for a number of further miles on sandy tracks through the insidious umbrella pines to yet another religious sanctuary there to be collected by our taxis.

I suppose a walker has to expect inclement weather at some point and that point was reached the following day. It had been cloudy and cool the previous afternoon and though the new day looked ominous with grey clouds sweeping across the usual blue sky and a chill wind blowing it wasn't actually raining as we boarded our taxis for the walk's startpoint. But it was when we got there. Our objective was Cape Trafalgar to which, we all being true Brits except Jim, the Canadian, were determined to pay our respects. The route led, once again, along the sandy coastal hinterland from Barbate, the sand this time being the consistency of thick soup beneath umbrella pines that failed to live up to their name. And it poured. Whether I'm walking in Iceland or India I invariably wear shorts; having wet trousers clinging to my legs is anathema. The trouble is the water runs down the legs to end up within one's boots, though I was not the only one with wet feet that sad morning in which we all experienced varying degrees of soaking. But we reached Cape Trafalgar via a final mile or two along a beach dodging, not always successfully, heavy ocean rollers that repeatedly washed ashore to drive us onto the rocks. Thereafter we aborted the walk returning waterlogged to Zahara. The rain ceased in the afternoon so, to reinforce the drying out of boots by hotel hair-drier, a few of us, with David and the hotel dog, set out on a further six-mile hike only to collect snow-shoes of mud which made even heavier going than did the wet sand. A beer at a local pub restored our shattered morale and we trudged, leg-weary, back to Zahara on hard mudless tarmac.

Sunday was all-change day, the one-weekers heading for Gibraltar and the UK; we two-weekers for pastures new in the fastness of the Andalucian mountains. Our numbers were down to 19, one couple having to be repatriated home, she with a broken arm sustained when the unfortunate lady fell awkwardly on soft sand while strolling on Zahara beach. Sand, wet and dry, had a lot to answer for this past week. For the survivors came a four-hour minibus journey along the shores of both Atlantic and Mediterranean oceans, then – from Marbella – inland and upwards on a winding road giving superb views across increasingly bucking terrain.

The new base was the Villa Turista, a ten-minute walk across the valley of the much-reduced Guadalete river from Grazalema. The villa was more of a self-catering unit than hotel; attainment of the reception and dining area necessitated an outdoor hike which included nearly a hundred stone steps. The individual bedroom suites were spacious but spartan and for a while the friendly, compact Gran Sol at Zahara was held in fond affection. But breakfasts and dinners – including free wine – were exceptional; factors which evened things out a bit. One Eileen from Edinburgh joined our ranks that Sunday night, arriving by taxi from Gibraltar, to bring our numbers up to a round 20.

I took to our new leader immediately. Bearded and tanned, Frank was neither particularly knowledgeable nor super-efficient having only taken over his beat a week or so earlier. He had an impish sense of humour, a qualification plainly popular with his charges. For what was left of the day he escorted us into town with the object of pointing out its salient points, i.e. the supermarket, bakery and post office.

Grazalema is not only picturesque but is a star representative of the Pueblos Blancos series of villages settled among the Sierras of El Pinar and El Endrinall, the two high ranges of the region. The township gives its name to the national park in which it stands and is, judging by the number of mostly Spanish Sunday excursionists flooding into the cafes and restaurants, a popular destination; a kind of Lavenham of Andalucia. And they weren't the only ones. The place was also a favoured settlement of the Romans and the Arabs, the latter calling it Ben-Zalema, and their legacies are scattered about the locality while two 17th century churches (one with a consumptive-sounding cracked bell) add to its attractions as does its superb setting cupped by weather-eroded limestone mountains and backed by the great Matterhorn-like Penon Grande peak. Here, I felt, even on that day of arrival, was a promise of more exciting walking than the flattish sandy pine groves of the Atlantic coast.

Though I didn't realise it at the time, our first walk was one along a mule track detailed and mapped in the Andalucian edition of Sunflower's excellent touring and walking guidebooks; bibles – or at least prayer books – for hikers. The book classed the route as strenuous but failed to mention that it was known as "The Leap of the Goatherd" and what and why this worthy leapt. The way wound up, round and down a spur of the Sierra de Pinar along faint paths that frequently vanished into thin air, a morass of stones or prickly entanglements of gorse causing those, like me, wearing shorts yelps of pain. This turned out to be a favourite trick of Andalucian mountain paths which was not greatly appreciated by the likes of us. The limestone rock paths – when they were visible – were often formed of cockscombs of narrow pointed boulders making walking that much more treacherous and where the rock had been worn smooth or was wet a walker had to watch every footfall.

Cattle roamed over much of the area so numerous makeshift gates – real Heath Robinson affairs – in dry stone walls were encountered and had to be painstakingly opened and closed. The surrounding rock walls, ridges, escarpments and gigantic boulders had been moulded into fantastic shapes by the elements and, in the most unlikely places, wild flowers, many strange to British eyes, grew and flourished. We even came across the occasional orchid.

On a fine day the temperature, even in March can be high though, as I said earlier, directly a cloud obscures the sun the cold air instantly re-asserts itself. Howeve, this time of year holds considerable advantages. The valleys are green and lush though come late Spring and Summer and the land is blasted brown and arid, the temperatures soar and walking becomes no longer a pleasure.

This walk ended at the sizeable village of Benaocaz standing close to the Via Romana, an old Roman highway. The place is another Pueblo Blanco of Arab origin alleged to contain the remains of a fortress though, sweating profusely, our objective lay on a less cultural plane – the village pub. Our return to Grazalema was effected by means of the local scheduled bus service that must have made a profit that afternoon.

The dry bed of the river Alemo guided us out of Grazalema the second day. Rivers hereabouts at this time of year seemed to be little more than a few slimy green ponds set among a tumbled mass of boulders and this one was no different though its banks were a carpet of wild irises. Initially we followed an old mule track, once the only "road" feeding the township, and it led us into a woodland of decrepit cork trees under which we consumed our packed "elevenses" while a flock of vultures circled hopefully overhead. The trunks of cork trees can be stripped of their bark but once every nine years; anything less than this period and the trees give up the ghost as these appeared to be doing. Crossing and re-crossing the riverbed we reached the head of a broad valley buttressed by impressive sheer rock walls eroded into the usual sculptured images; a wild lonely valley a million miles from today's world.

Possibly it is just this sort of environment that had helped, but right from the start of the first week our group had gelled into a tight group of friends with not the slightest indication of any friction amongst us. Maybe Ray, our oldest and senior participant, won't mind if I mention his occasional bouts of cantankerousness but at 80 years of age this is a permitted and accepted privilege.

The weather had been kind all day but caught us out with a short but sharp shower as we headed towards a road that hopefully would bring us to the village of Villaluenga del Rosario, there to catch our bus. Twice before a few drops of rain had fallen sending everyone diving for their waterproofs whereupon it stopped. The third time we ignored it – and paid the price of a wetting. Weather in the mountains is fickle indeed. Cloud can turn the terrain into a grey slash of brown hills. Then the sun reappears and there is a sudden retransformation as the scenery turns back into patterns of red, yellow, ochre and bright green.

The prospect of an urban day in Ronda, the largest town in the vicinity, was not universally greeted with great enthusiasm, particularly since there was an optional excursion to an even larger city – Seville – programmed for the following day. But Ronda was an included part of the schedule so to Ronda we went. And we loved it.

The town is unique. It sits astride a gigantic gorge, or *tajo* as they call it here, the two halves joined by an equally unique 17th century bridge known as the New Bridge. Its lower portions once housed prisoners, some of whom, even as recently as the Spanish Civil War, ended up very dead at the bottom of the gorge – as did the designer on the very day of the structure's opening ceremony though his descent was accidental. The only other town I know split by a similar gorge is Constantine in Algeria.

Ronda is one of the oldest towns in Spain as is its bullring which is a beautiful building whatever your views might be on bullfighting. It houses a museum of bullfighting too displaying relics of famous – and mostly extinct – matadors and even the more celebrated bulls.

Elsewhere there is a wealth of architectural magnificence concentrated within easy walking distance and mostly to be found on the southern and older section of the town. And the view across the great sheer cliffs to the west is stunning; one can stand looking at it for hours on a clear sunny day as was the one with which our visit was blessed.

About half the group chose to participate in the Seville excursion. I was not one of them having, again, been there before and being none too keen on city-visiting on warm sunny days. A lone walk in the hills made a better proposition. However, Seville should be seen, there's no doubt about that. The Old Town is a tangle of red roofs and low white houses, out of which a few tall palm trees act as green minarets to compete with the real thing. At the centre it masses round the huge cathedral – third largest in Europe – and there is a fine Moorish palace plus dozens of sedate churches. Above all, however, Seville is a place of secret gardens, a city of flowers, clean bright and crowded with lively people as has been the case for centuries.

The remainder of us stayed behind and went our own ways. My lone walk turned into a duo when Eileen chose to accompany me on a circuit of the Penon Grande massif again detailed in the Sunflower Andalucia guidebook. The going was classed as moderate, the distance quoted as eight kilometres or just over two and a half hours duration. Because we idiotically missed the correct turn-off at the top end of town we added an hour and four more kilometres to our walk which included some steep, rocky and prickly gorse-afflicted ascents and descents with the usual ankle-breaking potential while the path repeatedly disappeared playing its same old tricks. The near-end of the walk offered sensational views across the plains to the west and also of the great bulk of Penon Grande mountain at close quarters. An awesome sight. And just before entering Grazalema we passed through a grove of Pinsapai trees, a unique species of fir found only in this very locality.

On the penultimate walk we got ourselves lost. Well, kind of. We missed a marker and so we found ourselves in difficult terrain following cattle and sheep trails that, of course, led nowhere or in the direction we didn't want to go. It was a fine warm day with not a single cloud in the sky so nobody worried – except maybe Frank with his responsibilities. Gallantly he bade us halt and rest as he forged ahead on his own to reconnoitre the countryside even sacrificing his lunch break to do so.

Lunch break in Andalucia

Everywhere was a tumbled confusion of boulders, yellow gorse, dwarf oaks (bearing acorns which the pigs eat and maybe we too would if we were really lost), and the sound of sheep and cowbells on the still air. The valley in which we found ourselves was bordered by the customary buttresses of fissured limestone ensuring that there was only two directions we could go; straight on or back the way we had come. And retreat was not to our liking so there was no contest. So straight on we went. Then suddenly Frank recognised a landmark and, eventually, an outlying farm of the village we knew – Benaocaz – hove into view. The pigs could keep their acorns. The start of the walk had been the stiff and treacherous climb that Eileen and I had accomplished the previous day so, all in all, it was an exhausting hike though the spice of a small adventure had been appreciated by everyone. Maybe Ramblers had pre-arranged it. Anyway the beer in the pub at Benaocaz was nectar.

Our last walk was pleasant but something of an anti-climax. It didn't even take place in the mountains. Accompanied by one David Lanfear, who has lived in Andalucia for 13 years and knows the countryside around Grazalema like the proverbial back of the hand, we made what could almost be described as a leisurely stroll along the valley of the river Campoboche which, for once, had water in it. We left from the village of Montejaque, reportedly famous for a salami-type sausage, and followed the river through an undulating valley of cork trees and gorse clumps with barely a rocky patch to inconvenience our footsteps. All the while David aired his considerable knowledge of flowers, plants and trees which greatly pleased the botanists in our ranks. Towards the end of the walk, with the great Penon Grande in sight marking the home base, the fastest walkers forged ahead as if not to prolong the slow finale of a memorable Andalucian experience.

3. The Atlas Mountains of Morocco (two weeks, grade D+)

I have a special affinity with the Atlas Mountains of Morocco. Or that's what I like to think anyway. Over the years I have passed through them, round them, over them and even along them. I have climbed near 14,000-foot Mount Toubkal – no great feat in summer – to stand, shivering with cold, at the summit on snow that one imagines has no right to fall in Africa.

Actually the Atlas are not just Moroccan. They extend across both Algeria and Tunisia too for a distance of 1,500 miles running more or less parallel to the coast of northwest Africa and bounded on the north by the Mediterranean and on the south by the Sahara. But so far as Ramblers Holidays are concerned – and me too – it is the Moroccan Atlas that counts.

Known by Moroccans as *Idraren Draren* or "Mountains of Mountains", this section of them consists of five distinct ranges, varying in length and height, more or less parallel to one another. The main range, known as the Great Atlas, occupies a central position and is by far the longest and loftiest chain with an average height of 11,000 feet. The lower portion – or Middle Atlas – lying north of the Great Atlas has wooded slopes in which the lion is supposed to still exist – though I doubt it. The Anti-Atlas runs parallel to and south of the central range, and has a mean altitude of 5000 feet, although some peaks and even passes exceed 6,000 feet. These, then, are the salient points of the mountains upon which I was to join a Ramblers party for a two-week series of walks commencing the end of March.

Not so very long ago Morocco was a distant land visited, if ever, by travellers blessed with time and money to spare. Only a fortunate few could make it to Marrakech or even Tangier. But the rapid rise in popularity of Morocco as "the closest of the far-off places" has changed all this with the help of the package tour. Thus for the visitor from Europe, there is no land so near and yet so completely different as Morocco. It is the nearest Islamic country and the nearest African state; an entry point to another world.

The country enjoys a privileged climate all year round and its strange towns and glorious sandy beaches are accessible to all while the more intrepid traveller has the splendid interior in which to roam. This includes the Atlas Mountains which are equally accessible on the reasonably-maintained road system covering the whole country. Above all Morocco is a land of hospitality and friendliness; the courtesy of its people is proverbial as we group of ramblers were about to find out for ourselves.

I pronounced earlier that I had travelled along the Atlas. This, I think, needs short explanation. For reasons lost in the sands of time we – some eight or nine misguided souls – were attempting to drive a clapped-out Bedford three-ton lorry of World War Two vintage along part of the Moroccan section of the High Atlas on tracks where no wheeled vehicle – let alone a Bedford lorry – had ever been before. To cover some 50 miles took around a week, negotiating rivers into which we had to pile rocks to form bridges, inching along ledges with one side of the vehicle scraping the rock wall and the other overhanging sheer drops, traversing scree that had to be cleared so that the wheels could get a grip, and creeping along escarpments with one of us on foot in front guiding the steering so that embedded boulders didn't fracture the axles and innards of our sorely-tried lorry. Even in the few remote hamlets heavy tree boughs barred our way and had to be severed before we could continue. And for a day off from these ridiculous proceedings we found the energy to climb Toubkal. That particular journey was made nearly a quarter of a century ago. Now I was back in the Atlas with only my legs to worry about.

Because of a series of delayed flights from Heathrow we finally arrived at Marrakech around midnight. The group this time was 15-strong; a wider age-variation than hitherto with a younger element in the middle 30s, rising to 75 (me as usual) with a couple who likewise must have been close to my vintage. Our leader was Ann, a level-headed lady then sorely tried by lost baggage and missing participants courtesy of Royal Air Maroc at Marrakech Airport. Because of the vast emptiness of the High Atlas we also took on board a Moroccan guide who knew the terrain over which we would be walking. Thus we were introduced to 36-year old Hamid, a delightful Berber hailing from a village near Fez and, like all his Atlas tribal cousins, a rugged individualist..

The High Atlas act not only as a barrier but also as a refuge for one of the great tribal groups of North Africa, the Berbers. They are a people who have seen the world around them succumb to successive tides of influence while they have remained largely unchanged for over a quartet of centuries; they possess their own language, customs and dress. Yet, contrary to what one might expect, tourism is becoming a fast-growing source of income as the more adventurous of their foreign visitors come as climbers and trekkers into their realm. And the Berbers, perhaps the most agile mountain people in the world, have readily taken to this new industry. For a score of years they have catered for groups and individuals; a number have become qualified guides of the likes of Hamid, versed in geology, mountaineering techniques and speaking multiple languages. Yet in a range of mountains stretching so great a distance, among a people numbering over two million, those that have regular contact with what are Europe's more adventurous travellers are exceedingly few.

Largely unvisited and undisturbed, the majority of villages continue their lives untouched by tourism or even the central government of Morocco. Even those that do see the occasional foreign visitor slip back into their traditional life outside the tourist season – if anything had changed even during it. The Berber culture is a remarkably tough and stable creature.

An interminable post-midnight drive followed on an initially dead straight flat road running through moonlit olive groves. It then began to climb and spiral as we neared the small town of Asni which fancies itself as the "Chamonix of Morocco" sitting as it does at the southerly base of the Toubkal massif. The place is a base for hikers in the Toubkal National Park and it is also located near the somewhat limited ski slopes (I was told that a ski pass here entitles you not only to rides on the few chair lifts but also to uphill towing by mule-power!). Growing in stature as we ground up the hills were what appeared to be moon-illuminated white clouds but which eventually identified themselves as the snow-capped peaks of the High Atlas.

Our destination was the straggly village of Isni Wirgame, astride a much-reduced river in a rocky cleft. Here the Auberge au Sanglier qui Fume, an impressive title for a small hotel complex of basic but adequate rooms and facilities was to become home for the first four nights of the tour.

A late breakfast on the terrace of freshly-squeezed orange juice, warm sweet rolls and cold pancakes was taken in the company of a pair of expressionless storks who lived in a nest atop a tree nearby and were seemingly self-appointed honorary residents of the hotel. Hardly had we had time to digest this Alice-in-Wonderland scenario or scrape the diminished sleep from our eyes when we were off on our initial baptism of fire.

But the ensuing walk proved no great hardship. Dropped off by minibus just short of Asni, we made easy progress up a range of pink hills, the track – well-used but stony – leading initially to a village called Moulay

Brahim where we were "invited" to "morning coffee" – or, to be more precise – morning mint tea.

A word about these small compact villages linked by the roughest of tracks and often lying far from a tarmac road. Mud, stone and reed-built, and flat-roofed, the houses, piled together like square cardboard boxes divided by muddy alleyways, belong to a world of their own; a world of centuries gone by. There may be a tiny "shop" selling anything from Coca-Cola to shaving cream while in the larger communities a relatively impressive mosque, its tower square and solid, is by far a superior building to any other in the village. Children peer round corners ready to flee or wave shyly while the older and bolder boys emerge in force to demand money, cigarettes or pens before being shooed away by a disapproving adult. "Bon jour" is the staple greeting, French – a vestige of colonisation – being the second language after Arabic.

Our morning tea, well-sweetened, decanted back and forth between ornate silver teapot and small glass until the pourer was satisfied that the liquid was well impregnated with the sheaf of mint, was then poured solemnly into all the glasses which were then distributed for us to imbibe in small sips. On this occasion our tea party took place on the flat roof of a house with smoke issuing from a couple of holes that served as chimneys for the cooking operations being carried out below by the invisible lady of the household. The only women to be seen were carrying pitchers of water on their heads or undertaking some manual chore; the menfolk standing around smoking and chatting.

Refreshed, we pressed on, the view behind us of the huge Toubkal massif expanding as we gained height. Here you can lift your eyes up, up to towering snow walls, a maze of side valleys reaching up to cols that lead to parallel valleys, east and west, while straight on leads to Jbel Toubkal, Lord of all. Closer to hand was the Kik plateau on which we now stood. The red earth, studded with rocks, gave an impression of a parched land-scape though small plots of cultivation – mainly wheat – could be dis-cerned here and there. The countryside around these parts grips the imagination – or it does mine at any rate – a countryside of dried river-beds scattered with so many cacti they look like the stubble of a hay-field.

The stony track continued, leading us to Taddart, a larger village, this one graced with a square-towered mosque. Here we were mobbed by packs of children, mainly boys, with demands for anything we cared to give them; seemingly another ritual akin to the tea ceremony. These village children, well-dressed and cheerful, were not beggars; they simply looked upon us as richer than them – which, of course we undoubtedly were – and therefore fair game for the off-chance of a handout.

We were to pass two further villages in the afternoon as the track traversed the plateau before descending to the township of Tivili fed by a tarmac road and which, as a result, was afflicted by the trappings of urbanisation, the stone and wattle of the houses replaced by ugly concrete. Dust-covered cars stood in refuse-laden streets and hard-faced commercialism reared its head. We drank more tea at a decrepit cafe under the less-than-interested gaze of its bored male clients while awaiting our transport back to the hotel – in my case an overloaded Mercedes taxi with no seat-belts.

That the day's walk was no more than a warm-up was made abundantly clear. Tomorrow, we were gleefully informed, the going would be harder, longer and more arduous; well up to a D+ grade slog of which the tour had been classified. Thus, following an early breakfast – even too early for our companionable storks – we embarked upon it with slight trepidation.

And indeed it was a harder day but a greatly enjoyable one. We left on foot directly from the hotel to wend a way up and into the valley of the Azaden river, reduced at this time of year, to a fast-running but not quite leapable stream. Gradually the valley expanded enough to contain a village; thereafter it narrowed again forcing us to cross and re-cross the waters, a tricky business if attempting to do so without recourse to wet feet.

The path, well-defined and wide, began to climb steadily along the flank of the western wall of the valley by now taking on the guise of a gorge. It eventually offered superb views of the highest snow-clad peaks of the High Atlas. We were getting into our stride nicely when we had to turn off the track onto a barely-discernible path that took us steeply upwards in tight zigzags, clawing its way up the top of the valley wall. Under the midday sun it was tough going and we were soon sweating like the proverbial pig. Our picnic break on the summit was well-earned.

The route down the other side was easier; a gradual descent through, in the lower reaches, stubby trees that put me in mind, for some reason, of the African bush of Kenya. Tea was high on the agenda of the party's ladies so at the first village – Marighe – Hamid arranged a spontaneous invitation from the first occupant to appear. I can hardly envisage such an action in Britain where, of course, there are plenty of cafes and snack bars to hand but here, in these primitive brown villages, the producing of mint

The party walking in the Azaden river valley

tea for the passing stranger is taken for granted and provides a little extra income for the host.

A dry river bed with banks of loose soil and gravel made uncomfortable further walking and a longer homeward haul than expected and, for we men of the party, the beer back at the hotel barely touched the sides of our throats.

As mentioned earlier such a walk as this does wonders to cement the gelling process of a group of strangers such as we were upon arrival at Marrakech Airport. Inevitably one sizes up the varied individuals as they assemble, slotting into the mind those you think you are going to like and those that might be a pain in the neck. But first impressions are invariably false and those indexed first opinions are soon scattered to the winds. Metaphorically speaking, it is a similar process to a wary dog sniffing at another's backside and then running off happily with a new-found friend.

To compensate for a hard day's walking in and out of the Azaden river valley the subsequent perambulation almost lived up to the name of a ramble. In effect we walked a figure of eight that encompassed a range of hills in the Tahamout region beyond Asni. Much of it was dust-track walking with an optional ascent and descent of an escarpment that formed the top ring of the figure eight for which the reward was a stunning view of both the Toubkal and Oukaimeden massifs in their shining white livery. A gravelly descent by the whole group across scree overlooking the heat-shimmering Plain of Marrakech and a march through a wood littered with nature-decorated rocks brought us back to our waiting transport.

Boar, desert fox, mouflon and hyena are reputed to live in the Toubkal park region but with 17 of us chatting merrily plus one loud-voiced lady afflicted with – talking of hyenas – a guffaw to awaken the dead there was little chance of spotting anything beyond the odd tortoise.

Next morning we left early for pastures new. This involved a near 400-kilometre drive encompassing sections of both High and Middle Atlas including the negotiation of the Tizi-n-Tishka Pass of between six and seven thousand feet, the road here becoming a coiled serpent as it struggles for height. And beyond Ouarzazate the terrain switches in direct contrast to flat arid semi-desert broken around the towns of Skoura and Kelaa des M'Gouna where roses grow as thick as crabgrass on a suburban lawn; enough of them to provide the whole country with rose-water which is sold in virtually every shop in the two towns.

And so to the Dades Gorge in which we were to take up residence for the following eight days and nights. Here is truly a gorge with a capital "G", and surely one of the great spectacles of Morocco. By venturing into it you literally disappear into the bottom of a canyon, the road winding and twisting at the foot of sheer cliffs as straight and deep as knife wounds in the body of the plateau. In effect it is a narrow, intricately sculptured chasm that contains between its walls a multitude of imposing peaks and buttes, of smaller canyons within canyons and complex ramifying gulches and ravines. Through it runs the Dades river, fast-flowing and substantial, allowing on each bank a narrow band of cultivation; a shocking green blanket of fields and trees lit, here and there, by puffs of almond or cherry blossom sparkling with the glint of sun on water.

Our hotel was Le Vieux Chateau, a mile beyond Ait Oudinar, the last village of any substance in the most dramatic section of the gorge. It should have been the Auberge du Dades in the village itself but a German group got there first. However both hotels were run by the same management and equally lacked most of the amenities we consider vital in a hotel. But my room held a bed, it was clean, the kitchen was to produce simple but substantial meals and the staff were very friendly which, after all, is really all that matters. Electricity occasionally lit low-wattage electric bulbs and hot water materialised in the morning and evening while such items as towels, soap and toilet rolls had to be collected from reception. Since the rooms held not a stick of furniture except for a bed, items like chairs and tables had to be purloined from wherever they could be found while, with no cupboards, our belongings lay strewn around the floor or remained in suitcases. Someone mentioned that I was a writer so I won a table the first night. All this might sound off-putting but it has to be remembered that Morocco is a Third World country and the Dades Gorge way off the tourist circuit so such shortcomings form part of the experience of rural North Africa.

Our first walk in the gorge was an introductory one. The route followed the Dades river, our path occasionally requiring careful balancing acts on irrigation channels reminding me of the *levada* walkways of Madeira. It linked a number of villages hunched around their thick mud-walled *ksars* or village castles, many three centuries old yet still massive in ruin. Life here is more than medieval; it is positively Old Testament. Children waved to us, occasionally requesting bon-bons but without any aggressiveness. Flimsy log bridges took us, hesitatingly, across the river where frogs in the shallows croaked incessantly. But what held us spellbound was the fantastic shapes of the gorge walls with pinnacles of lava-impregnated limestone soaring chimney-like from tumbled rock formations that changed colour every hour of the day. Against these pink/red walls it was difficult to distinguish villages from the surrounding

The Plain of Marrakech

crags though, down at river-level, the vivid green of young corn and barley tipped by those bomb-bursts of blossom made startling contrast. We returned back to the hotel the same way we had come – and, of course, someone did fall into the irrigation canal.

A minibus ride of some eight kilometres taking us through the narrowest section of the gorge, where the river and road are compressed together like a nut in the jaws of a giant nut-cracker, delivered us next morning close to the village of Ait Oukhasine. Though the gorge continues for another 12 miles it is here that the grip of the stark mountain walls relent a little to turn it into a valley. Our path led through the village and up and over an escarpment then down to a neighbouring village astride the road along which we had come. In point of fact the object of the walk was to enable us to observe another section of the gorge, likened in some minds to a miniature version of America's Grand Canyon. And once we had gained height on the diagonal track that took us up the escarpment to the base of the vertical cliffs it was easy to see why. Huge bolsters of fissured brown/red lava-impregnated limestone moulded aeons ago by unimaginable forces hung over us as we consumed our picnic lunch in the warm sunshine watched by a couple of nomad women tending their sheep and camels.

The way down proved to be another of those ankle-breaking descents along the dry bed of a stream. There was no path as such; it was simply the fastest and most direct way back to the road. Our minibus awaited those who preferred to ride back to the hotel but a one and a half hour march along the dust road was small price to pay for the privilege of being amongst such astounding terrain.

On Saturday – at least I think it was Saturday, for in such a remote corner of the world as this one loses touch with mundane details like days of the week – we set out on what Ann described as the "Wet Walk". This involved a one and a half hour minibus journey at both ends of the walk which made exciting driving across a barren, arid and rock-studded desert on tracks that would offer a punishing challenge to any budding rally driver. At times we got stuck fast and had to bale out so that the empty – and lighter – vehicle could negotiate a particularly excruciating boulder-strewn gradient or wadi. All in all it made a good prelude and finale to the journey on foot we made between these activities.

The route from a village called Ait Maraoje followed the course of the M'Goun and Aindour rivers, fast-moving and, in parts, quite deep. Fording and re-fording – someone counted 22 fordings – against strong currents at frequent intervals as the river walls demanded we became adept at this form of water negotiation. And there is a method described in chapter 9 of this book for so-doing. In this case most of us chose to wear alternate and lighter footwear for those glorified paddles though, because of slippery and sharp stones as well as weed on the river bed, one's trekking boots make for safer fording. A stout stick is also a helpful accoutrement.

Though we were out of the gorge on this walk the brown/red rock walls of the valleys through which we passed held similar characteristics; limestone formations welded into weird shapes; a moon landscape if there ever was one. Yet alongside the rivers a gash of intense cultivation ensured easy and level hiking when we weren't wading through water. The only climbs and descents were those when transferring from one valley to another.

Villages, some dominated by turreted *kasbahs* the colour of dried red roses, still existed even in these remote parts and people popped up from nowhere to greet us. Friendly and cheerful children would accompany the group for a while until persuaded otherwise by adults who were invariably courteous and polite to us. As we had started out early we had a cross-valley view of one village coming to life: the goats pouring out to graze, young girls setting forth to collect scarce firewood or fodder, women going down to the stream to wash clothes, a mule bearing a man off on some errand; others with mattocks on their shoulders. In another gorge-like valley, with constricting rock walls hemming us in, a narrow mud walkway became our route high up above the river which lay on one side and a deep irrigation channel on the other. Progress along this treacherous path meant a degree of tightrope walking that put the wind up a few members of the group especially where the wall projected outwards threatening to push the unwary traveller over the edge. Hamid was of great help and comfort on such occasions. The walk ended at the village of Jourbeste reached via a communal well producing cool clear drinking water that nobody would touch except me; water sources such as this are almost certain to be safe; an overdone caution means missing a treat. So the "Wet Walk" came to an end. And under the hot sun the paddling had been the best part of it.

If yesterday's river walking had been designated the "Wet Walk" then Sunday's should surely be the "Nomad Circuit" though whether the edge-of-society family we intended to visit would be "at home" upon our arrival at their quarters remained to be seen. This was not a tourist gimmick but a genuine social call.

And the family was at home – or at least some of it was. An old blind man, a woman and a donkey greeted us while a second woman was weaving a rug on a home-made loom inside a dark, snug and surprisingly dirt-free cave. In fact the whole family, their goats and chickens all lived in a quartet of caves which we were permitted to inspect. Hamid brewed us mint tea on the hot embers of their dry scrub fire for which, in return, we donated fruit from our picnic lunch and a little money.

Many people associate nomads with gypsies but this is an erroneous conception. Whilst gypsy communities contentedly live close to urban areas the nomad family – not communities – never venture near a town preferring to be far away from the rest of human society. They make their living from rug-making or perhaps pottery-making which they sell through an agent who will visit them to negotiate terms. A nomad family will probably keep a certain number of sheep, goats and maybe a camel or two which will provide them with meat, milk and wool. Illness is treated by the use of herbs; a doctor would never be called. And when the family move from one location – like these caves we saw – they have no idea as to where their next extended sojourn will be. However they possess tents in which to reside in the meantime. In Morocco the nomad population refuse to be registered by the state; attempts were made but abandoned. These facts I gleaned from Hamid who was plainly in sympathy with a way of life that can hardly be closer to the environment and the land in which they – and we – live.

We had reached the nomad family by way of a steady climb from the hotel, crossing the Dades river to do so. Our social engagement completed we stumblingly followed the contours of a barren and stony hill, one of many that lay behind the gorge, then descended a rough zigzag donkey path to a dry river bed which proclaimed the beginnings of a deep ravine known, it seems, as "Death Canyon", one of the subsidiary gorges of the Dades. Within it we lunched, each to his own boulder as seat and table, and from there made our own way homeward since the canyon ends at a log bridge yards from the hotel, a final hour's dawdle.

This walk could have been extended but it would have meant missing out on the canyon. And this would have been a crying shame since this narrow slit of a gorge at right angles to its bigger brother is intensely dramatic with great multi-thousand ton boulders and sheer sculptured walls riddled with caves looming ominously overhead shutting out the bright afternoon sunshine.

Less than 25 miles separate the Dades and Todra gorges as the crow flies but mere mortals have to drive the best part of a 100, via Boumalne and Tinerhir, to reach Dades's neighbour. And that's what we did the following day. Mostly it was a day of sightseeing but to keep our limbs from seizing up a three-hour hike was included in the programme.

Most guidebooks reserve their purplest prose for the Todra rather than the Dades perhaps because it is easier and more convenient for excursion coaches to drive right into rather than taking the tortuous single track road, badly pot-holed and with little parking space, that feeds the latter. Yet the Dades Gorge displays more prolonged and varied sections of unbelievable rock scenery even if the walls are a mite lower. However, the Todra Gorge is not to be missed. Once the visitor decides to leave the date palm groves and kasbahs of Tinerhir for more startling spectacles, the Todra will provide it in full measure. The road virtually ends at the bottom of a narrow canyon, the walls of which rise well over a thousand feet. This and the enormous abyss separating the High Atlas from the Djebel Sarro, the dusty, lifeless plain over which we had driven from the Dades, is, so I am informed, the same kind of geological accident – albeit on a smaller scale – that produced the Grand Canyon to which, as already stated, the Dades is compared.

To me, and in fact to all of us, the high density of visitors plus a more aggressive hard-sell attitude to them by local touts in the gorge puts two nails into the Todra coffin. Even the central perpendicular walls were speckled with roped climbers doing their thing while a plethora of hotels and restaurants lay right at the base of this most spectacular section. The good old Dades with its kinder, gentler villagers, fewer amenities and visitors got our vote.

Tinerhir, the Todra township, holds a dusty, rakish air. A visit to the palmery, one of the biggest in southern Morocco, is worthwhile and it was through the greater part of its eight or nine kilometre length that we made our walk. The palm groves are interspersed with small cereal plots on a bigger scale than those of the Dades gorge; much of it putting me in mind of a giant set of allotments superimposed on, say, Richmond Park avec palm trees but sans deer. Across on the cliffsides there was a remarkable variety of soil colours; purple, red and yellow in turn, spotted with ilex trees. A shady restaurant was our venue for lunch making a pleasant alternative, again, from our midday picnic diet which seldom changed. We were pleased to leave the Todra for our happy hunting ground in the Dades Gorge which, somehow, had come to be our very own.

Our penultimate walk in the Dades region had the label of "Le Montagne du Dades" but it could well have been the "Switchback Walk" since it was something of a roller-coaster up and down a series of stony hills bare of foliage. The route was graded D+ but, with a discernible track for much of the distance the walk was hardly of great physical endurance in spite of one or two difficult bits where large boulders had accumulated. There was also some dry river-bed negotiation no worse than a hike along the shingle beach of Brighton. The single tree – standing out like a sore thumb – which we came across before the final descent to river-level at Ait Aubour village provided a minimum of shade for our picnic partaken in sight of another nomad cave settlement. Their two dogs enjoyed the hard crusts of our sandwich rolls.

We were supposed to be collected by minibus for return to the hotel but it was late arriving so, with energy to spare, some of us walked most of the way. It had been another warm and sunny day, as they had been all along, but cooler and cloudier weather built up in the late afternoon, the cloud beginning to form on the mountain tops to eventually clamp down as raw mist.

The *souk* of Boumalne with a traditional Moroccan *hammam* (steam bath) thrown in? Or try out an unscheduled, untried riverside walk upstream of the gorge? This was the choice of activities we were offered on our final day. With the sky blue and cloudless and showing no sign of unsettled weather the walk won hands down.

Here was a portion of the gorge we had passed by on the road a number of times. It contained what was assuredly the most extraordinary rock sculpture of all and now we had the chance to see it at close quarters.

It was, in the main, flat walking; nothing much in the way of long uphill plods though there were a couple of, for us, difficult sections involving a rock scramble to view a waterfall and a detour to avoid getting our feet wet in the river where it ran tight against the two walls of a subsidiary gorge. Some of us did in fact wade up to our thighs against a strong current, pushing ourselves through the deep cleft in the perpendicular walls. Otherwise it was a hike along the earthen banks of irrigation channels and alongside cereal plots often in the company of squads of village youngsters who took it upon themselves to act as guides when we were crossing their localities. Women were out washing by the river and they laughed and waved at us with a mixture of curiosity, shyness and friendliness. Women hereabouts are not veiled and wear bright garments often decorated with beads that look most attractive. Purple irises edged the cereal plots and the blossom advanced up the valley, the gorse and broom fully in bloom and the fig trees in leaf. Only the walnuts remained bare; always they are the last trees to burst into new life. I noticed a flight of kestrels calling above us on the crags while choughs showed off their acrobatic flying ability as we lunched beside the river. Noticing me draining the last dregs from my water bottle a dark-skinned Moroccan in a flowing white *jellaba* and skull cap offered me a bulbous orange which I accepted gratefully.

With this final walk of the tour we had the satisfaction of having seen in some detail the most sensational creations of nature in the gorge; great bulwarks of rock welded into shapes that the most imaginative artist or sculptor could never conjure up in his wildest dreams. And we likewise had seen much of the stony landscape that borders the gorge and which exhibits a harsh beauty all its own. It had been worth every footstep.

And so homeward via, once more, Ouarzazate, the Tizi-n-Tichka Pass, to Marrakech where we had time for a walking tour of a city described in one guidebook (written by a colleague of mine) as "a huge sun-baked sandwich with an exotic filling of palaces, *souks*, and colourful people". That this fabled city is today sold as a package resort is, to me, rather sad though at least I was privileged to have seen it, albeit briefly, more than a quarter of a century ago when it was a magic name, like Samarkand and Timbuctu.

We had been sorry to leave the Dades Gorge and its region, and, though few will admit it, I was unlikely to be the only one to feel a pang of perverted nostalgia for our friendly hotel with all its shortcomings. For ten days the hotel had become a tiny fragment of my life.

I would certainly miss my fellow-walkers, as I had those of earlier Ramblers parties. They had come from all walks of life as well as different parts of the UK and beyond. No one could fail to miss Hamid, our faithful, untiring guide, who accepted without a murmur our myriad idiosyncrasies . And this applies likewise to Ann whose duties – often self-imposed – multiplied far ahead of just those of group leader. But, speaking personally and possibly for all of us – I shall not miss our loud lady's strident guffaw reverberating across the valleys.

4. San Marcello, Tuscany

(one or two weeks, grade D+/C).

When I accepted an invitation to participate for a week of a one or two-week walking tour in Tuscany I was a mite nonplussed by the Ramblers brochure's indication of a slightly higher grade of physical effort required for this particular destination. And this puzzlement was reinforced when a former participant endorsed the alleged degree of endurance to be expected. Surely the gentle terrain of undulating countryside I remembered from a self-catering holiday Anna and I had experienced in the Chiantigiana district in the summer of 1984 was hardly a walking battleground? For many, Tuscany is a ravishing world of tranquility, of smooth hills, disciplined vineyards, olive groves, historic cities and stands of cyprus trees. Perhaps one is liable to forget that Tuscany is more than this. There are also the snow-capped peaks of the Apennines and Apuan Alps, with only one-tenth of Tuscany flat. Though many of its hills and minor mountains are rounded and curvaceous, the highlands of the northwest are a different story. Here rise the sheer Apuan Alps, often haughty, rough and jagged. Maybe I was in for a surprise.

Like nowhere else in Italy's heartland Tuscany reflects more than 3,000 years of history. Gigantic Etruscan walls stand guard over Renaissance palaces in its famed cities, Roman aqueducts soar past crenellated, medieval turrets. Every hilltop seems to be crowned by a castle, an ancient church or a crumbling ruin. And tucked away in the tiniest churches, as well as in the great cathedrals and palaces, is the world's most magnificent concentration of art. For this fertile heartland was the birth or workplace of the majority of the Italian masters; Leonardo, Michelangelo, Donatello, Fra Angelico, Cellini, and more.

When Charlemagne routed the Lombards, who had ruled Tuscany for two centuries, he annexed the region to his empire. But the restless cities tired of his rule and grabbed independence. Most of the splendid medieval cities were built in the 12th and 13th centuries during this era of assertiveness and so formed the chief bases for the ensuing rivalry between them; a struggle between Church and State that transformed Tuscany into a chessboard of competing interests.

However, the turbulence of democracy was wearing thin and, one by one, the mini-republics opted for a quieter life under a united rule from Florence and for three centuries there was comparative peace. Then in the 18th century Tuscany became part of the Habsburg empire before, on

Buttermere from Fleetwith Pike in England's Lake District

The beautiful Upper Inn Valley, Austria, from above Fiss

Walking the Aachener Hohenweg, Austria, with the splendid triple waterfall behind

Views on a walk to Kitzkopf, Austria

Taking a break on the way up Cathedral Peak, Drakensberg Mountains, South Africa

Ramblers on their way to Mushroom Rock, Drakensberg Mountains, South Africa

Ramblers on a contour path below the Cathedral Massif in the Drakensberg Mountains, South Africa

The Azat Gorge, Armenia

A "wishing tree" near the Gegard Monastery in Armenia

The Gegard Monastery, Armenia

A river crossing on the Highway of the Inca at La Union in Peru

Mount Chimborazo — the Mountain of Snow — in Ecuador

February 18, 1861, the kingdom of Italy, comprising Tuscany as a whole, was proclaimed; a prelude to eventual incorporation into the Italian state.

Here then was the geographical and historical background to my subsequent walking assignment.

Hardly had the minibus that met our group at Bologna Airport cleared the city suburbs when the flat terrain began to heave into ever-higher hills and I found myself gazing upon a very different Tuscany to that which was recorded in the memo-pad of my mind.

Given the commonly-held belief in the civilisation of the Tuscan landscape, "wild Tuscany" might seem a misnomer. But northwards of the classic chessboard of vineyards and cypress a rugged wilderness, only superficially tamed in parts, awaits the visitor. Here the woods covering the steep slopes of the expanding mountain flanks were thick as rainforests dissected only by jaunty torrents and the odd footpath that could be discerned from the road as our vehicle followed the abruptly winding tarmac. My feet began to itch; the more so when Jim, our infectiously-enthusiastic leader, gave us the opportunity of a 15-minute leg-stretch along part of the Reno river valley on one side of which the road ran. It came to me that no wonder Ramblers Holidays had chosen this gently wild countryside for a walking holiday. Here, though hiking in general is less well-organised than in Britain and France, northern Tuscany had the makings of a ramblers' paradise. Better mapped than most regions, it provides a huge variety of trails from relaxing to vigorous with paths waymarked by the Italian Alpine Club (CAI).

The Apennines here have not been ravaged by quarrying as have some of the coast-paralleling Apuan Alps. They include the range on the Emilian border – the loftiest in the northern Apennines – as well as those of Casentino and Mugello. Centred upon Abetone, one of the best ski resorts in the Apennines, specially favoured by Florentines and commanding the pass of the same name – itself originating from a huge long-gone fir tree – the rugged northern range is ideal summer hiking territory. The transition, for me, from undulating valleys to mountains, from olive groves to chestnut and oak forests, culminating in beechwoods and waterfalls, was striking.

Only a half dozen of us had been on the British Airways flight from London's Heathrow, a one and three-quarter hour flight fortuitously half-full and serving a succulent smoked fillet of salmon. The bulk of the 16-strong group departed from Manchester on a charter flight to Pisa. Fortuitously too, we reached the destination of San Marcello in time for a three-course hot evening meal while the late-arriving remainder had to make do with sandwiches.

Once more the assembled group comprised a mixed bag though containing more women than men. Al of them werel in the early- and mid-middle aged bracket. The non-British element was represented by a staid and disapproving Canadian lady from Vancouver and a game Jewish American couple from Chicago; the rest hailing from the length and breadth of the UK. All, as it turned out, were reasonably able walkers though the female half of the American couple sometimes found the long uphill grinds something of a trial.

Our base for the scheduled two-week holiday (of which I could only afford the time to partake of one) was the Hotel Giardini, a homely and comfortable four-storey hostelry situated behind a belt of trees within a three-minute stroll of San Marcello centre. Our room was small but bounded by a balcony on two sides and equipped with a slightly old-fashioned bathroom (some of the other bathrooms had recently been modernised), the suite giving views over the town and countryside. Though mid-May we were again the only clients, at least for a while, so were made exceedingly welcome by Maurizio, the owner, his wife and young daughter who, together, acted as chef, waiter, bar attendant and hotel staff in general. And most effectively too. During our stay Maurizio's older daughter and her family from Bologna turned up to make it a true family affair. The Giardini is that kind of hotel. And Jim, a long-term resident, was a walker of tremendous vitality and, as previously stated, enthusiasm; a fine and characteristic leader with a flamboyant abundance of facial hair, and in common with me, a devotee of shorts.

I would class San Marcello – or San Marcello Pistoiese to give it the full works – as either a large village or small town; possibly the latter since it is the capital of a commune of surrounding villages. Opposite the hotel is the old railway station, now the bus depot; the railway that once ran picturesquely between Mammiano and Pracchia having expired – though on several occasions we would be following on foot surviving sections of the single line trackbed. Some guidebooks class San Marcello as a ski resort though it hardly gives this impression and, while there are a number of ski lifts and skiing apparatus to be seen hereabouts, skiing conditions in winter are not of the highest order. But what the township is noted for is an annual event involving a *mongolfiera*, or hot air balloon, which, on September 8, is launched annually to mark the end of summer. According to local legend, if the balloon rises higher than the bell tower of the church, the harvest will assuredly be good.

It is the church which gives its name to San Marcello; one that is the most visible glory of the township. Roman in origin, one Tito Livio, a Roman historian, linked it to the name of the Roman consul, Marco Claudio Marcello in the second century AD. And in the fifth century a pope of the very same name, martyred in 310 AD, is said to have become the patron saint of the district. Anyway, needless to say, San Marcello has historic roots whilst its remaining fortifications are a reminder of the time of the Longobardi when, in company with other villages around, it lay on the oft-disputed route through the hilltop passes between Pistoia and Modena.

Our first morning, as has become the Ramblers custom, was given over to a whistle-stop tour of the township, Jim pointing out the more important facilities such as the supermarket, post office, information office and, in this particular case, a gem of a cobbler who can repair footwear that would be normally considered unrepairable elsewhere. Additionally, this paragon of leatherwork hand-stitches his own trekking boots which he sells at a very moderate cost.

The afternoon was devoted to another Ramblers innovation, the "warmer-upper" or introductory walk; a preparatory stroll to herald more formidable perambulations to come. This one involved a transit through a trio of villages and a route along both sides of the Lima valley. The first village was Mammiano, neighbouring San Marcello, and reached mainly by road. And road-walking on Italian pavement-less mountain roads is not to be recommended since their mechanical traffic holds little respect for the humble pedestrianised sort.

Mammiano possesses an old castle situated on a slope between the rivers Lima and Limestre. It dates back to the time of the city states of Tuscany and during the 18th and 19th centuries the village became a centre for iron-working, an industry of some importance during that period. But what is special today about the place, particularly for walkers, is its celebrated hanging bridge, a spectacular pedestrian suspension bridge 720 feet long spanning the wide Lima valley. Originally built in 1922 it connects the villages of Mammiano with Popiglio, the second village on our route. The present structure was hung in a slightly different site to its predecessor and on steel cables with guidelines to minimise the swaying motion when used, though not all members of our group were happy about crossing the narrow span.

On the opposite bank a path through woods followed by a short road walk brought us to minuscule Popiglio which contained a bar of which we made full use. A descent to the bottom of the valley led to another remarkable bridge, this one the lovely old 12th century stone structure traversing the Lima river which put me in mind of the famous Venetian Bridge of Mes in northern Albania though on a slightly smaller scale. Bridges, it seemed, were becoming the theme of this walk with the Mammiano suspension bridge dredging up, for me, recollections of hairy crossings of great chasms on far less sturdy construction in Nepal.

We picnicked in a wild-flower sprinkled meadow beside the river, then moved off along gently rising paths to skirt Migliorini, the third of the village trio. Our pace was moderate though, as usual, there was the fast element and the slower one plus the occasional general pause by the botanically-minded to inspect the more rarer species of flower which, at least, brought us together. Salvia, Star of Bethlehem, viola and a large mauve Iris we in Britain take the trouble to nurture in our gardens were the chief sources of interest and proved without doubt that spring is the perfect season for a northern Tuscan botanical stroll.

That the rugged northern range of the Apennines makes for ideal hiking country particularly, too, in spring is nowhere shown more strongly than in the leafy terrain centred upon the small resort of Abetone which commands the mountain pass separating Tuscany and Emilia. Abetone itself is no more than a ski resort somewhat barren out of season though proclaiming itself the "balcony over Tuscany". But the mountain air makes the region invigorating in even the most stifling Tuscan summer.

Ponte Castruccio at Popiglio on River Lima

And nowhere else in Italy is spring more productive in terms of the environment with forests hiding marmots, roe-deer, mouflons and boar while golden eagles and kites are to be spotted soaring over the rocky outcrops.

One such forest was to display its most vivid springtime apparel on a walk we made initially along path number 22 from the village of Gavinana, scene of the defeat of the Florentine army in 1530, in which both commanders of the opposing armies, Francesio Ferucci and Philibert, Prince of Orange, were killed. Just a three kilometre hike from San Marcello the village centre is marked by an impressive equestrian statue of Francesco Ferucci , Captain of the Florentine Republic, who had his throat cut en route to the village to join forces against the Imperial Army. The piazza is, of course, named after the famed warrior astride his horse as is the museum opposite that commemorates the battle and a comfortable-looking hostelry nearby.

Our path took us steeply and endlessly upward to the ridgetop of Monticelli of some 5,000 feet, the dark pines giving way to the deliciously fresh light green leaves of a chestnut canopy through which filtered the rays of brilliant sunshine. Before us stretched further and higher ranges, their flanks streaked with, as yet, unmelted snow.

The route down the other side was more gradual with beechwoods slowly thinning to reveal further panoramas to delight the eye. The small observatory of Pian dei Termini, together with the occasional tiny memorial to partisans killed in some long-forgotten saga of the Second World War, gave excuse for a halt.

And so back to San Marcello in plenty of time for a beer and bath before a treat of a meal served, as always, by the indefatigable Maurizio. Night life in the town is hardly a raver's delight but the English Bar, down the road, is not without its attractions.

The longest walk of the tour was one with an unscheduled twist that materialised later. The day commenced with a minibus drive, with a halfway pause at the historic village of Cutigliano situated on a high spur of Monte Cuccola. The fact that it is something of an upmarket township today perhaps comes about through a combination of it being a winter sports centre and possessing an aristocratic heritage marked by a series of haughty edifices. The medieval centre comprises the Piazzo Catilina, the coat-of-arms adorned Palazzo del Capitano – or, more fully, the Palace of the Captains of the Mountains, and a brace of majestic churches. The star exhibit is the Palazzo, now the town hall but once the seat of what was known as the Captain of the Mountains, a sort of administrative, military and judicial gauleiter at a time when the region was under Florentine control. And Cutigliano, being in a borderland, was a well-fortified centre as can be verified by a glance at the structure of the bell tower of St Bartholomew's Church which formed part of a network of look-out towers created as an aid to defence of the territory.

Our drive continued through Melo and a well-wooded countryside, known for an abundance of bilberries and other assorted fruits of the forest, to the Refuge of the Doganaccia, today the summit station of a leg of a funicular route at near 5,000 feet. Here the road petered out and we took to our feet. The snow we had seen from afar on earlier walks was now appearing beneath our feet as the path disappeared under heavy wedges of the stuff at every crevice of the hillside, but another refuge, the Rifugio della Croco Arcana, marked the route to a small lake. the Lago Scaffaiolo, that all but evaporates in the summer. Surrounded by snow its green waters looked particularly uninviting though this failed to deter Jim, a glutton for invigorating punishment, from taking a dip. Across a wide valley rose Mount Cimone, the highest peak in the Northern Apennines.

When we had left the hotel low, ominous cloud hid the hilltops and we were enveloped in its cold, clammy embrace for much of the way to the lake. But suddenly a warm sun broke through to dispel the mist and give us some spectacular views of the surrounding mountains, some of the peaks poking through heavy cloud at lower altitude. A steady descent followed by a pathless climb was rewarded by the presence of a sizeable cabin being prepared for the summer hiking season by a trio of workmen who brought out chairs and benches to form the perfect venue for our picnic lunch. More than that, they also contributed a bottle of sparkling wine as an aperitif for those so inclined. And I regret to report that, upon returning the empty bottle to our kind benefactors, Jim and I were persuaded to knock back further draughts of not only the wine but also a potent liquor hardly recommended as an aid to navigating treacherous mountain paths. But the steep and sweaty climb to the col at 6,000 feet made an adequate antidote to our over-indulgence.

The route up to then had been another botanists' delight with carpets of mauve and white crocuses plus the odd gentian and a sprinkling of viola, poppies and pasque flowers. But abruptly, at the Passo del Cancellino, flowers, hills and everything were blotted out by heavy, wet cottonwool cloud which appeared from nowhere. Plodding on in line it was even difficult to make out the walker in front.

Disorientated, Jim had us all looking for the red and white way-markers that now became a vital banister for onward progress while wide swathes of deep, melting snow obliterated all signs of the path. These considerable drifts set at steep angles and fiendishly slippery became severe

Trekkers' rest stop on Mount Monticelli

obstacles in themselves and had us sliding and slithering across each miniature snowfield which became still more difficult to negotiate amongst the trees through which the path was alleged to run. The best method of traversing such drifts is by taking them at a run and digging one's heels into the snow but few of the group, unnerved by the conditions, were prepared to undertake this for fear of a long, downward slide into invisible depths. Instead, the branches of the trees at least provided hand-holds for each tentative, nervous footstep which had many of my companions ending up spread-eagled on their backsides in the wet snow. It was a testing time for the quality of our footwear too and few of us could boast of dry feet at the conclusion of this painful passage.

Below the snowline, the path once more plain to see and the low cloud thinning, conditions reverted to normal and our descent to more hospitable climes was swift. With another ridge, this one called the Passagio dei Malandrini, behind us and a watery sun appearing between flakes of drifting cloud we found ourselves at a junction marked by further partisan memorials at a nowhere point the map called Maceglia. The materialisation of the observatory that had been a landmark on a previous walk was a reassuring sight and, by way of an easy descent through pine forests and via a series of short cuts across fields and along unmarked, little-used tracks that only Jim knew about, we staggered back into San Marcello as dusk closed in. All in all a hike of some excitement and incident – and one we would never have undertaken had we been aware beforehand of the appalling conditions that had lain in wait for us.

High altitude walking at this time of year is all too often accompanied by the sudden descent of cloud to obliterate the fine views that make fatiguing climbs worthwhile. So with a fine clear dawn showing optimistic signs of a cloudless day ahead we embarked on another walk, this one to the summit of a viewpoint ridge for the express purpose of basking in the glory of the panorama allegedly to be seen from it.

A public bus, bound for Abetone, dropped us off at La Lima, a hamlet astride the river of the same name, and, straightway, we were launched into an interminable climb up and up through the chestnut forest that enveloped the flank of the high ridge above the village. The path, well-marked with newly-painted signs, zigzagged tortuously, its surface cushioned by a thick layer of dead leaves and leaf-mould. And at the summit of one ridge came another until at last we stood, panting and sweating, on top of the world. And it was then of course, that cloud decided to descend; small wisps at first but, by the time we reached the best viewpoint clear of trees along a ridgetop track, the famous view was entirely blotted out.

The way down, however, was via a gently descending dust road that made easy, obstacle-free walking. And halfway to the village of Popiglio, to which it led, the cloud lifted and sunshine broke through as we consumed our picnic lunch. Fickle weather indeed but at least we had, so far, been spared rain.

Above Popiglio, we were to make a short detour to look upon a couple of Roman-built watchtowers that made a secondary objective of the day's walk. Stark, lonely and crumbling amongst the undergrowth, they made convenient subjects for the photographers of the group denied the celebrated view. All around were green meadows glowing with buttercups and a clump or two of wild orchids.

The final descent to the village in brilliant sunshine was swift and, with Popiglio visited on the first walk of the tour, we knew our way to its bar and our way home. The latter was via that foot suspension bridge across the Lima valley, enjoyable to most but disturbing again for those with no head for heights. And above us loomed the ridge upon which we had expended so much effort now completely clear of cloud – and probably laughing at the trick it had played on us.

As in all mountainous environments weather can be extraordinarily varied. On another day's circular walk, commencing from and returning to San Marcello, we awoke to a solid downpour with little sign, judging by the universally low black clouds that cloaked the scenery, of it letting up. Even at breakfast the rain hissed down, yet, barely 15 minutes later, the heavenly tap was turned off, the black clouds evaporated and sunshine bathed the steaming hillsides from a clear blue sky.

As with many Ramblers Holidays walking tours there is, each week, an included excursion to a nearby city of note. Thus the compact city of Lucca was to be honoured with our presence that first week. Our way there, one gloomy wet day, was assisted by a mixture of bus and train via Pistoia, the provincial capital.

Lucca, let it be said, is one of Tuscany's urban gems; an immediately likeable place of cobbled streets, Romanesque churches and lovely medieval buildings placed around a series of squares. In Henry James's words " it overflows with everything that makes for ease, for plenty, for beauty, for interest and good example".

The town began life as a Roman colony and, despite its propinquity to Florence, Lucca stood its ground for a long time. The Lombards had made it virtually the capital of Tuscany, and, later, unlike any other city in the region, it managed to hang onto autonomy for four whole centuries and was the only Tuscan city not to submit to Florence. But then Napoleon handed the town to his sister, Elisa, to be ruled by her for several years in the early 1800s.

Walking Lucca's streets, whatever the weather, is a pleasure in itself but, for Ramblers in particular, no visit to the city would be complete without covering the four-kilometre long city walls constructed during the 16th and 17th centuries as a defence against the Tuscan dukes. More solid and complete than many of those of other ancient cities, the tree-lined ramparts offer fine views over the pantiled rooftops. Music and opera-lovers will make a beeline for the Piazza San Michele, home of one of Italy's most unique churches, near which is the Casa Natale di Puccini, birthplace of Giacomo Puccini, now a rather disappointing (to me) museum. A visitor can hardly miss the cathedral of San Martino with its lofty Romanesque facade which, like most but not all its fellows, is more spectacular without than within.

A day's visit is adequate enough to gain a satisfactory impression of a city such as Lucca which is more than can be said for Florence, the included excursion destination during the second week. Imagine, if you will, that you had to pick just one city to represent all that humankind has achieved then you would be hard pushed to improve on Florence and Anna and I were only pleased that we had visited this paragon of cities before, albeit briefly. However, central Florence today is, in essence, the small city that, in one brief spell, can cast its mould in the mind.

How a quarrelsome city whose population was never more than 80,000 could, in barely a century, produce an explosion of genius that startled the world is an unsolved mystery. Yet Florence is not entirely devoted to art, and the visitor with just a day to spare should concentrate on the city's bridges (particularly, of course, the Ponte Vecchio spanning the Arno river), gardens and hidden squares of the old-world cafes. The reward will be adequate.

As readers will have noted there are also Ramblers Holidays so-called "rest or free days" on each week of a holiday giving opportunity to undertake one's own thing. On this tour some participants are likely to choose a local walk but, since we are on the subject of cities, it should be noted that others will catch the hourly bus from San Marcello to Pistoia, just an hour's ride away.

Here is a quite small city, its suburbs marred by industry, that is unfairly neglected by the fact of its situation midway between Florence and Pisa. Yet its heart is a delight, the Piazza del Duomo as captivating a medieval square to be found anywhere. It was the first city in Italy to draw up a democratic constitution in 1177 while its star shone the brightest in the 13th century when its banking houses prospered. But under repeated attack and siege by Lucca and Florence, it finally succumbed to the latter in the 14th century, by which time it had the most unsavoury repute in Italy for thuggery, murder and anarchy. Appropriately the name "pistol" derives from the town's name, a weapon that came into much use following that of the nasty little stilettos that everybody once carried.

As indicated earlier, Ramblers Holidays arrange both a one and two-week sojourn based at San Marcello; Anna and I only able to spare the time for one. The second week's walking, however, is of a similar calibre to that of the first with routes up the steep wooded flanks of the Northern Apennine ridges above Abetone and elsewhere with one hike, cloud base and snow banks permitting, at an altitude approaching 7,000 feet. I would have been only too happy to stay but a Ramblers assignment in New England, USA, was scheduled two days hence. Barely would I have time to remove from my boots the rich soil of Tuscany; or for that matter, even remove those boots from tired but well walking-accustomed feet.

5. Mountains and cities of New England, USA (two weeks, grade D/Ss)

I shall long remember my first ever touch-down in the United States. My sojourn lasted but a few uncomfortable hours and all I saw of the country was the sparse interior of the detention block of New York's then Idelwald Airport, now JFK. This was during the infamous McCarthy era, in the second half of the 1940s, when I had been intending to visit friends in California and New England. But there was a fly in the ointment in the guise of a communist-issued visa decorating a page of my passport and, at that time in the United States, such decoration was akin to waving a red flag at a bull. "Reds", "Fellow-Travellers" and "Subversive Characters" were alleged to be hiding behind every lamp-standard with the result that not only was I roughly handled by rude immigration officials but put aboard the next UK-bound flight. Back in my then Essex home town I reported this deplorable treatment to my member of parliament, Mr – later, Lord – RAB Butler, who was eventually to become deputy prime minister, the outcome being a rap over the knuckles for the US ambassador in London and, for me, a swift return to America. Aircraft in those days could only just make the trans-Atlantic crossing without running out of fuel so my four-engined Lockheed Constellation, after landings at Prestwick, Shannon and Gandar in Newfoundland, dropped me off in Boston, Mass, as I couldn't stomach the possibility of another hostile reception committee awaiting me at New York.

Hopefully my New England return 50 years later would be a little less fraught.

We Brits are apt to scoff at American history, though actually theirs goes back quite a long way; right back, in fact, to the year 1,000 when the Vikings, led by Eric the Red, landed on the coast of North America. It was "discovered" again in the 1490s by Christopher Columbus and John Cabot but, so far as New England is concerned, one Bartholomew Gosnold, an English navigator, was instrumental in putting Maine, one of the half-dozen present-day states, on the map around 1602. However, it was Captain John Smith, sailing on behalf of a group of London merchants, who became the first person to officially use the term "New England" in his despatches from that land.

Britain's migratory involvement in America started in 1620 with the arrival of the Pilgrim Fathers on the Mayflower at what is now Plymouth to found the first permanent English settlement in New England. Ten years later a group of Puritans under John Winthrop staked out Boston, today its chief city.

The six states of New England comprise Connecticut, Maine, Massachusetts, New Hampshire, Rhode Island and Vermont. The relatively small size of this corner of America is disproportionate to the influence the region has exerted on the political, cultural and economic development of the nation. Not only was it here that American independence was born, but the American culture and way of life arose, one of the best education systems in the world came into being, and the American economy first blossomed in the form of industrialisation.

Topographically the quite small region is divided by two low mountain chains, innumerable hills, a myriad lakes, and, on the 6,000-mile convoluted coastline, countless bays and inlets. All six states together would fit inside the borders of the single state of Texas though, measured by the ups and downs of its terrain, they equal a sizeable chunk of the American West. Each state too possesses a character all its own; Maine is very different to New Hampshire which could never be confused with Vermont, and so on. And, of course, with many of its towns named after their originals in England, together with the legacies of mostly British immigrants, there is a certain Englishness to be discerned in the look and feel of New England; one of the abiding recollections of my own long-ago sojourn in the town of Newhaven and thereabouts.

Returning after half a century I looked forward to a reacquaintance that would bring back into focus those past recollections and, hopefully, add new ones.

Fifty years on, today's Boston was, for me, a completely new and unfamiliar city; even its spiky skyline no more than just another American conurbation. Only the very English place-names – mostly suburban districts and towns as well as neighbouring counties – remained constant: Cambridge, Plymouth, Newbury, Malden, Braintree, as well as Essex and Suffolk, together with more or less the whole gamut of the English atlas.

Because I had, again, arrived 24 hours ahead of the main party, two whole days in New England's chief city were at my disposal; the first in the very pleasant company of one Ingram Paperny, mine host of the New Lebanon hostelry out in the sticks of the New England/New York State border where the group would be staying for much of the tour, and then with the 16-strong group itself and its leader, Margaret. In this varied company and on my own I walked Boston's so-called Freedom Trail – a pedestrian route (marked by a continuous red line on the, to use an American term, sidewalks) that connects the majority of the city's 18th and 19th century historic sites. One of these is the slender Bunker Hill monument with a narrow 300-step spiral stairway to the top which offered, for me, worthwhile leg-work in preparation for the more rural walking that lay ahead. I was also to sample the four-line metro (or Rapid Transport System – the "T" as the locals call it) and the double-decker trains of the suburban rail system. Together with Ingram I ate in Vietnamese, Chinese and Italian eateries in the different districts inhabited by these nationalities. And I searched out the site of a small but significant remnant of British-American history – the Boston Tea Party. Following these activities over a rainy day and a warm sunny one I felt no longer quite so much a stranger in the city.

Boston revels in its assumed role as the cradle of American civilisation and reflects this by being a city of spires, parks, a multitude of both ponderous and light-hearted statuary as well as a remarkably thriving culture. To this it has added, within the last three decades, an uncompromising American-looking high-rise silhouette, the new architecture blending surprisingly well with pockets of old world charm. The city, currently in a frenzy of highway reconstruction, looks smart and pleased with itself today, flaunting its gleaming office towers, elegant shops, refurbished wharves, historic edifices, and well-patronised restaurants and bars.

For Americans, Boston's history began 360 years ago with the coming of the European settlers headed by such as the Rev William Blaxton in 1624 and the Puritans led by John Winthrop in 1630 who changed the face of this land and, in particular, this "city upon a hill". There's a story beneath every cobblestone and behind every shuttered window, including what they still call the Boston Massacre (when English troops opened fire on a crowd and killed five people), the aforementioned and infamous Tea Party, Paul Revere's celebrated midnight ride to warn of the approach of an English Redcoat force, the fight for abolition of the slave trade and for women's rights, and more.

The settlers remained. The Irish control the city politics, the Italians characterise the district called North End, and in Chinatown it feels like a corner of Beijing. Boston is a truly international city and there's a lot of England – our England – here too. A golden lion and unicorn sneers down from atop the Old State House, and many a plaque and statue depicts our country's more negative roles: the repressions of colonisation, the Irish potato famine, and the Battle of Bunker Hill, which was the first major battle of the Revolution and which we won – but only just. However, as a park ranger who gave us a tour declared, "We still love you Brits".

But, begging its pardon, I had had enough of Boston for the moment. It was time to see what the New England countryside could inflict upon our feet.

Actually what we got next day was an amble rather than a ramble. This came about en route, along the Massachusetts Turnpike Interstate 90 highway by minibus – or maxi-van as they prefer to call it – to our walking base at New Lebanon. Turning off at Sturbridge we spent four hours strolling around a recreated farm village renowned in the locality as a carefully carried-out re-creation of a typical rural community that dominated the New England countryside between 1790 and 1840. Old Sturbridge Village, as it's called, is remarkable for the charm of its woodsy site and the authenticity of its buildings and atmosphere. Each exhibit provides a guide wearing 19th century costume who is proficient in and knowledgeable about the customs, activities and general life of the period.

At the end of the turnpike, though not Interstate 90, the first junction brought us to our base, Ingram Paperny's Inn at the Shaker Mill Farm. And in the holiday accommodation stakes his establishment must rank as unique. Situated beside a stream tumbling down the wooded hillside, carved out of the thickly-growing trees, and a mile out of the community of New Lebanon, stands a handsome stone building that was once a working mill built by members of the Shaker faith once predominant in the region and about which we would soon be learning more. The 150 year old building has been, to quote the brochure, "lovingly if casually rebuilt – much of it by Ingram himself, its furnishings sparse, functional and comfortable. It's homey and welcoming, and operated by a small staff whose idea of hospitality runs more to sharing moods than putting on airs. The Inn", to continue Ingram's own description, "is, unlike him, very tall and foursquare in its imposing plumpness. Built of stone in 1864, with walls a yard thick and 40 feet high, it now harbors (sic) about 20 very different rooms all with their own bathrooms, a large dining room and kitchen, and a huge lounge with an open fire that roars in the circular fireplace, which Ingram designed himself not only to bring his guests together but also to provide distance between them". There's even a quote within a quote too which goes "The Inn is like a man: a combination of rough and smooth. The rough texture – the coarseness of some of my jokes. The smoothness – a kind of charming presence, like a massage oil. The jug wine is what it is. The walls are rough; the woodwork too. Some of the food is highly sophisticated. The company is excellent. Some guests call the place rustic, others primitive. It's the difference between those who sense the wood and stone, and those who want electric heat and air-conditioning". End of double quote but they fit the Shaker Mill Inn like a glove and I make no apology for going on about it.

To all this I must add a few further details. A table is always laid out with fruit, cookies (i.e.biscuits), coffee, tea and herbal or fruit teas. Free wine is available at dinner. Breakfasts are substantial and include porridge. And, outside, fed by the stream, is a large pond, that is eminently swimmable. Altogether Ingram's pad is very much a home from home.

Surrounded, as we were, by fresh green woods calling out for walking I was all for taking off there and then next morning. We were in the Berkshires; a range of hills straddling the Massachusetts/New York State border that are, by and large, gentle hills; their grandeur more pastoral than wild. These uplands, part of a series of ranges extending northwards towards the Canadian border, put me in mind of a thickly-wooded version of Somerset's Quantocks; not a great deal higher bearing in mind we were already more than 1,000 feet up, but more extensive. This was to be, for the next eight or so days, our walking and sightseeing playground and, though our cosy base was right amongst this green and pleasant land, we were mostly to invoke the use of transport to attain the most advantageous of hiking routes and sightseeing venues. Hence, the first morning we took off for the Pleasant Valley Wildlife Sanctuary some nine miles distant.

The valley's longest trail of a complex of more than a dozen named short walking routes is the Overbrook, reached following an initial hike along the Bluebird Trail from the sanctuary office. It takes one to the top of the so-called Lenox Mountain of hardly alpine proportions but providing rewarding views of the neighbouring Taconic hill range and, on a clear day, hills near the Vermont border which we would be walking at a later date.

The path meanders through the hardwood forest following a mountain stream displaying, at intervals, tiny picturesque waterfalls that looked as if they had been installed for the benefit of passers-by. The route was easy underfoot, the ascent unfatiguing, though the subtle change in the plant life was noticeable as the elevation increased. Alas, our fine weather luck of the previous couple of days ran out as we approached the fire observation tower atop the hill and steady rain, coupled with increasing drops of water from wet tree cover, gave us a damping and denied our expected view. Weather conditions forced us to return the same way we had come, trying to avoid slipping on surface tree-roots, along the abruptly muddy path.

The Bash Bish Falls near Mount Greylock, Massachusetts

again, no more than an overgrown hill. The six-mile hike up and down a couple of initial ridges is hardly a climbing feat but, as usual, a very satisfying walk over some rocky patches and plank-bridged bogs with increasingly splendid views as excuse for a pause. And as one triumphantly attains the summit the Sherpa Tensing-like glow of accomplishment is quickly shattered by the demoralising sight of multiple cars and their day-tripper passengers – for there is a perfectly good road to the top. But, for us, the road had its advantages for it brought up Ingram with a fine pizza lunch.

As well as radio antenna masts and suchlike apparatus, Greylock is topped by a Massachusetts war memorial tower containing spiral stone and iron steps allowing visitors to climb another hundred feet. And the all-round view is stunning. The mountain was named after Chief Grey Lock who once hunted there with his tribe of Indians, while its tree-clothed slopes have served as inspiration to many of Berkshire's greatest poets and authors. These slopes are criss-crossed by trails of varying lengths, one of which – the Overlook – a few of us found the energy to follow though the ubiquitous trees hid whatever the trail was supposed to overlook. An hour and a quarter walk, it nearly doubled this for me when I was "volunteered" by leader Margaret to forge ahead to contact our vehicle and arrange for it to meet the group at one of the road/path crossing points. Alas, either I misheard the instructions or the maxi-van was not at the designated place – though probably the former – which resulted in my losing a gallon of sweat and causing much hilarity among the group.

Among the rare species of plant life found on Greylock is a number of 200 year old red spruce trees now protected by state law, while, so far as birdlife is concerned, it is the home of species usually only found hundreds of miles to the north. All in all, a hill of considerable virtue.

That evening, in lieu of a concert by an absent Boston Symphony Orchestra at Tanglewood, we attended a Virginia Woolf play at Lenox's celebrated Wharton **Theatre, a beautiful old family mansion set in another** lush green park; something on the lines of Glyndebourne in Sussex. A cultural end to the day.

Our final rural assignment was an appointment with the so-called Bash Bish Falls on the Massachusetts/New York State border. But first we had to climb another hill, this one grandly called Alender Mountain, an ascent decidedly easier than that of the previous day. A three and a half hour walk to an elevation of 2,239 feet and a vertical rise of 840 feet took us over flower-filled meadows and then up through assorted woodlands and across streams, the largest of which gave the less agile of us their baptism of water-full

Wall Street, New York

boots. The all-round view at the summit was, of course, superb and included, shimmering in the heat-haze, the distant Catskills.

The heatwave, which had brought out the national holiday crowds, sullied the look of the Bash Bish Falls where the Bash Bish river tumbles over a 275-foot gorge creating a double 50-foot waterfall and natural pool perfect for swimming were the state to allow it. Many youths were ignoring the rule and leaping dangerously from the rocks above the cascade. The walk to it, plus the earlier and longer one, took place in well over 90 degrees of heat which had many of us pondering wistfully upon those three cold, wet and cloudy days that had marred our initial hikes.

They say of New York City that you either hate it or love it. On my two previous, long-ago and brief visits I experienced slushy snow and prolonged rain which tended to switch my opinion firmly towards the former emotion. Now, for the final 50 hours of the tour, I was to experience this great metropolis sweating it out under a heatwave. And what a contrast it is to the rural Berkshires; even to villagey Boston. In place of soft, silent, verdant hillsides are great canyons of concrete and a cacophony of police sirens, hooting taxis and man-made noise that, initially, stuns the mind.

Under the guidance of Margaret we took a Circle Line cruise that circumnavigates Manhattan Island passing by much of the city's known and less-known sights, climbed (in a lift) the Empire State Building to see New York's layout from above, and explored, on foot, southern Manhattan's considerable attractions which included Wall Street, Battery Park, and Trinity Church. We also walked much of Central Park – which at least provided us with another sight of greatly-missed trees.

Okay, so the place is crowded, dirty, noisy and impolite as the Berlitz guidebook warns. But it's one of the world's most exciting and dramatic cities and, surprisingly, a very human one.

It made a fitting end to a fortnight for those who prefer a little walking to go with an introductory observation of rural as well as urban North America.

I write these words on the morning of our departure from JFK Airport and the flight home. But, from our hotel on the upper end of Broadway, I've just time for a $2 pint of beer at a bar, appropriately called The Dive , which I've found just around the corner. Cheers.

6. Walking on Samos, Greece

(one or two weeks, grade D)

When I was given the Aegean island of Samos as my next assignment I had never thought of it, or any of the small or medium-sized Greek islands, as particularly good walking territory; at least not in the same league as mainland Pindus (see chapter 4). Yet many of my fellow-Ramblers met on earlier tours had told me how enjoyable the walks were and even how relatively tough they had been in spite of the low walking grade indicated by the brochure. Maybe I was in for a surprise.

The Greek islands, they say, are what you want to make of them. One can wear a frilly shirt and flaunt oneself on fashionable Mykonos, play cricket on Corfu, visit Santorini to help experts prove that nearby Knossos is the lost city of Atlantis, or stretch out on the sun-blasted beaches of Kos to redecorate the body in an unhealthy shade of pink. For me it was to be hiking in Samos.

In all there are 1,425 Greek islands, comprising about a fifth of the nation's territory. However, only 166 are inhabited and quite a number of these seldom if ever visited by tourists. Some islands are lush; others barren; some raise mountains; others are predominately flat. Shorelines are more often rocky than sandy but conceal secluded coves ideal for swimming and snorkelling.

Samos, just over a mile from the Turkish coast, forms part of the East Aegean group of islands which include Lesbos, Lemnos, Chios, Ikaria, Aghios Efstratios and the Fournoi islands, with Lesbos as the largest. They are islands that came late to Greece – only after the 1912 Balkan War. They were originally settled around 1100 BC by Pelasgians and Ionians fleeing from the Peloponnese yet, by the seventh century AD, they had become centres of advanced civilisation as well as independent and powerful maritime states. But disunited, they fell, one by one, to a succession of invaders, notably the Genoese and the nearby Turks.

Samos itself, birthplace of, amongst other celebrities, Pythagoras, likes to be recognised as the one-time great power "when Athens was a young man". By car, the good road network allows a driver to span the centuries in a single day, visiting Pythagorion – the ancient capital – the 2,500-year old tunnel of Eupalinos, the site of the temple to Hera, the ancient marbles at Tigani, and the Palaeontological museum at Mytelene.

On foot it would take me a little longer; a week maybe.

As the Boeing 757 of Britannia Airways circled and banked steeply to avoid Turkish airspace, then dropped down towards the small Samos Airport I learnt my first lesson. Samos was *exceedingly* mountainous with craggy peaks rising above 5,000 feet almost straight from sea level; a very different kettle of fish, as one might say, to New England and the gentle Berkshires.

Since, without Anna with me, I can get a week's, or even two week's, clothing and hiking gear into one comparatively small bag I usually manage to persuade airline officials to class my baggage as hand-luggage; hence I was virtually the first passenger from a crowded flight through passport control and customs which, of course, resulted in a long wait for the rest of the group to assemble. Including myself we were 18-strong on this tour, all 17 others being members of a North East Hampshire Ramblers' Association branch; most of them from the Farnborough/Aldershot area. Thus, with Phil, the leader, I was the only outsider but was soon elected a *de facto* branch member and made to feel very much one of them. In fact, judging from first impressions which later never needed revising, these were by far the nicest bunch of companions I had come across on all my Ramblers Holidays tours so far. Phil, who met us at the airport, was ruddy-faced, middle-aged and knowledgeable on matters Greek in which country he had lived for many years though Belgium was another. It soon became apparent that he knew nearly all the residents on the island and, in particular, its restaurant, taverna and bar personnel, he smoked (though only when "off duty"), and was partial to Heineken lager.

The island, being only 476 square kilometres in size, meant that we were never far from the sea, its towns and places of interest. Thus the coach drive from the airport to the hotel in Vathi, the old quarter of the capital known, unimaginatively, as Samos Town (though the whole entirety is Vathi to the locals) was of only some 25 minutes. Our hotel, the Odysseas, was a pleasant, newly-whitewashed, three-storey building situated, not very distinctively, in Vlamaris Street, one of a maze of tiny streets at the higher rear end of Vathi within sight – and ten minutes fast walk – of the sea which, here forms the Bay of Vathi. The hotel rooms were simple, with baths or/and showers, but clean and entirely adequate; a bonus being that many possessed small balconies. The ever-smiling owner, Mr Odysseas, was invariably in attendance, mostly behind the bar. Breakfast was the only meal served and, in line with Greek breakfasts in general, was, to Brits, somewhat sparse, being a never-varied hard-boiled egg, white bread, packets of margarine/butter and jam plus tea or coffee.

We had been hit by the heat the moment of leaving the airport but the then near-90 degrees temperature was mitigated by a strong breeze, though this would lessen in later days. I was all for commencing our first day's walk – to the top of the nearby 850-foot peak of Rofitus Ileas which overlooks the town – with the cooler dawn; but the idea of such an early rise held little appeal within the group. So we started out direct from the hotel under an already blazing sun and sweated our way to the top; an easy uphill and downhill walk on a dirt road plus a few rocky path short cuts with no great exertion or difficulty beyond the heat. At the summit, with fine views of the town and a brace of islets in the bay, is a minuscule chapel used for services on certain saints' days when hundreds of locals come there via the dirt road. Close to the chapel are some radio antennae which the priest allowed to be raised on his patch with the condition that free floodlighting could be nightly directed onto his little church.

For the first time on one of these Ramblers walking tour assignments I was suffering a physical handicap. Two days before leaving home I dislocated something in the small of my back. This malady inflicted sharp pain, especially when sitting or lying down, but fortunately not so much when walking – though any steep downhill progress was hell. But I stuck it out and things gradually improved. However, my slight misfortune faded into insignificance compared with those of one lady member of the group who, following a series of operations, could walk only short distances. She was, therefore, unable to participate in any of the group hikes, though sometimes a taxi was arranged so that she could join us at the conclusion of the walk or for a taverna lunch and swim.

Our short ascent and descent of Rofitus Ileas gave us a free afternoon for a leisurely lunch at a seafront restaurant and sun and sea-bathing on a stony beach at the far end of Samos Town. Except for a cold Atlantic in Andalucia and the pond at the Shaker Mill in New England there had been no opportunity for swimming on the tours I had experienced so far but here in Samos the chance presented itself daily and many of us made the most of it. In fact all that we needed to carry in our day-sacks for each walk was a water-bottle and swimwear.

That first afternoon also gave us a chance to observe Samos Town. Built around the Bay of Vathi, one of Greece's largest natural harbours, the old quarter rises up an incline behind the mainly neo-classical port-city. The long esplanade is especially attractive at night with the lights of Vathi – though part of the main town – in the near distance. A central main street runs parallel to the esplanade and contains souvenir shops and rows of tourist restaurants, quite a few of which, I was told, were run by Greeks after a fast buck. On a more cultural level is the well-regarded Archaeological Museum housing a collection of finds from all eras of the considerable Samos store of history plus, beneath the magnificent Greek *kouros* statues, the figures of the Egyptian gods Osiris and Horus. However, it is Vathi, where we were based, that holds the real Greek character and sincerity. The narrow cobbled streets – their names sometimes only in Cyrillic lettering – separate 300-year old houses, their overhanging second stories and plaster-lath construction more akin to northern Greece and Anatolia than the Aegean. A peculiarity of Vathi too is this construction of its houses wherein the second storey often protrudes over the first and the roof over the second giving the tiny streets a tunnel-like aura. Many of our evening meals were taken in local Vathi tavernas and, though we ate earlier than do the Greeks, it was always dark when they ended so causing some difficulty in re-locating our hotel; a task perhaps made harder still following an overdose of retsina, ouzo and a very drinkable red and white wine and local brandy.

Our second walk was hardly more arduous than the first; possibly slightly longer at 11 kilometres but entirely on tarmac and dirt road surfaces. The only uphill section was that on the way out of Vathi where old men sitting smoking on the doorsteps of their homes greeted us with a wave or smile. Though at the time of our visit there was a considerable amount of anti-NATO sentiment in the country this never manifested itself in the slightest display of animosity towards visitors to Samos from NATO countries.

The tarmac road led to Paleokastro, a sizeable village, where we made a prolonged halt for liquid refreshment (in small bars and tavernas a litre bottle of beer costs only about 75 pence. There we sat, beneath an arbour of grape vines, and watched the elderly bar clients sipping their ouzo. A subsequent dirt road led to the resort of Psili Ammos, its bare-feet-singeing sand beach a disaster area of beach umbrellas and sun-burning flesh, though the sea made amends with its clear, initially-shallow water of a perfect temperature for swimming. At this point we were within spitting distance of the Turkish coast, villages and occasional passing vehicles plain to see. For those of us who didn't want to spend much of the rest of the day festooned on the beach, there was a bird-watching stalk led by Phil around a reed-sprouting lake – a nature sanctuary and protected area rife with bird-life. Flocks of ruddy shell ducks were rehearsing flying techniques in preparation for their long migratory flight to Siberia while small owls – which I always thought were creatures of the night – sat blinking on telegraph poles or the bare branches of dead trees. Of the flamingos said sometimes to inhabit the lake there was no sign. Lunch was taken in a surprisingly up-market beachside restaurant – the El Greco – which I recommend to anyone.

Walkers at Psili Ammos, close to the Turkish coast

It was becoming plain here on sunny, warm and sea-girthed Samos that, in general, the walks had been devised not only with an eye to the often intense heat but also to earn the reward of a beach sojourn and chance of immersion in a clear and refreshing sea at their conclusion. Thus, as we had found, they were of no great length or duration; the routes hardly severe. So our third ramble – and there's no other word for it – from Mytelene, to which we were taken by coach, to the pleasant coastal resort of Kokari was typical. Mostly level or downhill walking, it was a hike through what remained of the trees of a tree-shrouded valley; something of a catchment area for underground water supplies that fed a number of townships in the district.

We could see Kokari below us from the brow of the only slight hill of the route and during the gradual descent every turn presented a changing coastal vista as we ambled through quiet countryside bordering the eastern edge of the Ambelos mountain range. Though we were too late for the spring wildflower display, which includes various orchids and wild asparagus, there was plenty of colour left in the surrounding scrub though, in a very few weeks, this would vanish in the increasing heat. The rural idyll was broken only once by a passing convoy of Greek artillery, its dust-clouds toning us a uniform grey. The military have a very visible presence on Samos, particularly at its closest points to Turkey.

An old castle once overlooked Kokari but, through the centuries, its stones have melted into the rocks of the hillside with vegetation hiding any remnants, though a flight of lost steps to its site is alleged to exist. The small town was once a fishing village, the original centre cradled between twin headlands. Today it is an ebullient little resort, the long westerly pebble beach offering idyllic swimming with a choice of still or choppy water on either side of a natural narrow causeway to an island. We had almost to be dragged away to join our coach back to Vathi.

Walk number four held a slightly different theme and objective. A celebrated monastery became the chief objective with the bathing beach a secondary consideration – and with an optional but exhausting penalty attached. The walk to the Monastery of Zoodochou Pigis is detailed – together with our first walk of the tour up and down Rofitis Ileas – in the pages of the Sunflower series of guidebooks, this one Landscapes of Samos. The length of the basic hike from and back to Vathi is barely more than 10 kilometres and, to describe it, I can do no better than quote a paragraph of the narrative from this section. "Skilful positioning of the island's monasteries gives them an enormous sense of tranquillity and solitude. It is almost as if a bargain had been struck with nature whereby these gifts, together with their commanding views, have been bestowed on the *minis* in return for their blending so unobtrusively into a landscape of great natural beauty. And so it is with Zoodochou Pigis. The views from there are regarded by some as the finest on the island." The building is reached via an old trail since re-surfaced for military reasons, though cobbled sections and a steep, stepped path remain.

It was the hottest day, so far, of the tour and there was no breeze to mitigate the soaring temperatures. Thanks partly to the donation of an assortment of pills from a fellow Rambler my back pain had subsided by this time but, blow me, if I wasn't then struck down by another malady, the demon stomach-ache. This was coupled to my usual self-afflicted foible of not drinking enough liquid in high temperatures. I managed to stagger down to the pleasant halfway-home taverna where we were to lunch and there spent a couple of hours in the WC and pouring two litres of mineral water down my throat. My companions rallied round to help all they could and I felt heartily ashamed of myself; here was I with mammoth long-distance treks beneath my belt succumbing to a succession of minor ills on a short amble. The pay-off came when I missed my swim; the half-hour walk to the sea being beyond me at that juncture – especially as the return meant an uphill slog in temperatures nudging 100 degrees. Even the swimmers in the group balked at this and called on the services of a taxi.

Up until now we had patronised a series of different restaurants and tavernas for our evening meals. The first two were held in Vathi, the second two in Samos Town but, by Thursday of the first week, it was back to number one of the quartet. And it is a fact that we appreciated the simple cuisine and venues of the eateries in Vathi more than the elaborate ones in the main town. One of the former – the Gregori – was hosted by an English-speaking lady of formidable countenance. She showed her pleasure for our custom by plonking down on the table at the meal's end a gratis assortment of bottles of beer and wine which not only made a nice touch but got a few of us – alas, me included – into a very merry mood. That, I think, was one of the nights some of us were subsequently blundering around trying to find our hotel!

Friday was given over to exploration of some of the main man-made sights and sites resulting from the island's history, a catalogue of invasions and boundary disputes broken by that early "golden age" when, as an independent state, Samos was transformed by the tyrant Polycrates into a considerable imperial power. Traces of his ancient capital can be found in the hills above Pythagorion and it was to and up one of the hilltops we walked next on a mercifully fractionally cooler day. The surviving fortification walls reminded me of those raised by the Incas in Andean South America; Phil maintained the stones to be even more accurately placed but I could barely believe this. The all-round view was superb with the mountains of western Samos and, across the sea, Turkey's majestic Mount Mykale, stretching away into the heat haze. The path to the summit was narrow and prickly for bare legs but was greatly enjoyed by all participants in the walk. This eventually led down the other side of the hill into Pythagorion, the small town and resort on the south coast renamed, in 1955, to honour Mr Pythagoras who is alleged to have been born there. Both before and after we had negotiated the hill we looked in to see both mouths of the famous Eupalinos Tunnel, still in a remarkable state of preservation considering it was built as long ago as 687 BC for the purpose of providing a water supply and escape route in times of siege. Its further mouth, above Pythagorion, can be entered and the narrow tunnel followed on foot for several hundred yards. Unfortunately the centre has collapsed into one of the natural and extremely deep bore holes that exist in this region. The tunnel, or maybe it could be described as an underground aqueduct, was planned and constructed under one Eupalinos of Megara, an engineering genius of his time. Having made all the necessary measurements and calculations externally, he commenced boring a tunnel 1,046 metres in length using two work-teams of slaves who excavated simultaneously from north and south, meeting – perhaps surprisingly –

more or less in the middle, with only a very slight error. The work was rightly considered throughout antiquity to be a major technical feat; at least an achievement equal to today's Channel Tunnel.

We ended our cultural observations with a brief visit to the monastery of Moni Spilianis quite close to the tunnel mouth. The coolest spot on the whole island is its chapel in a cave with a temperature more suited to a crypt.

One of many restaurants in the town was our venue for lunch and, of course, there was time for a swim from a small sand and pebble beach adequate for the purpose. The immense harbour mole was constructed by classical slaves and has scarcely changed or needed repair since its original

Walkers making their way to the one-time city of Tigani

completion. In the harbour itself stands a modern statue of the celebrated mathematician (who made my schooldays arithmetic lessons a misery) looking a mite self-conscious. The port's shape suggested a frying pan to someone, hence Tigani was the town's former name – which was also that of the fortification ruins we looked upon on the hill.

I have already alluded to the composition of the group to which, for a week, I belonged and the fact that it was composed of a bunch of friends well-known to one another before arrival in Samos. This made it rather different to others where members were, initially, strangers. Besides the pleasure of their lively company I was now to learn something of the social whirl that a well-run branch of the Ramblers' Association creates in its home location. I heard of regular weekend walks, of social functions, excursions, committee meetings and the myriad doings of a vibrant fraternity. And here with me was the human core of it; characters all, including what I imagined could well be the father of the branch, the walks organiser, the branch humorist; even, surprisingly perhaps – and yet not – the loner as well as the widow and the widower finding solace within a tight fellowship. As a confirmed individualist I'm not a social animal; I had my fill of "belonging" during a half-century in my one-time Essex home town. But were I to join anything again I would look towards my own local branch of the RA. I see it could be fun.

Saturday was the proverbial "rest" or "free" day though whether this was for the benefit of the leader or his/her flock I was never sure since some leaders, as I have mentioned, use it to take volunteers on quite tough slogs. But here on Samos, the high temperatures alone give reason for a relaxing day for both leader and group, and with the enticing sea beaches nearby there was only one sensible place to spend it. Even so one energetic member took off early on a hired bicycle for a prolonged pedal around the interior of the island while a batch of us, conscience-struck at the idea of doing virtually nothing useful or educational, spent the morning exploring the exquisite and amicable little back streets of Vathi. The rest, as they say, did nowt.

For me, alas, that Saturday was my final day since, as with Tuscany, I could find the time to undertake only one week of what was a two-week tour. Our dinner that night, marking the halfway point, was held in Pythagorion's excellent harbour-side Manolis Tzeretas restaurant and it made, for me, a fitting end to an ailment-punctuated, over-heated but memorable week.

7. Hassness, the Lake District, UK (one week, grade D+/C or C+ or E)

Temperatures and weather conditions in England's Lake District were likely to be something of a contrast to those I experienced in Greece. And it was Cumbria to which I was assigned next. The quoted grades of this one-week series of perambulations amongst England's highest mountains offered the likelihood of more serious hiking than had been the case in New England, USA, and Samos.

Over the years I have sojourned, visited and passed through the Lake District any number of times, and, for me, its scenery never palls; its charm remains constant. I can vaguely remember my first holiday there as a schoolboy with my parents and brother in the late summer of 1939. We stayed in a far-from-anywhere self-catering establishment close to the Langdale Pikes and, following Neville Chamberlain's sombre broadcast to the nation on September 3 of that year, Britain went to war. This resulted in my father, a TA colonel, having to leave us to report to his unit.

On another, much later, occasion I made an April cycling circuit of the then just-inaugurated Cumbria Cycle Way, a route that took me around the Lake District via the coastal towns of Whitehaven, Workington, Maryport and Silloth, then inland to Carlisle and Brampton, and southwards via Appleby, Kirby Lonsdale and Grange-over-Sands. Between Silloth and Carlisle I was struck by a blizzard and it snowed heavily. After draping myself around a Carlisle station waiting room radiator to thaw out I continued to Brampton mostly on foot because of the drifting snow. My objective was a booked room in an apartment near Talkin Tarn, and somewhere between there and Brampton a rescue helicopter descended in a whirl of snow to attempt to persuade me to jettison the hire bike and be air-lifted to safety. But the bike wasn't mine so I declined and ploughed on remorselessly only to find my night's accommodation locked and barred; the owner having envisaged that no one in their right minds would even consider cycling anywhere in such conditions. Fortunately the occupants of the neighbouring apartment saw my plight, took me in, wrapped me in a blanket, topped me up with whisky, and phoned the absentee landlord who had the greatest difficulty in reaching me even in his chain-tyred, four-wheel-drive Landrover.

And since I'm in a reflective mood I might as well tell of the time when a colleague and I, on our way further north by car to attend a business meeting, stopped off for a leg-stretch which consisted of a jog to the summit and back of 3,116-foot Helvellyn attired in our best suits. The silly things one does.

The impact of the Lake District on the first-time visitor is seldom less than astonishing since it seems scarcely credible that this mountainous region of jagged crags can be an integral part of England's otherwise so gentle landscape. Though hardly Alpine, and certainly not Himalayan, in size and altitude – the highest peak, Scafell Pike, is but 3,210 feet – they form respectable mountains and are visually quite astounding. These Cumbrian heights enjoy real respect among climbers and it is a fact that only at close quarters – i.e. on foot – can their true awesome beauty be revealed.

Within an area of a mere 30 miles across and not much more from north to south can be found 16 major lakes squeezed between the steeply-pitched faces of these giant hills. Before the Neolithic age 5,000 years ago most of the now bare uplands were forested with pine and birch, and the valleys with oak and alder. Neolithic Man, the Romans and the Norse Vikings cleared these forests, the timber being used to shape flints into axes, for road-building, and the myriad uses that gave life and living to our ancestors. The Norse Vikings even added new words to the language like "fell" (mountain), "force" (waterfall) and the suffix "thwaite" indicating a clearing.

It was the outpourings of writers and poets of the likes of William Wordsworth, Samuel Taylor Coleridge, Robert Southey and, of more recent vintage, Alfred Wainwright, who probably made the greatest contribution to the promotion of the Lake District during the early 19th and into the 20th centuries. Wandering clouds, lonely or otherwise, still cast their shade over the lakes these poets and writers immortalised – Grasmere, Rydal Water, Brothers Water and more. In 1951, an area which includes the great majority of what is generally regarded as "The Lake District" was designated as a national park, though the region is not a park in the accepted sense in that it contains urban centres and working communities; nor is it national either because there's no central control. However, its popularity is not in doubt with some 18 million visitors annually homing in on the area.

"As a rule one can escape the summer crowds by getting around on foot – some of the country's most celebrated walks run through the Lake District, with an almost unchartable network of paths tracking the broken knife-edge ridges or weaving easier courses around the flanks onto the tops", enthuses the *Rough Guide to England*.

Since my week of walking with Ramblers had been scheduled for the start of the main summer holiday season I would be putting this declaration to the test.

This is the only walking tour that Ramblers Holidays run in Britain. Of varying walking grades, it is based on two neighbouring accommodations on the shores of Buttermere about a mile from its namesake village and midway between Keswick and Cockermouth, each approximately 10 miles distant. The tour is also the only one wherein transportation to and from the base is not pre-arranged and included since, being within our own English shores, most participants find it more convenient to arrive and depart by their own vehicles.

Not so, however, for my son, Paul and me, living in the far south of the country. Why drive all that distance when someone else can do it for you?, we asked ourselves. So we came and went by National Express who operate two coach services a day between London Victoria and Keswick offering, incidentally, a fine sightseeing drive through the more southerly parts of Cumbria and the Lake District including Lancaster, Morecambe, Kendal, Windermere, Ambleside and Grasmere with stunning views all round. Additionally, National Express services are far less expensive than is rail travel; the termini of the railway being Penrith, on the main line, and Windermere, both further afield than Keswick. And from Keswick to the base on Buttermere Paul and I obtained a lift by courtesy of Mountain Goat, the long-established Cumbrian mini-bus transportation company who arrange daily tours in the Lake District and elsewhere.

I don't quite know how to describe Hassness and Dalegarth, the two Ramblers-run establishments situated within a wooded park overlooking the lake. Ramblers call them guest houses though they are of hotel proportions with a touch of superior hostel about them. Paul and I were the last guests to arrive at Hassness and just in time for the early evening meal, a communal three-course repast, simple, tasty and substantial, followed by coffee or tea in the big drawing room equipped with comfortable armchairs, sofas andwell-stocked book cases. The bedrooms overlooked the lake and surrounding mountains, a drying room catered for wet clothing, while the whole atmosphere of the place was one of congeniality and informality.

My initial assessment of the 14-strong group added up to an exceedingly friendly, like-minded bunch with a sense of fun to match; a vital prerequisite when my son's somewhat earthy humour is taken into account. It is a characteristic that he doubtless inherited from his father. Judging from the first days run-in walk – considerably more arduous than most of the hikes in which I had participated over the previous couple of tours – the group comprised competent walkers, though one couple had imagined they had booked an E-grade tour which indicates little more than an amble. Our leader was Brian while the age-range enveloped a slightly younger element than usual.

The portent of the Hassness drying room became abundantly clear the next morning with rain belching from a low grey cloud ceiling. This, fortunately, turned to no more than frequent squally showers as we circled the southern end of Buttermere and by mid-afternoon even hesitant sunshine began to appear. Our first objective had been the modest summit of a near-2,000 foot mountain known as Haystacks, its name derived from the columnar buttresses that range in a series of rock towers along the northern fringe of the summit, the largest of which is called Big Stack. The mountain was one of Alfred Wainwright's favourites and he fervently defends its definition as a mountain in spite of its diminutive 1,900-odd feet when 2,000 feet is looked upon by some as the point when a hill becomes a mountain. "Those who say Haystacks is not a mountain", he retorts, "should go and see it. Or better still, climb it". We did both. It rises from the lake shore in a sheer, unassailable manner but, of course, there is a way round – as there usually is with mountains – though the stony path was steep and tending towards the vertical in places. The cloud relented enough as we rose higher to give us an idea of what a wonderful view could be had of lakes Buttermere and neighbouring Crummock Water on a finer day. Our ascent was made from Gatesgarth, no more than a farm (and, in summer, an ice-cream van) on the minor road to the Honister Pass, via Scarth Gap, where the path turns towards the summit and erosion has forced the fashioning of rough steps up a steep escarpment.

Beyond Haystacks rises a higher ridge known as Brandreth, our second objective, before which we sat amongst wet boulders to consume our picnic lunch overlooking Innominate Tarn, a tiny sheet of brackish water trapped in a saucer of rock. And as we trudged up the spongy, grassy incline to Brandreth even more stupendous potential panoramas opened up in two directions of both Buttermere and Ennerdale Water valleys. Brian knew his Lake District well (though Yorkshire-born and bred) , pointing out the vague shapes of lesser-known peaks with names like High Crag, Pillar, Glaramara and Dale Head; peaks that we too would come to know before long. Further afield rose the flanks of the bigger guns of

Skiddaw, Helvellyn and the Langdale Pikes, their heads still hidden by cloud. We were told that Wainwright had stipulated that, after death, his ashes were to be scattered hereabouts, with the proviso that, should a walker suffer a smut in his or her eye, that it be treated with respect!

From Brandreth the path led across a boggy grass plateau and then downwards to the resurrected slate mines and surface workings of Dubs Quarry, the soaring cost of slate and its popularity as a material for house construction having given the mine a new lease of life. Of the old tramway at Drumhouse, that once transported the slate down to road level, only the track bed remained; today four-wheel drive lorries do the job. And so, descending the excruciating, ankle-breaking miner's path, each of us attempting not to slip on the still-wet cockscombs of slatey rock, we made our slow way back to Buttermere as the sun dissipated the last of the cloud to reveal a clear, blue sky in a manner that asserted that it never rains in the Lake District.

With no in-house bar at Hassness there was only one thing to do of an evening following dinner – a mile-long tramp to and from The Fish Inn, one of two pubs in Buttermere village, for a pint of Theakson's Old Peculiar. Being so far north there was, in July, still dim daylight as we trudged homeward at 11.00 pm under a clear sky promising fine weather ahead.

And it was no false omen either. As we tramped the lakeside path into the village again for the start of the second day's walk clear blue sky gave us a warm ascent of the northern flank of Sail Beck valley leading us to Crag Hill. Though only a mile or so longer than yesterday's plod it was tougher going with prolonged stony climbs and if the weather-limited views of the earlier walk were superb then those that materialised as we gained altitude were utterly magnificent with virtually all the ranges of the Lake District, The cumbrian coast, the Solway Firth, the Scottish Borders and the Yorkshire Dales presenting themselves in stark clarity. Even the Isle of Man was faintly visible beneath a white puff of cloud.

Only nine of us, plus Brian, participated in the walk; the remainder of the group choosing to do their own thing – and they missed a treat of a hike. Below us, Keswick and Borrowdale with Derwent Water spread themselves out like a map while, behind them, rose the Helvellyn Ridge. In another direction Skiddaw allowed itself to be seen; in another Great Gable's bald summit shone like an old gentleman's pate. Our descent was via Whiteless Edge leading to Whiteless Pike and steep but, mercifully, mostly grassy downward progress – though hard on the knees – back to Buttermere village. A late afternoon pint here for some of us, a swift cool

Ramblers on the summit of Great Gable

dip in the lake for Paul and I, and so back to Hassness at the end of an exceptionally rewarding day.

Came the ubiquitous rest day, its true purpose finally revealed by Brian. It was, he told us, not only so that the leader could have a rest from his charges but, equally, so that the charges could have a rest from their leader! Which I suppose is as good a reason as any.

And lo and behold too came another morning of glorious sunshine, the air clear as champagne. But the bucking countryside was not to be mollycoddled by such prolonged fine weather and the sky clouded over later. However, the absence of rain allowed Paul and me to make our way along Fleetwith Edge towards Fleetwith Pike and then complete a circuit of

Buttermere on the waterside footpath fretted with gates, each of which latches according to its own ingenious system. We were not alone on this easy saunter; nor had we been so on the previous more onerous two hikes. These days, especially in the Lake District and the more foot-itching portions of the British countryside, groups of walkers are everywhere. They saunter along the roadside near their bed & breakfast bases and clamber over the hills armed with inadequate maps and spurred onward by Kendal Mint Cake. Perhaps in the Lake District more than anywhere in England, the great appeal is the amazing variety of terrain found in a relatively small area. One can wander from real heat, below, to sub-arctic chill, above, in just a few hours. Even unambitious routes are full of surprising prospects, from cool damp glade to soaring, naked crag. I have to agree with one writer on the Lake District who found it likely that few places on earth are more fickle, more blissful, more maddening, more lovely; changing, as it does, from grey tears to shining laughter in one flick of a misty curtain; and with another flick reducing miles of high splendour to a narrow arc of vague, damp sadness.

Low cloud – but no rain – prevented the subsequent planned ascent of 2,947-foot Great Gable so we had to be content with a 10-mile low altitude hike in Borrowdale which turned out to be no disappointing alternative whatsoever. The Borrowdale valley penetrates to the very heart of Lakeland, with dramatic mountain scenery contrasting with woodland, water and green meadows; in fact it is difficult to overstate the beauty of this valley with its bucolic river flats at the head of Derwent Water overshadowed by the peaks of Scafell and Scafell Pike.

We reached, and returned from, the starting point of the walk – Rosthwaite village – by car via the 1,176-foot Honister Pass cupped by sweeping hill flanks of scree. And from Rosthwaite the path led along a bracken-bordered path to the only serious incline of the route passing the so-called Resting Stone where, once upon a time, coffins were placed as their bearers took a breather en route to the cemetery. Shapely geographical features such as Belt Knott, Birkett's Leap and Puddingstone Bank became the most eye-catching landmarks on a route of easy walking to Watendlath, a tiny farming hamlet set high on a ledge in the fells beside its tarn. Here we stopped for elevenses, watching sheep being sheared as we sipped our coffee.

Continuing across a stone bridge, officially opened quite recently by Prince Charles, we skirted the Lodore Falls where the Watendlath Beck tumbles abruptly down a precipitous rock face and made for Shepherd's Crag. Its diminutive stature tried to make up for a lack of serious height with an aggressively steep rocky upthrust to provide us with a short but

Picnic lunch on Shepherd's Crag above Derwent Water

near-perpendicular scramble to the top. And picnicking there our eyes frequently turned towards Great Gable still wreathed in grey, damp cloud. Perhaps tomorrow...

An uncomfortable descent brought us to the riverside meadows at lake-level, the lake being Derwent Water approached by way of a lengthy plank walkway. The shoreline was speckled with thick clumps of yellow daisies, bog asphodel, bog myrtle (its strong scent a midge deterrent) and marsh orchids, while water lilies punctured the still clear waters of the lake.

A mile or so of road-walking and we were in Grange-in-Borrowdale, with its fine stone double-arched bridge over the river Derwent providing our view at one of the two village tea-rooms where we enjoyed toffee-fudge and blueberry ice cream watched by beady-eyed robins and chaffinches. And so down the Jaws of Borrowdale, as the narrowest, gorge-like section of the valley is called, in which the path closely hugged the river to show us the way back to Rosthwaite. Above us the clouds were fast dispersing as sunshine once more rent them asunder to herald a clearer day ahead.

But, again, the ascent of Great Gable was not to be. Though slowly rising, grey cloud still clung to the summit so a lower mountain called Robinson became the penultimate day's objective. It rose, directly behind

Buttermere and formed, together with Hindscarth and Dale Head, a hefty barrier between Buttermere valley together with the Honister Pass and the Vale of Newlands, a parallel valley the other side. A doddle, I thought, but I had failed to hear Brian's continued proposition that we carry on from atop Robinson to Dale Head, descend to the top of the pass, climb the opposite flank of hills at the head of Buttermere to Fleetwith Pike and so down back to the lake from there, a slog firmly in the C grade scale and of considerable onerousness.

Mountain summits have an infuriating habit of not only presenting the climber with false crests but also of often unseen dips in the ridges between them. Hence, by the time we had ground our way to the stone cairn that was Robinson's crown, the way ahead along the crest of the ridge to Dale Head, which had earlier offered the impression of a pleasant barely undulating stroll on a soft, grassy plateau, instead turned fiendishly into a stony descent and ascent from virtually halfway back to lake level.

Finally, however, we stood upon the crest of Dale Head to witness magnificent views over the Vale of Newlands with slithers of sunshine shafting down upon it from a torn cloud ceiling. It was probably so named by early Newlands settlers since the head terminates the upper reaches of the lovely valley with an immense barrier of forbidding cliffs in perpetual shadow while, for us, it became the focal point of a semicircle of fells that together provided a horseshoe walk of infinite variety.

There followed a lengthy but easy descent to the top of the Honister Pass where we crossed the road to wend our way past the still operating slate quarry and up, up, up a winding dirt road to a new ridge forming the opposite arm of the horseshoe. This eventually led to the head of Fleetwith Pike sensationally overlooking the Buttermere valley with its lake the centrepiece.

At least we were blessed with full sunshine and pale blue skies for the scaling of the pike and, more to the point, the climb down from it. A fine mountain, its dominance belies its comparatively modest height of 2,127 feet but the direct descent of it is a beast of a steep and moderately dangerous operation. It took some of the group considerable time to negotiate the sharp, precipitous rocky sections. To be back on flat ground, even the tarmac road, was a pleasure – as was the swim Paul and I rewarded ourselves with using our underpants as swimming trunks.

One evening a week at Hassness is given over to what might be termed as after-dinner entertainment; in our case, entertainment with serious overtones as we were lectured light-heartedly by a member of the Cockermouth Mountain Rescue unit on the hazards of their unpaid and so very worthwhile job. Most other after-dinner activities revolved around the stroll to and from the pub or simply involved sitting around chatting in the Hassness lounge. Strangers no longer, with group members from all walks of life and interests, there were a myriad tales to be recounted and heard. Our most vocal member was the good-natured Alan, a British resident of Florida who seemed to have lived in most countries of the world at one time or another. Our most proficient walker was assuredly Philip on his third consecutive holiday at Hassness in a Lake District he plainly loved. And there was down-to-earth Nigel, ex marine, swarthy, tanned and with a fading tattoo on his arm, who invariably brought a raw touch to the conversation. His partner was Sandra, who, unable to participate in most of the walks because of an injury, gamely and stubbornly still insisted on a footslog around both the lakes of Buttermere and Crummock Water. Amongst the ladies was Ann, always the rearguard on the excruciating hill climbs and descents but never giving up, and Wendy with a bottomless rucksack full of "might need" items. Finally, mention must be made of, if a not too surreptitious holding of hands, stroking of arms and legs, and the faraway look reflected in two pairs of eyes is anything to go by, a budding romance within the group. May it flourish more successfully than the string of failed love-affairs recounted with relish by my own son, Paul, that had his amazed listeners in stitches.

Our final day dawned fine and clear. Great Gable here we come (we would have gone there anyway since, as the highest mountain we would be climbing, it makes a good climax to the tour). As Alfred Wainwright confirms, Great Gable is everybody's favourite; the very name a compelling magnet, the aspect of the mountain on all sides is challenging and its ascent a highlight in the itineraries of all walkers in Lakeland.

There are a number of approaches to the near 3,000-foot summit of one of the "Big Six" of the Lake District. The *Rough Guide* enthuses thus: "The rugged area of fells at the head of Borrowdale contains one of the finest-looking mountains in England – Great Gable", and elsewhere I've heard it described as the most beautiful of all England's mountains. But I beg to disagree. Its rounded bulk looks more like London's Millennium Dome than anything else; the summit not even a peak. But the views from it are astounding with much of the high ground of the Lake District, together with the lovely valleys of Wasdale and Ennerdale at its feet. But such views have to be earned with sweat and a certain amount of tears.

Only seven of us, plus Brian, made the ascent commencing from the top of Honister Pass, thus cheating a little by saving nearly a thousand feet. The slate quarry here is not a pretty sight though it's nice to see a rebirth of an industry, particularly around Honister which is honeycombed by dead mines. The one-time mine tramway bed led us to the top of the ridge (along which we had walked earlier to Fleetwith Pike), from which we branched off on a faint path designated as Moses' Trod, Moses being, it transpired, a slate miner who supplemented his wages by flogging illicit alcohol from a secret still. The stony path that contours both the lower girth of the smaller Green Gable as well as that of Great Gable makes for quite easy going; a prelude to a stiff steep climb from Beck Head which becomes progressively stiffer and steeper near the summit where a maelstrom of boulders and rock ledges require the aid of hands as well as feet. An untidy pile of stones, surmounted by a cairn – affixed to which is a War memorial tablet of the Fell and Rock Climbing Club – marks the highest point.

Our way down – and descending such precipitous walls is more risky and difficult than ascending them – took us over Windy Gap, a cleft between the two Gables which often lives up to its name, then up to Green Gable's summit at 2,628 feet and gradually back over some boggy and ankle-turning rocky descents to Brandreth, along which we had walked in the rain on the first day of the tour. And so back, down yet another knee-aching escarpment, to the top of the pass.

I was sadder to leave Hassness more than any other Ramblers' accommodations of my experience. It is a happy place beautifully run by Ann (no hostel or boarding house matron she) and her hard-working staff who do everything to keep their guests content. Brian too I shall miss for his wisdom (there's not a summit, a peak or a rock pimple of which he doesn't know the name) and his plain niceness.

I have already referred to the beauty of the Lake District and this latest sojourn there recharged my earlier memories. And it holds a special sort of beauty; one so chaste and innocent in one place, so dark and terrible in another. The whole world is here in this small corner of England.

8. The Upper Inn Valley, Austria

(one or two weeks, grade D+)

If the highest mountain in England is not much over 3,000 feet, they get a little higher in the Austrian Tirol where the Alps here rise to around 12,500 feet. And Mont Blanc in the French Alps, the highest mountain in Europe, rears up to an awesome 15,771 feet. But I didn't envisage slogging it to such altitudes as these on a series of walks that formed my next assignment over the mid-July holiday season.

My walking experiences in Austria have not been wide. Besides the 50-mile stomp that Paul and I made from the Czech border to Vienna, described in chapter 7, my hikes have been no more than half-day peregrinations in Carinthia (Karnten) to the south, Burgenland to the east, and Vorarlberg to the west. And bordering the Tirol in the province of Salzburg, I can faintly remember afternoon meanderings while on holiday with my parents at Zell-am-See shortly before the outbreak of the Second World War. But in the Tirol itself my feet were even less active. Now was the opportunity to see where they could carry me.

Though today a fairytale playground filled with craggy peaks, verdant pastures and onion-domed churches, the Tirol has had less than a fairytale history. Settled by Bavarian tribes in the 8th century, it began life as a medieval dukedom centred on Meran (now Merano in Italy) falling under Habsburg rule in 1363. When the 1805 Treaty of Pressburg awarded the Tirol to Bavaria a local patriot, one Andreas Hofer, led his ready-made army of schutzen (riflemen) – a force raised as a result of a 16th century decree requiring the region to defend its own borders – against the Bavarians and their French allies. This revolt, dubbed the Tirolean War of Independence, was crushed and the province remained under Franco-Bavarian control until Napoleon's defeat in 1815, when it was returned to the Austrian fold. Later, South Tirol was awarded to Italy in the aftermath of the First World War and renamed Alto Adige by the Italians though, to this day, it remains a predominantly German-speaking region. And to add to this fragmentation of the province the portion now known as East Tirol has been left geographically isolated by the province of Salzburg.

The Tirolean provincial capital is Innsbruck, situated at the junction of the rivers Inn and Sill. The city is girdled by a trio of Alpine massifs and its ornate centre of Austrian baroque is little changed over the centuries. On my rail tours around Europe I invariably find myself in Innsbruck which is always a pleasure. But on this Ramblers walking tour we would be a long way west of the city; our nearest town being Landeck of far less attraction. Nevertheless, there is compensation in the fact that the Oberinntal, or Upper Inn Valley, is on the doorstep, and this harbours a string of small Alpine resort villages including the one called Ladis which was to be our base. And it would be from Ladis that my well-worn feet would once more be leading me into a walking wonderland.

Ladis, at almost 4,000 feet, lies at a higher altitude than any of the summits of England's mountains and on a broad terrace of meadow and woodland high above the western slopes of the valley, here guarded by a 13th century castle. Mother earth has been particularly kind to western Austria, endowing it with an improbable picture postcard beauty. The landscape, almost too good to be true, of majestic snow-crested mountains, sparkling lakes and wild gorges, is complemented by villages such as Ladis, colourful with carved and painted chalets hung with flowers. And all around are meadows tinkling with the sound of cow bells (I nearly got carried away and wrote "music"!).

Though Innsbruck is probably the nearest international airport, Ramblers Holidays use Zurich, in Switzerland, as the air terminus of this tour, a destination that holds two advantages. One is that, since Switzerland is not in the European Union, full duty-free allowances are permitted at Heathrow; the other being the three-and-a-half-hour coach drive between Zurich and Ladis, a highly picturesque journey via Bregenz on the Bodensee and the dramatic Arlberg Pass – a sightseeing excursion in itself. We reached our accommodation, the Hotel-Pension Goies, by late evening expecting a cold snack in lieu of dinner but here we got the full works, a four-course repast of fine cuisine that set the standard for all future evening meals, most of which were actually of five courses.

The Goies is an absolute delight. Constructed in the traditional Swiss and Tirolean Alpine chalet style of wide overhanging roofs with balconies brimming with flowers, its solid timber interior softened by heavy warm furnishings, I rated the hotel as probably the most pleasant base – equalled perhaps by the Shaker Mill in the USA's New England – of all eight Ramblers walking tours so far sampled. And like all of them it is family-owned and run, this one by the Larcher family with Frau Larcher very much in evidence in reception, bar and dining rooms while her husband, behind the scenes, is the chef who produces the ever-changing fare.

The usual introductory walk on the first – Sunday – morning was heralded by another fine, sunny, warm day; the first being that of yesterday and our arrival at Zurich sweltering in the high 80s. And this was fortunate since, over the previous week, it had rained every day at some point. The walk commenced with a swift tour of Ladis, a spa village no less sprouting a health-giving spring, with our leader, Eddie, pointing out its salient points of interest and practicalities. Echoing our hotel, the alpine village is another delight with the square bulk of the castle keep rising above it from a flanking cliff. Ladis has been a settlement with a history going back to Roman times, the castle – the fortress of Landeck – being, for 300 years, the seat of the oldest judicial court in the Inn valley. Today its keep, main hall and chapel are open at certain hours to the public. Another remarkable building is the Stockerhaus, its painted facade – particularly that of the central bay window – virtually unique in the Tirol which possesses artistically-painted houses in abundance. The overall theme of the paintings of the Stockerhaus show assorted examples of confrontation such as those of the Old and New Testament, God and man, good and evil, death and life, in vivid detail. A fine white church bell tower, several examples of outdoor bread oven and a sizeable pond add to the attractions while our arrival in the village coincided with a weekend festival involving much trumpeting by the never-out-of-puff village band and much beer-consumption that had pretensions of equalling a Bavarian beer festival.

Two other associated nearby villages of similar ilk but, to me, less attraction, situated on this plateau of the Inn valley are Fiss and Serfaus which we would likewise come to know to a lesser degree over the ensuing week. And across the valley on a smaller plateau of its own is Fendels, another typical small Tirolean village backed by woods and high mountains. But it was from Ladis, and in particular its central cafe-restaurant Bad Ladis (known to Ramblers as Bad Ladies) that we commenced our first hike.

This involved a steady 800-foot climb on a well-designated footpath, sustaining few rocky pitfalls, up the grassy and well-wooded slopes of the foothills of what I believe was the Samnaun range which rose behind the village. Possibly because of the preceding severe winter the spring wild flower display was still much in evidence with meadows ablaze with black vanilla, spotted and marsh orchids in considerable profusion together with occasional gentians and a variety of yellow and orange daisy-like blooms. Across the valley the jagged 10,000-foot peaks of the opposite mountain range, that of the Otztaler Alps, streaked with snow, provided a magnificent backcloth to the intense green meadows below, some with their lush grass already mown. Following a halt for refreshments at a ridge-top restaurant beside a salmon-stocked pond our descent was rapid, the route, somewhat boggy in parts, ending in Fiss from which a tarmac path led us smoothly back to Ladis. Not much more than a test amble this so that Eddie could gain an idea of the walking abilities of his charges.

Monday produced another glorious morning as the two dozen of us – yes, there were 24 members in the group on this occasion – caught the public bus from Ladis to Serfaus for the start of a higher altitude and longer hike that would take us upwards close to 6,500 feet. Serfaus is considerably bigger than either Fiss or Ladis and certainly more touristy particularly, it would seem, during the winter skiing season. We spent a while individually investigating its shops, supermarkets and churches – not necessarily in that order – before taking the two cable car lifts, one after another, to a point called Lazid at nearly 6,000 feet, then walking a further few hundred feet higher to a point the map showed as Scheid on the flank of a peak that formed part of the craggy bulwark of Mount Furgler. The all-round views from here were stupendous with not only the high Otztaler ranges we could see from Ladis but also the equally high ones of the Samnaun mountains to the south which, up to then, had been hidden by foothills.

We then made our way, stumbling and slithering, along a ragged, rock-studded and often flooded path that meandered and zigzagged along the flanks of Furgler to a small lake, the Furglersee, completely hidden by a thick but fast-melting snow-crust. Because of its treacherous nature, Eddie insisted upon us crossing it singly in case the crust gave way, a sensible precaution even if other smaller parties of walkers were less prudent. As had been the case in Tuscany we periodically had to traverse substantial wedges of unmelted snow that remained in the hollows, slipping and sliding as we did so. And, in spite of these snowy patches the display of wild flowers never faltered, some determinedly pushing their blooms through the white shroud. Anemone, pulsatilla, nymphaea, primula, saxifrage, iris, the whole range of wild orchids (including one allegedly known as birds nest), aquilegia and two sizes of gentian all spread their colours over the brilliant green of the marshy grasslands on a scale I have never seen before in Europe, the gentians occasionally appearing in lovely deep blue clumps amongst nuggets of rock. Unfortunately, though many individuals were greatly intrigued and delighted with this botanical paradise, no member of the group professed to be a horticulturist so the names of many of these plants escaped us – though I resolved there and then to have my wife, who is knowledgeable on the subject, participate at a future date in one of the flower-lovers' tours which Ramblers Holidays run in various countries.

Views on a walk to Kitzkopf

This display remained with us over much of the walk which continued with the sometimes fading path leading us in a wide arc around the Komperdellalpe valley veined by inoperative ski lifts and rushing meltwater torrents, the latter donating tricky obstacles to progress and, where Eddie led us off the path, any number of boot-clinging bogs. At intervals we could hear the squawks of marmots, while sitting cows, showing no timidity, permitted a light pat on their noses and flanks as we passed them by, their bells tinkling as they shook their heads as if in disbelief at the line of pleasure-seeking masochists roaming their hillsides. Nor were we the only ones; other clusters of hikers tramped the skein of footpaths too, though our group of two dozen was by far the largest. However, the somewhat taciturn Eddie was faultless in ensuring the safety of his flock, taking every care to see that nobody got too far behind and regularly counting us as we passed by. Not a great talker was Eddie; his evening assembly meetings in the hotel during which he announced the next day's programme were of the briefest. An amusing incident that was a consequence of this brevity occurred as we followed him into the cable car station at Serfaus that morning. Eddie made no mention of the fact that he was not going straight to the ticket office and we followed him lemming-like into the cavernous building – where all 24 of us found ourselves in the gents toilet!

The descending route took us around the wooded bulk of a headland shown on my map as Plansegg, and indicated on another as Beutelkops, to then slowly wind down towards Fiss which we could make out far below. We hopped across more streams fed by the melting snow and passed huts where cowherds used to spend the summer minding their beasts before, eventually, reaching another high-altitude cafe and chair lift station where we halted for well-earned refreshment. Thereafter, under storm clouds spitting rain and with thunder reverberating amongst the massifs and saw-blade crests of the Otztaler Alps, we retraced our steps of the previous day to Ladis as the late-afternoon sun reappeared to fleetingly bathe the ranges in a blaze of orange and copper. So ended a walk of considerable length, much of it at a higher altitude than that of my previous three walking tours.

Tuesday and, in spite of the previous afternoon's storm and a wet evening, the weather held its own with a fine sunny morning albeit a fraction cooler and cloudier. Breakfasts at the Goiers are a vast buffet, a full consumption of which – and here my son Paul excelled – negates the necessity of lunch beyond the lightest snack.

The walk that day was a lesser one both in altitude and length and it took place on the opposite side of the Inn valley which gave satisfying views of the plateau – or "sun terrace" as the tourist brochures choose to call it – on which Ladis, Fiss and Serfaus sit with its background of mountains. A hired coach carried us, via Ried on the valley floor, where we paused for provisioning, to Fendels, the village on the same level as Ladis. From Fendels we were carried by chair lift to a point called Sattele at around 2,000 feet. A trail, here and there blocked by more snow wedges, led to the Renk refuge cabin, our objective, directly beneath the peaks of Gamskopf and Feichtener Karlspitze. The trail was named the Aachener Hohenweg and it took us in a haphazard manner across the grain of the foothills of the Glockturmkamm ranges of the Otztaler Alps, its marshy meadows again a carpet of flowers. Above the tree line the path turned into a side valley, known, according to my map, as Zermesgrat, headed by a splendid three-pronged waterfall as melt water cascaded over a sheer 200-foot cliff. Directly in front of us rose the near 7,000 foot Gamskopf and its slightly higher brother, the Feichtener Karlspitze, snow-flecked and scowling and, as we attained the cabin, haloed by angry cloud that, once more, spat rain. Beneath the eaves of the stout timber building we consumed our picnic lunches, watching the thundering waters of the falls.

Our return initially involved a retracing of steps along the rim of the Zermesgrat valley and back across the undulating meadows, bright with the usual orchids, and saxifrage as well as buttercups twice the size of

English ones, to the point indicated as Zirmeskopf which is no more than a junction of footpaths. Here, by way of another refuge cabin – the Jagehutte – where we halted for a few blissful moments, we wended our way ever downwards through forest land and across fallen trees to finally end up on a dirt road that terminated at Ried. Just once – as had happened on yesterday's tramp – we were struck by a sudden shower of rain which ceased barely had we donned our rainwear.

Wednesday was the customary free or rest day for doing our own thing, some taking themselves off by public transport to Innsbruck, the Weisser Glacier near the Italian border, or, closer to hand, Nauders where the Inn valley narrows into a spectacular gorge. Others, including Paul and myself, made it, unashamedly, a rest day, doing no more than pottering about Ladis, giving ourselves a leg-stretch with a four-mile stomp to and from the astoundingly-situated Hotel restaurant Newegg visible, white and remote, from afar, and partaking of a midday beer at the "Bad Ladies" bar. After dinner, which included a course the menu pronounced as "Tirolean Gristle" (actually fried egg on roast potatoes), most of us visited an old farmhouse in the village that has been preserved for posterity as a private-enterprise museum. The brief tour of the rooms included an issue of schnapps which at least warmed us up for a scurrying return to the hotel under a downpour of rain.

Thursday dawned dry but with low cloud hiding the hills and mountains; not the perfect conditions for the further high altitude walk planned. We delayed making the final decision to the last moment which followed our arrival at Serfaus on the local bus. Alas, though a few desultory rays of sunshine managed to pierce the grey ceiling, the clouds stayed put, prompting Eddie to instigate an alternative, low altitude hike. And actually a very enjoyable alternative it turned out to be.

We left the township on a footpath labelled Argenweg which zigzagged down the thickly-wooded flank of the Inn valley, the tall pine trunks rising from a steeply angled ground well endowed with mushrooms sprouting from damp pine-needled earth. On a small grassy plateau clear of the tree-cover stood the little 10th century church of St Georg, one of the oldest such edifices in the Tirol containing some remarkable 15th century wall paintings. Reaching the valley floor we made a detour to see the Romanbrucke, the Roman bridge that spanned the Argen torrent alongside of which we had walked for much of the route so far. Here it enters the fast-flowing, cold grey waters of the Inn which would be our close companion for the remainder of the hike. Retracing our steps, we joined another named footpath, this one the grandly-titled Via Claudia Wanderweg, hugging the Inn as if its life depended on it. This gave us a pleasantly level trudge all the way to Prutz, a village beyond - and north – of Ried. Low grey cloud continued to shroud the hilltops as we entered the village and a mouth-watering cake-serving cafe which offered an all too adequate refuge from a prolonged downpour. A footpath leads directly up the hillside to Ladis, an hour's ascent, but the lowering weather prompted an excuse to take the bus.

Weather conditions were only slightly improved on Friday, the last walking day for those of us on the one week-only tour which included Paul and myself. Once more we took the bus into Serfaus and there decided to go ahead with the higher altitude walk abandoned earlier. This commenced with the double cable car ride to its summit terminus at Lazid followed by a muddy slog to the point called Scheid, a couple of hundred feet higher, that had been the turning-off point for our warm and sunny hike the previous Monday. But it was warm and sunny no longer; instead it was now snowing and bitterly cold as if the elements had decided to give us a dose of their contrasting capabilities. And on such a day as this the full regalia of the outdoor clothing market's waterproof clothing range appeared on display, transforming individuals into unrecognisable hooded and caped anonymities. Five of the group, rather sensibly, decided to abort the walk and return to the cable car station and less disagreeable climes; the remaining 19 of us pressing on across boggy grassland deficient of any path or marker but liberally scattered with wet rocks. In such terrain a certain amount of care has to be taken; not least in where one places each foot. Wet rocks can be slippery and a resulting fall painful; bogs hold deep wet patches that can fill one's boots with muddy water which is merely uncomfortable. Thus the latter is the better of two evils. The trick is to avoid both though few of us succeeded. Floundering on, we struggled, a mite miserably, through the murk, mist and falling snow. Then miraculously, the sky lightened as sunshine attempted to spread a little joy into the proceedings; it surely raised our morale. But it didn't last though the snow turned to sleet and then rain while the clouds lifted enough for us to make out where we were going. We began to descend – which was heartening – but the rain changed back to snow – which was not. A refuge cabin, the Boderhutte, however, was visible and as we made our way towards it a herd of at least 50 Haflinger horses, light brown, handsome and exceedingly friendly, galloped towards us, the thunder of their hoofs giving a fair imitation of the Charge of the Light Brigade. This caused momentary concern within our ranks but the animals' desire for human companionship became apparent as they nuzzled our rucksacks as if they knew where our picnic apples might be stored. This brief interval of light relief over, we repaired to the limited shelter of the small locked cabin to rest awhile as the new snow shower turned back again to rain.

Reluctantly emerging, we continued the descent, following and crossing at intervals the hastening water of the Moosbach torrent, which flowed as if it too wanted to get off the afflicted mountain tops. Then, contouring around the cap of the high ground called Lazidgrat that tumbles precipitously to Serfaus and its plateau, and then climbing again under ceaseless rain, we halted briefly for a damp picnic. Another muddy track guided us to the Kolner Haus, the sizeable summit station of the lower – Kamperdell – cable car lift where, in its warm, fuggy restaurant an intake of apfelstrudel and thick creamy hot chocolate did much to raise our spirits. And they were raised even higher with Eddie's decision to finally abort the walk and proceed back to Ladis by cable car and bus. A disappointing end to a week's walking in and about one of the Tirol's loveliest valleys.

Though, to my mind, rather large in size, the group comprised the nicest of participants. I deemed it a privilege to have been their companion. Again the age ratio was little different from that of earlier groups; in this particular instance it lay between Paul, at 38, and myself, at 75, with life styles and interests equally varied. In terms of occupation, the group included an architect, a British Telecom technician based in Germany, a dentist, a traffic warden who was once a railway policeman and customs officer, and two Irish lady schoolteachers. We also boasted a church bell-ringer, a one-time prison social worker and a couple of scout masters (male and female).

From total strangers we had, in the space of a week, become the closest of friends who discussed the most intimate of subjects. Yet, upon leaving the homeward-bound aircraft back at Heathrow, we were to go our differing ways, like birds at dusk, probably never to meet again.

The Drakensberg Mountains, South Africa (17 days, grade D+/C)

So to my final walking holiday assignment, the last of nine all undertaken within a six-month period, and this one within sight of my 76th year. As befits a climax reached by my worn but still willing feet, the destination was to be a far-away one – South Africa; the venue – the Drakensberg Mountains, the highest ranges in southern Africa. Together, again, with Paul, I was going there in August – late summer here, the prelude to spring there – for the full 17-day holiday which was to be a two-centre one; three if you include the final couple of days on the coast at Durban. I had been to this great country twice before, even passing through the Drakensbergs by rail: once in super luxury on the famous Blue Train and, later, in a lot less luxury on an oft-stopping, late-arriving train which South African Railways grandly called the Trans-Natal Express – though I think they were joking.

I have some interesting friends in Greater Johannesburg. The exiled royal family of Albania have known me for many years and I stay with them whenever I go to South Africa. Since it is Her Majesty the Queen of the Albanians who has kindly supplied the foreword to this book I crave a paragraph to relate how this came about, though she does make mention of it herself. My first of a number of incursions into Albania undertaken with the greatest difficulty was during the communist Enver Hoxha regime when its borders were tightly closed to Westerners. More or less legally crossing this border I was read the "riot act" by the authorities which listed activities that transgressed various laws for which the punishment was summary execution. The list covered virtually everything worthwhile, though I noted that foreigners riding the Albanian State Railway without special permission were rewarded with no more than 25 years hard labour. So I took to the railway and criss-crossed the country by the most diabolical set of trains imaginable – and lived to tell the tale. (I repeated this on a subsequent visit but on that occasion was removed from my broken-down coach to be taken to the Ministry of Foreign Affairs in Tirana for a severe reprimand.) About this time I wrote a book – actually two books, the most recent of which is The Great Railway Adventure , narrating these and other incident-full world rail journeys of mine. His Majesty King Leka by chance picked up a copy in a Jo'burg bookshop, read it and contacted me in the hope I knew more about his afflicted country than he did at the time; he and his family having had to flee, just days after his birth, from the invading Italian and German armies during the Second World War.

But back to the subject of South Africa and, in particular, Natal, in which province the bulk of the Drakensberg Mountains are located. Except for Gauteng, it is the smallest of the country's provinces but within it lies a huge diversity of geography from snow-prone peaks to well-baked Indian Ocean beaches. Its peoples range from Anglo to Zulu.

It was the Portuguese explorer Vasco da Gama who gave Natal its name, having set eyes on its coast on Christmas Day 1497, "Natal", in his language meaning "Christmas". Subsequently, for over 200 years, there were few landfalls on this coast despite the presence of a fine natural harbour where Durban now stands. Gradually, however, the Cape Town-based Dutch East India Company began to hear favourable reports of Natal's fertility, friendly inhabitants and abundance of game, so it set up a coastal provisioning post in the bay which, by 1750, had become well-known to ships from all over Europe.

In the 1800s came much strife to disrupt Natal's peaceful existence with a number of dominant tribes emerging from the mass of small chiefdoms in the region, some gaining sufficient power to maintain standing armies of warriors used to mount large-scale raids on their neighbours. From this simmering cauldron of conflict the Zulus proved their superiority to the extent that the two, by then, contenders for the colonisation of Natal – the British and the Voortrekker Boers – were, in turn, on a head-on collision course with them. Thus the stage was set for both the Anglo-Zulu and Anglo-Boer wars, the former of which saw the Zulu kingdom subjugated.

Since these troubled times and following the formation of the Union of South Africa in 1910, Natal has prospered and, with apartheid officially out of the way, it was recently renamed Kwa Zulu/Natal in belated recognition of the fact that the Zulu heartland of Kwa Zulu comprised a substantial part of the province; a step towards the ideal of the equality of Man.

The Drakensberg Mountains – the Great Drakensberg or Dragon Mountains as they are also known – stretch for hundreds of miles along the eastern margins of the interior plateau, from the Eastern Cape to the Transvaal, with the highest summits on the border between Natal and Lesotho. As another friend of mine, John Cleare, the eminent mountaineering photographer, points out in his book *Mountains and Mountaineering*

(Collins,1979), the chief crags and pinnacles are formed of weathered basalt, rising above the sandstone of the foothills known as the "Little Berg". These rolling hills are covered by grasslands, green in the wet summer months and dry and cold in winter when snow and ice appear on the peaks. The Drakensbergs abound with wildlife, including eland, baboon and even leopard, while the rare African lammergeier is sometimes seen.

The highest peaks rear upward to nearly 11,500 feet making them not only the highest in southern Africa but, with the exception of Kilimanjaro and Mount Kenya in East Africa and the Toubkal massif in North Africa, the highest ranges in the whole African Continent. As with the Tirolean Alps of my previous assignment, I didn't imagine we would be walking at such rarefied altitudes on this tour though my recollections of attaining the fairly easily-reached summit of Toubkal and the less-so easy third highest of the treble peaks of 17,000-foot Mount Kenya in my only slightly younger days offer me wry moments of contemplation. I had done no more than look upon Kilimanjaro in Tanzania but I had done better with a hellish ascent of Chimborazo, of nearly 22,000 feet, in South America's Ecuador (see chapter 13).

But, again, I digress; I'm now older still, perhaps a little wiser, and assuredly less nimble. In this closing year of the 19th century I'm content to allow my legs to carry me around terrain of more modest altitude.

Though Paul and I would be arriving at Johannesburg Airport 24 hours ahead of the main Ramblers group, as well as returning to it from Durban for a change of aircraft at the conclusion of the tour, I didn't think any of us would see much of the city on either occasion. And, for me at least, this would be no loss. Years before I had spent a night at its once-celebrated Carlton Hotel in the heart of what then was called "town", a city centre now a sea of dereliction. The Carlton has long closed and the city has become a dangerous place, almost a no go area after dark if you are on your own, as I discovered on my second visitation in 1997. The high-rise skyline remains impressive; it's the largest conurbation in Africa south of Cairo, and still growing. Jo'burg's devotees will point out its redeeming features – wealth, energy and a sublime climate – but omit the paralleling ugliness of the poverty to be seen in the shanty towns – a cause for infinite sadness.

For us the rural Drakensbergs would make a happier destination.

For Paul and me, our brief sojourn with the Royal Family of Albania made a restful interlude between a near-sleepless overnight flight from

London and the five-hour coach drive to the Central Drakensbergs where our first of three sets of accommodation was located. We met the main group – a very manageable one dozen (including ourselves) strong – back at Jo'burg Airport from a BA flight that arrived fractionally early. The previous day had been cloudy and decidedly cool but now the sun shone brightly if not warmly. The composition of the group hardly varied from those of earlier tours except in quantity, though amongst us were a couple of fanatical 'birders' and a leavening of amateur botanists. The group leader was Fred, a wildly enthusiastic and knowledgeable South African from the Cape.

As expected, we were to see nothing of central Jo'burg as we headed out of the eternal suburbs of this mega-city but I was heartened to glimpse vast new housing estates made up of row after row of small, compact dwellings that were mushrooming everywhere as the government attempted to alleviate the chronic housing shortage that was – and still is – the ugly blight on all South African conurbations, particularly Jo'burg.

The first hours of the drive took us at high speed over a dead-straight highway that traversed a draughty plain; virtually a semi-desert, the wind blowing eddies of sand and dust across the tarmac. And the wind was bitter which, for me, boded ill since the clothing I had brought was only that suitable for what I hoped would be a warm and balmy African spring. Here and there we could see the circular crop fields we had noted from the aircraft as we came into land, the uncommon shape of them making for easier irrigation by spider-like water-spraying machines. Gradually the featureless landscape began to buck itself into low, oddly-shaped mounds; some flat-topped, others rounded, a few sharp-pointed; terrain that slowly expanded in a similar pattern first into hills and then mountains to reach a climax of an awesome range of almost lunar-like peaks and summits chiselled into fantastic shapes and linked by jagged escarpments. We had arrived at the foot of the great barrier, or Battlement of Spears (Quathlamba) as the Zulus called these spectacular Drakensberg Mountains, the highest range of South Africa's Great Escarpment curving eastwards from Lesotho into Natal in a giant buttress whose cliffs fall sheer to the bare green foothills of the Natal Midlands.

From a distance, only the highest ridges are visible, a thin blue line suspended above the horizon and hung with shifting cloud. As we were soon to see, their scale is dwarfing. At some points, river gorges fall over a 1,000 feet while above soar cliffs of equal height. There is a crystal quality in the air; waterfalls and cold streams cascade down hidden forest *kloofs* (water chutes) to wild open plateaux of montane grassland grazed by small herds of shy antelope. Balancing rocks and toothlike columns, bizarrely-shaped and hundreds of metres high, jut from the huge massifs of the square-topped basalt peaks. And that we were in the heart of Zululand was plain to see from the myriad small settlements of mostly circular wattle-walled and thatched dwelling huts constructed at random on hillside ledges bordering the road.

Our first base was the three-star Cathedral Peak Hotel, assuredly the most luxurious establishment of all those I had sampled on the previous eight tours. More a mountain resort than a plain hotel it consists of a spaced-out series of bedroom suites centred on a main building housing an extensive dining hall, bars, games rooms and lounges, the whole complex surrounded by sports and activity facilities such as swimming pool, horse-stables, mini-golf course, a chapel and even the hotel's own helicopter; a complex as out-of-place among the simple Zulu-inhabited surroundings as it is possible to be. But who's complaining?! However, I have to admit that the small, homely, family-run pensions and hostelries experienced on the other tours are, to me, more fitting a Ramblers walking holiday, but it's nice to have a change of pad once in a while. More to the point, the army of staff required to run such a place gives much-needed employment to the local people. And to wipe away any further lingering misgiving the cuisine was as awesome as the scenery; the range of dishes for the buffet breakfasts and dinners startling in their variety, quality and quantity.

The hotel was the vision of the Albert Van der Riet family who purchased the area from a local farmer. Initial developments began in 1936 and the hotel opened on Christmas Day 1939. When the whole region was declared a national park the der Riets donated their portion of it to the park on condition that no other hotel should be raised thereon. And so, right up to the present day, there is no alternative accommodation to be found within the Cathedral Peak park with the exception of a couple of self-catering chalets and a camping site.

At the pre-dinner briefing Fred gave us the low-down on not only the customary next day's walking programme but a myriad matters that concerned our six-day sojourn at Cathedral Peak. The thoroughness of his briefing impressed me greatly; few other leaders had been so meticulous or so informative when it came to imparting facts concerning the routes we would be taking, the risks we should avoid and precautions we should take. The first day's walk, he affirmed, would be the usual preliminary acclimatising run-in from which the walking standard of the group could be judged. It would be a doddle; just a ramble to a nearby waterfall, some cave-paintings and a short ascent to a local headland.

In the event, though hardly a marathon accomplishment, the walk was considerably more than the doddle or ramble expected. The sun glowed warmly from a clear blue sky with the wind of the previous day no more than a pleasant breeze. Cathedral Peak, is the highest mountain in the region and one of the highest in the Drakensbergs at nearly 10,000 feet, while its group of attendant buttresses (which resembles a Gothic cathedral with twin towers) is only fractionally lower. But our first walk took us to more modest altitudes though, by choosing a route and an almost non-existent path, the way degenerated into quite rough-going.

We left the hotel on a well-trodden track that led up the Umhlonhlo valley following the stream of the same name which brought us eventually to the modest Doreen Waterfall. From there we contoured around the flanks of a couple of rocky headlands to attain a distinctive crag known as Mushroom Rock.Een route we climbed a near-vertical rock escarpment, traversed an area of ankle-turning tufted grass and bare leg-scratching undergrowth and, on a less arduous section, ascended to a broad cave mouth to view some 600-year old cave paintings. All the while Fred pointed out strange – to European eyes – birds, flowers and shrubs. The birders of the group had something of a field day, their binoculars picking out birds they had never seen before, including jackal buzzards, black shrouded kites and even a comparatively rare lammergeier soaring effortlessly overhead. And this plus a host of smaller birds of vivid plumage and strange song. Our botanists too were not to be excluded as they perceived the startlingly crimson blooms of the Natal bottlebrush tree, the dry flowers of various species of protea and countless smaller blooms such as miniature wild iris and what was thought to be Erica peeping from various delicately-designed grasses. Maybe it was too early in the season for the full wild flower display such as I had observed in the Austrian Tirol and assuredly nothing could compare with the staggering sight of vivid acres of colour that characterises the Cape further south. We also spotted a couple of kudu leaping from rock to rock on the other side of the valley.

Though I had looked upon much better and seldom-seen examples in the Libyan Desert, the cave paintings we saw on that first walk were interesting. Here in the Natal Drakensberg the walls of sandstone caves and overhangs often display evidence of bushman art, many of which can be reached on foot. These San bushmen inhabited much of Southern Africa when the first whites arrived in the 15th century, and cling on in scattered communities in Botswana and Namibia even today. Traditional San hunting and ritual pictures sometimes alternate with scenes from the later white settler invasion, such as ox-wagons and horsemen with guns. The San had occupied the Drakensberg since being driven there by African pastoralists around the 14th century and it was this range that provided the South African San with their last mountain stronghold before they were virtually wiped out by both white settlers and black tribes, neither of whom would tolerate the San's practice of hunting cattle when there was insufficient game elsewhere (though, being a gentle and hospitable people they would willingly share the resulting meat with the victims of their robbery).

All around us as we walked were strange rock formations, the rock comprising soft easily-weathered sandstone and hard wear-resisting basalt, the panorama of mountains viewed from the top of Mushroom Rock spreading out before us in startling clarity. The Cathedral range, as this massif is called, is formed by a high corridor of basalt, sand and limestone eroded over millions of years to form well-known peaks and summits with names like the Chessman, the Horns, the Bell, the Organ Pipes and the impressive Cathedral Peak itself.

The way down from Mushroom Rock was steep but easily negotiable since, in days gone by, rough steps had been cut which, though eroded, made convenient stepping stones. And with a quite short but reasonably strenuous first day's hike beneath our belts we were back in time for a highly civilised hotel afternoon tea on the terrace.

Next day we "scaled" Baboon Rock. David Bristow's fine book *Drakensberg Walks* quotes the duration of this walk as five hours but, according to Fred, Bristow is a confirmed jogger and so covers at a jog-trot many of the 120 walking routes which he detailed. This put the wind up a few members of the group while a forecast of 28 degrees of temperature hardly added encouragement – though it allayed my concern about a deficiency of cold-weather clothing.

Actually the new day's hiking, though strenuous, was not too much for any of us. It started easily enough with an undulating path leading from the foot suspension bridge spanning the Mlambonja river, near the hotel, and up and along the Ganabu Ridge. Only when directly beneath the pinnacle that is Baboon Rock does the ascent become arduous, the path rocky with one or two perpendicular barriers necessitating a little climbing technique and firm hand-holds. The rock is well-named; its lower slopes were well populated by baboons of all sizes, mostly in family groups. They scampered about, stopping at intervals to take a long hard look at us. At least on this route the path was well-defined though, here and there, not recommended to sufferers of vertigo. Near the top the path wound round the back of Baboon Rock to bring us quite gently to the grassy plateau that forms the summit.

The views are spectacular in all directions, particularly those of the Cathedral massif and across the Little Berg plateau (most South Africans refer to the Natal Drakensbergs as the "Berg"). Except for the occasional tiny wild iris and a few unidentified yellow daisy-like blooms, flowers were conspicuous by their absence while, on the bird front, jackal buzzards kept many binoculars glued to the sky whenever their owners were not looking where they placed their feet on the difficult path. The descent, like all steep descents in mountainous districts, needed our full concentration.

Day 3 spelt Rainbow Gorge which Fred gleefully described as a fun walk. And the weather entered into the spirit of things by again being sunny and warm. The initial section of the walk followed the Ndumeni river which rises below the Organ Pipes bulwark of the Cathedral massif. The route then skirts the base of Tryme Hill (which we Brits would class as a mountain) before turning into Mike's Pass and doubling back on itself to descend slowly into the forested valley of the river, the waters of which, in spite of snow-melt, were not unduly high. The tree cover was more jungle than forest with thick creepers hanging from yellow-wood and other lichen-sheathed trees, while rocky outcrops forced the path to twist and turn, rise and fall, between feeder streams. A kilometre of this brought us to Mermaid Pool, an enchanting basin of water fed by a couple of waterfalls cascading down around both sides of a huge, moss-covered boulder. Here we halted for a while, three members of the group electing to remain there to await our return since the valley that we were following was fast narrowing to a gorge – Rainbow Gorge – that promised some tricky legwork with a virtual no through road at its end. The remainder of us proceeded forward – and that's where the heralded fun started. A further kilometre ahead the wildly-gyrating and frequently boulder-blocked track gives up the ghost to tip the hiker into the boulder-strewn river now becoming increasingly compressed by awesomely-tall and sheer sandstone cliffs. From here onwards our progress became a series of boulder balancing acts as we crossed and re-crossed the river to arrive finally at what is described as a hanging rock – a gigantic chockstone boulder wedged between the narrowing walls of the gorge – the first of two such occurrences of nature. The way forward here was barred by smooth-faced walls of rock which had to be negotiated not without some difficulty, the successful negotiation only leading us to the second similar barrier. This one lay under a second hanging rock while the barrier itself was guarded by a waist-deep pool of exceedingly cold melt water.

To surmount this new barrier it was necessary to enter the water waist-deep to reach an iron-stepped, chain-hung ladder that led perpendicularly to the top of the array of great boulders down which the river cascaded.

Only three of us, including Paul, myself and a colleague named Eugene, plus Fred, made it to the base of the makeshift ladder which someone with a warped sense of humour had arranged to hang nearly out of reach from the surface of the water. The trick was to attain this point before the cold water paralysed your legs whereupon, in desperation, the bottom rung had to be jumped for and grabbed. By brute strength of the arms, you then pulled yourself out of the freezing water, feet scrabbling for the slightest footholds on the slippery surface of the boulder up which the ladder mounted until the feet too could attain the bottom rung. Thereafter it was simply a matter of hauling yourself upwards to the top.

This was virtually the terminus of the outward route of the walk though it is possible, I learnt, to continue to a path that leads back to the summit of Tryme Hill. Instead we had to return the way we had come, descending the accursed ladder, dropping into the ice-cold water and re-negotiating all the geographical impediments met on the outward journey.

Thus the Rainbow Gorge perambulation; a barrel of er, fun!

With only two more days before leaving our present location for pastures new, Fred resolved that we should undertake a longish walk that circuited the Oqalweni valley taking us right up close to the base of the Cathedral massif, a total distance of about 12 miles. The first section of the route would be that of the initial portion of the slog to the peak itself.

Following the usual cold night a warm sun blazed down from the thankfully monotonous blue sky; how different from shivery Jo'burg and, from what we heard, rainy Cape Town. And yet, contrary to what I intimated earlier, this was still winter; albeit the end of it, spring not officially commencing until September 1.

Boulder-hopping the Miambonje river, climbing a hill to a grassy plain, our path took us in zigzags to the top of a plateau. This in turn guided us on a gentle incline across another plateau towards the ridge that lay between us and the cliffs that form the base of Cathedral Peak. Halfway up the ridge the track inherits the designation of the Contour Path at the junction with one leading towards the Peak. I gazed wistfully at this further footway. David Bristow in his book warns that the ascent of this evocative mountain is "severe to extreme and should be attempted only by experienced climbers" which, though I'm not even an amateur climber, offered something of a challenge. There and then I resolved to have a go at it and, in this, I was fully supported by Paul who is a chip off the old block. After all we could always return if things got too difficult, I told myself with little conviction.

Living up to its name our present path stuck closely to the 100-metre contour line around the head of the valley with the gigantic bulk of the Cathedral massif looming overhead. Except for a landslide obliterating the path and requiring a detour at one point and a few stream crossings, the route made for easy going with long sharp grass, shrubs and occasional clumps of so-called breakfast fruit, to observe or/and curse as their stems speared bare legs. At the further valley wall the path climbs again to the grassy plateau of One Tree Hill where there is not a tree to be seen though, instead, there were, in our case, plenty of baboons in evidence as well as eland. We also noted the footprints of jackal together with what purported to be the droppings of a leopard. Across on the opposite flank of the valley our path wound slowly downward across the green swathe following a route that was in fact becoming a great horseshoe of a walk.

The descent of One Tree Hill is steep and uncomfortable while large proteus bushes repeatedly have to be avoided, their scratchy black branches liable to inflict painful jabs. Except for the tiny irises there were few wild flowers to excite the botanists of the group while the birders had to be content with the odd soaring kite and buzzard. At the bottom of the hill the Oqalweni joins the Miambonja river flowing down from the adjoining valley, their combined waters little more than an overgrown stream which we crossed by the customary boulder-hopping at which we were becoming adept. Back at the hotel before dusk we had broken no records – except, maybe, in the case of one of our Irish members, Don, for the size of his blisters.

There is no rest or free day as such on this tour; only a transfer day and even on that there was time for an afternoon hike. However, on the final day at Cathedral Peak there were a number of options available – an excursion to a concert given by the Drakensberg Boys' Choir (reputed to be finer even than that of Vienna) at Winterton, an hour's drive distant or/and a morning walk with time to nurse blisters and other ailments. For Paul and me Cathedral Peak beckoned.

Since the ascent of this mountain is far beyond the physical grade of the tour and is therefore not included in the programme I will not dwell too long on our efforts. Suffice to say we made it, reaching the near 10,000-foot summit in four hours of intense slog which had my poor near-76 year old heart and lungs working overtime while the final virtually-sheer section of the peak had both Paul and me in spasms of mortal terror as we traversed near-perpendicular smooth rock faces desperately searching for non-existent finger-holes but relying entirely on the ability of the Vibram soles of our boots to prevent us from sliding downwards into oblivion. However, in Francis, our black Lesotho guide, we had a man of great climbing ability; but for him we would never have attained the summit. And the view from it is out of this world. All around us mountain ranges spread into a blue haze. Sharp against the sky their outlines and long stark ridges crowned by jagged outcrops had a force and a significance bordering upon the sinister. Yet in the sunlight, with the sun stroking every fold of ground and sharpening every edge of rock, what lay before our astounded eyes had a variety and beauty impossible to resist.

David Bristow quotes the 20-kilometre trek and ascent as of "six to seven hours duration" so, by accomplishing it in seven, including half an hour on the summit consuming a banana and undertaking a celebratory pee, wasn't bad going. Additionally I seem to have set up a record by being the oldest person to have reached the top. And the trouble with reaching the top of a mountain is that one then has to go down, an operation equally hazardous.

For me transfer day was opportune. With two 20-kilometre walks on consecutive days plus the climb my legs felt as if they were made of jelly, while my blooded hands (resulting from scrabbling for rock-face finger-holes) were painful in the extreme. The move from Central to North Drakensberg in this instance involved little more than an hour-and-a-half drive via the township of Bergville; the destination being the Royal Natal National Park. The scenery here is among the most dramatic in Africa, particularly that of the so-called Amphitheatre, the main geographical feature of the area, which is an awesome rock wall some seven kilometres in length over which the Tugela river plunges in three gigantic leaps. With its protea woodland, fast-running streams, waterfalls and flat-topped heights, Royal Natal is picture-postcard Drakensberg. It provides hiking trails through mountains where Zulu women can sometimes be seen cutting reed for basket-making, as they have done since before the park existed. The park itself is only a little over 22,000 acres in extent, the southern boundary being formed by the Amphitheatre. Looming up behind is 11,000-foot Mont-aux-Sources, so-called because the Tugela, Elands and Western Khubedu rivers rise here. Other notable summits in the district include the Devil's Tooth, the Sentinel, the Crocodile and a variety of peaks with names often hard to reconcile with their shape.

Our base in this delectable countryside was the Royal Natal National Park Hotel which likes to call itself a "hotel", not a "resort", though I could detect little difference. Both park and hotel were proclaimed "royal" following our present queen's visit in 1947 when, as Princess Elizabeth, she was accompanied by the whole royal family. There are plenty of mementoes of that visit in both the main building of the hotel and in its flowering shrub-bedecked grounds. Alas the slightly run-down complex of

Fred talking to the party with The Crack in the background

faded glories is to close down in April 2,000 so there is little point in my penning a long account of its delights beyond, perhaps, praising the cuisine which manifested itself in seven-course served repasts every evening.

An afternoon toddle along a steeply-inclined concrete path (laid down to arrest erosion) to a huge circular boulder known as Lookout Rock was no more than a leg-stretcher after the drive and an appetiser for the first gastronomic intake.

In general the mountains hereabouts are slightly lower than those of the Cathedral Peak range and our walk next day reflected this as we made our way, via a rock pool on the Golide stream called Fairy Glen, to the Gudu Falls. The only stiff climb and, later, descent, was made in forested slopes on a rock-strewn zigzag path, a mite confusing to follow amongst fallen trees and thick, snake-like creepers. Near Gudu Pool, into which the Gudu river plunges some 120 feet, is a majestic view of four massifs including that of the flat-topped but domineering Sentinel. Gudu Pool never attracts a single ray of sunshine so is shockingly cold – though this failed to deter my son from taking a dip. Come to think of it, all the water in the Drakensberg is pretty numbing at this time of year; even that of the hotel pool was disturbed only by madmen such as Paul and myself.

Back on lower ground and away from the Gudu fraternity the route continued via a level and well-worn path through diverse vegetation including the usual silver-tinted bracken, thick stiff grass, tree ferns and the occasional yellow-wood tree sheltered by huge boulders. Above us rose giant cliffs featuring characteristic forms such as the Crack, Ploughman's Kep and Broome Hill – if I've got their pet names right. And so, by way of a currently dried-up waterfall caller Tiger Falls (with baboons peeping down at us from its lip), back to the hotel in time for a late snack lunch for those who needed it.

Fred warned of a long – 26-kilometre – hike on the cards for the following day which resulted in our two bird fanatics, Owen and the Irishman Don, hurriedly electing to remain behind to undertake a little local bird-watching instead. The rest of us, a few with some trepidation, embarked upon a path that, for much of the way, contoured the impressive Mahai valley headed by the falls of the same name though the cascade held little water. But the views were superb as we rose higher with the whole mighty Amphitheatre revealing itself together with lesser rock formations while, above and around us, rose stark, sheer cliffs of savage visage. The air was clear enough even to allow us to glimpse the backside of Cathedral Peak, 70 kilometres away.

Above the falls the path swung upwards taking us to and over the Basutholand (Lesotho) border and into a new country. Literally on this border stands the Witsieshhoek Mountain resort, something on the lines of a miniature and simpler version of the Cathedral Peak complex, where we paused for a coffee watching a lammergeier circling lower and lower to finally alight on burnt grass only to be disturbed by a flock of goats. Puffy white clouds in the sky had turned to ominous grey heralding rain to come.

The walk continued along the South African side of the border marked by a light barbed-wire fence and, on a headland overlooking the magnificent panorama, we consumed the substantial picnic lunch supplied by the hotel. After a walk of the kind we had just undertaken, such views as those that lay before us here are very special and richly rewarding. To stand alone on top of any hill or mountain is to look upon an apparently unpeopled world. And yet it is there that you may suddenly experience the conviction of having a place in a chain longer than history.

Fred then offered us a choice of three routes home: a retracing of steps, or via one of two geographical components – the Crack or the Mudslide – we had seen on earlier walks. The vote went to the Mudslide (which actually has nothing to do with its nomenclature, the slide having

Ramblers descending the Mudslide

taken place some distance away) – and thereby lay the sting in the tail of this particular walk.

From the headland the path led steeply down to a rocky plateau that forms the summit of more immense basalt and sandstone cliffs, over which the Gudu river plunges. Here, however, we were looking down on the fall whilst yesterday we had looked up at it. As always our downward progress had to be paid for, now by a stiff upward climb to the top of another plateau. This one turned out to be the summit of the so-called Mudslide which is a wooded crevice slicing down the cliff wall the other side of the Gudu Falls. The first of two vertical iron ladders supported by chains was our introduction to a somewhat hairy and very steep descent of this vertical cliff, the way down being strewn with large boulders, loose stones and a maze of tree-roots forming a course that was more chute than a path. Tree-roots are frequently a bane to the walker, being slippery particularly when wet, but here they were a blessing since they provided much-needed handholds and footholds as we slowly inched our way down the cliff-face, mostly on our bottoms. It was a difficult descent but we all reached the bottom safely; the second vertical iron chain ladder becoming the last serious test of agility before the path re-asserted itself to slowly level out and lead us to the hotel.

The weather predictions proved false the following morning, the ominous clouds of the day before giving way to the blue skies we had come to expect (though it should be noted that it can be wet at this time of year). The new day's walk commenced from Fairy Glen. We continued round the head of the valley to the opposite flank, negotiated a headland and climbed an escarpment, carpeted by rocks and tufted grass, to Surprise Ridge, so-called for the surprising and varied views to be seen from it. The sky had clouded over by midday and the wind had risen. The latter at least sent the more threatening clouds packing, though, equally, it did its best to topple us over the ridge. On that day it could be more appropriately called Windy Ridge, particularly at its highest point known as the Camel's Hump.

Down the other side, crossing the odd rivulet, and into another valley – this one containing amongst the ubiquitous black-stemmed protea trees a fern forest – to the Cavern Berg Resort which, from April 2,000, would be the Ramblers Holidays' second base following the closure of the Royal National Park Hotel. Before descending to it for lunch we made a detour around the head of the new valley to observe briefly the elongated horizontal cavern called Cannibal Cave. It has an interesting history. During the mid-19th century the cave was reputed to have been used as a lair by one of the cannibal bands which roamed the area of present-day Lesotho. Passing travellers were frequently abducted, then strung up in the cave mouth to keep them fresh for eating. And should travellers be in short supply, the cannibals even ate their own wives and children. Thus the popular image of missionaries gazing unhappily out of stewing pots and of cannibals chanting songs around the fire were derived largely from tales brought back to Europe by surviving travellers in this region.

A more hospitable and less gruesome "cavern" is that of the resort which we reached after a long downward passage made uncomfortable by erosion. And at this point I must beg a few lines to describe briefly this enchanting mountain resort looking out onto fine alpine-like views. The Carte family has owned The Cavern for nearly 60 years, initially running it as a guest farmhouse accommodating 15 people in thatched rondavels. The rondavels have long since gone but the thatch remains; virtually all the buildings are handsomely thatch-roofed. Again a smaller and more concentrated version of the Cathedral Peak resort, it offers a variety of indoor and outdoor activity and sports facilities within its grounds while the bedroom suites and service rooms are light and airy, many with balconies. And if the massive Sunday buffet lunch on the front lawn was anything to go by the cuisine is superb too, the staff attentive and exceedingly friendly. The resort is just outside the Royal Natal National Park but set in perfect walking terrain. I envy future Ramblers who will be staying in this tight little corner of paradise.

We left with some reluctance and over-stretched stomachs to wend our way back from whence we came taking a slightly different initial route back to Surprise Ridge. And from here we were rewarded with a long gentle downhill march back to our quarters, plus the sight of a herd of rhebok we surprised on the ridge.

The penultimate day's walking could almost be described as a rest day involving, as it did, no more than a toddle along Otto's Walk from the hotel and up the flank of a hill to see further examples of San bushman art. These these paintings, also faded and indistinct, were on the sheltered rock overhang of the Sigubudo valley. Otto's Path overlooks the site of the film *Zulu* depicting the Battle of Rorke's Drift in which 4,000 Zulu warriors were repulsed by 150 defending British troops who, between them, won 11 Victoria Crosses for this feat of arms. The real battlefield is situated no more than 50 kilometres away but the Amphitheatre mountain region was found more photogenic and the Royal Natal National Park Hotel a convenient and suitably luxurious pad for Michael Caine and his fellow actors.

The weather was gradually deteriorating, the sky clouding over with heavy gusts of wind, which boded ill for the proposed 28-kilometre hike on our last day in the Drakensbergs. And, for once, the omens proved correct and we were greeted next morning with heavy rain though the wind had dropped. We were thus given opportunity to sample the indoor games facilities of the hotel, such as they were (much better ones existed at Cathedral Peak and the Cavern Berg).

Providentially, by midday, the rain ceased and the sun emerged again but the temperature had dropped to a nippy six degrees (and by nightfall to zero) while grey cloud blotted out the mountain tops. In need of fresh air and exercise nine of us, together with Fred, set off on a reduced version of the aborted hike which took us, at a fair rate of knots, along a flank of the Tugela valley; what water there was in its river coming straight from the Amphitheatre. The path contoured the valley side with a minimum of inclines so that, within a couple of hours, we had attained the bottom of the Tugela Gorge at the base of the great Amphitheatre wall, which reared upwards into the cloud, a sprinkling of new snow on its exposed extremities. Had we been able to complete the hike we would have descended to river level, boulder-hopped through the narrowing gorge, and climbed another of those perpendicular chain ladders to a point some way up the gigantic wall of the Amphitheatre itself. Instead we had to be content with gazing at what might have been and returning to the hotel likewise at double quick time; a four and a half hour near-jog which at least gave us an appetite for dinner. And of course it was Sod's Law that had the Amphitheatre completely clear of cloud by the time we were halfway home.

Leaving the Drakensberg Mountains was a wrench. There is something about their summits that is irresistible; more so than some other mountain ranges of the world. Not that they are of immense altitude or more remote than those of Asia or South America and elsewhere outside of Europe. Perhaps it is the incredible shapes of the summits, the truly awe-inspiring sheerness of the cliffs that provides their magnetism. As David Bristow intimates, all mountains from Olympus to Everest have long been associated with spiritual involvement. Perhaps this is what drives us to sweat and curse our way up long mountain paths.

Bristow has a warning too that we should all heed. How is it that people still manage to litter paths, deface cave walls and cause erosion by taking short cuts in spite of all efforts to persuade them otherwise? Only a true love of mountains and their environment will act as a guide and persuasion to treat this delicate ecosystem in the manner befitting this inspirational terrain which has been bequeathed to us.

We left the Royal Natal National Park in cold but brilliant sunshine for our final brief sojourn in South Africa, this one an urban seaside one. I equate Durban, the country's third largest city, with my own home town of Brighton; a Brighton with a port, a greener promenade and an Indian quarter instead of the Royal Pavilion. Perhaps, for that reason, I like the place though I've only been there once before. People come from all parts of South Africa to ride the surf or the roller-coaster or both; Durban combines the "fun" atmosphere of the nation's premier beach resort with the restlessness of Africa's busiest port. And as a shopping centre it is supreme, whether your choice lies in malls like the Workshop or the myriad food stalls of the Indian Market.

The three hour drive gave us our last views of the slowly reducing Drakensbergs, a sad farewell. With two nights and two and a half days to go most of the group chose an optional full day excursion to Umfolozi Game Reserve, four hour's drive away, and, on the day of departure, there was plenty of time for shopping and a city tour before the short intermediate flight back to Jo'burg.

The members of the group had not only been delightful companions but virtually all were competent walkers good-naturedly tolerant of those of slower pace. The rotund, ever-smiling Don – he of the blisters – invariably made up the rearguard of every hike, having joined the tour imagining it to be a bird-watching amble. Yet in spite of his infirmities he never uttered a word of complaint, plodding along gamely, a big smile on his face; a man with a lot of Irish guts. Eugene possessed a gammy knee, the result of an earlier injury, but he too never faltered. Cyril and Wendy – he lanky, she petite – were both good walkers though never hurrying. I've already mentioned Owen, birder supreme, with a sardonic sense of humour, ex-army and erudite, always near the front of the walking file together with Paul and myself, closely followed by the elegant Sylvia, the perfect lady who, in company with Elisabeth, somehow never sweated buckets like the rest of us; not even a gentle perspiration sullied her fair brow.

And so homeward, the Heathrow-bound, British Airways Boeing 747 levelling off above the clouds in a night sky that would stretch all the way to London.

PUBLISHER'S NOTE Christopher joined a relatively high grade Ramblers party for his trip to the Drakensberg Mountains. However, Ramblers Holidays is planning to develop a lower grade holiday for the year 2001, so that people who prefer less strenuous walking can also enjoy the Drakensberg paradise. Details can be obtained from the Ramblers Holidays office in Welwyn Garden (see the Ramblers Holidays details on page 351).

10. New Horizons — Armenia

(two weeks, grade D)

Keep going eastwards in Turkey and you'll find yourself in Armenia; at least you would were there a permitted crossing point between the two countries. There wasn't when I was riding the trains in eastern Turkey a year or two ago, though Cook's Overseas Timetable shows a tenuous rail link from Kars, and there was emphatically no form of contact back even further in the days of the Soviet Union when I arrived by train at that remote Turkish town with ideas of proceeding onwards into the USSR. Hopefully, however, cross-border relations will improve as Armenia opens up to tourism.

In the bad old days of European communism I visited a number of those Soviet republics that have since, and with various degrees of hassle, become independent states. These included Uzbekistan and other eastern then constituent republics but never had I been to Armenia, Georgia and the smaller southern ones. So when Ramblers Holidays invited me to make a brief tour of Armenia to observe and report upon the forming of a new walking holiday to be inaugurated in the year 2000, I jumped at the chance.

History has been exceptionally unkind to a country no larger than Belgium. Its struggle for independence against the imperialist expansion of, first, Babylonia and, later, Assyria goes back to before the ninth century. A high point in the country's history – perhaps the highest point – came about under satrap – governor – Artaxias who not only unified the nation but wrested territories from Parthia, Syria and Cappadocia; even occupying Syria itself. However, it was the neighbouring Turks who caused the greatest grief by establishing their rule over Armenia.

At the beginning of the 17th century further developments arose from a new direction as the Russians appeared in Transcaucasia and occupied Georgia while, resulting from their war of 1828 against Persia, they brought under their rule the whole plain of Erivan (now Yerevan), extending it to further Armenian territory later. Britain then came into the picture with a pro-Turkish, anti-Russian stance which raised the hackles of the Russians. The latter promptly became hostile to the Armenians in Armenia, while the Turks were to subject the minority Armenians living in eastern Turkey to open suppression during which some 80,000 Armenians perished.

The consequential hostility to Turkey continued into the 20th century although the Armenian leadership assured the Turks of their support on the outbreak of the First World War. So with Turkey allied to Germany, Russia proceeded to conquer Turkish Armenia proclaiming "the liberation of Armenia from the Turkish yoke", while subsequent border changes first added to and then reduced Armenia's territory in eastern Turkey. These border changes resulted from various treaties which, again, involved British statesmen.

After the Russian revolution of November 1917 the Armenians experienced a short-lived independence but, in September 1920, Turkey attacked the new republic and, at the same time, the Russians advanced from Azerbaijan to end this moment of sovereignty. Thereafter, Armenia slid into the Soviet camp to become the Armenian Soviet Socialist Republic from which it has only recently emerged to become an independent nation once more.

Thus, in a very small nutshell, the convulsive, not to say tragic, history of a minuscule country, an allegedly beautiful land of sophisticated people, a people who were caught between competing great powers but who became friends of neither. Yet, in spite of the vicissitudes, Armenia remains a land of culture; its people known for extending great hospitality to visitors. All in all a favourable basis for a Ramblers destination at the start of the 21st century.

As readers might have noticed I'm a great one for gauging and, later, comparing, first impressions. My subject is usually individual members of a party as each arrives at airport or hotel. In a more general sense I do the same for, to me, new hotels, cities and towns. But arriving, as I did, in Yerevan at three o'clock in the morning on the relatively mew direct British Airways service, I was hard-pressed to gain any kind of coherent impression as the young driver of the Russian jeep, who collected me at the airport, hurled me at breakneck speed through the shadowy outskirts of the Armenian capital dodging horrendous potholes in a highway fortunately devoid of traffic.

The hotel at which I was eventually, and thankfully, dropped appeared, in the darkness, to be a beacon of respectability situated in an urban slum. Actually the area has been designated as a future residential neighbourhood and, as I observed in the all too rapidly arriving light of the new day, already a number of villas were blossoming. But none, I declare, could hold a candle to the White Castle, a six-bedroom suite-equipped private pension of sumptuous exclusiveness; probably the most expensive pad in town. From the ornately sculptured marble reception hall I was ushered into a suite, the bedroom of which was frugally but richly furnished. Yet that room was but half the size of a palatial black and white marble-tiled bathroom containing a veritable swimming pool-sized bath alternating as a jacuzzi with an array of controls for all sorts of potential water-bearing pleasures and surprises. And breakfast, later in the morning, was a banquet of exotic fruits, juices, yoghurts, not to mention a substantial fry-up taken on the patio beside the delicately-shaped swimming pool with decorative pheasants strutting on the lawn. Had the White Castle been in the city centre instead of seven kilometres from it the establishment would have been a truly sensational place to stay.

As it is, the Marriott-adopted Hotel Armenia, currently the premier sizeable hotel in Yerevan, and in the process of having a face-lift, holds this position by bordering Republic Square, the city's heart. And it is in this establishment that Ramblers Holiday guests will be based while in the city region. However, since this tour is designated as a P for Pioneer classification, anything can happen in the meantime regarding hotel sojourning as new structures rise, while, in the realm of transportation, more congenial flight times than mine are negotiated.

Expecting cool, if not cold autumnal weather in early September I was launched on my full-day tour of the capital in a veritable heatwave with temperatures nudging 30 degrees. Again my Stirling Moss-inspired driver, Robert, together with Ramblers' enthusiastic and knowledgeable local guide, Ara, rocketed me into and around a city of equally crazily-driven Ladas, Trabants and other assorted one-time East-Bloc vehicular abominations ably supported by dented trams and buses; a hubbub of motor horns and highway intersection anarchy.

When I wasn't pushing my feet against the jeep's floorboards or closing my eyes in anticipation of a high-speed collision I perceived a city that might have shed its stifling mantle of communism only yesterday – though I think it was but my imagination that conjured the depressing aroma of boiled cabbage and low octane petrol I long remembered from Stalinist days in eastern Europe. And yet not quite. Grey dusty buildings with occasional pink, brown volcanic tufa walls. A cat's cradle of telephone, electric and tramway wires and cables festooned from broken or leaning posts. The once-compulsory parade ground – across which Soviet tanks rolled on special occasions – now known as Republic Square after decades as Lenin Square – bordered by frowning state edifices. A sudden splash of colour where some capitalist enterprise has invaded a fragment of street and held its own. Cracked and broken pavements retreating in the face of an advance of jigsaw puzzle paving. Phalanxes of jerry-built flats with

Memorial to the Armenian genocide of 1915 at Yerevan

cracked walls and tiny corrugated-iron fenced balconies. These made my initial impressions of a city far behind the likes of Prague, Budapest and Warsaw in the race to clean its grimy face of the dross of communism but showing clear signs of setting about the job of doing so. Despite a favoured locale overlooked by the twin snow-capped peaks of Mount Ararat, 55 miles southwest in Turkey, Yerevan is not a beautiful city – the drab orderliness of the Soviet era sees to that – but it flaunts an extraordinary vitality.

The ancient city fortress of Erebuni (hence Yerevan) was founded in the year 783 BC by King Argishti I of Urartu, according to a stone title deed that is the city's proudest possession. Falling at different times under Romans, Parthians, Arabs, Tartars, Turks, Persians and Georgians, Yerevan was a place of considerable importance in old Armenia, mushrooming, in more recent times, from a pre-First World War population of just 30,000 to around a million and a quarter today. In spite of 1988 political strife and a terrible earthquake, plus, currently, political friction with neighbouring Azerbaijan, the city is ripe for small-scale tourism. And there's plenty to see.

Pride of place is taken by the History and Art Museums on Republic Square where, on seven floors, are exhibits of exemplary interest and fascination. In the northeast is the Matenadaran, the Ancient Manuscript

Library housing over 12,000 Armenian manuscripts from the 9th century onwards collected from all over the world. The Armenian Opera House is a reminder that Khachaturyan lived in Yerevan; his home – now a museum – is open to all who are devoted to opera and ballet. And in half-wild Tsitsernakaberd Park on the hills overlooking the city from the west is Yerevan's memorial to the victims of the 1915 genocide, its skyward-pointing needle marking a circle of basalt pillars leaning around an eternal flame. Overshadowed by more recent acts of genocide from the holocaust of World War Two through Cambodia and central Africa to the Kosovo killing fields, this monument to a near century-old slice of history still remains intensely moving.

On a more prosaic level the colourful sunshades of a myriad pavement cafes do much to brighten this struggling city. Its confectionery emporiums will have a visitor drooling at the mouth at the sight of serried rows of fresh cream cakes that taste as good as they look, while the cost of such inspired sweetmeats can be measured in pence. Modern shopping malls with western goods on sale are fast appearing in side streets and plazas. And if it's the celebrated Armenian brandy that tickles the taste buds then there are stalls and shops laid out with nothing but. And taking coffee – or a full-blown meal – at the Hotel Armenia in its open-air restaurant, overlooking the square that comes to life at dusk with an array of fountains spraying upwards to musical accompaniment, offers a touch of Paris – but without the cost. Ramblers will have at least one evening meal at the Eastern Kitchen, a truly Armenian enterprise with an almost wholly Armenian clientele.

Capital cities seldom reflect the country they head except in the most superficial sense, so I set off, initially southward, accompanied by Ara in our jeep driven, as usual, like a bat out of hell by Robert, to gain an idea of what the Armenian countryside could offer.

At first the terrain was flat; the double lane highway out of Yerevan in reasonable condition once clear of the suburbs. The scenery was dullish; enlivened only by fruit stalls and fish tanks lining the road plus the great double bulk of the two Mount Ararats faint in the heat haze but seemingly within strolling distance though barred by a heavily-guarded Turkish/Armenian frontier reminiscent of the old Iron Curtain. This border accompanied us for the first hour before we were forced northward by another, that of Azerbaijan, which, at the time I was there, was in a spasmodic shooting conflict with Armenia. Our highway, now reduced to a single lane, held sparse traffic but compensated for this with liberal amounts of potholes as if to keep drivers on their toes. The terrain changed too, abruptly becoming mountainous, the expanding hills dry

Pleasure lake at Jermuk

and rock-bound with, where a river flowed through them, valleys of lush greenery which reminded me of the Moroccan Atlas. At one point on the highway, resurfacing was in progress over a longish section requiring traffic to crawl over roadless terrain that not even a self-respecting T54 tank would tolerate. To Robert, of course, this was a challenge and he took it at speed, his vehicle – with us in it – occasionally taking to the air.

Two hours out of Yerevan brought us to a turn-off to the newly-restored monastery of Noravank. One of my tasks on this assignment was to access and report upon some of the walking routes planned for the Armenian tour, though I had but a few days at my disposal in which to do so. And here was the location of one of them; in fact the introductory walk of the tour to give the leader an idea of the hiking standard of the group. The Noravank walk is but a gently inclined traffic-free road ramble some eight kilometres long through a picturesque gorge with the monastery buildings as the pot of gold at the end of the rainbow. These monasteries and churches are mostly unoccupied, but many are still in use on regular or specific occasions. Their exteriors are more attractive than are their plain interiors, while they are usually situated in spectacular locations – as is Noravank overlooking, in both directions, the gorge of the same name.

Back on the main highway leading to Goris we travelled for another hour through towns and villages seemingly devoid of speed limits. We eventually turned off onto an even worse-afflicted lesser road that wound its way to Jermuk. And in Jermuk is to be found something of profound interest. In effect it is a ghost town; a town of enormous sanatoria blocks, columned spa buildings from which sprout mineral water of varying degrees of temperature, an airport runway capable of handling the largest aircraft, and a lake on and around which can be discerned the basics for a host of recreational facilities. All this is within overgrown parkland and encircled by modest-sized mountains. Once upon a time the elite of the Soviet Union flew here direct from Moscow for rest and treatment but with the demise of the USSR Jermuk has been allowed to die. Yet, who knows, one day a rich entrepreneur could discover its rich potential and give the place a new lease of life as a holiday resort for the ordinary people. Currently there is no accommodation available here fit for holiday sojourning which is a crying shame since Jermuk would make a fine Ramblers base for a few days in a country woefully short of hotels.

Thankfully leaving the jeep for a brief period, Ara and I walked a little way down Jermuk canyon bordered by strangely-sculptured rock walls and pinnacles together with several arched caverns, not to mention an impressive waterfall injecting a further torrent of water into the river that lay at the bottom. Ramblers will see all this for themselves as well as another and larger gorge a few miles away to which Robert whisked us following our departure from this sad ghost city and its few present-day apathetic inhabitants.

The new gorge was that of the Apa river, a majestic canyon of towering and, again, peculiarly-shaped cliffs between which runs the old road which, like Jermuk, has been allowed to expire. As a result there is little tarmac remaining so that, in effect, it is a dust road offering easy and gently downhill walking with much to observe en route. To me the Apa Gorge reflected a kinship with the Dades Gorge in, again, the Moroccan Atlas, though the walls in the former are not so high or sheer.

An hour and a half's stroll is rewarded by a bridge which offers a dry crossing of the river though, at the time I was there, a boulder hopping traverse would have sufficed. And thereafter it is but 15 minutes to the monastery church of Gandevank and its interesting out-buildings – once inhabited by the monks – that have survived destruction under the Soviet regime. Some of the interiors of those monastery buildings would not be entirely unsuitable for overnight camping had one a sleeping bag and suchlike, since there were fireplaces, plenty of available firewood and a nearby source of fresh cold water. However, Ramblers Holidays aims for higher standards of accommodation though, as I have already made clear, hotels outside of Yerevan are, at present, far too thin on the ground.

There is a winding footpath leading to the top of the southern wall of the gorge and the village of Gandevaz but we never found it until after we had struggled, sometimes on hands and knees, up steeply-angled semi-scree to the lip, a somewhat arduous ascent well beyond the D hiking grade of the tour. It was therefore recommended that this walk should end at the monastery.

North of Yerevan, barely 40 minutes fast driving away, lies the southern shore of Lake Sevan fed by 30 rivers but with only one outlet, the Razdan river. The lake has a shoreline of 120 miles and is some 45 miles long so is looked upon as one of the largest mountain lakes in the world. We halted at the Sevan Peninsula with, at its head, two ninth century monastery churches currently under restoration, from which are sublime views in all directions over the lake and its surroundings. Guidebooks express the opinion that the water is exceptionally cold but I enjoyed a relaxing swim in it without turning blue. Ramblers will spend an hour or two here so can find this out for themselves and, since this shore is a favourite weekend bolthole for Yerevan citizens, there are plenty of boating and other recreation facilities available as well as small cafes and restaurants. At one time the monastery stood on an island but, because of the tapping of the Razdan river for hydro-electricity and irrigational purposes, the lake shrank thus allowing the peninsula to be formed.

The second accommodation base of the tour is that of what is known as the Writers' House just outside the winter ski resort of Tzahkadzor amongst the hilly countryside south of the lake. A haunt of Armenian writers, the building contains a grandiose vestibule and reception area, service rooms and sleeping quarters combined with a very willing management and staff. Ramblers will assuredly enjoy their four-night stay here away from the bustling capital. One of the hikes, which I sampled in its entirety, led from the hotel through pleasant mushroom-smelling woodland out onto an open plateau and headland. From here are fine views over not only Tzahkadzor and its summer-operating ski-lift traversing countryside but also the industrial city of Razdan, its new section afflicted by the all-too-common Soviet-built high-rise apartment blocks. The old part of town is more attractive with fewer hideous dwelling houses. It is centred by the obligatory and typical monastery church with its rounded tower. Such ecclesiastical establishments are the inevitable destination of many of the walks in Armenia though they are invariably worth seeing. And, since I am on the subject, the Kecharis monastery complex in Tzahkadzor, likewise under current restoration, is well worth a visit. Most of the ski-resort accommodation buildings to be seen on the hillsides around the township are, at present, occupied by refugees from Baku in war-torn Azerbaijan.

Back on the Tbilisi-Yerevan highway, another Robert-challenging race-track, I realised that pothole dodging must form an integral part of Armenian driving technique. Eventually we returned to the capital, in preparation for a foray towards the north-east of the country.

Except in the immediate Yerevan district all highway direction signs are in Armenian and Russian hieroglyphics, though English is fast appearing as the third language. However, my escort knew the way to Garni and Gegard, our ruptured minor road leading us, via the villages of Avan, Dzhrvezh and Vokhchaberd, through Garni to Gegard where it terminated. The route twisted and turned through an utopian landscape along the ridge of the Gegami range of hills before descending over a pass into the Garni valley. En route we halted briefly to gaze across the dry hilly terrain to distant Yerevan from the vantage point of the arched memorial to the dissident and avant garde poet Charentz, one of millions of victims of the Soviet era. The rock walls of the Garni pass are honeycombed with caves, today almost inaccessible, though once a regular refuge from invaders and persecutors.

At the end of the road stood – yes – another monastery, this one of startling originality. The Gegard (which means Holy Lance or Spear, the one that is supposed to have pierced the side of Christ) is partly built into the great cliff face of a ravine at the bottom of which flows the Karmirget river. Here too the rock walls are indented with partly-walled caves, some of which have been transformed into fourth century living quarters for the monks, while the free-standing church and its monastery buildings, dating back to the 11th century, are themselves a depository of stone chambers. The carved figure of a lion attacking an ox, high above the elaborate south portal of the church, is the coat of arms of the Zakarian princely family which built it as a combined meeting chamber and a place of worship. Most of the nine chambers – open to visitors – are divided by arches; their ceilings and walls displaying finely-carved figures. Until quite recently Gegard was a working monastery but now only the church is used for services though the whole complex exudes a religious aura as may be noted from the abundance of "wishing trees" – hung Christmas tree-like with strips of cloth, each tied onto a branch to accompany a wish or a prayer.

Again tour participants will have plenty of time to explore this complex before moving back to the township of Garni in which is situated the Greek-like temple to the Roman god Mithras. Built by the Armenian King

Tiridates 1 in the first century AD with the aid of funds and artisans from Rome, this mini-Acropolis is unique in the country. It stands 1,000 feet above the Azat river on a plateau which had supported a near impregnable fortress since the third century BC. Much of the fortification has disappeared but a third century bathhouse with a mosaic floor can still be seen. The edifice makes a striking sight with the Azat gorge below and the mountains all around. Nearby a row of walnut trees provide shade and shelter for the proposed group picnic which will take place here prior to a three and a half hour walk from the township down to and along the gorge.

I only had time for an hour's perambulation but it was enough to gauge the slightly downhill walk along a dust road to be a doddle. It is taken alongside some of the most fantastically-shaped cliff faces you are ever likely to see. And at the bottom of the gorge the end of the hike is marked, not by the ubiquitous monastery, but by a lake; actually a reservoir.

The time at my disposal in Armenia allowed me to observe and sample but a limited number of destinations, edifices, hotels, restaurants and walking routes that will form the basis for the programme and itinerary of the quartet of Ramblers tours within the country throughout the year 2000. However, it was enough to enable me to assure potential participants that, whatever their specific interests might be, this fascinating nation that has so recently opened its doors to the world in general, is one that should be seen and appreciated as it emerges from the scourges it suffered from nearly a century of tyranny and various grades of oppressive communism. Many of you probably have, in recent times, looked upon the changing faces, and marvelled at their transformation, of such as the Czech Republic, Poland, Hungary, and even Bulgaria and Romania, which endured only 40 years of communism. Now it is the turn of Armenia to show what it can do. I cannot emphasise too strongly the kindliness and welcoming attitude of its people as well as their determination to give to their land a lifestyle and prosperity that we in Britain, Europe and North America take for granted. In a way the walking side of the holiday programme is subordinate to that of simply experiencing a new country; the hikes, which are not arduous, offer a vehicle for doing so, since their routes take you through the most beautiful and spectacular countryside together with simple villages exhibiting the Armenian rural way of life.

In addition to a leader, the parties will have as a guide Ara, who knows and loves his country. His command of English is improving rapidly and he has a wife and small son whom Ramblers will no doubt meet too.

Additionally, he is a talented artist whose works are on display in Yerevan's picture galleries – which means that the perfect souvenir of the tour is at hand for those who appreciate art.

For me, alas, my short flying visit to Armenia was at an end. A last, Robert-inspired race to the airport, a final glimpse of the country from the aircraft window. And following the landing in London of the British Mediterranean Airlines Airbus I, just for once, had occasion to bless the dull smoothness of the M25 as I rode home in one of the comfortable Jetlink twice-hourly coaches between Heathrow, Gatwick and Brighton – thanking God that Robert wasn't driving it.

Epilogue

With the exception of that of the World War Two episode in German-occupied Poland, narrated in chapter 6, all the walks described in this book were carried out when I was well over 50 years old. The most recent long-distance hike - that of the near-1200 kilometres between the Baltic and the Danube (chapter 7) – I undertook when I was almost 74. But age is no barrier to such a method of locomotion and I like to think that using my feet has kept me as fit as I am.

As I write this I am in my seventy-sixth year and my eyes still frequently stray to the map of the world, my mind mulling over possible venues for future journeying on foot or bicycle. There is no mystique about walking. It can be as easy or as demanding as you could wish and, at any level, it is one of the most healthy activities available - in spite of many of the vicissitudes I suffered on some of my longer treks. Yet many of us abhor the very idea of going anywhere except on wheels, water or in the air.

So if my narrative gives a reader, young or old, a pair of itchy feet such as mine and sets him or her off on a walk, long or short, then this book will have served its purpose.

Appendix

Appendix

For those who may wish to follow in my footsteps this brief list of guidebooks, contacts and other items of information may be of some initial assistance:

Chapter 1
Bibliography: *Roman Roads in Britain* by Ivan Margary (Barker)
                The Great North Road by Norman Webster (Adams & Dart)
                Along the Roman Roads of Britain by J H B Pees (Pan)
                Walker's Britain (AA Publishing)
Contacts   Northumbria Tourist Board, Aykley Heads, Durham DH1 5UX
                Scottish Borders Tourist Board, Shepher's Mill, Selkirk TD7 5DT
Maps   Ordnance Survey Landranger sheets 80, 92, 93, 99, 105

Chapter 2
Bibliography   *Footsteps* by Richard Holmes (Hodder & Staughton)
                Walkers by Miles Jebb (Constable)
                Travels with a Donkey by Robert Louis Stevenson (OUP)
                Classic Walks in France by Rob Hunter/David Wickes (Oxford University Press)
                The Elf book of Long Walks in France by Adam Nicholson (Weidenfeld)
Contacts   French Government Tourist Office, 178 Piccadilly, London W1V 0AL
Maps   IGN 1:50 000, sheets 2836, 2736, 2737, 2738, 2739, 2740
                IGN Carte Vert, 1:100 000, sheets 50, 58, 59

Chapter 3, part 1
Bibliography   *Classic Walks in Europe* edited by Walt Unsworth (Oxford Illustrated Press)
                Visitor's Guide to Southern Germany (MPC)
Contacts   The Bavarian Tourist Board, Prinzregentenstrasse 18/1V, 8000 Munich 22, Germany
                The German National Tourist Office, Nightingale House, 65 Curzon Street, London W1Y 7P
Maps   Kompass Wanderkarte 1:50 000, sheets 180, 179, 4

Chapter 3, part 2
Bibliography   *Der Rennsteig* (Fremdenverkehrsverband Thuringer Wald e.V) (in German)
                Kompass Wanderfuhrer
                Thuringer Wald 2 (in German)

Contacts	Thuringer Landesfremdenverkehrsverband e.V, Stauffenbergallee 18, PSF 219, 99005 Erfurt, Germany
	German National Tourist Office (as above)
Maps	Kompass Wanderkarte 1:50 000 Westlicher Thuringer Wald, Mittlerer Thuringer Wald, Schwarzatal
	Also Karte des Rennsteig by J Buhring

Chapter 4

Bibliography	*Classic Walks of the World* edited by Walt Unsworth (Oxford Illustrated Press)
	Epirus by Arthur Foss (Faber)
	Exploring Rural Greece by Pamela Westland (Helm)
Contacts	The Greek National Tourist Organisation, 4 Conduit Street, London W1R 0DJ
Maps	Michelin Road Map no. 980 (red) 1:700 000 (1cm to 7 km)
	A series of Freytag & Berndt maps covers the region in more detail

Chapter 5, part 1

Bibliography	*Iceland, Greenland and the Faroe Isles* (Lonely Planet)
	Iceland in a Nutshell (Iceland Travel Books)
	Last Places by Lawrence Millman (Abacus)
Contacts	Iceland Tourist Information Bureau, Icelandair, 172 Tottenham Court Road, London W1P 9ZG
	Mr Dick Phillips, Icelandic Travel Specialist, Whitehall House, Nenthead, Alston, Cumbria CA9 3PS
Maps	Obtainable from Dick Phillips

Chapter 5, part 2

Bibliography	*Guide to Spitsbergen* by Andreas Umbreit (Bradt)
Contacts	Norwegian Tourist Board, Charles House, 5 Lower Regent Street, London SW1Y 4LR
Maps	a comprehensive range available from Stanfords Books & Maps, 12-14 Long Acre, London WC2E 9LP

Chapter 6

Bibliography	*Pedal for Your Life* by Christopher Portway (Lutterworth Press)

Chapter 7

Bibliography	*Poland* (Lonely Planet)
	Poland (Rough Guides)
	Czech Republic (Berlitz)
	Visitor's Guide Czechoslovakia (MPC)
	Essential Austria (AA)
	Exploring Rural Austria by Gretel Beer (Helm)
	Vienna (Berlitz)
	Vienna (Thomas Cook Travel)

	Austria (Fodor)
	Eastern Europe on a Shoestring (Lonely Planet)
	Eastern Europe (Fodor)
	On the Loose in Eastern Europe (Berkeley)
	People to People – Poland (Canongate Press)
	People to People – Czechoslovakia, Hungary, Bulgaria (Canongate Press)
Contacts	Polish National Tourist Office, Remo House, 310-312 Regent Street, London W1R 5AJ
	The Czech Republic Tourist Authority, The Czech Centre, 95 Great Portland Street, London W1N 5RA
	Austrian Tourist Office, 14 Cork Street, London W1X 1PF
Maps	Hungary, Czechoslovakia, Poland 1:1000 000 (Hallwag) (Bartholomew)
	Road Atlas Europe (Collins)

Chapter 8	
Bibliography	*The Story of the Great American West* (Reader's Digest)
Contacts	Dakota, South: Rocky Mountain International, Garden Studios, 11-15 Betterton Street, London WC2 H6R
	Travel Division, North Dakota Highway Department, Capital Grounds, Bismark, ND 58506, USA
	Fort Seward Wagon Train, Fort Seward Inc, Box 244, Jamestown, ND 58401, USA
Maps	North and South Dakota highway maps available free at petrol stations and elsewhere in the states concerned

Chapter 9	
Bibliography	*Canada* (Lonely Planet)
	Canada (Rough Guides)
	Visitor's Guide to Canada (MPC)
	Canada (Insight Guides)
	Canada (Michelin Green Guides)
	Milepost – Alaska & West Canada (Box 4-EE Anchorage, Alaska 99509, USA)
Contacts	Canadian Tourist Office, MacDonald House, 1 Grosvenor Square, London W1X 0AB
Maps	Official Road Map Yukon 1:2,500 000 obtainable at petrol stations and elsewhere

Chapter 10, part 1	
Bibliography	*India Handbook* (Footprint)
	India (Lonely Planet)
	India, Nepal & Sri Lanka (Fodor)
	India by James Elliott (Batsford)
	Into India by John Keay (Murray)

	Trekking in the Indian Himalayas (Lonely Planet)
	India (Rough Guides)
	Western Himalaya (Insight)
Contacts	Government of India Tourist Office, 7 Cork Street, London W1X 1PB
Chapter 10, part 2	
Bibliography	*The Trekker's Guide to the Himalaya Karakoram* by Hugh Swift (Hodder & Stoughton)
	A Guide to Trekking in Nepal by Stephen Bezruchka (Cordee)
	Trekking in the Nepal Himalaya (Lonely Planet)
Contacts	Royal Nepalese Embassy, 12a Kensington Palace Gardens, London W8 4QU
Chapter 11	
Bibliography	*Kenya* (Rough Guides)
	Kenya (Insight Guides)
	Kenya (Lonely Planet)
	Kenya (Berlitz)
	A Kenyan Adventure by Christopher Portway (Impact Books)
	East Africa Handbook (Footprint)
	The Great Travelling Adventure by Christopher Portway (Oxford Illustrated Press)
Contacts	Kenya National Tourist Office, 25 Brooks's Mews, Off Davies Street, London W1Y 1LG
Maps	Africa North-East, sheet 154 – 1:4000 000 (Michelin)
	Mount Kenya Ordnance Survey – 1125 000 (World Maps)
Chapter 12	
Bibliography	*South American Handbook* (Footprint)
	Peru (Insight Guides)
	Peru (Rough Guides)
	Peru Handbook (Footprint)
	Peru (Lonely Planet)
	Backpacking and Trekking in Peru & Bolivia (Bradt)
	Conquest of the Incas by Dr John Hemming (MacMillan)
	Realm of the Incas by Victor von Hagen (New American Library)
	Tears of the Sun God by J H Moore (Faber)
	The Rucksack Man by Sebastian Snow (Hodder & Stoughton)
	Half a Dozen of the Other by Sebastian Snow (Hodder & Stoughton)
	Four Faces of Peru by W Byford-Jones (Hale)
	Journey Along the Andes by Christopher Portway (Impact Books)
	Eight Feet in the Andes by Dervla Murphy (Murray)
	Cucumber Sandwiches in the Andes by John Ure (Constable)
	South America (Lonely Planet)

Contacts	Embassy of Peru (Tourist Department), 52 Sloane Street, London SW1X 9SP
Chapter 13	
Bibliography	See Chapter 12 plus:
	Ecuador Handbook (Footprint)
	Ecuador (Insight Guides)
	Ecuador & Galapagos (Lonely Planet)
Contacts	Embassy of Ecuador, Flat 3b, 3 Hans Crescent, London SW1X 0LS
Chapter 14	
Part 1: Sicily	
Bibliography	*Landscapes of Sicily* (Sunflower Books)
	Sicily, A Traveller's Guide (Murray)
	Sicily (Cadogan Island Guides)
	Blue Guide: Sicily (A & C Black)
	Sicily (Berlitz Travel Guides)
Contacts	Italian State Tourist Board, 1 Princes Street, London W1R 8AY
Part 2: Andalucia	
Bibliography	*Landscapes of Andalucia* (Sunflower Books)
	Andalucia Handbook (Footprint)
	Andalucia (Rough Guides)
	Walking Through Spain by Robin Neillands (McDonald, Queen Anne Press)
	Explorer Spain (AA)
Contacts	Spanish National Tourist Office, 22-23 Manchester Square, London W1M 5AP
	Gibralter Tourist Board, Arundel Great Court, 179 Strand, London WC2R 1EH
Part 3: Morocco	
Bibliography	*Morocco* (Blue Guide)
	Essential Morocco (AA)
	Morocco (Cadogan)
	Morocco Handbook (Footprint)
	Morocco (Insight Guides)
	Morocco (Lonely Planet)
	Morocco (Rough Guides)
	Independent Traveller: Morocco by Christine Osborne (MPC)
	The Great Walking Adventure by Hamish Brown (Oxford Illustrated Press)
	Lords of the Atlas by Gavin Maxwell
Contacts	Moroccan National Tourist Office, 205 Regent Street, London W1R 7DE

Part 4: Tuscany
Bibliography   *Blue Guide: Northern Italy* (A & C Black)
                Blue Guide: Tuscany (A & C Black)
                Exploring Rural Italy by Michael Leech (Helm)
                Essential Tuscany & Florence (AA)
                Tuscany (Insight Guides)
                Tuscany (Michelin Green Guides)
                Tuscany in your Pocket (Michelin)
Contacts   Italian State Tourist Board, 1 Princes Street, London W1R 8AY

Part 5: New England and New York
Bibliography   *New England* (Insight Guides)
                New England (Michelin)
                New England (Lonely Planet)
                Boston and New England Essential Explorer (AA)
                New England (Berlitz Traveller's Guide)
                New England (Michelin Green Guide)
                New York in your Pocket (Michelin)
                New York (Berlitz)
                New York State (Insight Guides)
Contacts   New York Travel Advisory Bureau Inc, 11 Berkeley Street, London W1X 6BU

Part 6: Samos
Bibliography   *Landscapes of Samos* (Sunflower Books)
                Greek Islands of the Aegean (Michelin)
                Essential Greek Islands (Berlitz Travel Guides)
                Greek Islands (Insight Guides)
Contacts   Greek Hellenic Tourist Organisation, 4 Conduit Street, London W1R 0DJ

Part 7: Lake District
Bibliography   *Lake District* by Norman Buckley (Landmark Publishing)
                English Lake Country by Dudley Hoye (Batsford)
                Wainwright's Favourite Lakeland Mountains (Michael Joseph)
                Discover Britain (Berlitz)
                Exploring England & Wales by Christopher Peck (Helm)
                Walking in Britain (Rough Guides)
                England and Wales (Berlitz Traveller's Guide)
Contacts   Cumbria Tourist Board, Ashleigh, Holly Road, Windermere LA23 2AQ
Maps   Ordnance Survey Outdoor Leisure series (1:25 000) nos.4-7 (for walkers)
                Ordnance Survey Landranger series (1:50 000) nos. 89, 90, 96, 97 (for walkers)

Leisure Map of the Lake District (1:75 000) (Estate Publications) (touring)

Part 8: Austria	
Bibliography	*Austria* (Insight Guides)
	Austria (Rough Guides)
	Off the Beaten Track – Austria (MPC)
	The Visitor's Guide to Austria (MPC)
Contacts	Austrian National Tourist Office, 14 Cork Street, London W1X 1PE
Part 9: South Africa	
Bibliography	*South Africa, Swaziland & Lesotho* (Cadogan)
	Baedeker's South Africa (AA)
	South Africa, Lesotho & Swaziland (Lonely Planet)
	South Africa (Berlitz)
Contacts	South African Tourist Board, 5-6 Alt Grove, London SW19 4DZ
Part 10: Armenia	
Bibliography	At present there are no guidebooks specifically on Armenia except for brief mention in guides about the former USSR
Contacts	With no tourist office yet in the UK the Armenian Embassy is the only source of information (and also visas which are required). The address is 25a Cheniston Gardens, London W8 6TG

This contact and information list is of necessity sketchy. Fuller information can be gleaned from *The Traveller's Handbook* (Wexas Publications) while map information can be obtained likewise from this handbook and also from such stockists as Stanfords, 12-14 Long Acre, Covent Garden, London WC2E 9LP and also from the Royal Geographical Society, 1 Kensington Gore, London SW7 2AR.

Finally, readers may be interested to know that, as well as organising all the walking holidays described in chapter 14 of this book, Ramblers Holidays also currently (i.e. for the year 2000) offer walking holidays to venues in several countries mentioned in chapters 1-13 – namely, Britain, Canada, the Czeck Republic, France, Germany, Greece, Hungary, Iceland, Nepal, Poland, Ecuador, Peru and the USA.

Information about Ramblers Holidays' full range of tours, and on how to contact the company, is given on page 351.

THE RAMBLERS' ASSOCIATION was founded in 1935 to protect public paths, encourage walking, campaign for freedom to roam in uncultivated open country and defend the beauty of the countryside. It exists to enable everyone to enjoy and discover Britain on foot.

Joining the Ramblers is inexpensive and is a great way to make new friends, get fit and discover your local surroundings.

BENEFITS OF MEMBERSHIP INCLUDE

☆ *The Rambler*, our quarterly colour magazine with its celebrity columnists, breathtaking photography and campaigning journalism

☆ *The Rambler's Yearbook and Accommodation Guide* (which is sold in shops but is free to members) containing over 3,500 places to stay and information on maps, long distance paths, equipment shops and much more

☆ Regional newsletters

☆ Discretionary discounts in many outdoor equipment shops

☆ Free membership of one of our 417 local walking groups which offer led walks most weekends and often mid-week as well.

There is also the opportunity to involve yourself in practical conservation activities in your area. Many of our past successes have been built on the efforts of Ramblers' volunteers; it's work that is worthwhile — and truly satisfying.

Whether you're a serious hiker pushing yourself to the limits, an occasional walker blowing away the cobwebs, or you simply want to support the leading charity working to encourage walking and protect the countryside... the Ramblers is for you.

The Ramblers' Association, 1-5 Wandsworth Road,
London, SW8 2XX
☎ 0207 339 8500.
E-Mail: ramblers@london.ramblers.org.uk
Web site address: www.ramblers.org.uk

You can go "Walking the World" with

RAMBLERS HOLIDAYS

RAMBLERS HOLIDAYS is an independent company which offers walking, sightseeing, trekking and cross-country skiing holidays in countries across the globe.

Ramblers Holidays is the principal trading arm of its parent company, Ramblers' Association Services Ltd, the publishers of Christopher Portway's *A Good Pair of Legs*.

Since its holidays began in 1946, Ramblers Holidays has developed a reputation for offering:

◆ A wide choice of beautiful and fascinating holiday locations

◆ Reasonable prices and value for money

◆ Experienced holiday leaders

◆ A friendly party atmosphere

The holidays organised by Ramblers Holidays are open to everyone, not just to Ramblers' Association members. But all customers of Ramblers Holidays are ultimately helping The Ramblers' Association. This is because, each year, Ramblers Holidays transfers a large part of its profits to a trust fund which helps to finance The Ramblers' campaigns for protecting footpaths, access and the countryside in Great Britain.

For a free copy of Ramblers Holidays' current brochure, please call, write, fax, telephone or e-mail the Ramblers Holidays office at:

2 Church Road (Box 43), Welwyn Garden, Herts, AL8 6PQ

Direct brochure line: 01707 339039

Telephone: 01707 331133

Fax: 01707 333276

E-mail: brochures@ramblersholidays.co.uk